The History of Archery

Contents

1 Introduction   **1**

     1.1 Medieval archery 1

         1.1.1 Prehistory 1

         1.1.2 Ancient history 2

         1.1.3 Middle Ages 4

         1.1.4 Decline of archery 5

         1.1.5 Recreational revival 6

         1.1.6 A modern sport 7

         1.1.7 See also 8

         1.1.8 References 8

         1.1.9 Further reading 10

         1.1.10 External links 10

     1.2 Arab archery 10

         1.2.1 Release Style 10

         1.2.2 Arab Archery History 11

         1.2.3 Archery in Islam 11

         1.2.4 Arab Archery Today 11

         1.2.5 References 11

         1.2.6 Bibliography 11

         1.2.7 See also 12

     1.3 Archery butt 12

         1.3.1 Towns with areas known as 'The Butts' 12

         1.3.2 Notes and references 13

         1.3.3 External links 13

     1.4 Assize of Arms of 1252 13

         1.4.1 See also 13

         1.4.2 Notes 13

         1.4.3 References 13

     1.5 Battle of Crécy 13

		1.5.1	Campaign background	14
		1.5.2	Battle	14
		1.5.3	Aftermath	17
		1.5.4	Nobles and men at arms at the battle	19
		1.5.5	Fictional accounts	20
		1.5.6	See also	20
		1.5.7	References	20
		1.5.8	Further reading	22
		1.5.9	External links	23
	1.6	Crossbow		23
		1.6.1	Construction	24
		1.6.2	History	28
		1.6.3	Modern use	32
		1.6.4	Comparison to conventional bows	33
		1.6.5	Legal issues	33
		1.6.6	See also	34
		1.6.7	Notes	34
		1.6.8	References	36
		1.6.9	External links	36
	1.7	English longbow		36
		1.7.1	Description	37
		1.7.2	Use and performance	38
		1.7.3	History	41
		1.7.4	Tactics	42
		1.7.5	Surviving bows and arrows	42
		1.7.6	Social importance	43
		1.7.7	See also	43
		1.7.8	Notes	43
		1.7.9	References	45
		1.7.10	Further reading	46
	1.8	Gorytos		47
		1.8.1	External links	47
	1.9	History of crossbows		47
		1.9.1	China and South East Asia	48
		1.9.2	Europe	49
		1.9.3	Islamic World	51
		1.9.4	Africa and in the Americas	52
		1.9.5	Use of crossbows today	52

		1.9.6	See also	52

- 1.9.6 See also . . . 52
- 1.9.7 References . . . 52
- 1.9.8 Sources . . . 53
- 1.9.9 Further reading . . . 54
- 1.10 Mary Rose . . . 54
  - 1.10.1 Historical context . . . 54
  - 1.10.2 Construction . . . 55
  - 1.10.3 Design . . . 55
  - 1.10.4 Military career . . . 60
  - 1.10.5 Causes of sinking . . . 64
  - 1.10.6 History as a shipwreck . . . 65
  - 1.10.7 Archaeology . . . 69
  - 1.10.8 Display . . . 72
  - 1.10.9 See also . . . 73
  - 1.10.10 Notes . . . 73
  - 1.10.11 References . . . 76
  - 1.10.12 Further reading . . . 77
  - 1.10.13 External links . . . 77
- 1.11 Medieval archery . . . 77
  - 1.11.1 Prehistory . . . 78
  - 1.11.2 Ancient history . . . 79
  - 1.11.3 Middle Ages . . . 81
  - 1.11.4 Decline of archery . . . 81
  - 1.11.5 Recreational revival . . . 83
  - 1.11.6 A modern sport . . . 83
  - 1.11.7 See also . . . 84
  - 1.11.8 References . . . 84
  - 1.11.9 Further reading . . . 87
  - 1.11.10 External links . . . 87
- 1.12 Mongol bow . . . 87
  - 1.12.1 Pre-Qing Mongol Bow . . . 87
  - 1.12.2 Influence of the Qing Dynasty . . . 87
  - 1.12.3 Construction . . . 88
  - 1.12.4 The arrows . . . 88
  - 1.12.5 Range . . . 88
  - 1.12.6 Mongolian draw and release . . . 89
  - 1.12.7 See also . . . 89
  - 1.12.8 References . . . 89

- 1.12.9 External links ... 89
- 1.13 Mounted archery ... 90
  - 1.13.1 Basic features ... 90
  - 1.13.2 Appearance in history ... 91
  - 1.13.3 Technology ... 93
  - 1.13.4 Modern revival of mounted archery ... 93
  - 1.13.5 Chinese mounted archery ... 93
  - 1.13.6 Traditional Korean school ... 94
  - 1.13.7 Traditional Japanese horseback archery ... 94
  - 1.13.8 Mounted archery in the United States ... 95
  - 1.13.9 Horseback Archery in the United Kingdom ... 95
  - 1.13.10 See also ... 95
  - 1.13.11 References ... 95
  - 1.13.12 Further reading ... 97
  - 1.13.13 External links ... 97
- 1.14 Pítati ... 97
  - 1.14.1 A letter example--no. 337 ... 97
  - 1.14.2 "Archers and myrrh" ... 98
  - 1.14.3 Analysis ... 98
  - 1.14.4 See also ... 98
  - 1.14.5 References ... 98
- 1.15 Scorton Arrow ... 98
  - 1.15.1 References ... 98
- 1.16 Shooting an apple off one's child's head ... 99
  - 1.16.1 Examples ... 99
  - 1.16.2 Related stories ... 100
  - 1.16.3 Scholarly study ... 100
  - 1.16.4 See also ... 101
  - 1.16.5 References ... 101
  - 1.16.6 Sources ... 102
  - 1.16.7 External links ... 102
- 1.17 Society of Archers ... 102
  - 1.17.1 References ... 102
- 1.18 St Mary's Butts ... 102
  - 1.18.1 History ... 102
  - 1.18.2 References ... 103
  - 1.18.3 External links ... 103
- 1.19 Stone wrist-guard ... 103

- 1.19.1 Description 103
- 1.19.2 Original use 103
- 1.19.3 Terminology 103
- 1.19.4 References 104
- 1.20 The Archer's Craft 104
- 1.21 The Witchery of Archery 104
  - 1.21.1 Background 104
  - 1.21.2 See also 105
  - 1.21.3 Notes 105
  - 1.21.4 References 105
- 1.22 Thumb ring 105
  - 1.22.1 Use 106
  - 1.22.2 Historic specimens 106
  - 1.22.3 Variants 106
  - 1.22.4 Gallery 107
  - 1.22.5 References 107
  - 1.22.6 External links 107
- 1.23 Toxophilus 107
  - 1.23.1 Influence on English 108
  - 1.23.2 History of archery 108
  - 1.23.3 Editions 108
  - 1.23.4 See also 108
  - 1.23.5 References 108
  - 1.23.6 Further reading 109
  - 1.23.7 External links 109
- 1.24 Turkish archery 109
  - 1.24.1 History 109
  - 1.24.2 Equipment 109
  - 1.24.3 Technique 110
  - 1.24.4 See also 110
  - 1.24.5 External links 110
  - 1.24.6 References 110
- 1.25 Unlawful Games Act 1541 111
  - 1.25.1 Section 5 111
  - 1.25.2 See also 111
  - 1.25.3 References 111
- 1.26 William Tell 112
  - 1.26.1 Legend 112

- 1.26.2 Earliest mentions (15th century) 113
- 1.26.3 Early Modern period 114
- 1.26.4 Reception 1789–1945 115
- 1.26.5 Historicity debate 117
- 1.26.6 Comparative mythology 118
- 1.26.7 See also 119
- 1.26.8 Notes and references 119
- 1.26.9 Bibliography 120
- 1.26.10 External links 120
- 1.27 Yabusame 120
  - 1.27.1 History 120
  - 1.27.2 Ritual 121
  - 1.27.3 Famous schools 122
  - 1.27.4 Decline and revival 122
  - 1.27.5 Contemporary practice 123
  - 1.27.6 See also 123
  - 1.27.7 Notes 123
  - 1.27.8 External links 123
- 1.28 Yeoman 123
  - 1.28.1 Etymology 124
  - 1.28.2 History of Yeomen 124
  - 1.28.3 United States 124
  - 1.28.4 Other references 125
  - 1.28.5 See also 126
  - 1.28.6 Notes 126
  - 1.28.7 Further reading 126
  - 1.28.8 External links 126

2 Medieval Archery — 127

- 2.1 Arbalest 127
  - 2.1.1 Nomenclature 127
  - 2.1.2 References 127
- 2.2 Archer's stake 128
  - 2.2.1 Origins 128
  - 2.2.2 Deployment 128
  - 2.2.3 Usage 128
  - 2.2.4 References 128
- 2.3 Franc-archer 128
  - 2.3.1 Recruitment and composition 129

		2.3.2	Organization and equipment	129

- 2.3.2 Organization and equipment . . . 129
- 2.3.3 Service . . . 129
- 2.3.4 Franc-archers in literature . . . 129
- 2.3.5 References . . . 129
- 2.3.6 Bibliography . . . 129
- 2.4 Gakgung . . . 130
  - 2.4.1 History of Military Origin and Usage . . . 130
  - 2.4.2 Transition to Recreational Sport . . . 131
  - 2.4.3 Construction and competition . . . 131
  - 2.4.4 See also . . . 132
  - 2.4.5 References . . . 132
  - 2.4.6 External links . . . 132
- 2.5 Newington Butts . . . 132
  - 2.5.1 Toponymy . . . 133
  - 2.5.2 History . . . 133
  - 2.5.3 Theatre . . . 133
  - 2.5.4 See also . . . 133
  - 2.5.5 Notes and references . . . 134
  - 2.5.6 Further reading . . . 134
  - 2.5.7 External links . . . 134
- 2.6 Yumi . . . 134
  - 2.6.1 History . . . 135
  - 2.6.2 Shape . . . 135
  - 2.6.3 String . . . 136
  - 2.6.4 Care and maintenance . . . 136
  - 2.6.5 Bow lengths . . . 136
  - 2.6.6 Yumi history . . . 136
  - 2.6.7 Gallery . . . 136
  - 2.6.8 See also . . . 137
  - 2.6.9 References . . . 137
  - 2.6.10 Further reading . . . 137
  - 2.6.11 External links . . . 137

3 Text and image sources, contributors, and licenses   **138**
- 3.1 Text . . . 138
- 3.2 Images . . . 144
- 3.3 Content license . . . 154

Chapter 1

Introduction

1.1 Medieval archery

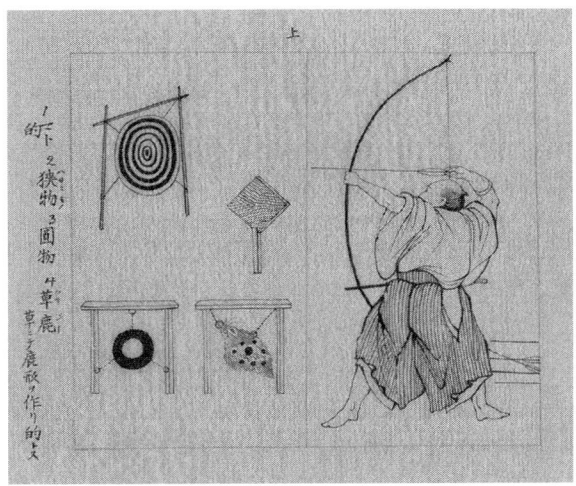

A Japanese archer with targets. Ink on paper, 1878.

The bow and arrow are known to have been invented by the end of the Upper Paleolithic, and for at least 10,000 years archery was an important military and hunting skill, and features prominently in the mythologies of many cultures.

Archers, whether on foot, in chariots and on horseback were a major part of most militaries until about 1500 when they began to be replaced by firearms, first in Europe, and then progressively elsewhere.

Archery continues to be a popular sport; most commonly in the form of target archery, but in some places also for hunting.

1.1.1 Prehistory

Epipaleolithic

Based on indirect evidence, the bow seems to have been invented near the transition from the Upper Paleolithic to the Mesolithic, some 10,000 years ago. The oldest direct evidence dates to 8,000 years ago. The discovery of stone points in Sibudu Cave, South Africa, has prompted the proposal that bow and arrow technology existed as early as 64,000 years ago.*[1]

In the Levant, artifacts which may be arrow-shaft straighteners are known from the Natufian culture, (ca. 12,800-10,300 BP) onwards. The Khiamian and PPN A shouldered Khiam-points may well be arrowheads.

The oldest indication for archery in Europe comes from Stellmoor in the Ahrensburg valley north of Hamburg, Germany. They were associated with artifacts of the late Paleolithic (11,000-9,000 BP). The arrows were made of pine and consisted of a mainshaft and a 15-20 centimetre (6-8 inches) long foreshaft with a flint point. They had shallow grooves on the base, indicating that they were shot from a bow.*[2]

The oldest definite bows known so far come from the Holmegård swamp in Denmark. In the 1940s, two bows were found there, dated to about 8,000 BP.*[3] The Holmegaard bows are made of elm and have flat arms and a D-shaped midsection. The center section is biconvex. The complete bow is 1.50 m (5 ft) long. Bows of Holmegaard-type were in use until the Bronze Age; the convexity of the midsection has decreased with time.

Mesolithic pointed shafts have been found in England, Germany, Denmark, and Sweden. They were often rather long, up to 120 cm (4 ft) and made of European hazel (*Corylus avellana*), wayfaring tree (*Viburnum lantana*) and other small woody shoots. Some still have flint arrow-heads preserved; others have blunt wooden ends for hunting birds and small game. The ends show traces of fletching, which was fastened on with birch-tar.

The oldest depictions of combat, found in Iberian cave art of the Mesolithic, show battles between archers.*[4] A group of three archers encircled by a group of four is found in Cueva del Roure, Morella la Vella, Castellón, Valencia. A depiction of a larger battle (which may, however, date to the early Neolithic), in which eleven archers are attacked by seventeen running archers, is found in Les Dogue, Ares

Cave painting of a battle between archers, Morella la Vella, Valencia, Spain.

del Maestrat, Castellón, Valencia.[5] At Val del Charco del Agua Amarga, Alcañiz, Aragon, seven archers with plumes on their heads are fleeing a group of eight archers running in pursuit.[6]

Archery seems to have arrived in the Americas via Alaska, as early as 6000 BCE,[7] with the Arctic small tool tradition, about 2,500 BCE, spreading south into the temperate zones as early as 2,000 BCE, and was widely known among the indigenous peoples of North America from about 500 CE.[8]

Neolithic

The oldest Neolithic bow known from Europe was found in anaerobic layers dating between 7,400-7,200 BP, the earliest layer of settlement at the lake settlement at La Draga, Banyoles, Girona, Spain. The intact specimen is short at 1.08m, has a D-shaped cross-section, and is made of yew wood.[9] European Neolithic fortifications, arrow-heads, injuries, and representations indicate that, in Neolithic and Early Bronze Age Europe, archery was a major form of interpersonal violence.[10] Stone wrist-guards, interpreted as display versions of bracers, form a defining part of the Beaker culture and arrowheads are also commonly found in Beaker graves.

Bronze Age

Chariot-borne archers became a defining feature of Middle Bronze Age warfare, from Europe to Eastern Asia and India. However, in the Middle Bronze Age, with the development of massed infantry tactics, and with the use of chariots for shock tactics or as prestigious command vehicles, archery seems to have lessened in importance in European warfare.[10] In approximately the same period, with the Seima-Turbino Phenomenon and the spread of the Andronovo culture, mounted archery became a defining feature of Eurasian nomad cultures and a foundation of their military success, until the massed use of guns. In China, crossbows were developed, and Han Dynasty writers attributed Chinese success in battles against nomad invaders to the massed use of crossbows, first definitely attested at the Battle of Ma-Ling in 341 BCE.[11]

1.1.2 Ancient history

Further information: Mounted archery, Composite bow, Perso-Parthian bow, Parthian shot, Sassanid army, Rashidun army, Mongol military tactics and organization, Mongol bow, Turkish archery, Turkish bow, and English longbow

Ancient civilizations, notably the Persians, Parthians,

Archers with recurve bows and short spears, detail from the archers' frieze in Darius' palace in Susa. Siliceous glazed bricks, c. 510 BC.

Indians, Koreans, Chinese, and Japanese fielded large

numbers of archers in their armies. Arrows were destructive against massed formations, and the use of archers often proved decisive. The Sanskrit term for archery, dhanurveda, came to refer to martial arts in general. Mounted archers were used as the main military force for many of the equestrian nomads, including the Cimmerians and the Mongols.

Ancient Near East

The ancient Egyptian people took to archery as early as 5,000 years ago. Archery was widespread by the time of the earliest pharaohs and was practiced both for hunting and use in warfare. Legendary figures from the tombs of Thebes are depicted giving "lessons in archery".*[12] Some Egyptian deities are also connected to archery.*[13] The "Nine bows" were a conventional representation of Egypt's external enemies. One of the oldest representations of the Nine bows is on the seated statue of Pharaoh Djoser (3rd Dynasty, 27th century BCE).*[14]

Female acrobat shooting an arrow with a bow in her feet; Gnathia style pelikai *pottery; 4th century BC*

Archer wearing feather headdress. Alabaster. From Nineveh, Iraq. Reign of Ashurbanipal II, 668-627 BCE. The Burrell Collection, Glasgow, UK

The Assyrians and Babylonians extensively used the bow and arrow; the Old Testament has multiple references to archery as a skill identified with the ancient Hebrews. Xenophon describes long bows used to great effect in Corduene.

The Chariot warriors of the Kassites relied heavily on the bow. The Nuzi texts detail the bows and the number of arrows assigned to the chariot crew. Archery was essential to the role of the light horse-drawn chariot as a vehicle of warfare.*[15]

Three-bladed (trilobate) arrowheads have been found in the United Arab Emirates, dated to 100BCE-150CE.*[16]

Greco-Roman antiquity

The people of Crete practiced archery and Cretan mercenary archers were in great demand.*[17] Crete was known for its unbroken tradition of archery.*[18]

The Greek god Apollo is the god of archery, also of plague and the sun, metaphorically perceived as shooting invisible arrows, Artemis the goddess of hunting. Heracles and Odysseus and other mythological figures are often depicted with a bow.

During the invasion of India, Alexander the Great personally took command of the shield-bearing guards, foot-companions, archers, Agrianians and horse-javelin-men and led them against the Kamboja clans—the Aspasios of Kunar valleys, the Guraeans of the Guraeus (Panjkora) valley, and the Assakenois of the Swat and Buner valleys.*[19]

The early Romans had very few archers, if any. As their empire grew, they recruited auxiliary archers from other

Apollo and Artemis. Tondo of an Attic red-figure cup, ca. 470 BC.

Scythian bowmen on gold plaque from Kul Oba kurgan, in Crimea, 4th century BC.

nations. Julius Caesar's armies in Gaul included Cretan archers, and Vercingetorix his enemy ordered "all the archers, of whom there was a very great number in Gaul, to be collected".[20] By the 4th century, archers with powerful composite bows were a regular part of Roman armies throughout the empire. After the fall of the western empire, the Romans came under severe pressure from the highly skilled mounted archers belonging to the Hun invaders, and later Eastern Roman armies relied heavily on mounted archery.[21]

East Asia

Main articles: Chinese archery, Gungdo, Kyudo, and Yabusame

For millennia, archery has played a pivotal role in Chinese history.[22] In particular, archery featured prominently in ancient Chinese culture and philosophy: archery was one of the Six Noble Arts of the Zhou dynasty (1146–256 BCE); archery skill was a virtue for Chinese emperors; Confucius himself was an archery teacher; and Lie Zi (a Daoist philosopher) was an avid archer.[23][24] Because the cultures associated with Chinese society spanned a wide geography and time range, the techniques and equipment associated with Chinese archery are diverse.[25]

In East Asia Joseon Korea adopted a military-service examination system from China,[26] and South Korea remains a particularly strong performer at Olympic archery competitions even to this day.[27][28]

India

The bow and arrow constituted the classical Indian weapon of warfare, from the Vedic period, until the advent of Islam.[29][30] Some Rigvedic hymns lay emphasis on the use of the bow and arrow.[31]

Detailed accounts of training methodologies in early India concern archery, considered to be an essential martial skill in early India.[32] Legendary figures like Drona, are depicted as masters in the art of archery.[33] Arjuna, Eklavya, Karna, Rama, Lakshmana, Bharata and Shatrughna the great warrior are also associated with archery.

1.1.3 Middle Ages

A complete arrow of 75 cm[34] (along with other fragments and arrow heads) dated back to 1283 CE, was discovered inside a cave[35] situated in the Qadisha Valley,[36] Lebanon.

A treatise on Saracen archery was written in 1368. This was a didactic poem on archery dedicated to a Mameluke sultan by ṬAIBUGHĀ, al-Ashrafī.[37]

A 14th century treatise on Arab archery was written by Hussain bin Abd al-Rahman.[38]

A treatise on Arab archery by Ibn Qayyim Al-Jawziyya, Muḥammad ibn Abī Bakr (1292AD-1350AD) comes from the 14th century.[39] Another treatise, *A book on the excellence of the bow & arrow* of c. 1500 details the practices and techniques of archery among the Arabs of that

1.1. MEDIEVAL ARCHERY

time.*[40] An online copy of the text is available.*[41]

Skilled archers were prized in Europe throughout the Middle Ages. The Assize of Arms of 1252 tells us that English yeomen were required by law, in an early version of a militia, to practice archery and maintain their skills. We are told that 6,000 English archers launched 42,000 arrows per minute at the Battle of Crecy in 1346.*[42] The Battle of Agincourt in 1415 is notable for Henry V's introduction of the English longbow into military lore. Henry VIII was so concerned about the state of his archers that he enjoined tennis and other frivolous pursuits in his Unlawful Games Act 1541.

1.1.4 Decline of archery

Panels depicting Archery in England from Joseph Strutt's 1801 book, The sports and pastimes of the people of England from the earliest period. *The date of the top image is unknown; the middle image is from 1496 and the bottom panel is circa fourteenth century.*

Archery game outside the town. Jan Lamsvelt in Van Heemskerk: Batavische Arcadia, *1708.*

The advent of firearms eventually rendered bows obsolete in warfare. Despite the high social status, ongoing utility, and widespread pleasure of archery, almost every culture that gained access to even early firearms used them widely, to the relative neglect of archery.

> "Have them bring as many guns as possible, for no other equipment is needed. Give strict orders that all men, even the samurai, carry guns."
> —Asano Yukinaga, 1598*[43]

In Ireland, Geoffrey Keating (c. 1569 - c. 1644) mentions archery as having been practiced "down to a recent period within our own memory" *[44]

Early firearms were inferior in rate-of-fire (a Tudor English author expects eight shots from the English longbow in the time needed for a "ready shooter" to give five from the musket),*[45] and François Bernier reports that well-trained mounted archers at the Battle of Samugarh in 1658 were "shooting six times before a musketeer can fire twice".*[46] Firearms were also very susceptible to wet weather. However, they had a longer effective range (up to 200 yards for the longbow, up to 600 yards for the musket),*[45]*[47] greater penetration,*[48] and were tactically superior in the common situation of soldiers shooting at each other from behind obstructions. They also penetrated steel armour without any need to develop special musculature. Armies equipped with guns could thus provide superior firepower, and highly trained archers became obsolete on the battlefield. The Battle of Cerignola in 1503 was won by Spain mainly by the use of matchlock firearms, marking the first time a major battle was won through the use of firearms.

The last regular unit armed with bows was the Archers' Company of the Honourable Artillery Company, ironically a part of the oldest regular unit in England to be armed with gunpowder weapons. The last recorded use of bows in battle in Britain seems to have been a skirmish at Bridgnorth; in October 1642, during the English Civil War, an impromptu militia, armed with bows, was effective against unarmoured musketmen.*[49] (A more recent use of archery in war was in 1940, on the retreat to Dunkirk, when Jack Churchill, who had brought his bows on active service, "was delighted to see his arrow strike the centre German in the left of the chest and penetrate his body").*[50]

Archery continued in some areas that were subject to limitations on the ownership of arms, such as the Scottish Highlands during the repression that followed the decline of the Jacobite cause, and the Cherokees after the Trail of Tears. The Tokugawa shogunate severely limited the import and manufacture of guns, and encouraged traditional martial skills among the samurai; towards the end of the Satsuma Rebellion in 1877, some rebels fell back on the use of bows and arrows. Archery remained an important part of the military examinations until 1894 in Korea and 1904 in China.

Within the steppe of Eurasia, archery continued to play an important part in warfare, although now restricted to mounted archery. The Ottoman Empire still fielded auxiliary cavalry which was noted for its use of bows from horseback. This practice was continued by the Ottoman subject nations, despite the Empire itself being a proponent of early firearms. The practice declined after the Crimean Khanate was absorbed by Russia; however mounted archers remained in the Ottoman order of battle until the post 1826 reforms to the Ottoman Army. The art of traditional archery remained in minority use for sport and for hunting in Turkey up until the 1820s, but the knowledge of constructing composite bows, fell out of use with the death of the last bowyer in the 1930s. The rest of the Middle East also lost the continuity of its archery tradition at this time.

An exception to this trend was the Comanche culture of North America, where mounted archery remained competitive with muzzle-loading guns. "After... about 1800, most Comanches began to discard muskets and pistols and to rely on their older weapons." *[51] Repeating firearms, however, were superior in turn, and the Comanches adopted them when they could. Bows remained effective hunting weapons for skilled horse archers, used to some extent by all Native Americans on the Great Plains to hunt buffalo as long as there were buffalo to hunt. The last Comanche hunt was in 1878, and it failed for lack of buffalo, not lack of appropriate weapons.*[52]

Ongoing use of bows and arrows was maintained in isolated cultures with little or no contact with the outside world. The use of traditional archery in some African conflicts has been reported in the 21st century, and the Sentinelese still use bows as part of a lifestyle scarcely touched by outside contact. A remote group in Brazil, recently photographed from the air, aimed bows at the aeroplane.*[53] Bows and arrows saw considerable use in the 2007–2008 Kenyan crisis.

1.1.5 Recreational revival

A print of the 1822 meeting of the "Royal British Bowmen" archery club.

The British initiated a major revival of archery as an upper-class pursuit from about 1780-1840.*[54] Early recreational archery societies included the Finsbury Archers and the Kilwinning Papingo, established in 1688. The latter held competitions in which the archers had to dislodge a wooden parrot from the top of an abbey tower. The Company of Scottish Archers was formed in 1676 and is one of the oldest sporting bodies in the world. It remained a small and scattered pastime, however, until the late 18th century when it experienced a fashionable revival among the aristocracy. Sir Ashton Lever, an antiquarian and collector, formed the Toxophilite Society in London in 1781, with the patronage of George, the Prince of Wales.

Archery societies were set up across the country, each with its own strict entry criteria and outlandish costumes. Recreational archery soon became extravagant social and ceremonial events for the nobility, complete with flags, music and 21 gun salutes for the competitors. The clubs were "the drawing rooms of the great country houses placed outside" and thus came to play an important role in the social networks of local elites. As well as its emphasis on display and status, the sport was notable for its popularity with females. Young women could not only compete in the contests but retain and show off their sexuality while doing so. Thus, archery came to act as a forum for introductions, flirtation and romance.*[54] It was often consciously styled in the manner of a Medieval tournament with titles and laurel wreaths being presented as a reward to the victor. General meetings were held from 1789, in which local lodges convened together to standardise the rules and ceremonies. Archery was also co-opted as a distinctively British tradition, dating back to the lore of Robin Hood and it served as a patriotic form of entertainment at a time of political tension in Europe. The societies were also elitist, and the new middle class bourgeoisie were excluded from the clubs due to their lack of social status.

After the Napoleonic Wars, the sport became increasingly popular among all classes, and it was framed as a nostalgic reimagining of the preindustrial rural Britain. Particularly influential was Sir Walter Scott's 1819 novel, *Ivanhoe* that depicted the heroic character Lockseley winning an archery tournament.*[55]

Picture of Pope taken while grizzly hunting at Yellowstone

1.1.6 A modern sport

The 1840s saw the first attempts at turning the recreation into a modern sport. The first Grand National Archery Society meeting was held in York in 1844 and over the next decade the extravagant and festive practices of the past were gradually whittled away and the rules were standardised as the 'York Round' - a series of shoots at 60, 80, and 100 yards. Horace A. Ford helped to improve archery standards and pioneered new archery techniques. He won the Grand National 11 times in a row and published a highly influential guide to the sport in 1856.

Towards the end of the 19th century, the sport experienced declining participation as alternative sports such as croquet and tennis became more popular among the middle class. By 1889, just 50 archery clubs were left in Britain, but it was still included as a sport at the 1900 Paris Olympics.

In the United States, primitive archery was revived in the early 20th century. The last of the Yahi Indian tribe, a native known as Ishi, came out of hiding in California in 1911.*[56]*[57] His doctor, Saxton Pope, learned many of Ishi's traditional archery skills, and popularized them.*[58]*[59] The Pope and Young Club, founded in 1961 and named in honor of Pope and his friend, Arthur Young, became one of North America's leading bowhunting and conservation organizations. Founded as a nonprofit scientific organization, the Club was patterned after the prestigious Boone and Crockett Club and advocated responsible bowhunting by promoting quality, fair chase hunting, and sound conservation practices.

In Korea, the transformation of archery to a healthy pastime was led by Emperor Gojong, and is the basis of a popular modern sport. The Japanese continue to make and use their unique traditional equipment. Among the Cherokees, popular use of their traditional longbows never died out.*[60]

In China, at the beginning of the 21st century, there has been revival in interest among craftsmen looking to construct bows and arrows, as well as in practicing technique in the traditional Chinese style.*[61]*[62]

In modern times, mounted archery continues to be practiced as a popular competitive sport in modern Hungary and in some Asian countries but it is not recognized as an international competition.*[63] Archery is the national sport of the Kingdom of Bhutan.*[64]

From the 1920s, professional engineers took an interest in archery, previously the exclusive field of traditional craft experts.*[65] They led the commercial development of new forms of bow including the modern recurve and compound bow. These modern forms are now dominant in modern Western archery; traditional bows are in a minority. In the 1980s, the skills of traditional archery were revived by American enthusiasts, and combined with the new scientific understanding. Much of this expertise is available in the *Traditional Bowyer's Bibles* (see Additional reading). Modern game archery owes much of its success to Fred Bear, an American bow hunter and bow manufacturer.*[66]

1.1.7 See also

- Archery
- Kyūdō, Japanese archery
- Yabusame, Japanese horseback archery
- Gungdo, Korean archery
- Turkish archery
- Chinese archery
- Archery in India

1.1.8 References

[1] Backwell, Lucinda; d'Errico, Francesco; Wadley, Lyn (2008). "Middle Stone Age bone tools from the Howiesons Poort layers, Sibudu Cave, South Africa". *Journal of Archaeological Science*. **35** (6): 1566–1580. doi:10.1016/j.jas.2007.11.006. "Explicit tests for distinctions between thrown spears and projected arrows have not yet been conducted, and many of the segments could have been employed equally successfully as insets for spears or arrows (Lombard & Pargeter 2008)." Lombard, Marlize; Phillipson, Laurel (2010). "Indications of bow and stone-tipped arrow use 64 000 years ago in KwaZulu-Natal, South Africa". *Antiquity*. **84**: 635–648. doi:10.1017/s0003598x00100134.

[2] McEwen E, Bergman R, Miller C. Early bow design and construction. Scientific American 1991 vol. 264 pp76-82.

[3] Charles E. Grayson, Mary French, Michael J. O'Brien. Traditional Archery from Six Continents: The Charles E. Grayson Collection. University of Missouri Press 2007. ISBN 978-0-8262-1751-6 p=1

[4] Keith F. Otterbein, *How War Began* (2004), p. 72.

[5] Christensen J. 2004. "Warfare in the European Neolithic", *Acta Archaeologica* 75, 129–156.

[6] S.L. Washburn, *Social Life of Early Man* (1962), p. 207.

[7] Blitz, John. "Adoption of the Bow in Prehistoric North America. *North American Archaeologist*, vol 9 no 2, 1988" (PDF).

[8] Brian Fagan. The first North Americans. Thames and Hudson, London, 2011. ISBN 978-0-500-02120-0 Hodge, Frederick Webb (1907). *Handbook of American Indians North of Mexico, Vol 1* pg 485. Government Printing Office

[9] accessed The oldest Neolithic Bow discovered in Europe, Universitat Autònoma de Barcelona 2012. 1 July 2012

[10] Bronze Age Warfare. Richard Osgood and Sarah Monks with Judith Toms. The History Press 2000. pp.139-142

[11] Needham (1986), Volume 5, Part 6, 124–128.

[12] Wilson, John (1956). *The Culture of Ancient Egypt* pg 186. University of Chicago Press

[13] Traunecker, Claude (2001). *The Gods of Egypt* pg 29. Cornell University Press

[14] "Enemies of Civilization: Attitudes toward Foreigners in Ancient Mesopotamia, Egypt, and China", Mu-chou Poo, Mu-chou Poo Muzhou Pu. SUNY Press, Feb 1, 2012. p. 43. Retrieved 7 jan 2017

[15] Drews, Roberts (1993). *The End of the Bronze Age: Changes in Warfare and the Catastrophe Ca. 1200 B.C.* pg 119. Princeton University Press

[16] "A trilobate arrowhead can be defined as an arrowhead that has three wings or blades that are usually placed at equal angles (i.e. c. 120°) around the imaginary longitudinal axis extending from the centre of the socket or tang. Since this type of arrowhead is rare in southeastern Arabia, we must investigate its origin and the reasons behind its presence at ed-Dur."Delrue, Parsival (2007). "Trilobate Arrowheads at Ed-Dur (U.A.E, Emirate of Umm Al-Qaiwain)"." . *Arabian Archaeology and Epigraphy*. **18** (2): 239–250. doi:10.1111/j.1600-0471.2007.00281.x.

[17] Cambridge University Press (2000). *Cambridge Ancient History* pg 174.

[18] Kirk, Geoffrey etc (1993). *The Iliad: a commentary* pg 136. Cambridge University Press

[19] The Ashvayanas living on river Guraeus (modern river Panjkora), which are the Gauri of Mahabharata, were also known as Gorys or Guraios, modern Ghori or Gori, a wide spread tribe, branches of which are still to be found on the Panjkora and on both sides of the Kabul at the point of its confluence with Landai (See: *History of Punjab*, Vol I, 1997, p 227, Publication Bureau, Punjabi University, Patiala (Editors) Dr L. M. Joshi, Dr Fauja Singh). The clan name Gore or Gaure is also found among the modern Kamboj people of Punjab and it is stated that the Punjab Kamboj Gaure/Gore came from the Kunar valley to Punjab at some point in time in the past (Ref: These Kamboja People, 1979, 122; Kambojas Through the Ages, 2005, p 131, Kirpal Singh).

[20] gutenberg.org Caius Julius Caesar. *Caesar's Commentaries*. Translated by W. A. Macdevitt.

1.1. MEDIEVAL ARCHERY

[21] *Greece and Rome at War*, Peter Connolly, Adrian Keith Goldsworthy. Greenhill Books 1998 ISBN 1-85367-303-X ISBN 978-1853673030

[22] "Archived copy". Archived from the original on 31 January 2011. Retrieved 26 December 2010.

[23] Six Arts of Ancient China

[24] Chinese Archery (Paperback). Stephen Selby. Hong Kong University Press 2000. ISBN 962-209-501-1 ISBN 978-962-209-501-4

[25] The Bows of China. Stephen Selby. Journal of Chinese Martial Studies, Winter 2010 Issue 2. Three-In-One Press, 2010.

[26] Korea archery at anthromuseum.missouri.edu "During the Choson period (1392-1910), Korea adopted a military-service examination system from China that included a focus on archery skills and that contributed to the development of Korean archery as a practical martial art."

[27] Archery in South Korea at lycos.com/info/archery

[28] "South sweep," 28 September 2000 at sportsillustrated.cnn.com

[29] Zimmer, Heinrich and Campbell, Joseph (1969). *Philosophies of India* pg 140. Princeton University Press.

[30] Drews, Robert (1993). *The End of the Bronze Age: Changes in Warfare and the Catastrophe Ca. 1200 B.C.* pg 119. Princeton University Press

[31] With the bow let us win cows, with the bow let us win the contest and violent battles with the bow. The bow ruins the enemy's pleasure; with the bow let us conquer all corners of the world. -- Drews, Roberts (1993). *The End of the Bronze Age: Changes in Warfare and the Catastrophe Ca. 1200 B.C.* pg 125. Princeton University Press

[32] Scharfe, Hartmut (2002). *Education in Ancient India* pg 271. Brill Academic Publishers

[33] Van Buitenen, J. A. B. (1980). *The Mahabharata: The Book of the Beginning* pg 153. University of Chicago Press

[34] Abi Aoun B., Baroudy F., Ghaouch A. Khawaja P and alias Momies du Liban: Rapport préliminaire sur la découverte archaéologique de 'Asi-al-Hadat (XIIIe siècle), France, Édifra, 1994

[35] http://www.cavinglebanon.com/asi-l-hadath-fortified-cave

[36] http://www.whc.unesco.org/en/list/850

[37] Boudot-Lamotte, A. 1972. "J. D. Latham et Lt. Cdr. W. F. PATERSON, Saracen Archery, An English version and exposition of a mameluke work on Archery (ca. A.D. 1368), with Introduction, Glossary, and Illustrations, London (The Holland Press) 1970, XL + 219 pp". Arabica. 19, no. 1: 98-99.

[38] Jallon, A.D. Kitab Fi Ma "Rifat "Ilm Ramy Al-Siham, a Treatise on Archery by Husayn B. "Abd Al-Rahman B. Muhammad B. Muhammad B. "Abdallah Al-Yunini AH 647 (?) - 724, AH 1249-50 (?) - 1324: A Critical Edition of the Arabic Text Together with a Study of the Work in English. University of Manchester, 1980. OCLC: 499854155.

[39] Ibn Qayyim al-Jawzīyah, Muḥammad ibn Abī Bakr. kitab ʻuniyat al-ṭullāb fī maʻrifat al-rāmī bil-nushshāb. [Cairo?]: [s.n.], 1932. OCLC: 643468400.

[40] Faris, Nabih Amin, and Robert Potter Elmer. Arab archery. An Arabic manuscript of about A.D. 1500, "A book on the excellence of the bow & arrow" and the description thereof. Princeton, N.J.: Princeton University Press, 1945. Translation of "Kitāb fī bayān faḍl al-qaws w-al-sahm wa-awsāfihima," no. 793 in Descriptive catalog of the Garrett collection of Arabic manuscripts in the Princeton university library.

[41] [tuba-archery.com/article/arab-archery.pdf Arab Archery].

[42] Rhoten, R.: "Trebuchet Energy Efficiency - Experimental Results" AIAA 2006-775

[43] Asano Yukinaga, 1598 CE, letter to his father, quoted in The Samurai, by S.R. Turnbull, Osprey, London 1977. ISBN 0-85045-097-7

[44] Geoffrey Keating. The History of Ireland, translated into English and preface by David Comyn, Patrick S. Dinneen. Accessed 9 December 2007

[45] A right exelent and pleasaunt dialogue, betwene Mercury and an English souldier contayning his supplication to Mars: bevvtified with sundry worthy histories, rare inuentions, and politike deuises. wrytten by B. Rich: gen. 1574. Published 1574 by J. Day. These bookes are to be sold [by H. Disle] at the corner shop, at the South west doore of Paules church in London. https://bowvsmusket.com/2015/07/14/barnabe-rich-a-right-exelent-and-pleasaunt-dialouge-1574/ accessed 21 April 2016

[46] as attributed to Bernier by Dirk H.A. Kolff. Naukar, Rajput, & Sepoy. The ethnohistory of the military labour market in Hindustan, 1450-1860. University of Cambridge Oriental Publications no. 43. Cambridge University Press 1990., p.23

[47] Korean Traditional Archery. Duvernay TA, Duvernay NY. Handong Global University, 2007

[48] Gunn, Steven; Gromelski, Tomasz (2012). "For whom the bell tolls: accidental deaths in Tudor England". *The Lancet*. **380** (9849): 1222–1223. doi:10.1016/S0140-6736(12)61702-4. "The mean depth of arrow wounds, for example, was an inch and a half, that of gunshot wounds six inches, not counting balls that went right through the body or head"

[49] John Norton, letter dated 5 October 1642. As printed in The Garrisons of Shropshire during the Civil War, Leake and

Evans publishers, Shrewsbury, 1867, page 32. "every man from 16 to 50 and upwards, gott himself into such armes as they could presently attaine, or could imagine be conduceable for the defence of the towne". "some companies of foote.. with their musketts... began to wade foarde, which being descried, we, with our bowes and arrows did so gaule them (being unarmed men) that with their utmost speed they did retreate" accessed 7 August 2012

[50] The archer's craft: A sheaf of notes on certain matters concerning archers and archery, the making of archers' tackle and the art of hunting with the bow. Adrian Eliot Hodgkin. Faber 1951

[51] T.R. Fehrenbach. Comanches, the history of a people. Vintage Books. London, 2007. ISBN 978-0-09-952055-9. First published in the USA by Alfred Knopf, 1974. Page 125.

[52] T.R. Fehrenbach. Comanches, the history of a people. Vintage Books. London, 2007. ISBN 978-0-09-952055-9. First published in the USA by Alfred Knopf, 1974. Page 553.

[53] "Amazonian archers". *BBC News*. 2008-05-30. Retrieved 2010-01-05.

[54] Johnes, Martin. "Archery—Romance-and-Elite-Culture-in-England-and-Wales —c-1780-1840 Martin Johnes. Archery, Romance and Elite Culture in England and Wales, c. 1780–1840". Swansea.academia.edu. Retrieved 2013-03-26.

[55] "The Royal Company of Archers". Retrieved 2012-12-17.

[56] Allely, Steve; et al. (2008), *The Traditional Bowyer's Bible, Volume 4*, The Lyons Press, ISBN 978-0-9645741-6-8

[57] Kroeber, Theodora (2004), *Ishi in Two Worlds: a biography of the last wild Indian in North America*, Berkeley: University of California Press, ISBN 978-0-520-24037-7

[58] Pope, Saxton (1925), *Hunting with the Bow and Arrow*, New York: G. P. Putnam's Sons

[59] Pope, Saxton (1926), *Adventurous Bowmen: field notes on African archery*, New York: G. P. Putnam's Sons

[60] Cherokee Bows and Arrows: How to Make and Shoot Primitive Bows and Arrows. Al Herrin. White Bear Pub (Nov 1989). ISBN 978-0962360138

[61] Article about the 2009 Chinese Traditional Archery Seminar

[62] News coverage of the 2010 Chinese Traditional Archery Seminar

[63] "Magyar index".

[64] "Bhutanese Traditional Archery".

[65] Hickman, C. N.; Nagler, Forrest; Klopsteg, Paul E. (1947), *Archery: The Technical Side. A compilation of scientific and technical articles on theory, construction, use and performance of bows and arrows, reprinted from journals of science and of archery*, National Field Archery Association

[66] Bertalan, Dan. *Traditional Bowyers Encyclopedia: The Bowhunting and Bowmaking World of the Nation's Top Crafters of Longbows and Recurves*, 2007. p. 73.

- uiowa.edu

*[1]

1.1.9 Further reading

- *The Traditional Bowyers Bible Volume 1*. The Lyons Press, 1992. ISBN 1-58574-085-3
- *The Traditional Bowyers Bible Volume 2*. The Lyons Press, 1992. ISBN 1-58574-086-1
- *The Traditional Bowyers Bible Volume 3*. The Lyons Press, 1994. ISBN 1-58574-087-X
- *The Traditional Bowyers Bible Volume 4*. The Lyons Press, 2008. ISBN 978-0-9645741-6-8

1.1.10 External links

- Archery Library Online Archery Books with historical content

[1] Crombie, Laura (2016). *Archery and Crossbow Guilds in Medieval Flanders*. Woodbridge: Boydell and Brewer.

1.2 Arab archery

Arab archery is the traditional style of archery practiced by the Arab peoples of the Middle East and North Africa from ancient to modern times.

1.2.1 Release Style

The style of Arab archery described in the extant texts (all of which date long after the Mongol conquests and the widespread use of Turkish Mamluk slaves as soldiers) is similar to the styles used by Mongol and Turkish archers, drawing with a thumb draw and using a thumb ring to protect the right thumb.*[1]*[2]

1.2.2 Arab Archery History

In 70 ce the town of Emesa (modern-day Homs, some 160 kilometers north of Damascus) sent archers to aid the Roman siege of Jerusalem. Hadrian knew Syria, having first visited in 117 and again in 123, shortly after his visit to Britannia. A Headstone of a Syrian archer was found along Hadrian's Wall, and dates from the 2nd century Common Era, when 200 Syrian archers were sent to reinforce the 8,000 Roman soldiers. The tombstone is now displayed at the Great North Museum: Hancock. Field archaeologist Mike Bishop, however, contends that everyone hunted, and the primary value of the Syrian archers was tactical — on the battlefield. Their bows, he explains, were Composite bows (also called "recurved"), capable of longer range than common longbows. "Correct and effective use of the composite bow," Bishop adds, "took a lifetime to master, so Eastern recruits were essential." *[3]

Arab archers used composite bows from foot, horse, and camel, to good effect from the 7th century.*[4]

1.2.3 Archery in Islam

Muhammad was quite good with a bow, and appreciated the benefits of archery in sports and warfare. A recurved bow made of bamboo, and ascribed to Muhammad, is held in the Sacred Relics (Topkapı Palace) in the Chamber of the Sacred Relics in the Topkapi Museum in Istanbul.*[5]

There are several comments by Mohammad concerning archery in the Hadith. Umm Salama told of Muhammed coming upon two groups practicing archery, and he praised them.*[6]

Malik ibn Anas spoke about when at the battle of Uhud, the troops left Muhammad behind, where the archer, Abu Talhah, remained behind and protected the Prophet with his shield.*[7]

Uqbah ibn Amir relates how Muhammad said that archery shooting was more dear to him than riding.*[8]

The Prophet owned six bows: az-Zawra', ar-Rauha', as-Safra', al-Bayda', al-Katum – which was broke during the battle of Battle of Uhud, and was taken by Qatadah bin an-Nu'man – and as-Saddad. The Prophet had a quiver called al-Kafur, and a strap for it made from tanned skin, as well as three silver circular rings, a buckle, and an edge made of silver. We should mention that Ibn Taymiyyah said that there are no authentic narrations that the Prophet ever wore a strap around his waist.*[9]

1.2.4 Arab Archery Today

There are a number of Arab Archery clubs and societies today. Some practice the traditional Arab archery, while others use Western styles of archery in sport competition and hunting. The main organization is FATA, or the "Fédération Arabe de Tir a L'Arc" of Lebanon, a member of the World Archery Federation. The Pan Arab Games usually have an archery competition, and the 12th Arab Games*[10] in Qatar held in 2011 had 60 archers from nine Arab countries compete.

1.2.5 References

[1] Paterson, W. F. 1966. "The Archers of Islam." Journal of the Economic and Social History of the Orient. Vol. 9, No. 1/2 (Nov., 1966), pp. 69-87.

[2] Marcelo Muller. "XLII. On thumb-tips and the various kind thereof, from: Arab Archery, by N.A. Faris and R.P. Elmer, 1945.". *archerylibrary.com*.

[3] Cecil, Charles O. 2017. Hadrian's Syrians. Aramco World. August 2017.

[4] KUNSELMAN, DAVID E. 2007. ARAB-BYZANTINE WAR, 629-644 AD. Page 53.

[5] "Sacred Relics". *bilkent.edu.tr*.

[6] Volume 4, Book 56, Number 710.

[7] Volume 5, Book 58, Number 156.

[8] Book 14, Number 2507.

[9] Abu Maryah. 2008. "Weapons of the Prophet Muhammad". February 20, 2008.

[10] http://www.worldarchery.org/OTHEREVENTS/Others/2011/Doha-ArabGames/TabId/1124/ArtMID/1567/ArticleID/470/Successful-Archery-Competition-at-the-12th-Arab-Games-.aspx

1.2.6 Bibliography

- Boit, Bernard A. 1991. THE FRUITS OF ADVERSITY: TECHNICAL REFINEMENTS, OF THE TURKISH COMPOSITE BOW DURING THE CRUSADING ERA. (PDF) A Thesis Presented in Partial Fulfillment of the Requirements for the degree Master of Arts in the Graduate School of The Ohio State University by Lt. Bernard A. Boit, USAF.

- Faris, Nabih Amin, and Robert Potter Elmer. Arab Archery: An Arabic Manuscript of About A.D. 1500, "A Book on the Excellence of the Bow & Arrow" and the Description Thereof. Princeton, N.J.: Princeton University Press, 1986. 182 pages. Translation of "Kitāb fī bayān fadl al-qaws w-al-sahm wa-awsāfihima," no. 793 in Descriptive catalog of the Garrett collection of Arabic manuscripts in the Princeton University library.

- Latham, J. D., W. F. Paterson, and Ṭaybughā. Saracen Archery: An English Version and Exposition of a Mameluke Work on Archery (Ca. A.D. 1368). (PDF) London: Holland P., 1970.

- McLeod, Wallace E. 1962. "Egyptian Composite Bows in New York." American Journal of Archaeology. Vol. 66, No. 1 (Jan., 1962), pp. 13–19

- Paterson, W. F. 1966. "The Archers of Islam." Journal of the Economic and Social History of the Orient. Vol. 9, No. 1/2 (Nov., 1966), pp. 69–87.

- Sukenik, Yigael. 1947. "The Composite Bow of the Canaanite Goddess Anath." Bulletin of the American Schools of Oriental Research. No. 107 (Oct., 1947), pp. 11–15.

- The Art of Shooting a Short Reflexed Bow with a Thumb Ring. 2012. By Adam Swoboda. Gdynia Press.

- A treatise on Arab archery is by Ibn Qayyim Al-Jawziyya, Muḥammad ibn Abī Bakr (1292AD-1350AD) and comes from the 14th century.[1]

1.2.7 See also

- Chinese archery
- Kyūdō
- Turkish archery
- English longbow

[1] Ibn Qayyim al-Jawzīyah, Muḥammad ibn Abī Bakr. kitab 'uniyat al-ṭullāb fī ma'rifat al-rāmī bil-nushshāb. [Cairo?]: [s.n.], 1932. OCLC: 643468400.

1.3 Archery butt

A **butt** is an archery shooting field, with mounds of earth used for the targets. The name originally referred to the targets themselves, but over time came to mean the platforms that held the targets as well. For instance *Othello*, V,ii,267 mentions "Here is my journey's end, here is my butt". In medieval times, it was compulsory for all yeomen in England to learn archery; see for example An Act concerning shooting in Long Bows, passed in the 3rd year of Henry VIII.

Several English towns have districts called "The Butts", but they may not always take their names from archery. The Middle English word "butt" referred to an abutting strip of land, and is often associated with medieval field systems.[1] An example is Newington Butts in south London where contrary to popular belief, the 1955 *Survey of London* published by London County Council could find no historical reference to archery butts.[2] It concluded that the name probably derived from the triangle of land between the roads, as the word "butts" is used elsewhere in Surrey to refer to odd corners or ends of land.[2]

The word is also used today for the earthwork mounds on, or before, which targets are mounted on a rifle range, with the object of stopping the flight of bullets beyond the range.

1.3.1 Towns with areas known as 'The Butts'

- Alston, Cumbria
- Alton, Hampshire
- Ashover, Derbyshire
- Barry, South Glamorgan
- Brentford, Middlesex
- Bromfield, Shropshire
- Clearwell, Gloucestershire

Chippenham, Wiltshire

- Chobham, Surrey
- Coventry, West Midlands
- Cowbridge, Glamorganshire
- Dunsford, Devonshire
- Fordingbridge, Hampshire
- Frome, Somerset
- Hexton, Hertfordshire
- Kidsgrove, Staffordshire
- Kilkenny, Ireland
- Lutterworth, Leicestershire
- Madley, Herefordshire

- Nether Alderley, Cheshire
- Newton Ferrers, Devon
- Rochdale, Greater Manchester
- St Mary's Butts, Reading, Berkshire
- Shaftesbury, Dorset (Butts Knapp)
- Worcester, Worcestershire
- Walsall, Staffordshire
- Westbury, Wiltshire
- **also** the village of Wootton-by-Woodstock, Oxfordshire

1.3.2 Notes and references

[1] "Archery butts - 3 General description". English Heritage. Archived from the original on 2012-03-01. Retrieved 2010-08-22.

[2] Darlington, Ida (1955), *Survey of London Volume 25 - St George's Fields, the Parishes of St. George the Martyr Southwark and St. Mary, Newington*, London County Council, pp. 83–84

1.3.3 External links

- "Archery butts". English Heritage. Archived from the original on 2006-09-05. Overview including a definition
- Archery butts definition
- Old engraving showing archery butts

1.4 Assize of Arms of 1252

The **Assize of Arms of 1252**, also called the **Ordinance of 1252**, was a proclamation of King Henry III of England concerning the enforcement of the Assize of Arms of 1181, and the appointment of constables to summon men to arms, quell breaches of the peace, and to deliver offenders to the sheriff.*[1]*[2]*[3]

Along with the Ordinance of 1233 that required the appointment of watchmen, the appointment of constables has been cited as one of the earliest creation of the English police, as has the Statute of Westminster 1285.*[2]*[4]*[5]

1.4.1 See also

- Assize of Arms of 1181

1.4.2 Notes

[1] Clarkson & Richardson 1889, p. 1.

[2] Pollock & Maitland 1898, p. 565.

[3] Delbrück 1990, p. 177.

[4] Clarkson & Richardson 1889, pp. 1-2.

[5] Rich 1977, p. 50.

1.4.3 References

- Clarkson, Charles Tempest; Richardson, J. Hall (1889). *Police!*. OCLC 60726408.
- Pollock, Frederick; Maitland, Frederic William (1898). *The History of English Law Before the Time of Edward I*. **1** (2 ed.). ISBN 978-1-58477-718-2.
- Delbrück, Hans (1990). Renfroe, Walter J., Jr, ed. *Medieval Warfare*. History of the Art of War. **3**. ISBN 0-8032-6585-9.
- Rich, Robert M. (1977). *Essays on the Theory and Practice of Criminal Justice*. ISBN 978-0-8191-0235-5. The origin of the exception goes back in English history to the Ordinance of 1233 which instituted night-watchmen, and directed them 'to arrest those who enter vills at night and go about armed.' Later the Ordinance of 1252 mentions 'disturbers of our peace.'

1.5 Battle of Crécy

"Crecy" and "Crécy" redirect here. For other uses, see Crecy (disambiguation).

The **Battle of Crécy** (1346), also called **Battle of Cressy**, was an English victory during the Edwardian phase of the Hundred Years' War. Married with the later battles of Poitiers in 1356, and Agincourt in 1415, it was the first of the trifecta of famous English successes during the conflict.

The battle was fought on 26 August 1346 near Crécy, in northern France. An army of English, Welsh, and allied mercenary troops led by Edward III of England, engaged and defeated a much larger army of French, Genoese and Majorcan troops led by Philip VI of France. Emboldened by the lessons of tactical flexibility and utilisation of terrain learned from the earlier Saxons, Vikings, Muslims and the recent battles with the Scots, the English army won an important victory.*[6]*[7]

The battle heralded the rise of the longbow as the dominant weapon on the Western European battlefield, and helped to continue the rise of the infantryman in medieval warfare. Crécy also saw the use of the ribauldequin, an early cannon, by the English army. The heavy casualties incurred by the French knightly class at the hands of peasants wielding ranged weapons was indicative of the decline of chivalry, and the emergence of a more practical, pragmatic approach to conducting warfare.*[8]

The battle crippled the French army's ability to come to the aid of Calais, which fell to the English the following year. Calais would remain under English rule for over two centuries, falling in 1558.

1.5.1 Campaign background

On the death of the French monarch Charles IV in 1328, Edward III of England was his closest male relative and legal successor. But a French court decreed that Charles' closest relative was his first cousin, Philip, Count of Valois. Philip was crowned as Philip VI of France. Reluctantly, Edward paid homage to Philip in his role as the Duke of Aquitaine, which he had inherited, in 1329. Populated by Gascons with a culture and language separate from the French, the inhabitants of Aquitaine preferred their relationship with the English crown. However, France continued to interfere in the affairs of the Gascons in matters both of law and war. Philip confiscated the lands of Aquitaine in 1337, precipitating war between England and France. Edward declared himself King of France in 1340, and set about unseating his rival from the French throne.

An early naval victory at Sluys in 1340 annihilated the French naval forces, giving the English domination at sea.*[9] Edward then invaded France with 12,000 men through the Low Countries, plundering the countryside. After an aborted siege of Cambrai, Edward led his army on a destructive chevauchée through Picardy, destroying hundreds of villages all the while shadowed by the French. Battle was given by neither side and Edward withdrew, bringing the campaign to an abrupt end. Edward returned to England to raise more funds for another campaign and to deal with political difficulties with the Scots, who were fighting for their independence.

On 11 July 1346, Edward set sail from Portsmouth with a fleet of 750 ships and an army of 15,000 men.*[10] With the army were Edward's sixteen-year-old son, Edward, the Black Prince, a large contingent of Welsh soldiers, and allied knights and mercenaries from the Holy Roman Empire. The army landed at St. Vaast la Hogue, 20 miles from Cherbourg. The intention was to undertake a massive chevauchée across Normandy, plundering its wealth and severely weakening the prestige of the French crown. Carentan, Saint-Lô and Torteval were all razed, after which Edward turned his army against Caen, the ancestral capital of Normandy. The English army sacked Caen on 26 July, plundering the city's huge wealth. Moving off on 1 August, the army marched north to the River Seine, possibly intending to attack Paris. The English army crossed the Seine at Poissy;*[11] however it was now between the Seine and the Somme rivers. Philip moved off with his army, attempting to entrap and destroy the English force.

Fording the Somme proved difficult: all bridges were either heavily guarded or burned. Edward vainly attempted to probe the crossings at Hangest-sur-Somme and Pont-Remy before moving north. Despite some close encounters, the pursuing French army was unable to bring to bear against the English. Edward was informed of a tiny ford on the Somme, likely well defended, near the village of Saigneville, called Blanchetaque. On 24 August, Edward and his army successfully forced a crossing at Blanchetaque with few casualties. Such was the French confidence that Edward would not ford the Somme that the area beyond had not been denuded, allowing Edward's army to resupply and plunder: Noyelles-sur-Mer and Le Crotoy were burned. Edward used the respite to prepare a defensive position at Crécy-en-Ponthieu while waiting for Philip to bring up his army.*[12] The position was protected on the flanks by the River Maye to the west, and the town of Wadicourt to the east, as well as a natural slope, putting cavalry at a disadvantage.

1.5.2 Battle

Preparation

Edward deployed his army facing south on a sloping hillside at Crécy-en-Ponthieu; the slope put the French mounted knights at an immediate disadvantage. The left flank was anchored against Wadicourt, while the right was protected by Crécy itself and the River Maye beyond. This made it impossible for the French army to outflank them. The army was also well-fed and rested, giving them an advantage over the French, who did not rest before the battle.*[13]

The English army The English army was led by Edward III; it mainly comprised English and Welsh troops along with allied Breton, Flemish and German mercenaries. The exact size and composition of the English force is not known. Andrew Ayton suggests a figure of around 2,500 men-at-arms: nobles and knights, heavily armoured and armed men, accompanied by their retinues. The army contained around 5,000 longbowmen, 3,000 hobelars (light cavalry and mounted archers) and 3,500 spearmen.*[14] Clifford Rodgers suggests 2,500 men-at-arms, 7,000 longbowmen, 3,250 hobelars and 2,300 spearmen.*[15] Jonathon Sumption believes the force was some-

1.5. BATTLE OF CRÉCY

Battle of Crécy (19th-century engraving)

what smaller, based on calculations of the carrying capacity of the transport fleet that was assembled to ferry the army to the continent. Based on this, he has put his estimate at around 7,000–10,000.*[16]

The power of Edward's army at Crécy lay in the massed use of the longbow: a powerful tall bow made primarily of yew. Upon Edward's accession in 1327, he had inherited a kingdom beset with two zones of conflict: Aquitaine and Scotland. England had not been a dominant military force in Europe: the French dominated in Aquitaine, and Scotland had all but achieved its independence since the Battle of Bannockburn in 1314. Previously, pitched battles in the medieval era had largely been decided by the massed charge of heavily armoured mounted knights, a widely feared force in their heyday. However, battles such as Manzikert had demonstrated their vulnerability to nimble mounted archers on fast horses, while engagements such as the Golden Spurs, Stirling, and Bannockburn, heralded the rise of the infantryman in effectively countering the armoured charge. Infantry did have significant advantages over heavily armoured cavalry; they were far cheaper to train and equip by comparison, and offered greater tactical flexibility, in that they could be deployed on almost any terrain.*[17]

Longbows had been effectively used before by English armies. Edward I successfully used longbowmen to break up static Scottish schiltron formations at the Battle of Falkirk in 1298; however it was not until Edward III's reign that they were accorded greater significance in English military doctrine. Edward realised the importance of inflicting severe damage upon an enemy force before melée combat began; at Halidon Hill in 1333, he used massed longbowmen and favourable terrain to inflict a significant defeat on the Scots forces to very few casualties of his own—in some ways a harbinger of his similar tactics at Crécy. To ensure he had a force of experienced and equipped archers to call upon, Edward ingrained archery into English culture. He encouraged archery practice, and the production of stocks of arrows and bows in peacetime, as well as war. In 1341, when Edward led an expedition to Brittany, he ordered the gathering of 130,000 sheaves, a total of 2.6 million arrows; an impressive feat on such short notice.*[18]

A common claim for the longbow was its ability to penetrate plate armour due to its draw weight, a claim contested by contemporary accounts and modern tests. A controlled test conducted by Mike Loades at the Royal Military College of Science's ballistics test site for the programme *Weapons That Made Britain - The Longbow* found that arrows shot at a speed of around 52 metres per second against a plate of munition-quality steel (not specially hardened) were ineffective at a range of around 80 metres, enough to mildly bruise/wound the target at 30 metres, and lethal at a range of 20 metres.*[19] Archery was described as ineffective against plate armour by contemporaries at battles such as Bergerac in 1345, Neville's Cross in 1346 and Poitiers in 1356. Later studies also found that late period plate armour such as that employed by Italian city-state mercenary companies was effective at stopping contemporary arrows.*[20]*[21] Horses, however, were almost wholly unprotected against arrows, and arrows could penetrate the lighter armour on limbs. Clifford Rodgers, commenting on the later, similar Battle of Agincourt, argues that the psychological effect of a massive storm of arrows would have broken the fighting spirit of the target forces.

Archers were issued with around 60-72 arrows before a battle began. Most archers would not shoot at the maximum rate, around six per minute for the heaviest bows,*[22] as the psychological and physical exertion of battle strained the men. As the battle wore on, the arm and shoulder muscles would tire from exertion, the fingers holding the bowstring would strain and the stress of combat would slacken the rate of fire.*[23]

The English army was also equipped with five ribauldequin, an early form of cannon.*[24]

The French army The French army was led by Philip VI and the blind John of Bohemia. The exact size of the French army is less certain as the financial records from the Crécy campaign are lost, however there is a prevailing consensus that it was substantially larger than the English. The French army likely numbered around 30,000 men. Contemporary chronicler Jean Froissart places the French numbers at 100,000, Wynkeley suggests 80,000 and Henry Knighton claimed the king of France brought 72,000.*[25] These numbers have been described as unrealistic and exaggerated by historians, going by the extant war treasury records for 1340, six years before the battle.*[26] Ayton suggests around 12,000 mounted men-at-arms as the core soldiery of the French army, several thousand Genoese crossbowmen and a "large, though indeterminate number of common infantry".*[3] Most historians have accepted the figure of 6,000 Genoese crossbowmen.*[27] However, Schnerb questions this figure, based on the estimates of 2,000 available crossbowmen in all of France in 1340. That Genoa on its own could have put several thousand mercenary crossbowmen at the disposal of the French monarch is described by Schnerb as "doubtful".*[28] The contingent of common infantrymen is not known with any certainty, except that it outnumbered the English and was in the thousands.*[29]

Longbow versus crossbow The Battle of Crécy is often exemplified as a battle in which the longbow defeated the rival crossbow. The crossbow had become the dominant ranged infantry weapon on the continental European battlefield: the choice weapon for expert mercenary companies. The crossbow was favoured as it required less physical strength to load and shoot than a longbow, and could release more kinetic energy than its rival, making it deadlier at close range. It was, however, hampered by slower, more difficult loading, its cumbersome shape and its range, in which the longbow had the advantage. Later developments in more powerful crossbows in the 15th century, such as the windlass-span crossbow, negated these advantages, while advances in bow technology brought to Europe from armies on crusade introduced composite technology; decreasing the size of the crossbow while increasing its power. A common claim about the crossbow is a reload time of one bolt every 1–2 minutes. A test conducted by Mike Loades for *Weapons That Changed Britain - The Longbow* found that a belt-and-claw span crossbow could discharge 4 bolts in 30 seconds, while a longbow could shoot 9.*[19] A second speed test conducted using a hand-span crossbow found that the weapon could shoot 6 bolts in the same time it took for a longbow to shoot 10.*[30]

Initial deployments

The English army was deployed in three divisions, or "battles". Edward's son, Edward, the Prince of Wales commanded the vanguard with John de Vere, the Earl of Ox-

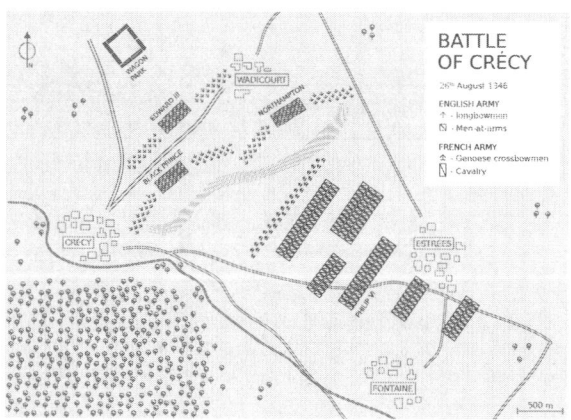

Map of the Battle of Crécy

ford, Thomas de Beauchamp, the Earl of Warwick and Sir John Chandos. This division lay forward from the rest of the army and would bear the brunt of the French assault. Edward himself commanded the division behind, while the rear division was led by William de Bohun, Earl of Northampton. Each division composed of spearmen in the rear, men-at-arms in the centre and the longbowmen arrayed in front of the army in a jagged line.*[31]*[32] The exact location of the English baggage train is not known. Edward ordered his men-at-arms to fight on foot rather than stay mounted.*[33] The English also dug a series of ditches, pits and caltrops to maim the French cavalry.

The French army came north from Abbeyville, the advance guard arriving at the Crécy ridgeline at around midday on 26 August. After reconnoitering the English position, it was advised to Philip that the army should encamp and give battle the following day. Philip met stiff resistance from his senior nobles, but decided that the attack would be made that day. This put them at a significant disadvantage; the English army was well-fed after plundering the countryside and well-rested, having slept in their positions the night before the battle.*[13] The French were further hampered by the absence of their Constable. It was the duty of the Constable of France to lead its armies in battle, however, the Constable Raoul II of Brienne, Count of Eu had been taken prisoner when the English army sacked Caen, depriving them of his leadership. Philip formed up his army for battle; the Genoese under Antonio Doria and Carlo Grimaldi formed the vanguard, followed by a division of knights and men-at-arms led by Charles II, Count of Alençon accompanied by the blind King John of Bohemia. The next division was led by Rudolph, Duke of Lorraine and Louis II, Count of Blois, while Philip himself commanded the rearguard.*[32]

The French attack

The French army moved forward late in the afternoon, around 4pm after it had formed up. As it advanced, a sudden rainstorm broke over the field of battle. The English archers de-strung their bows to avoid the strings becoming slackened; the Genoese with their crossbows could take no such precautions, resulting in damage to their weapons.*[34] The crossbowmen began their advance; however, they had left their pavises back in the baggage train, and thus had no means of protection as they loaded their weapons.*[35]*[36] The Genoese moved within range and discharged their crossbows. Damaged by the rain, their efforts had little effect on the English line. The English archers shot their bows in retaliation, inflicting heavy casualties on the Genoese, causing them to retreat. The knights and nobles following in Alençon's division, seeing the routed mercenaries, hacked them down as they retreated. Froissart writes of the event:

> The English, who were drawn up in three divisions and seated on the ground, on seeing their enemies advance, arose boldly and fell into their ranks... You must know that these kings, earls, barons, and lords of France did not advance in any regular order... There were about fifteen thousand Genoese crossbowmen; but they were quite fatigued, having marched on foot that day six leagues, completely armed, and with their wet crossbows. They told the constable that they were not in a fit condition to do any great things that day in battle. The Count of Alençon, hearing this, was reported to say, "This is what one gets by employing such scoundrels, who fail when there is any need for them." *[37]
> —Chateaubriand, after Froissart's middle French, gives: "On se doit bien charger de telle ribaudaille qui faille au besoin" *[38]

The clash of the retreating Genoese and the advancing French cavalry threw the army into disarray. The longbowmen continued to discharge their bows into the massed troops, while five ribauldequin, early cannon, added to the confusion, though it is doubtful that they had inflicted any significant casualties.*[39] Froissart writes that such guns fired "two or three discharges on the Genoese", likely large arrows or primitive grapeshot. Giovanni Villani writes of the guns:

> The English guns cast iron balls by means of fire...They made a noise like thunder and caused much loss in men and horses... The Genoese were continually hit by the archers and the gunners... [by the end of the battle], the whole plain was covered by men struck down by arrows and cannon balls.*[40]

English gun used at the Battle of Crécy

With the Genoese defeated, the French cavalry mounted a charge upon the English ranks. However, the slope and obstacles laid by the English disrupted the attack. Successive charges had to be made through ever-increasing numbers of dead and wounded, hampering their subsequent effectiveness. Despite the repeated attacks, the French cavalry could not break the English position. The Black Prince's division was particularly hard-pressed during the fighting. When reinforcements were requested from Edward, the king famously said; "*I am confident he will repel the enemy without my help. Let the boy win his spurs*". During the fighting along the Black Prince's division, the blind king John of Bohemia was struck down and killed.

The assault continued well into the night, with the French nobility stubbornly refusing to yield. Finally, Philip abandoned the field of battle. The French king had two horses killed from underneath him, and had taken an arrow to the jaw. His sacred and royal banner, the Oriflamme, was captured and taken, one of the five occasions this occurred during the banner's century-long history.*[41] The battle ended soon after Philip withdrew, with the majority of the French army melting away from the field. The following day, after the morning fog had lifted, 2,000 longbowmen, supported by 500 spearmen, advanced down the slope and drove away the French levies who had remained.*[42]

1.5.3 Aftermath

Casualties

The losses in the battle were highly asymmetrical. All contemporary sources give very low casualty figures for the English.*[43] Geoffrey le Baker gives around 300 English soldiers killed at a highest estimate.*[4] While some consider the low English casualty figures to be improbably low,

Edward III counting the dead on the battlefield of Crécy

Rogers argues that they are consistent with reports of casualties on the winning side in other medieval battles. Most casualties in medieval battles were incurred during the retreat, often resulting in heavily lopsided victories. Thus far, only two Englishmen killed at the battle have been identified: the squire Robert Brente and the newly anointed knight Aymer Rokesley.*[44] Two English knights were also taken prisoner, although it is unclear at what stage in the battle this happened.*[4]

Contemporary sources provide casualty figures for the French that are generally considered to be highly exaggerated. An estimate by Geoffrey le Baker deemed credible by Michael Prestwich states that 4,000 French knights were killed.*[45] According to a body count made after the battle, 1,542 French knights and squires were found in front of the lines commanded by the Black Prince, Sumption assumes another "few hundred" men-at-arms were killed in the pursuit which followed.*[46] Ayton estimates at least 2,000 French men-at-arms were killed, noting that over 2,200 heraldic coats were taken from the field of battle as war booty by the English.*[47]

According to Ayton, the heavy losses of the French can also be attributed to the chivalric ideals held by knights at the time; nobles would have preferred to die in battle, or be captured and then accorded for ransom, rather than dishonourably flee the field.*[48] Although considered to be heavy, no reliable figures exist for losses among the common French soldiery. Froissart writes that the French army suffered a total of 30,000 killed or captured, though these numbers are likely exaggerated.*[5] Several secondary sources place an estimate on 12,000 killed or wounded, though it should be noted this number is not substantively reinforced by academics.*[49]*[50]*[51]

Campaign and Legacy

The battle crippled the French army's ability to come to the aid of Calais, which was besieged by Edward's army the following month. Calais fell after a year-long siege and would become an exclave of England, remaining under English rule until 1558.

In subsequent engagements, French men-at-arms would dismount to assail English longbowmen rather than stay mounted, as was advised to John II at Poitiers. The majority of the French soldiery at Agincourt also fought dismounted. Despite this, the French suffered similarly catastrophic defeats at those engagements as they did at Crécy.

The revolution in tactics heralded the rise of the longbow as the dominant weapon in Western Europe, and signalled a dramatic shift away from the focus of prior medieval battles; that of the mounted knight. The slaughter of the French nobility at the hands of longbowmen, who were commoners and peasants in English society, caused a huge shock in France, as infantrymen began to play a greater role in medieval warfare. Though the Hundred Years' War would feature clashes that have been since held as the model of chivalry, such as the Combat of the Thirty, the combined-arms approach of the English at Crécy saw the emergence of a more practical, pragmatic approach to conducting warfare; one where tactics and achieving victory held greater importance than observing chivalric codes of knightly conduct.*[8] The battle helped to contribute to the infantry revolution, where innovations and shifts in military thinking began to erode the importance of the heavily armoured mounted knight.

After the equally disastrous French defeat at Poitiers, the Edwardian phase of the Hundred Years' War would draw to a close, with very favourable terms for the English.

Renaissance Florence

To finance the army for the campaign, Edward III had relied on loans from Florentine bankers, in particular the three largest banks in Florence (and Europe) at the time — the banks of the families of Bardi, Peruzzi, and Acciaiuoli. Despite being victorious, Edward III largely defaulted on England's debt which led to the bankruptcy and destruction of all three banking houses.*[52] Their closure enabled the rise of the house of Medici, later founded by Giovanni di

1.5. BATTLE OF CRÉCY

Bicci de' Medici, which would define early modern European banking, create modern accounting, and finance many of the greatest artists of the Renaissance along with Galileo.

1.5.4 Nobles and men at arms at the battle

Crécy village sign

The young Prince of Wales had with him:

- Thomas de Beauchamp, 11th Earl of Warwick
- John de Vere, 7th Earl of Oxford
- Sir Godfrey de Harcourt
- Reginald de Cobham, 1st Baron Cobham
- Thomas Holland, 1st Earl of Kent
- Ralph de Stafford, 1st Earl of Stafford
- Lord Mauley
- Lord de la Warre
- Sir John Chandos
- Bartholomew de Burghersh, 2nd Baron Burghersh
- Lord Robert Neville
- Lord Thomas Clifford
- Robert Bourchier, 1st Baron Bourchier
- William Latimer, 4th Baron Latimer
- Richard FitzAlan, 10th Earl of Arundel
- William de Ros, 3rd Baron de Ros
- Willoughby, Basset, St Albans, Sir Lewis Tufton, Lord Multon and the Lord Lascels.*[33]
- Sir Thomas Felton, a member of the Order of the Garter, fought at Crécy and Poitiers.*[53]*[54]

Others included:

- Sir Richard Fitz-Simon
- Sir Miles Stapleton of Bedale
- William de Bohun, 1st Earl of Northampton
- Earl Bowden
- Sir John Sully
- Sir John Giffard of Twyford
- Sir Richard Pembrugge (Pembroke).*[55]

In front of the French army were the Moisne of Basle, the Monk of Bazeilles, the lords of Beaujen and Noyles and Louis of Spain. The French army was led by Phillip VI; surrounding him were:

- Charles II, Count of Alençon
- Louis I, Count of Flanders
- Louis II, Count of Blois
- Rudolph, Duke of Lorraine
- Jean de Hainaut and de Montmorency, and a gathering of the lords.

Moisne of Basle related the location and formation of the English forces.*[56] Charles, king of the Romans, son of John of Bohemia, was also present and lightly wounded in the battle.

1.5.5 Fictional accounts

A fictional portrayal of the Battle of Crécy is included in the Ken Follett novel *World Without End*. The book describes the battle from an English knight's perspective, that of an archer, and from that of a neutral observer. This novel was made into a telefilm in 2012 and the Battle of Crécy is included, albeit in a very summarized form.

Another depiction can be found in Warren Ellis' & Raulo Caceres' graphic novel *Crécy*, which frames the battle as a narration by a Suffolk archer; or in Bernard Cornwell's fictional account of an archer in the Hundred Years' War, *Harlequin* (UK title), part of the Grail Quest novel series, or *The Archer's Tale* (US title). The lead character Thomas of Hookton, is an English archer who fights in the battle.

The battle appears in "The campaign of 1346, as an historical drama" by Christopher Godmond.

It is also portrayed in Ronald Welch's *Bowman of Crécy* and in David Gilman's *Master of War*.

The protagonist, Edmund Beche, in P.C. Doherty's *The Death of a King* (1985) is present at the battle and describes it from the perspective of a bowman on the right flank near the village of Crécy.

In G. A. Henty's historical fiction book, *St. George for England* the main character is present at the battles of Cressy and Poitiers.[*][57]

The battle is a crucial episode in the life of the hero Hugh de Cressi (his name is apparently a coincidence), in the H. Rider Haggard novel "Red Eve". The battle is described in some detail, including, for example the failure of the Genoese bowmen, attributed in the book, as above, to wet strings; and also the merciless treatment of the French wounded.[*][58]

In Michael Jecks 2014 book *Fields of Glory*, the entire campaign is viewed from the point of view of a vintaine of archers under the command of the non fictional Sir John de Sully commencing with the landing in Normandy and terminating with a detailed description of the eventual final battle at Crecy.[*][59] It highlights the devastating effects of the chevauchée as the English laid waste to the countryside in an attempt to bring the French army into the field to protect its inhabitants.

The battle features at the climax of another 2014 novel, *Son of the Morning*, by Mark Barrowcliffe writing as Mark Alder. A fantasy take on the Hundred Years' War, the novel depicts English and French forces as being supported by devils and angels.[*][60]

1.5.6 See also

- Medieval warfare
- Battle of Agincourt in 1415 for a similar battle won by English/Welsh longbowmen
- Battle of Poitiers (1356)

1.5.7 References

[1] Ayton, "The English Army at Crécy" in Ayton & Preston (2005), p. 189; Rogers (2000), p. 423

[2] Geoffrey (eds. & trans.), Martin (1995). Knighton's Chronicle, 1337-1396. Oxford: Clarendon Press. p. 63. ISBN 0-19-820 503-1

[3] Ayton, "The Battle of Crécy: Context and Significance" in Ayton & Preston (2005), p. 18

[4] Ayton, "The English Army at Crécy", in Ayton & Preston (2005), p. 191

[5] Froissart, Jean. The Chronicles of Froissart, John Bourcher [Lord Berners], tr., G.C. Macaulay, ed. (London : Macmillan, 1908), pp. 99-107

[6] Henri de Wailly. Introduction by Emmanuel Bourassin, *Crecy 1346: Anatomy of a Battle* (Blandford Press, Poole, Dorset 1987) Introduction p. 8

[7] Henri de Wailly. Introduction by Emmanuel Bourassin, *Crecy 1346: Anatomy of a Battle* (Blandford Press, Poole, Dorset 1987) pp. 8, 12

[8] Santosuosso 2004, pp. 130-36

[9] Henri de Wailly. Introduction by Emmanuel Bourassin, *Crecy 1346: Anatomy of a Battle* (Blandford Press, Poole, Dorset 1987) p. 10

[10] Prestwich. Plantagenet England. p. 315

[11] Rothero (2005), pp. 4–6

[12] Curry (2002), pp. 31-39.

[13] Rothero (2005), pp. 2–6

[14] Ayton, "The English Army at Crécy" in Ayton & Preston (2005), p. 189; Rogers (2000), p. 423

[15] Rogers (2000), p. 423

[16] Sumption (1990) p. 497

[17] Nicholson (2004), p. 14

[18] https://crecymuseum.wordpress.com/about/battle-of-crecy/

[19] *Midieval Weapons and Combat - The Longbow (Middle Ages Battle History Documentary)*. 11 May 2014 – via YouTube.

[20] Strickland & Hardy 2005, pp. 272–278

[21] Kaiser 2003

[22] Strickland & Hardy 2005, p. 31

[23] Barker 2006

[24] Ayton & Preston (2005

[25] Geoffrey (eds. & trans.), Martin (1995). *Knighton's Chronicle, 1337-1396*. Oxford: Clarendon Press. p. 63. ISBN 0-19-820 503-1.

[26] Schnerb, "The French Army before and after 1346"in Ayton & Preston (2005), p. 269

[27] Lynn (2003), p. 74; Sumption (1990), p. 526

[28] Schnerb, "The French Army before and after 1346"in Ayton & Preston (2005), pp. 268–69

[29] Curry (2002), p. 40; Lynn (2003), p. 74

[30] *The Longbow Vs The Crossbow Speed Test - Video 17*. 11 April 2009 – via YouTube.

[31] Rothero (2005), pp. 5–6

[32] Neillands, Robin (2001). *The Hundred Years War*. Routledge. ISBN 978-0415261319.

[33] *Chronicles of England, France and Spain and the Surrounding Countries, by Sir John Froissart, Translated from the French Editions with Variations and Additions from Many Celebrated MSS, by Thomas Johnes, Esq; London: William Smith, 1848. pp. 160–171.*

[34] Henri de Wailly. Introduction by Emmanuel Bourassin, *Crecy 1346: Anatomy of a Battle* (Blandford Press, Poole, Dorset 1987) pp. 49, 50

[35] Henri de Wailly. Introduction by Emmanuel Bourassin, *Crecy 1346: Anatomy of a Battle* (Blandford Press, Poole, Dorset 1987) p. 66

[36] Jean Birdsall edited by Richard A. Newhall. *The Chronicles of Jean de Venette* (N.Y. Columbia University Press. 1953) p.43

[37] Amt (2001), p. 330.

[38] Chateaubriand, 'Invasion de la France par Edouard', in Volume 7 from the complete works of 1834; p.37.

[39] Ayton & Preston (2005)

[40] Nicolle (2000)

[41] Osprey Publishing (2000) *Crécy 1346: Triumph of the Longbow*, Osprey Publishing. p72

[42] Henri de Wailly. Introduction by Emmanuel Bourassin, *Crecy 1346: Anatomy of a Battle* (Blandford Press, Poole, Dorset 1987) pp. 76–77

[43] Prestwich (1996), p. 331; Rogers (2008), p. 215; Sumption (1990), p. 530

[44] Rogers (2007), p. 215

[45] Prestwich (1996), p. 331

[46] Sumption (1990), p. 530

[47] Ayton, "The Battle of Crécy: Context and Significance" in Ayton & Preston (2005), pp. 19-20

[48] Ayton, "The Battle of Crécy: Context and Significance" in Ayton & Preston (2005), pp. 25-26

[49] http://www.history.com/this-day-in-history/battle-of-crecy

[50] http://www.longbow-archers.com/historycrecy.html

[51] https://www.thoughtco.com/hundred-years-war-battle-of-crecy-2360728

[52] De Roover, Raymond *The Rise and Decline of the Medici Bank: 1397-1494*. Beard Books, Washington, D.C.; 1999. Introduction p.2

[53] *Dictionary of National Biography p308 col. 2*

[54] *67 (app c.1381) List of Members of the Order of the Garter*

[55] *The chronicles of Froissart. Translated by John Bourchier, Lord Berners. Edited and reduced into one volume by G. C. Macauly former fellow of Trinity College, Cambridge. (Macmillan & Co., Ltd 1904 not in copyright) Chpt. CXXX pps. 104–106*

[56] Henri de Wailly. Introduction by Emmanuel Bourassin, *Crecy 1346: Anatomy of a Battle* (Blandford Press, Poole, Dorset 1987) p. 58

[57] "Saint George for England".

[58] "Red Eve". *Project Gutenberg*.

[59] "Fields of Glory - Kindle edition by Michael Jecks. Literature & Fiction Kindle eBooks @ Amazon.com.".

[60] Orion Books publisher page for *Son of the Morning*

Bibliography

- Ayton, Andrew; Preston, Philip; et al. (2005). *The Battle of Crecy, 1346*. Boydell Press.

- Amt, Emilie, ed. (2001). *Medieval England 1000–1500: A Reader*. Peterborough, Ontario: Broadview Press. ISBN 1-55111-244-2.

- Barber, Richard W. *Edward III and the Triumph of England: The Battle of Crécy and the Company of the Garter*. London: Allen Lane, 2013. ISBN 9780713998382 OCLC 839314940

- Curry, Anne, *Essential Histories: The Hundred Years' War 1337-1453.* Osprey Publishing, Oxford; 2002. ISBN 1841762695 OCLC 59427611

- De Roover, Raymond *The Rise and Decline of the Medici Bank: 1397-1494.* Beard Books, Washington, D.C.; 1999. ISBN 1893122328

- Lansing & English *A Companion to the Medieval World.* Wiley-Blackwell, Oxford; (editors 2009). ISBN 9781405109222 OCLC 276930478

- Lynn, John A. (2003), *Battle: A History of Combat and Culture.* Cambridge, MA: Westview Press. ISBN 0813333725 OCLC 58548315

- Matthews, Rupert. *The Battle of Crecy.* Stroud: Spellmount, 2007. ISBN 9781862273696 OCLC 78989699

- Nicolle, David (2000). *Crécy 1346: Triumph of the longbow.* Oxford: Osprey Publishing. ISBN 1-85532-966-2.

- Rogers, Clifford. *War Cruel and Sharp: English Strategy under Edward III, 1327–1360,* Chapter 11. Woodbridge, UK: Boydell Press, 2000. ISBN 0851158048 OCLC 44420496

- Rogers, Clifford J, *Soldiers' Lives through History: The Middle Ages.* Westport, CT: Greenwood Press, 2007. ISBN 9780313333507 OCLC 464726482

- Rothero, Christopher *The Armies of Crecy and Poitiers.* Osprey Publishing, Oxford; 2005. ISBN 0850453933 OCLC 8698451

- Sumption, Jonathan. *The Hundred Years War, Volume I: Trial by Battle.* Philadelphia, PA: University of Pennsylvania Press, 1990. ISBN 0812216555 OCLC 46838615

Primary sources

- *The Anonimalle Chronicle, 1333–1381.* Edited by V.H. Galbraith. Manchester: Manchester University Press, 1927.

- Avesbury, Robert of. *De gestis mirabilibus regis Edwardi Tertii.* Edited by Edward Maunde Thompson. London: Rolls Series, 1889.

- *Chronique de Jean le Bel.* Edited by Eugene Deprez and Jules Viard. Paris: Honore Champion, 1977.

- Dene, William of. *Historia Roffensis.* British Library, London.

- *French Chronicle of London.* Edited by G.J. Aungier. Camden Series XXVIII, 1844.

- Froissart, Jean. *Chronicles.* Edited and Translated by Geoffrey Brereton. London: Penguin Books, 1978.

- *Grandes chroniques de France.* Edited by Jules Viard. Paris: Société de l'histoire de France, 1920–53.

- Gray, Sir Thomas. *Scalacronica.* Edited and Translated by Sir Herbert Maxwell. Edinburgh: Maclehose, 1907.

- Le Baker, Geoffrey. *Chronicles* in *English Historical Documents.* Edited by David C Douglas. New York: Oxford University Press, 1969.

- Le Bel, Jean. *Chronique de Jean le Bel.* Edited by Jules Viard and Eugène Déprez. Paris: Société de l'historie de France, 1904.

- *Rotuli Parliamentorum.* Edited by J. Strachey et al., 6 vols. London: 1767–83.

- *St. Omers Chronicle.* Bibliothèque Nationale, Paris, MS 693, fos. 248-279v. (Currently being edited and translated into English by Clifford J. Rogers)

- Venette, Jean. *The Chronicle of Jean de Venette.* Edited and Translated by Jean Birdsall. New York: Columbia University Press, 1953.

Anthologies of translated sources

- *Life and Campaigns of the Black Prince.* Edited and Translated by Richard Barber. Woodbridge: Boydell Press, 1997.

- *The Wars of Edward III: Sources and Interpretations.* Edited and Translated by Clifford J. Rogers. Woodbridge: Boydell Press, 1999.

1.5.8 Further reading

- Barber, Richard. *Edward, Prince of Wales and Aquitaine: A Biography of the Black Prince.* Scribner, 1978. ISBN 0684158647 OCLC 4360312

- Belloc, Hilaire *Crécy.* Covent Garden, London: Stephen Swift and Co., LTD. https://www.gutenberg.org/ebooks/32196, 1912.

- Burne, Alfred H. *The Crecy War: A Military History of the Hundred Years War from 1337 to the peace of Bretigny, 1360.* New York, NY: Oxford University Press, 1955. ISBN 7400020129 OCLC 962690

- DeVries, Kelly. *Infantry Warfare in the Early Fourteenth Century*. Woodbridge, UK: Boydell Press, 1996. ISBN 0851155677 OCLC 34356019

- Fowler, Kenneth (editor), *The Hundred Years War*. Suffolk, UK: Richard Clay. The Chaucer Press, 1971.

- Hewitt, H.J. *The Organization of War under Edward III*. Manchester: Manchester University Press, 1966. OCLC 398232

- Keen, Maurice (editor), *Medieval Warfare: A History*. Oxford, UK: Oxford University Press, 1999. ISBN 0198206399 OCLC 41581804

- Livingston, Michael, and Kelly DeVries, eds. *The Battle of Crécy: A Casebook* (2016). ISBN 9781781382646

- Nicolle, David, *Crecy 1346: Triumph of the Longbow*. (Osprey, 2000). ISBN 978-1-85532-966-9

- Ormrod, W.D. *The Reign of Edward III*. Charleston, SC: Tempus Publishing, Inc, 2000.

- Packe, Michael. *King Edward III*. (Routledge & Kegan Paul, 1985).

- Prestwich, Michael. *Armies and Warfare in the Middle Ages: The English Experience*. (Yale UP, 1996).

- Prestwich, Michael. *The Three Edwards: War and State in England, 1272–1377*. (St. Martin's Press, 1980).

- Reid, Peter. *A Brief History of Medieval Warfare: The Rise and Fall of English Supremacy at Arms, 1314–1485*. Philadelphia: Running Press, 2007.

- Rogers, Clifford J. *Essay on Medieval Military History: Strategy, Military Revolution, and the Hundred Years War*. Surrey, UK: Ashgate Variorum, 2010. ISBN 9780754659969 OCLC 461272357

- Seward, Desmond. *The Hundred Years War: The English in France 1337–1453*. London, UK: Constable and Company Ltd, 1996.

- Tuchman, Barbara. *A Distant Mirror: The Calamitous 14th Century*. Random House, 1987 ISBN 0345349571

- Waugh, Scott L. *England in the reign of Edward III*. Cambridge: Cambridge University Press, 1991.

1.5.9 External links

- Crecy 1346 by Jeffery P. Berry
- "An animated map of the Battle of Crecy" by David Crowther
- "An animated map of the Crecy campaign" by David Crowther

1.6 Crossbow

This article is about the weapon. For other uses, see Crossbow (disambiguation).

A **crossbow**, also known as horizontal bow, is a type of

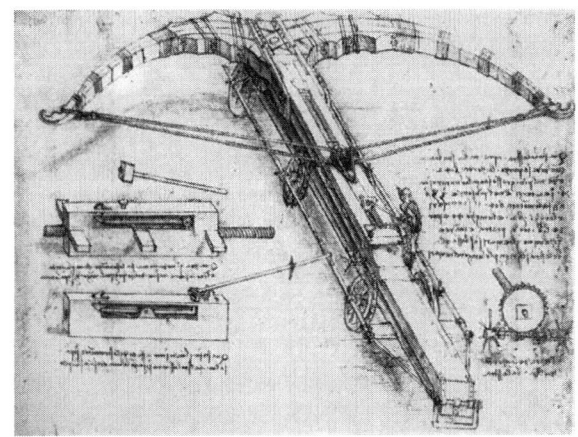

Sketch by Leonardo da Vinci, c. 1500

weapon based on the bow and consisting of a horizontal bow-like assembly mounted on a stock. It shoots projectiles called bolts or quarrels. The medieval crossbow was called by many names, most of which were derived from the word ballista, a torsion siege engine resembling a crossbow.*[1]

Historically, crossbows played a significant role in the warfare of East Asia, Europe, and the Mediterranean.*[2] The earliest crossbows in the world were invented in ancient China and caused a major shift in the role of projectile weaponry. The traditional bow and arrow had long been a specialized weapon that required a considerable training, physical strength, and expertise to operate with any degree of efficiency. In many cultures, bowmen were considered a separate and superior caste, despite usually being drawn from the common class, as their archery skill-set was essentially developed from birth (similar to many horseman cultures) and was impossible to reproduce outside a pre-established cultural tradition, which many nations lacked. In contrast, the crossbow was the first projectile weapon to be simple, cheap, and physically undemanding enough to be operated by large numbers of conscript soldiers, thus enabling virtually any nation to field a potent force of ranged crossbowmen with little expense beyond the cost of the weapons themselves.*[3]

In modern times, crossbows have been largely supplanted by firearms in most roles, but are still widely used for shooting sports, hunting, and when shooting in relative silence is an important consideration.

1.6.1 Construction

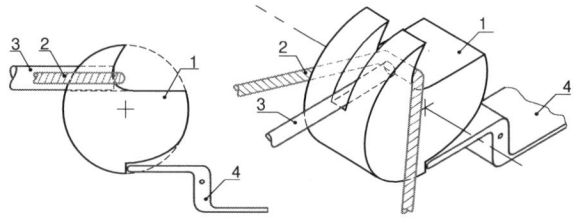

Crossbow nut:

1. *Nut.*
2. *String.*
3. *Quarrel.*
4. *Trigger.*

A crossbow is a bow mounted on a stick (called a tiller or stock) with a mechanism in it that holds the drawn bow string. The earliest designs featured a slot in the stock, down into which the string was placed. To shoot this design, a vertical rod is thrust up through a hole in the bottom of the notch, forcing the string out. This rod is usually attached perpendicular to a rear-facing lever called a trigger or *tickler*. A later design implemented a rolling cylindrical pawl called a *nut* to retain the string. This nut has a perpendicular centre slot for the bolt, and an intersecting axial slot for the string, along with a lower face or slot against which the internal trigger sits. They often also have some form of strengthening internal *sear* or trigger face, usually of metal. These *roller nuts* were either free-floating in their close-fitting hole across the stock, tied in with a binding of sinew or other strong cording; or mounted on a metal axle or pins. Removable or integral plates of wood, ivory, or metal on the sides of the stock kept the nut in place laterally. Nuts were made of antler, bone, or metal. Bows could be kept taut and ready to shoot for some time with little effort, allowing crossbowmen to aim better.*[4]

The bow (called the *prod* or *lath* on a crossbow) of early crossbows was made of a single piece of wood, usually ash or yew. Composite bows are made from layers of different material, often wood, horn, and sinew glued together and bound with animal tendon. These composite bows made of several layers are much stronger and more efficient in releasing energy than simple wooden bows. As steel became more widely available in Europe around the 14th century, steel prods came into use.

The crossbow prod is very short compared to ordinary bows, resulting in a short draw length. This leads to a higher draw weight in order to store the same amount of energy. Furthermore, the thick prods are a bit less efficient at releasing energy, but more energy can be stored by a crossbow. Traditionally, the prod was often lashed to the stock with rope, whipcord, or other strong cording. This cording is called the *bridle*.

The strings for a crossbow are typically made of strong fibres that would not tend to fray. Whipcord was very common; however linen, hemp, and sinew were used as well. In wet conditions, twisted mulberry root was occasionally used.

Very light crossbows can be drawn by hand, but heavier types need the help of mechanical devices. The simplest version of mechanical cocking device is a hook attached to a belt, drawing the bow by straightening the legs. Other devices are hinged levers, which either pulled or pushed the string into place, cranked rack-and-pinion devices called *cranequins**[5] and multiple cord-and-pulley cranked devices called windlasses.

-  Stirrup

- 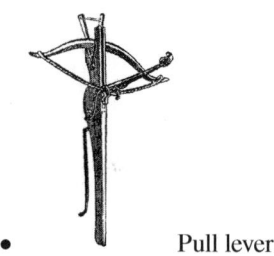 Pull lever

- 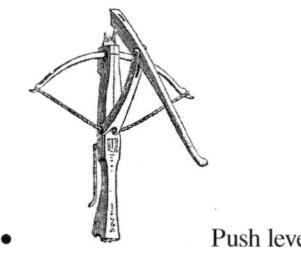 Push lever

1.6. CROSSBOW

- 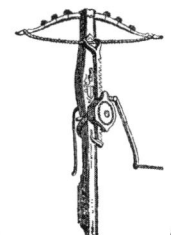 Cranequin (rack & pinion)

-  Cranequin (rack & pinion)

-  Windlass

- 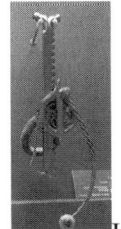 Iron cranequin, South German, late 15th century

- 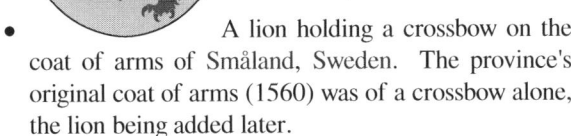 A lion holding a crossbow on the coat of arms of Småland, Sweden. The province's original coat of arms (1560) was of a crossbow alone, the lion being added later.

Modern recurve crossbow

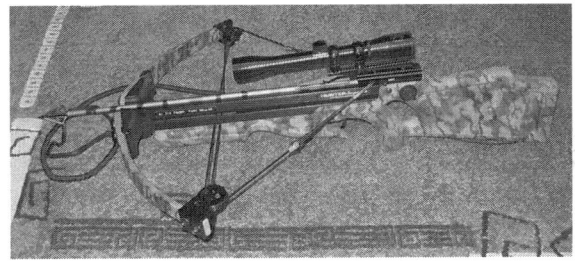

Modern compound crossbow

Variants

Crossbows exist in different variants. One way to classify them is the acceleration system, while another is the size and energy, degree of automation or projectiles.

A recurve crossbow is a bow that has tips curving away from the archer. The recurve bow's bent limbs have a longer draw length than an equivalent straight-limbed bow, giving more acceleration to the projectile and less hand shock. Recurved limbs also put greater strain on the materials used to make the bow, and they may make more noise with the shot.

Multiple bow systems have a special system of pulling the sinew via several bows (which can be recurve bows). The workings can be compared to a modern compound bow system. The weapon uses several different bows instead of one bow with a tackle system to achieve a higher acceleration of the sinew via the multiplication with each bow's pulling effect.

A compound crossbow is a modern crossbow and is similar to a compound bow. The limbs are usually much stiffer than those of a recurve crossbow. This limb stiffness makes the compound bow more energy efficient than other bows, but the limbs are too stiff to be drawn comfortably with a string attached directly to them. The compound bow has the string attached to the pulleys, one or both of which has one or more cables attached to the opposite limb. When the string is drawn back, the string causes the pulleys to turn. This causes the pulleys to pull the cables, which in turn causes the limbs to bend and thus store energy. Other types of compound bows use either (one or both) cam shaped or eccentrically mounted pulleys in order to provide a "let off", such that the archer is not holding against the maximum draw weight of the bow while trying to aim. But, in a crossbow, the string is held back mechanically, so there is no advantage in providing a let off. Therefore, compound crossbows generally only use pulleys that are both round and concentrically mounted, in order to capture the maximum available energy from the relatively short draw length.

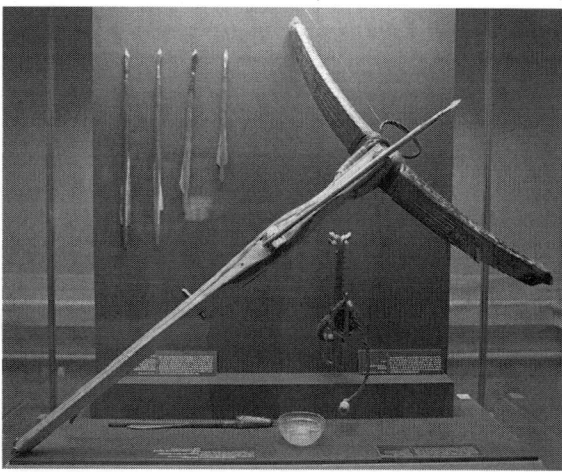

15th-century Wallarmbrust, *a heavy crossbow used for siege defense.*

The smallest crossbows are pistol crossbows. Others are simple long stocks with the crossbow mounted on them. These could be shot from under the arm. The next step in development was stocks of the shape that would later be used for firearms, which allowed better aiming. The arbalest was a heavy crossbow that required special systems for pulling the sinew via windlasses. For siege warfare, the size of crossbows was further increased to hurl large projectiles, such as rocks, at fortifications. The required crossbows needed a massive base frame and powerful windlass devices. Such devices include the oxybeles. The ballista has torsion springs replacing the elastic prod of the oxybeles, but later also developed into smaller versions.*[6] Ballista* is still the root word for crossbow in Romance languages such as Italian (*balestra*) and Spanish (*ballesta*).

The repeating crossbow automated the separate actions of stringing the bow, placing the projectile and shooting. This way the task can be accomplished with a simple one-handed movement, while keeping the weapon stationary. As a result, it is possible to shoot at a faster rate compared to an unmodified version. The Greek Polybolos was an ancient repeating ballista reputedly invented by Dionysius of Alexandria in the 3rd century BC. The Chinese repeating crossbow, Chu Ko Nu, is a handheld crossbow that accomplishes the task with a magazine containing a number of bolts on top. The mechanism is worked by moving a rectangular lever forward and backward. The weapon was mainly used as a weapon against lightly armored soldiers, since it shot small bolts that were often dipped in poison.

A bullet crossbow is a type of handheld crossbow that, instead of arrows or bolts, shoots spherical projectiles made of stone, clay or lead. There are two variants; one has a double string with a pocket for the projectile, and the other has a barrel with a slot for the string.

A slurbow is a type of crossbow with a wood or metal barrel over the top of the stock that is arguably influenced by the emergence of the pistol.

- Cocking of a Greek *gastraphetes*

- 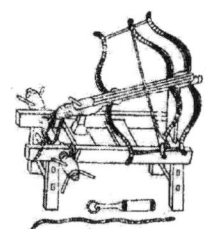Arsenal of ancient mechanical artillery in the Saalburg, Germany; left: polybolos reconstruction by the German engineer Erwin Schramm (1856-1935)

- Chinese *Chuangzi Nu* stationary windlass device with triple bow arcuballista

- Chinese repeating crossbow with pull lever and automatic reload magazine

1.6. CROSSBOW

- 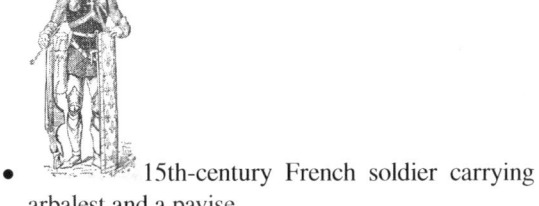 Chinese Lian Nu (連弩), multiple shot crossbow without a visible nut or cocking aid

- 15th-century French soldier carrying an arbalest and a pavise

- Early modern four-wheeled ballista drawn by armored horses (1552)

- 16th-century French mounted crossbowman (*cranequinier*). His crossbow is drawn with a rack-and-pinion *cranequin*, so it can be used while riding.

- Pistol crossbow for home recreational shooting. Made by Frédéric Siber in Morges, early 19th century. On display at Morges military museum.

- 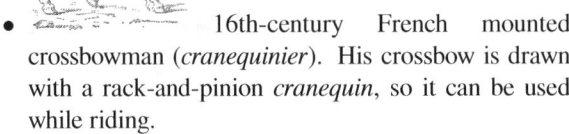 French cross-bow grenade thrower Arbalète sauterelle type A d'Imphy circa 1915

Projectiles

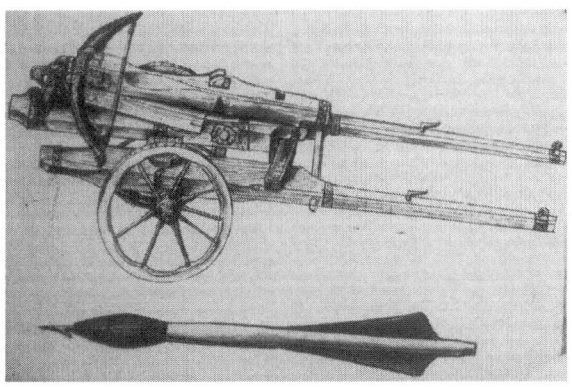

Arcuballista on wheels with a steel bow and incendiary bolt (15th century)

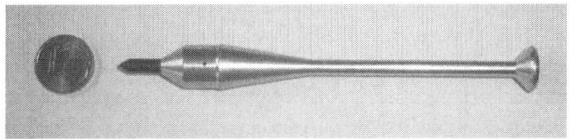

Modern crossbow bolt compared to a 1 eurocent coin

The arrow-like projectiles of a crossbow are called bolts. These are much shorter than arrows, but can be several times heavier. There is an optimum weight for bolts to achieve maximum kinetic energy, which varies depending on the strength and characteristics of the crossbow, but most could pass through common mail. In ancient times, the bolts of a strong crossbow were usually several times heavier than arrows. Modern bolts are stamped with a proof mark to ensure their consistent weight and do not have fletching, i.e. feathered ends like those commonly seen on arrows.*[7] Crossbow bolts can be fitted with a variety of heads, some with sickle-shaped heads to cut rope or rigging; but the most common today is a four-sided point called a quarrel. A highly specialized type of bolt is employed to collect blubber biopsy samples used in biology research.

Most modern crossbows are designed to shoot arrows instead of bolts.*[7] Crossbow arrows are of similar construction to ordinary bow arrows, just shorter in length because of reduced power stroke.

Crossbows can also be adapted to shoot lead bullets or rocks, in which case they are called **stone-bows**. Primarily used for hunting wildfowl, these usually have a double string with a pouch between the strings to hold the projectile.

Even relatively small differences in arrow weight can have a considerable impact on its drop and, conversely, its flight trajectory.*[8]

Accessories

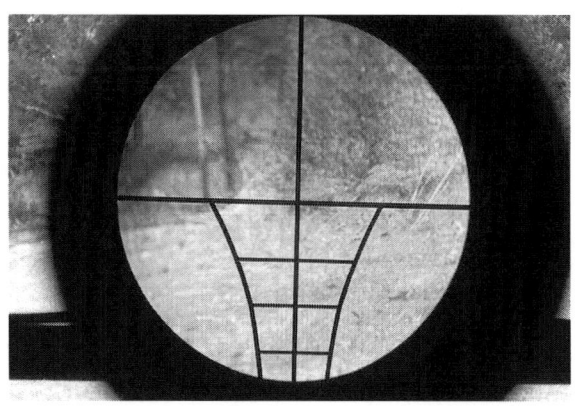

The reticle of a modern crossbow telescopic sight allows the shooter to adjust for different ranges

The ancient Chinese crossbow often included a metal (i.e. bronze or steel) grid serving as iron sights. Modern crossbow sights often use similar technology to modern firearm sights, such as red dot sights and telescopic sights. Many crossbow scopes feature multiple crosshairs to compensate for the significant effects of gravity over different ranges. In most cases, a newly bought crossbow will need to be sighted for accurate shooting.*[9]

Quivers can be mounted to hold ammunition. These are often made from plastic and usually hold the bolts in fixed positions along the structure. A popular detachable design consists of a main arm that is attached to the weapon, a plate on one end that secures four or more individual bolts at a point on their shafts and at the other end a cover that secures their heads. This kind of quiver is attached under the front of the crossbow, parallel to the string and is designed to be quickly detached and reattached. Other designs hold bolts underneath the crossbow parallel to the stock, sometimes on either side of the crossbow.

A major cause of the sound of shooting a crossbow is vibration of various components. Crossbow silencers are multiple components placed on high vibration parts, such as the string and limbs, to dampen vibration and suppress the sound of loosing the bolt.*[10]

1.6.2 History

Main article: History of crossbows

East Asia

A bronze crossbow trigger mechanism and butt plate that were mass-produced in the Warring States period (475-221 BC)

The earliest evidence of crossbows comes from ancient China in the form of crossbow triggers dating back to the 6th century BC.*[11] According to Sir Joseph Needham in his Science and Civilisation in China, it is not possible to pinpoint exactly which of the East Asian peoples invented the crossbow. However, there is unquestionable evidence that the crossbow was used for military purposes at least as far back as the Warring States period from the second half of the 4th century BC onwards.*[12]

In terms of archaeological evidence, bronze crossbow bolts dating from as early as the mid-5th century BC have been found at a Chu burial site in Yutaishan, Hubei.*[13] The earliest handheld crossbow stocks with bronze trigger, dating from the 6th century BC, were found in Tomb 3 and 12 at Qufu, Shandong, previously the capital of Lu, ancient China.*[11]*[14]*[15] Other early finds of crossbows were discovered in Tomb 138 at Saobatang, Hunan, dating to the mid-4th century BC.*[16]*[17] Ammunition for crossbows could have also been spherical. In discussing the astronomical topics such as solar and lunar eclipses, the Western-Han era mathematician and music theorist Jing Fang (78-37 BC) wrote that the moon, shaped like a ball, produced no light and was illuminated only by the sun, which he compared to the shape of a round crossbow bullet.*[18]

Repeating crossbows, first mentioned in the *Records of the Three Kingdoms*, were discovered in 1986 in Tomb 47 at Qinjiazui, Hubei, and were dated to around the 4th century BC.*[19] The earliest Chinese document mentioning a crossbow were texts from the 4th to 3rd centuries BC attributed to the followers of Mozi. Sun Tzu's influential treatise on war, *The Art of War* (first appearance dated to sometime between 500 BC to 300 BC*[20]) refers in chapter five to the traits of crossbows and in chapter twelve, to the usage of crossbows.*[21] One of the earliest reliable descriptions of this weapon in warfare is of an ambush in 341 BC, the Battle of Ma-Ling. In the opinion of one authority, the crossbow (Chinese: 弩; pinyin: nǔ) had become "nothing less than the standard weapon of the Han armies" by the 2nd century BC.*[22]

A miniature guard wielding a handheld crossbow from the top balcony of a model watchtower, made of glazed earthenware during the Eastern Han era (25–220 AD) of China, from the Metropolitan Museum of Art.

The earliest textual evidence of the *handheld* crossbow used in battle dates to the 4th century BC.*[23] Handheld crossbows with complex bronze trigger mechanisms have also been found with the Terracotta Army in the tomb of Qin Shihuang (r. 221–210 BC) that are similar to specimens from the subsequent Han Dynasty (202 BC–220 AD), while crossbowmen described in the Qin and Han Dynasty learned drill formations, some were even mounted as cavalry units, and Han Dynasty writers attributed the success of numerous battles against the Xiongnu to massed crossbow volleys.*[24]*[25] The bronze triggers were designed in such a way that they were able to store a large amount of energy within the bow when drawn, but was easily shot with little recoil when the trigger were pulled (this allowed it for precision shooting). The metal portions of the crossbow were also mass-produced with precision, with the bronze mechanisms being interchangeable. Finally, the Qin and Han Dynasties also developed crossbow shooting lines, with alternating rows of crossbowmen shooting and reloading in a manner similar to a musket firing line. Many archaeological specimens of the crossbow (ranging from 2 to 1 BC) were excavated near Pyongyang. The books of Samgukhsagi (三國史記), Gikhguandji (職官志), Muguahnjo (武官條) and Goryeodjeon (高麗傳) of the Book of Zhou (周書) records detailed descriptions of the usage of crossbows of Goguryeo and Silla. Goguryeo used greatly large versions of the crossbow, called Pohnoh (砲弩) (Stationary) and Geauhnoh (車弩). Korean craftsmanship of crossbows and all other bows were renowned in China. The Tang, who had terrible relations with Goguryeo and Beakje, relied on Silla for high quality crossbows. A Sillan craftsmen, Nosa (弩師) Gutchindjeon (仇珍川) in particular, was taken by the Tang for him to produce high quality crossbows for China.

In Vietnamese historical legend, general Thục Phán, who ruled over the ancient kingdom of Âu Lạc from 257 to 207 BC, is said to have owed his power to a magic crossbow, capable of shooting thousands of bolts at once.

Crossbow technology for multi-proded crossbows was transferred from the Chinese to Champa, which Champa used in its invasion of the Khmer Empire's Angkor in 1177. China transferred crossbow technology to Champa.*[26] When the Chams sacked Angkor they used the Chinese siege crossbow.*[27]*[28] Crossbows were given to the Chams by China.*[29] Crossbows and archery while mounted were instructed to the Cham by a Chinese in 1171.*[30]

Different varieties of crossbows were also developed, such as the repeating crossbow, multi-shot crossbow, and repeating multi-shot crossbow.

Ancient Greece

The earliest reasonably reliable date for the utilization of crossbows in Europe is in ancient Greece from the 5th century BC.*[31] The historian Diodorus Siculus (fl. 1st century BC), described the invention of a mechanical arrow shooting catapult (*katapeltikon*) by a Greek task force in 399 BC.*[32]*[33] According to the inventor Hero of Alexandria (fl. 1st century AD), who referred to the now lost works of the 3rd-century BC engineer Ctesibius, this weapon was inspired by an earlier hand crossbow, called the *gastraphetes* (*belly shooter*), which could store more energy than the Greek bows. A detailed description of the *gastraphetes*, along with a drawing, is found in Heron's technical treatise *Belopoeica*.*[34]*[35] The *gastraphetes* was powered by a composite bow. It was cocked by resting the stomach in a concavity at the rear of the stock and pressing down with all strength. In this way, considerably more energy can be summoned up than by using only one arm of the archer as in the hand-bow. The heavy weight and bulk of the *gastraphetes* may have necessitated a prop to keep it standing, i.e. by mounting it on a defensive wall or using a portable prop.*[36]

A third Greek author, Biton (fl. 2nd century BC), whose reliability has been positively reevaluated by recent scholarship,*[33]*[37] described two advanced forms of the *gastraphetes*, which he credits to Zopyros, an engineer from southern Italy. Zopyrus has been plausibly equated with a

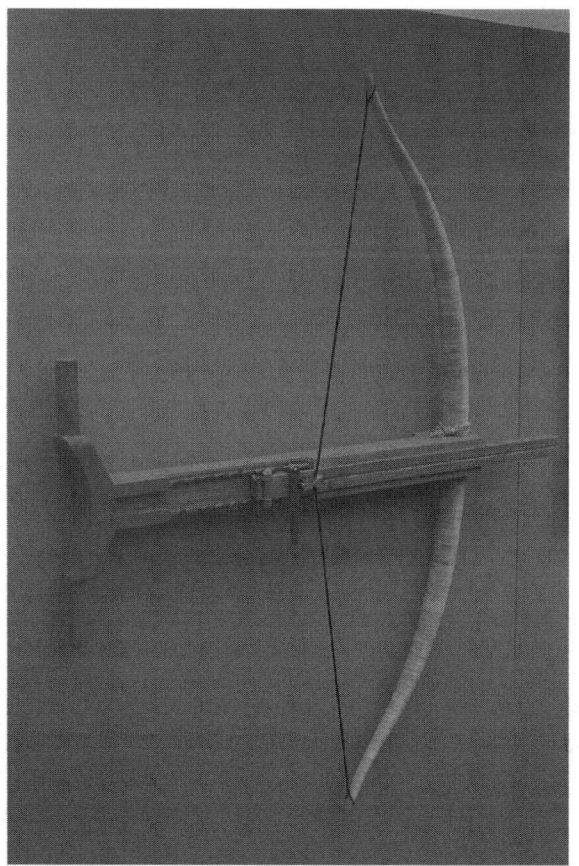

Greek gastraphetes

Pythagorean of that name who seems to have flourished in the late 5th century BC.*[38]*[39] He probably designed his bow-machines on the occasion of the sieges of Cumae and Milet between 421 BC and 401 BC.*[40]*[41] The bows of these machines already featured a winched pull back system and could apparently throw two missiles at once.*[42]

From the mid-4th century BC onwards, evidence of the Greek use of crossbows becomes more dense and varied: Arrow-shooting machines (*katapeltai*) are briefly mentioned by Aeneas Tacticus in his treatise on siegecraft written around 350 BC.*[42] An Athenian inventory from 330–329 BC includes catapults bolts with heads and flights.*[43] Arrow-shooting machines in action are reported from Philip II's siege of Perinthos in Thrace in 340 BC.*[44] At the same time, Greek fortifications began to feature high towers with shuttered windows in the top, presumably to house anti-personnel arrow shooters, as in Aigosthena.*[45]

The transition to torsion catapults, which are not considered crossbows and came to dominate Greek and Roman artillery design, is first evident in inventories of the Athenian arsenal from between 338 and 326 BC.*[42]*[43]

Roman Empire

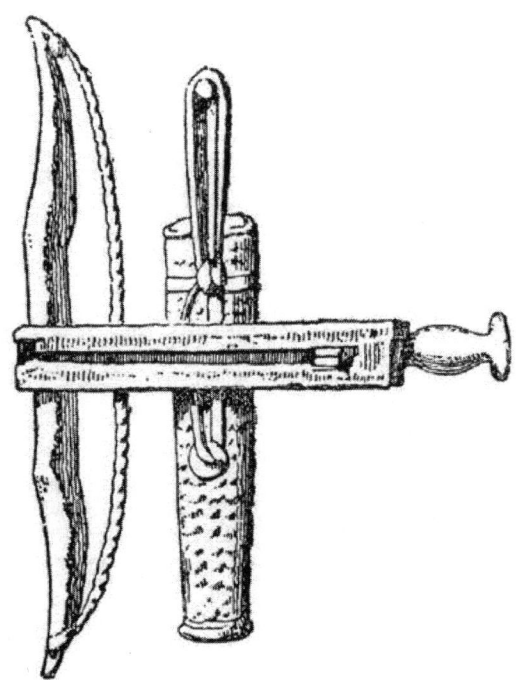

Fig. 467. Arbalète et carquois.

Roman crossbow

The ancient world knew a variety of mechanical hand-held weapons similar to the later medieval crossbow. The exact terminology is a subject of continuing scholarly debate. Roman authors like Vegetius (fl. 4th century) note repeatedly the use of arrow shooting weapons such as *arcuballista* and *manuballista* respectively *cheiroballista*. While most scholars agree that one or more of these terms refer to handheld mechanical weapons, there is disagreement whether these were flexion bows or torsion powered like the recent Xanten find.*[46]

The Roman commander Arrian (c. 86 – after 146) records in his *Tactica* Roman cavalry training for shooting some mechanical handheld weapon from horseback.*[47] Sculptural reliefs from Roman Gaul depict the use of crossbows in hunting scenes. These are remarkably similar to the later medieval crossbow.*[48]

Medieval Europe

The crossbow is portrayed as a hunting weapon on four Pictish stones from early medieval Scotland (6th to 9th centuries): St. Vigeans no. 1, Glenferness, Shandwick, and Meigle.*[49] The use of crossbows in European warfare is

1.6. CROSSBOW

A Medieval crossbowman drawing his bow behind his pavise. A hook on the end of a strap on his belt engages the bowstring. Holding the crossbow down by putting his foot through the stirrup, he draws the bow by straightening his legs

Usually they engaged the enemy in offensive skirmishes before an assault of mounted knights. Crossbowmen were also valuable in counterattacks to protect their infantry. The rank of commanding officer of the crossbowmen corps was one of the highest positions in any army of this time. Along with polearm weapons made from farming equipment, the crossbow was also a weapon of choice for insurgent peasants such as the Taborites.

Mounted knights armed with lances proved ineffective against formations of pikemen combined with crossbowmen whose weapons could penetrate most knights' armor. The invention of pushlever and ratchet drawing mechanisms enabled the use of crossbows on horseback, leading to the development of new cavalry tactics. Knights and mercenaries deployed in triangular formations, with the most heavily armored knights at the front. Some of these riders would carry small, powerful all-metal crossbows of their own. Crossbows were eventually replaced in warfare by more powerful gunpowder weapons, although early guns had slower rates of fire and much worse accuracy than contemporary crossbows. Later, similar competing tactics would feature harquebusiers or musketeers in formation with pikemen (pike and shot), pitted against cavalry firing pistols or carbines.

Elsewhere

Wheelmounted and elephantmounted double-bow-arcuballistae of the Champa kingdom.

The Saracens called the crossbow *qaws Ferengi*, or "Frankish bow", as the Crusaders used the crossbow against the Arab and Turkic horsemen with remarkable success. The adapted crossbow was used by the Islamic armies in defence of their castles. Later, footstrapped versions became very popular among the Muslim armies in Iberia. During the Crusades, Europeans were exposed to Saracen composite bows, made from layers of different material—often wood, horn and sinew—glued together and bound with animal ten-

again evident from the Battle of Hastings until about the year 1500. They almost completely superseded hand bows in many European armies in the 12th century for a number of reasons.

In modern tests, longbows showed a higher rate of shot than crossbows of the same energy, due to the difficulty of the shooter in handling the mechanical parts for loading in the same time as the bow was pulled. With lots of training, a longbowman can achieve a high degree of accuracy that is comparable to the much steeper learning curve in aimed shooting with the crossbow. Despite strength training, there are physical limits to the longbow, unlike the crossbow, which can store several times the energy, but will be less efficient in translating stored into kinetic energy due to the thicker spring material. There is no record from the Middle Ages comparing longbowmen and crossbowmen shooting in one army from a similar position, although such occasions are known with visiting Englishmen in the Baltic and Scots in the French army.

In the armies of Europe,*[50] mounted and unmounted crossbowmen, often mixed with slingers, javelineers and archers, occupied a central position in battle formations.

don. These composite bows could be much more powerful than wooden bows, and were adopted for crossbow prods across Europe. Crossbow prods could be more easily waterproofed than hand bows, which was essential in the humid European climate.

In Western Africa and Central Africa,*[51] crossbows served as a scouting weapon and for hunting, with enslaved Africans bringing this technology to natives in America.*[52] In the American South, the crossbow was used for hunting and warfare when firearms or gunpowder were unavailable because of economic hardships or isolation.*[52] In the North of Northern America, light hunting crossbows were traditionally used by the Inuit.*[53] These are technologically similar to the African derived crossbows, but have a different route of influence.

The native Montagnards of Vietnam's Central Highlands were also known to have used crossbows, as both a tool for hunting, and later, an effective weapon against the Viet Cong during the Vietnam War. Montagnard fighters armed with crossbows proved a highly valuable asset to the US Special Forces operating in Vietnam, and it was not uncommon for the Green Berets to integrate Montagnard crossbowmen into their strike teams.*[54]

The French, and the British used a Sauterelle (French for grasshopper) in World War I. It was lighter and more portable than the Leach Trench Catapult, but less powerful. It weighed 24 kg (53 lb) and could throw an F1 grenade or Mills bomb 110–140 m (120–150 yd).*[55] The Sauterelle replaced the Leach Catapult in British service and was in turn replaced in 1916 by the 2 inch Medium Trench Mortar and Stokes mortar.*[56]

1.6.3 Modern use

Hunting, leisure and science

Crossbows are used for shooting sports and bowhunting in modern archery and for blubber biopsy samples in scientific research. In some countries such as Canada or the United Kingdom, they may be less heavily regulated than firearms, and thus more popular for hunting; some jurisdictions have bow and/or crossbow only seasons.*[57]

Modern military and paramilitary use

In modern times, crossbows are no longer used for assassinations, but there are still some applications. For example, in the Americas, the Peruvian army (Ejército) equips some soldiers with crossbows and rope, to establish a zipline in difficult terrain.*[58] In Brazil the CIGS (Jungle Warfare Training Center) also trains soldiers in the use of

Fisheries scientist obtaining tissue samples from dolphins swimming in the bow wave of a NOAA ship (2010).

A whale shot by a modified crossbow bolt for a blubber biopsy sample.

crossbows.*[59]*[60] In the United States, SAA International Ltd manufacture a 150 ft·lb crossbow-launched version of the U.S. Army type classified Launched Grapnel Hook (LGH), among other mine countermeasure solutions designed for the middle-eastern theatre. It has been successfully evaluated in Cambodia and Bosnia.*[61] It is used to probe for and detonate tripwire initiated mines and booby traps at up to 50 meters. The concept is similar to the LGH device originally only fired from a rifle, as a plastic retrieval line is attached.*[62] Reusable up to 20 times, the line can be reeled back in without exposing oneself. The device is of particular use in tactical situations where noise discipline is important.*[63]

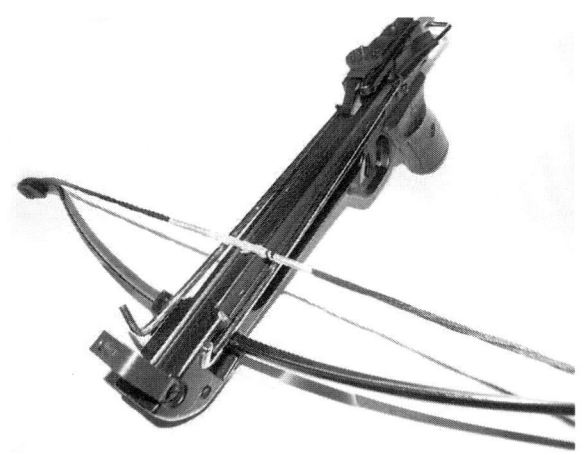

A pistol crossbow

In Europe, British-based Barnett International supplied crossbows to Serbian forces which according to *The Guardian* were later used "in ambushes and as a counter-sniper weapon", against the Kosovo Liberation Army during the Kosovo War in the areas of Pec and Djakovica, south west of Kosovo.*[64] Whitehall launched an investigation, though the department of trade and industry established that not being "on the military list" crossbows were not covered by such export regulations. Paul Beaver of Jane's defence publications commented that, "They are not only a silent killer, they also have a psychological effect". On 15 February 2008, Serbian Minister of Defence Dragan Sutanovac was pictured testing a Barnett crossbow during a public exercise of the Serbian army's Special Forces in Nis, 200 km south of capital Belgrade.*[65] Special forces in both Greece and Turkey also continue to employ the crossbow.*[66]*[67] Spain's Green Berets still use the crossbow as well.*[68]

In Asia, some Chinese armed forces use crossbows, including the special force Snow Leopard Commando Unit of the People's Armed Police and the People's Liberation Army. One justification for this comes in the crossbow's ability to stop persons carrying explosives without risk of causing detonation.*[69] During the Xinjiang riots of July 2009, crossbows were used alongside modern military hardware to quell protests.*[70] The Indian Navy's Marine Commando Force were equipped until the late 1980s with crossbows supplied with cyanide-tipped bolts, as an alternative to suppressed handguns.*[71]

1.6.4 Comparison to conventional bows

With a crossbow, archers could release a draw force far in excess of what they could have handled with a bow. Furthermore, the crossbow could hold the tension for a long time, whereas even the strongest longbowman could only hold a drawn bow for a short period of time. The ease of use of a crossbow allows it to be used effectively with little training, while other types of bows take far more skill to shoot accurately. The disadvantage is the greater weight and clumsiness compared to a bow, as well as the slower rate of shooting and the lower efficiency of the acceleration system, but there would be reduced elastic hysteresis, making the crossbow a more accurate weapon.

Crossbows have a much smaller draw length than bows. This means that for the same energy to be imparted to the arrow (or bolt), the crossbow has to have a much higher draw weight.

A direct comparison between a fast hand-drawn replica crossbow and a longbow show a 6:10 rate of shooting*[72] or a 4:9 rate within 30 seconds and comparable weapons.*[73]

1.6.5 Legal issues

Main article: Laws on crossbows

Can. 29 of the Second Lateran Council under Pope In-

Modern competition crossbow

nocent II in 1139 banned the use of crossbows, as well as slings and bows, against Christians.*[74]

Today, the crossbow often has a complicated legal status due to the possibility of lethal use and its similarities to both firearms and archery weapons. While some jurisdictions regard crossbows the same as firearms, many others do not require any sort of license to own a crossbow. The legality of using a crossbow for hunting varies widely around the world, and even within different jurisdictions of some federal countries.

For example, in Canada you do not need a valid licence or registration certificate to possess any other type of bow, including a crossbow that is longer than 500 mm and that requires the use of both hands.*[75]

1.6.6 See also

- Arbalist (crossbowman)
- Bow (weapon)
- History of crossbows
- Master of Crossbowmen
- Modern competitive archery and target archery for bows
- Shooting sport
- Sauterelle
-

1.6.7 Notes

[1] Payne-Gallwey, Ralph (2007) [1903], *The Crossbow*, Skyhorse Publishing Inc., p. 2, ISBN 1-60239-010-X

[2] Tom Ukinski (23 May 2013). "Drones: Mankind's Always Had Them". *Guardian Liberty Voice*. Retrieved 1 March 2015.

[3] "Facts and interesting information about Medieval Weapons, Armor and arms, specifically, the Crossbow". *medieval-life-and-times.info*. Retrieved 1 March 2015.

[4] Hanafi et al. 2011: 23

[5] Ixax, belle. "Crossbow Reviews 2017". *Archer's Café*. Retrieved 9 March 2017.

[6] O'Connell, Robert L. (1989). *Of Arms and Men: A History of War, Weapons, and Aggression*. Oxford University Press. ISBN 0-19-505359-1, p. 65

[7] Bolts and Arrows: The Lighter Side of Hunting Projectile Name Calling. Foremosthunting.com. Retrieved on 24 June 2011.

[8] Crossbow Arrow Drop - Charted Test Results. BestCrossbowSource.com

[9] "Sighting a Crossbow". *Best Crossbow Source*. Retrieved 28 October 2014.

[10] "Crossbow". *reference.com*. Columbia University Press. Retrieved 1 March 2015.

[11] Teun Koetsier; Marco Ceccarelli (2012), *Explorations in the History of Machines and Mechanisms*, Springer Science & Business Media, p. 214, ISBN 9789400741324

[12] Needham, Joseph (2004), *Science and Civilisation in China, Vol 5 Part 6*, Cambridge University Press, p. 135, ISBN 9780521327275.

[13] Wagner (1993), 153, 157–158.

[14] You (1994), 80.

[15] A Crossbow Mechanism with Some Unique Features from Shandong, China. Asian Traditional Archery Research Network. Retrieved on 20 August 2008.

[16] Mao (1998), 109–110.

[17] Wright (2001), 159.

[18] Needham, Joseph (1986). *Science and Civilization in China: Volume 3, Mathematics and the Sciences of the Heavens and the Earth*. Taipei: Caves Books Ltd, p. 227.

[19] Lin (1993), 36.

[20] James Clavell, *The Art of War*, prelude

[21] Sun Tzu, *The Art Of War*

[22] Graff 2002, p. 22.

[23] Wright (2001), 42.

[24] Needham (1986), Volume 5, Part 6, 124–128.

[25] Lewis (2000a), 45.

[26] R. G. Grant (2005). *Battle: A Visual Journey Through 5,000 Years of Combat*. DK Pub. p. 100. ISBN 978-0-7566-1360-0.

[27] Stephen Turnbull (20 August 2012). *Siege Weapons of the Far East (1): AD 612-1300*. Osprey Publishing Limited. pp. 42–. ISBN 978-1-78200-225-3.

[28] Stephen Turnbull (20 August 2012). *Siege Weapons of the Far East (1): AD 612–1300*. Bloomsbury Publishing. pp. –. ISBN 978-1-78200-225-3.

[29] Joseph Needham; Ling Wang; Robin D. S. Yates; Gwei-Djen Lu; Ping-Yü Ho (1994). *Science and Civilisation in China: Vol. 5, Chemistry and chemical technology ; Pt. 6, Military technology : missiles and sieges*. Cambridge University Press. pp. 145–. ISBN 978-0-521-32727-5.

[30] Stephen Turnbull (20 August 2012). *Siege Weapons of the Far East (1): AD 612–1300*. Bloomsbury Publishing. pp. –. ISBN 978-1-78200-225-3.

[31] Gurstelle, William (2004).*The Art of the Catapult*. Chicago Review Press. ISBN 1-55652-526-5, p. 49

[32] Diod. Sic. 14.42.1

[33] Duncan Campbell: *Greek and Roman Artillery 399 BC-AD 363*, Osprey Publishing, Oxford 2003, ISBN 1-84176-634-8, p.3

[34] Duncan Campbell: *Greek and Roman Artillery 399 BC-AD 363*, Osprey Publishing, Oxford 2003, ISBN 1-84176-634-8, p.4

[35] Stanley M. Burstein, Walter Donlan, Sarah B. Pomeroy, and Jennifer Tolbert Roberts (1999). *Ancient Greece: A Political, Social, and Cultural History*. Oxford University Press. ISBN 0-19-509742-4, p. 366

[36] Campbell (2003), 4.

[37] M.J.T. Lewis: *When was Biton?*, Mnemosyne, Vol. 52, No. 2 (1999), pp. 159–168

[38] Peter Kingsley: Ancient Philosophy, Mystery and Magic, Clarendon Press, Oxford 1995, p.150ff. Plato.stanford.edu. Retrieved on 24 June 2011.

[39] Lewis established a lower date of no later than the mid-4th century (M.J.T. Lewis: *When was Biton?*, Mnemosyne, Vol. 52, No. 2 (1999), pp. 159–168 (160)). Same de Camp (L. Sprague de Camp: *Master Gunner Apollonios*, Technology and Culture, Vol. 2, No. 3 (1961), pp. 240–244 (241)

[40] Biton Biton 65.1–67.4 & 61.12–65.1

[41] Duncan Campbell: *Greek and Roman Artillery 399 BC-AD 363*, Osprey Publishing, Oxford 2003, ISBN 1-84176-634-8, p.5

[42] Duncan Campbell: *Greek and Roman Artillery 399 BC-AD 363*, Osprey Publishing, Oxford 2003, ISBN 1-84176-634-8, p.8ff.

[43] Eric William Marsden: *Greek and Roman Artillery: Historical Development*, The Clarendon Press, Oxford 1969, ISBN 978-0-19-814268-3, p.57

[44] Eric William Marsden: *Greek and Roman Artillery: Historical Development*, The Clarendon Press, Oxford 1969, ISBN 978-0-19-814268-3, p.60

[45] Josiah Ober: *Early Artillery Towers: Messenia, Boiotia, Attica, Megarid*, American Journal of Archaeology, Vol. 91, No. 4. (1987), S. 569–604 (569)

[46] Romanhideout.com: Manuballista found near Xanten

[47] Arrian Tact. 43.1; Baatz 1999, pp. 11–15; Campbell 1986, pp. 117–132

[48] Dictionnaire des antiquites grecques et romaines: Arcuballista, Manuballista

[49] John M. Gilbert, *Hunting and Hunting Reserves in Medieval Scotland* (Edinburgh: John Donald, 1979), p. 62.

[50] Verbruggen, J.F; Second revised and enlarged, edition, in English translation (1997), *The art of warfare in Western Europe during the Middle Ages*, Boydell&Brewer, ISBN 0-85115-570-7

[51] Baaka pygmy with crossbow. Photographersdirect.com. Retrieved on 24 June 2011.

[52] Notes On West African Crossbow Technology. Diaspora.uiuc.edu. Retrieved on 24 June 2011.

[53] Hunting Network (10 February 2009). "The Crossbow: Four thousand years of traditional archery". bowhunting.com. Retrieved 1 March 2015.

[54] John Friedman. "The Crossbow History". www.cacciaebalestra.altervista.org. Retrieved 1 March 2015.

[55] *The Royal Engineers Journal*. The Institution of Royal Engineers. **39**: 79. 1925. Missing or empty |title= (help)

[56] Hugh Chisholm (1922). *The Encyclopædia Britannica: The New Volumes, Constituting, in Combination with the Twenty-nine Volumes of the Eleventh Edition, the Twelfth Edition of that Work, and Also Supplying a New, Distinctive, and Independent Library of Reference Dealing with Events and Developments of the Period 1910 to 1921 Inclusive, Volume 1*. Encyclopædia Britannica Company Limited. p. 470.

[57] https://dr6j45jk9xcmk.cloudfront.net/documents/3311/2014-ontario-hunting-regulations.pdf

[58] Ejercito prepare for deployment.

[59] CIGS information thread.

[60] CIGS photograph.

[61] Jane's LGH Mine Clearance by US forces Jul 2009. Janes.com (9 June 2011). Retrieved on 24 June 2011.

[62] LGH Plastic Retrieval Line. None. Retrieved on 24 June 2011.

[63] SAA Crossbow Launched Grapnel Hook Archived 15 July 2011 at the Wayback Machine.. Saa-intl.com. Retrieved on 24 June 2011.

[64] The Guardian.

[65] Day Life Serbia report. Daylife.com (15 February 2008). Retrieved on 24 June 2011.

[66] Greek soldiers uses crossbow.

[67] Turkish special ops.

[68] Spanish Green Beret 2005 photo.

[69] *New crossbow shoots with great accuracy*, archived from the original on 2 February 2014

[70] Bingham, John. (9 July 2009) "Xinjiang riots: Modern Chinese army displays ancient preference for crossbow". Daily Telegraph (UK). Retrieved on 24 June 2011.

[71] Marine Commandos[dead link]

[72] Video comparing longbow and crossbow Retrieved 16 September 2010

[73] longbow vs crossbow behind a pavese Retrieved 16 September 2010

[74] The sources are collected in Hefele, Histoire des conciles d'apres les documents originaux, trans. and continued by H. Leclerq 1907–52., 5/1, 721–722; but see also, Bernhardi Jahrbuecher der deutschen Geschichte, I Leipzig 1883, 154–160: *Tenth Ecumenical Council: Lateran II 1139*, Internet Medieval Source Book, 1 November 1996, retrieved 5 May 2007

[75] Police, Government of Canada, Royal Canadian Mounted; Canada, Gouvernement du Canada, Gendarmerie royale du. "Language selection - Royal Canadian Mounted Police".

1.6.8 References

- Baatz, Dietwulf (1994), "Die römische Jagdarmbrust", *Bauten und Katapulte des römischen Heeres*, Stuttgart: Franz Steiner Verlag, pp. 284–293, ISBN 3-515-06566-0

- Graff, David A. (2002), *Medieval Chinese Warfare, 300-900*, Warfare and History, London: Routledge, ISBN 0415239559

- Payne-Gallwey, Ralph, Sir, *The Crossbow: Mediaeval and Modern, Military and Sporting; its Construction, History & Management with a Treatise on the Balista and Catapult of the Ancients and An Appendix on the Catapult, Balista & the Turkish Bow*, New York : Bramhall House, 1958.

- The Crossbows of South-West China, by Stephen Selby, 1999

- African crossbow, Donald B. Ball, 1996

- How to Use a Crossbow Effectively

1.6.9 External links

- How To Make A Crossbow - Online Video Course

- International Crossbow Shooting Union (IAU)

- World Crossbow Shooting Association (WCSA)

- The Crossbow by Sir Ralph Payne-Gallwey, BT

- Designing crossbows

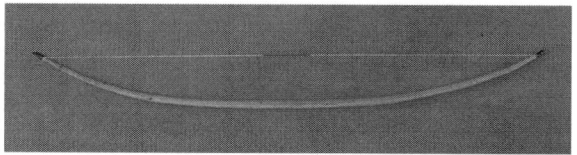

Self-yew English longbow, 6 ft 6 in (1.98 m) long, 470 N (105 lbf) draw force.

A period illustration of the Battle of Crécy. Anglo-Welsh longbowmen figure prominently in the foreground on the right, where they are driving away Italian mercenary crossbowmen.

1.7 English longbow

The **English longbow** was a powerful medieval type of longbow (a tall bow for archery) about 6 ft (1.8 m) long used by the English and Welsh for hunting and as a weapon in medieval warfare. English use of longbows was effective against the French during the Hundred Years' War, particularly at the start of the war in the battles of Sluys (1340), Crécy (1346), and Poitiers (1356), and perhaps most famously at the Battle of Agincourt (1415). They were less successful after this, with longbowmen having their lines broken at the Battle of Verneuil (1424), and being completely routed at the Battle of Patay (1429) when they were charged before they had set up their defensive position.

The earliest longbow known from England, found at Ashcott Heath, Somerset, is dated to 2665 BC,[1] but no longbows survive from the period when the longbow was dominant (c. 1250–1450 AD),[2] probably because bows became weaker, broke and were replaced, rather than being handed down through generations.[3] More than 130 bows survive from the Renaissance period, however. More than 3,500 arrows and 137 whole longbows were recovered from the *Mary Rose*, a ship of Henry VIII's navy that sank at Portsmouth in 1545.

1.7.1 Description

Length

A longbow must be long enough to allow its user to draw the string to a point on the face or body, and the length therefore varies with the user. In continental Europe it was generally seen as any bow longer than 1.2 m (3.9 ft). The Society of Antiquaries of London says it is of 5 or 6 feet (1.5 or 1.8 metres) in length.[4] Richard Bartelot, of the Royal Artillery Institution, said that the bow was of yew, 6 feet (1.8 m) long, with a 3-foot (910 mm) arrow.[5] Gaston III, Count of Foix, wrote in 1388 that a longbow should be "of yew or boxwood, seventy inches [1.8 m] between the points of attachment for the cord".[6] Historian Jim Bradbury said they were an average of about 5 feet and 8 inches.[7] All but the last estimate were made before the excavation of the *Mary Rose*, where bows were found ranging in length from 1.87 to 2.11 m (6 ft 2 in to 6 ft 11 in) with an average length of 1.98 m (6 ft 6 in).[8]

Draw weights

Estimates for the draw of these bows varies considerably. Before the recovery of the *Mary Rose*, Count M. Mildmay Stayner, Recorder of the British Long Bow Society, estimated the bows of the Medieval period drew 90–110 pounds-force (400–490 newtons), maximum, and Mr. W.F. Paterson, Chairman of the Society of Archer-Antiquaries, believed the weapon had a supreme draw weight of only 80–90 lb_f (360–400 N).[2] Other sources suggest significantly higher draw weights. The original draw forces of examples from the *Mary Rose* are estimated by Robert Hardy at 150–160 lb_f (670–710 N) at a 30-inch (76.2 cm) draw length; the full range of draw weights was between 100–185 lb_f (440–820 N).[9] The 30-inch (76.2 cm) draw length was used because that is the length allowed by the arrows commonly found on the *Mary Rose*.

A modern longbow's draw is typically 60 lb_f (270 N) or less, and by modern convention measured at 28 inches (71.1 cm). Historically, hunting bows usually had draw weights of 50–60 lb_f (220–270 N), which is enough for all but the very largest game and which most reasonably fit adults can manage with practice. Today, there are few modern longbowmen capable of using 180–185 lb_f (800–820 N) bows accurately.[10][11][12]

A record of how boys and men trained to use the bows with high draw weights survives from the reign of Henry VII.

> [My yeoman father] taught me how to draw, how to lay my body in my bow ... not to draw with strength of arms as divers other nations do ... I had my bows bought me according to my age and strength, as I increased in them, so my bows were made bigger and bigger. For men shall never shoot well unless they be brought up to it.
> —Hugh Latimer.[13]

What Latimer meant when he describes laying his body into the bow was described thus:

> the Englishman did not keep his left hand steady, and draw his bow with his right; but keeping his right at rest upon the nerve, he pressed the whole weight of his body into the horns of his bow. Hence probably arose the phrase "bending the bow," and the French of "drawing" one.
> —W. Gilpin.[14]

Construction and materials

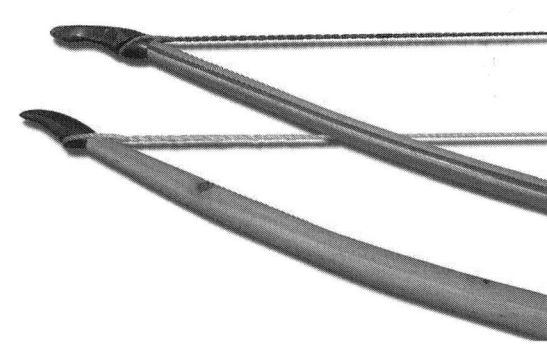

Self (bottom) and laminated (top) bows for comparison

The bowstave The preferred material to make the longbow was yew, although ash, elm and other woods were also used. Gerald of Wales speaking of the bows used by the Welsh men of Gwent, says: "They are made neither of horn, ash nor yew, but of elm; ugly unfinished-looking weapons, but astonishingly stiff, large and strong, and equally capable of use for long or short shooting".[15] The traditional construction of a longbow consists of drying the yew wood for 1 to 2 years, then slowly working the wood into shape, with the entire process taking up to four years. (This can be done far more quickly by working the wood down when wet, as a thinner piece of wood will dry much faster.) The bow stave is shaped into a D-section. The outer "back" of sapwood, approximately flat, follows the natural growth rings; modern bowyers often thin the sapwood, while in the *Mary Rose* bows the back of the bow was the natural surface of the wood, only the bark being removed. The inner side ("belly") of the bow stave consists of rounded heartwood. The heartwood resists compression and the outer sapwood performs better in tension. This combination in a single piece of wood (a self bow) forms a natural "laminate", somewhat similar in effect to the construction of a composite bow. Longbows will last a long time if protected with a water-resistant coating, traditionally of "wax, resin and fine tallow".

The trade of yew wood to England for longbows was such that it depleted the stocks of yew over a huge area. The first documented import of yew bowstaves to England was in 1294. In 1350 there was a serious shortage, and Henry IV of England ordered his royal bowyer to enter private land and cut yew and other woods. In 1470 compulsory practice was renewed, and hazel, ash, and laburnum were specifically allowed for practice bows. Supplies still proved insufficient, until by the Statute of Westminster 1472, every ship coming to an English port had to bring four bowstaves for every tun.*[16] Richard III of England increased this to ten for every tun. This stimulated a vast network of extraction and supply, which formed part of royal monopolies in southern Germany and Austria. In 1483, the price of bowstaves rose from two to eight pounds per hundred, and in 1510 the Venetians obtained sixteen pounds per hundred.

In 1507 the Holy Roman Emperor asked the Duke of Bavaria to stop cutting yew, but the trade was profitable, and in 1532 the royal monopoly was granted for the usual quantity "if there are that many". In 1562, the Bavarian government sent a long plea to the Holy Roman Emperor asking him to stop the cutting of yew, and outlining the damage done to the forests by its selective extraction, which broke the canopy and allowed wind to destroy neighbouring trees. In 1568, despite a request from Saxony, no royal monopoly was granted because there was no yew to cut, and the next year Bavaria and Austria similarly failed to produce enough yew to justify a royal monopoly.

Forestry records in this area in the 17th century do not mention yew, and it seems that no mature trees were to be had. The English tried to obtain supplies from the Baltic, but at this period bows were being replaced by guns in any case.*[17]

The string Bowstrings are made of hemp, flax or silk, and attached to the wood via horn "nocks" that fit onto the end of the bow. Modern synthetic materials (often Dacron) are now commonly also used for strings.

The arrow A wide variety of arrows were shot from the English longbow. Variations in length, fletchings and heads are all recorded. Perhaps the greatest diversity lies in hunting arrows, with varieties like broad-arrow, wolf-arrow, dog-arrow, Welsh arrow and Scottish arrow being recorded.*[18] War arrows were ordered in the thousands for medieval armies and navies, supplied in sheaves normally of 24 arrows.*[19] For example, between 1341 and 1359 the English crown is known to have obtained 51,350 sheaves (1,232,400 arrows).*[20]

Only one significant group of arrows, found at the wreck of the *Mary Rose*, has survived. Over 3500 arrows were found, mainly made of poplar but also of ash, beech and hazel. Analysis of the intact specimens shows their length to vary from 61 to 83 centimetres (24–33 in), with an average length of 76 centimetres (30 in).*[21] Because of the preservation conditions of the *Mary Rose* no arrowheads survived. However, many heads have survived in other places, which has allowed typologies of arrow heads to be produced, the most modern being the Jessop typology.*[22] The most common arrowheads in military use were the short bodkin point (Jessop M10) and a small barbed arrow (Jessop M4).*[23]

1.7.2 Use and performance

Training

Longbows were very difficult to master because the force required to deliver an arrow through the improving armour of medieval Europe was very high by modern standards. Although the draw weight of a typical English longbow is disputed, it was at least 360 newtons (81 pounds-force) and possibly more than 600 N (130 lb_f). Considerable practice was required to produce the swift and effective combat shooting required. Skeletons of longbow archers are recognisably adapted, with enlarged left arms and often osteophytes on left wrists, left shoulders and right fingers.*[24]

It was the difficulty in using the longbow that led various monarchs of England to issue instructions encouraging their ownership and practice, including the Assize of Arms of 1252 and Edward III of England's declaration of 1363:

> Whereas the people of our realm, rich and poor alike, were accustomed formerly in their games to practise archery – whence by God's help, it is well known that high honour and profit came to our realm, and no small advantage to ourselves in our warlike enterprises... that every man in the same country, if he be able-bodied, shall, upon holidays, make use, in his games, of bows and arrows... and so learn and practise archery.

If the people practised archery, it would be that much easier for the King to recruit the proficient longbowmen he needed for his wars. Along with the improving ability of gunfire to penetrate plate armour, it was the long training needed by longbowmen that eventually led to their being replaced by musketeers.

Range

The range of the medieval weapon is not accurately known, with much depending on both the power of the bow and the type of arrow. It has been suggested that a flight arrow of a professional archer of Edward III's time would reach 400 yd (370 m)[25] but the longest mark shot at on the London practice ground of Finsbury Fields in the 16th century was 345 yd (315 m).[26] In 1542, Henry VIII set a minimum practice range for adults using flight arrows of 220 yd (200 m); ranges below this had to be shot with heavy arrows.[27] Modern experiments broadly concur with these historical ranges. A 667 N (150 lbf) *Mary Rose* replica longbow was able to shoot a 53.6 g (1.89 oz) arrow 328 m (359 yd) and a 95.9 g (3.38 oz) a distance of 249.9 m (273.3 yd).[28] In 2012, Joe Gibbs shot a 2.25 oz (64 g) livery arrow 292 yd (267 m) with a 170 lbf yew bow.[29] The effective combat range of longbowmen was generally lower than what could be achieved on the practice range as sustained shooting was tiring and the rigors of campaigning would sap soldiers' strength. Writing 30 years after the Mary Rose sank, Barnabe Rich estimated that if 1000 English archers were mustered then after one week only 100 of them would be able to shoot farther than 200 paces, while 200 would not be able to shoot farther than 180 paces.[30]

Armour penetration

Modern testing   In an early modern test by Saxton Pope, a direct hit from a steel bodkin point penetrated Damascus mail armour.[31][32]

A 2006 test was made by Matheus Bane using a 75 lbf (330 N) draw (at 28") bow, shooting at 10 yards; according to Bane's calculations, this would be approximately equivalent to a 110 lbf (490 N) bow at 250 yards.[33] Measured against a replica of the thinnest contemporary "Jack coat" armour, a 905 grain needle bodkin and a 935 grain curved broadhead penetrated over 3.5 inches (89 mm). ("Jack coat" armour could be up to twice as thick as the coat tested; in Bane's opinion such a thick coat would have stopped bodkin arrows but not the cutting force of broadhead arrows.) Against "high quality riveted maille", the needle bodkin and curved broadhead penetrated 2.8". Against a coat of plates, the needle bodkin achieved 0.3" penetration. The curved broadhead did not penetrate but caused 0.3" of deformation of the metal. Results against plate armour of "minimum thickness" (1.2mm) were similar to the coat of plates, in that the needle bodkin penetrated to a shallow depth, the other arrows not at all. In Bane's view, the plate armour would have kept out all the arrows if thicker or worn with more padding.

Other modern tests described by Bane include those by Williams (which concluded that longbows could *not* penetrate mail, but in Bane's view did not use a realistic arrow tip), Robert Hardy's tests (which achieved broadly similar results to Bane), and a *Primitive Archer* test which demonstrated that a longbow **could** penetrate a plate armour breastplate. However, the *Primitive Archer* test used a 160 lbf (710 N) longbow at very short range, generating 160 joules (vs. 73 for Bane and 80 for Williams), so probably not representative of battles of the time.

Tests conducted by Mark Stretton[34] examined the effects of heavier war shafts (as opposed to lighter hunting or distance-shooting 'flight arrows'). The quarrel-like 102 gram arrow from a yew 'self bow' (with a draw weight of 144lbs at 32 inches) while travelling at 47.23 metres per second yielded 113.76 joules, more kinetic energy than the lighter broad-heads while achieving 90% of the range. The short, heavy quarrel-form bodkin could penetrate a replica brigandine at up to 40° from perpendicular.

In 2011, Mike Loades conducted an experiment in which short bodkin arrows were shot at a range of 10 yd (9.1 m) by bows of 140 lbf (620 N) - powerful bows at less than normal battlefield range. The target was covered in a riveted mail over a fabric armour of deerskin over 24 linen layers. While most arrows went through the mail layer, none fully penetrated the textile armour.[35]

Other research has also concluded that later medieval armour, such as that of the Italian city state mercenary companies, was effective at stopping contemporary arrows.[36]

Contemporary accounts   Gerald of Wales commented on the power of the Welsh longbow in the 12th century:

> [I]n the war against the Welsh, one of the men of arms was struck by an arrow shot at him by a Welshman. It went right through his thigh, high up, where it was protected inside and outside the leg by his iron chausses, and then through the skirt of his leather tunic; next it penetrated that part of the saddle which is called the alva or seat; and finally it lodged in his horse, driving so deep that it killed the animal.[37][38]

Against massed men in armour, massed longbows were murderously effective on many battlefields.[39]

Strickland and Hardy suggest that "even at a range of 240 yards heavy war arrows shot from bows of poundages in the mid- to upper range possessed by the Mary Rose bows would have been capable of killing or severely wounding men equipped with armour of wrought iron. Higher-quality armour of steel would have given considerably greater protection, which accords well with the experience of Oxford's men against the elite French vanguard at Poitiers in 1356, and des Ursin's statement that the French knights of the first ranks at Agincourt, which included some of the most important (and thus best-equipped) nobles, remained comparatively unhurt by the English arrows".*[40]

Archery was described by contemporaries as ineffective against plate armour in the Battle of Neville's Cross (1346), the siege of Bergerac (1345), and the Battle of Poitiers (1356); such armour became available to European knights of fairly modest means by the late 14th century, though never to all soldiers in any army. Longbowmen were however effective at Poitiers, and this success stimulated changes in armour manufacture partly intended to make armoured men less vulnerable to archery. Nevertheless, at the battle of Agincourt in 1415 and for some decades thereafter, English longbowmen continued to be an effective battlefield force.*[39]

Shields Following the Battle of Crécy, the longbow did not always prove as effective. For example, at the Battle of Poitiers (1356), the French Men-at-Arms formed a shieldwall with which Geoffrey le Baker recounts " 'protecting their bodies with joined shields, [and] turned their faces away from the missiles. So the archers emptied their quivers in vain".*[41]

Summary Modern tests and contemporary accounts agree therefore that well-made plate armour could protect against longbows. However this did not necessarily make the longbow ineffective; thousands of longbowmen were deployed in the English victory at Agincourt against plate armoured French knights in 1415. Clifford Rogers has argued that while longbows might not have been able to penetrate steel breastplates at Agincourt they could still penetrate the thinner armour on the limbs. Most of the French knights advanced on foot but, exhausted by walking across wet muddy terrain in heavy armour enduring a "terrifying hail of arrow shot", they were overwhelmed in the melee.

Less heavily armoured soldiers were more vulnerable than knights. For example, enemy crossbowmen were forced to retreat at Crécy when deployed without their protecting pavises. Horses were generally less well protected than the knights themselves; shooting the French knights' horses from the side (where they were less well armoured) is described by contemporary accounts of the Battle of Poitiers (1356), and at Agincourt John Keegan has argued that the main effect of the longbow would have been in injuring the horses of the mounted French knights.

Shooting rate

A typical military longbow archer would be provided with between 60 and 72 arrows at the time of battle. Most archers would not shoot arrows at maximum rate, as it would exhaust even the most experienced man. "With the heaviest bows [a modern war bow archer] does not like to try for more than six a minute." *[42] Not only do the arms and shoulder muscles tire from the exertion, but the fingers holding the bowstring become strained; therefore, actual rates of shooting in combat would vary considerably. Ranged volleys at the beginning of the battle would differ markedly from the closer, aimed shots as the battle progressed and the enemy neared. On the battlefield English archers stored their arrows stabbed upright into the ground at their feet, reducing the time it took to nock, draw and loose.

Arrows were not unlimited, so archers and their commanders took every effort to ration their use to the situation at hand. Nonetheless, resupply during battle was available. Young boys were often employed to run additional arrows to longbow archers while in their positions on the battlefield.*[43] "The longbow was the machine gun of the Middle Ages: accurate, deadly, possessed of a long range and rapid rate of fire, the flight of its missiles was likened to a storm".*[2]

In tests against a moving target simulating a galloping knight*[34] it took some approximately seven seconds to draw, aim and loose an armour-piercing heavy arrow using a replica war bow, that in the seven seconds between the first and second shots the target advanced 70 yards and that the second shot occurred at such close range that, if it was a realistic contest, running away was the only option.

A Tudor English author expects eight shots from a longbow in the same time as five from a "ready shooter" with the musket,.*[30] He points out that the musket also shoots at a flatter trajectory, so is more likely to hit its target and its shot is likely to be more damaging in the event of a hit. The advantage of early firearms lay in the lower training requirements, the opportunity to take cover while shooting, flatter trajectory,*[30] and greater penetration.*[44]

Treating arrow wounds

The only way to remove an arrow cleanly was to tie a piece of cloth soaked in water to the end of it and push it through the victim's wound and out the other side —this was extremely painful. Specialised tools have existed since ancient times: Diocles (successor of Hippocrates) devised the graphiscos, a form of cannula with hooks, and the duck-billed forceps (allegedly invented by Heras of Cappadocia[45]) employed during the medieval period to extract arrows from places where bone prevented the arrow being pushed through.

Henry, Prince of Wales, later Henry V, was wounded in the face by an arrow at the Battle of Shrewsbury (1403). The royal physician John Bradmore had such a tool made, which consisted of a pair of smooth tongs. Once carefully inserted into the socket of the arrowhead, the tongs screwed apart till they gripped its walls and allowed the head to be extracted from the wound. Prior to the extraction, the hole made by the arrow shaft had been widened by inserting larger and larger dowels of elder pith wrapped in linen down the entry wound. The dowels were soaked in honey, now known to have antiseptic properties.[46] The wound was then dressed with a poultice of barley and honey mixed in turpentine (pre-dating Ambroise Paré but whose therapeutic use of turpentine was inspired by Roman medical texts that may have been familiar to Bradmore). After 20 days the wound was free of infection.[47]

1.7.3 History

Etymology

The first recorded use of the term 'longbow', as distinct from simply 'bow', occurs in a Paston Letter of the 15th century.

Origins

The origins of the English longbow are disputed. While it is hard to assess the significance of military archery in pre-Norman Conquest Anglo-Saxon warfare, it is clear that archery played a prominent role under the Normans, as the story of the Battle of Hastings shows. Their Anglo-Norman descendants also made use of military archery, as exemplified by their victory at the Battle of the Standard in 1138. During the Anglo-Norman invasions of Wales, Welsh bowmen took a heavy toll of the invaders and Welsh archers would feature in English armies from this point on. However, historians dispute whether this archery used a different kind of bow to the later English Longbow.[48] Traditionally it has been argued that prior to the beginning of the 14th century, the weapon was a self bow between four and five feet in length, known since the 19th century as the shortbow. This weapon, drawn to the chest rather than the ear, was much weaker. However, in 1985, Jim Bradbury reclassified this weapon as the *ordinary wooden bow*, reserving the term shortbow for short composite bows and arguing that longbows were a developed form of this ordinary bow.[49] Strickland and Hardy in 2005 took this argument further, suggesting that the shortbow was a myth and all early English bows were a form of longbow.[50] In 2011, Clifford Rogers forcefully restated the traditional case based upon a variety of evidence, including a large scale iconographic survey.[51] In 2012, Richard Wadge added to the debate with an extensive survey of record, iconographic and archaeological evidence, concluding that longbows co-existed with shorter self-wood bows in England in the period between the Norman conquest and the reign of Edward III, but that powerful longbows shooting heavy arrows were a rarity until the later 13th century.[52] Whether or not there was a technological revolution at the end of the 13th century therefore remains in dispute. What is agreed, however, is that the English longbow as an effective weapon system evolved in the late 13th and early 14th centuries.

Fourteenth and fifteenth century

The longbow decided many medieval battles fought by the English and Welsh, the most significant of which were the Battle of Crécy (1346) and the Battle of Agincourt (1415), during the Hundred Years' War and followed earlier successes, notably at the Battle of Falkirk (1298) and the Battle of Halidon Hill (1333) during the Wars of Scottish Independence. They were less successful after this, with longbowmen having their lines broken at the Battle of Verneuil (1424), and being routed at the Battle of Patay (1429) when they were charged before they had set up their defenses.

The longbow was also used against the English by their Welsh neighbours. The Welsh used the longbow mostly in a different manner than the English. In many early period English campaigns, the Welsh used the longbow in ambushes, often at point blank range that allowed their missiles to penetrate armour and generally do a lot of damage.[53]

Although longbows were much faster and more accurate than the black-powder weapons which replaced them, longbowmen always took a long time to train because of the years of practice necessary before a war longbow could be used effectively (examples of longbows from the *Mary Rose* typically had draws greater than 637 N (143 lb_f)). In an era in which warfare was usually seasonal, and non-noble soldiers spent part of the year working at farms, the year-round training required for the effective use of the longbow was a challenge. A standing army was an expensive proposition to a medieval ruler. Mainland European armies seldom trained a significant longbow corps. Due to their specialized training, English longbowmen were sought as mercenaries in other European countries, most notably in the Italian city-states and in Spain. The White Company,[54] comprising men-at-arms and longbowmen and commanded by Sir John Hawkwood, is the best known English Free Company of the 14th century. The powerful Hungarian king, Louis the Great, is an example of someone who used longbowmen in his Italian campaigns.

Sixteenth century and later

Longbows remained in use until around the 16th century, when advances in firearms made gunpowder weapons a significant factor in warfare and such units as arquebusiers and grenadiers began appearing. Despite this, the English Crown made numerous efforts to continue to promote archery practice by banning other sports and fining people for not possessing bows.*[55] Indeed, just before the English Civil War, a pamphlet by William Neade entitled *The Double-Armed Man* advocated that soldiers be trained in both the longbow and pike; although this advice was followed only by a few town militias.

The Battle of Flodden (1513) was "a landmark in the history of archery, as the last battle on English soil to be fought with the longbow as the principal weapon..." *[56] The last recorded use of bows in an English battle may have been a skirmish at Bridgnorth, in October 1642, during the Civil War, when an impromptu town militia, armed with bows, proved effective against un-armoured musketeers.*[57] The Battle of Tippermuir (1644), in Scotland, may have been the last battle involving the longbow.*[58] Longbowmen remained a feature of the Royalist Army, but were not used by the Roundheads.

Longbows have been in continuous production and use for sport and for hunting to the present day, but since 1642 they have been a minority interest, and very few have had the high draw weights of the medieval weapons. Other differences include the use of a stiffened non-bending centre section, rather than a continuous bend.

Serious military interest in the longbow faded after the seventeenth century but occasionally schemes to resurrect its military use were proposed. Benjamin Franklin was a proponent in the 1770s; the Honourable Artillery Company had an archer company between 1784 and 1794; and a man named Richard Mason wrote a book proposing the arming of militia with pike and longbow in 1798.*[59] Donald Featherstone also records a Lt. Col. Richard Lee of 44th Foot advocated the military use of the longbow in 1792.*[60] There is a record of the use of the longbow in action as late as WWII, when Jack Churchill is credited with a longbow kill in France in 1940.*[61] The weapon was certainly considered for use by Commandos during the war but it is not known whether it was used in action.*[62]

1.7.4 Tactics

Battle formations

The idea that there was a standard formation for English longbow armies was argued by Alfred Byrne in his influential work on the battles of the Hundred Years' War, *The Crecy War*.*[63] This view was challenged by Jim Bradbury in his book *The Medieval Archer*[64] and more modern works are more ready to accept a variety of formations.*[65]

In summary, however, the usual English deployment in the 14th and 15th centuries was as follows:

- Infantry (usually dismounted knights and armoured soldiers employed by the nobles and often armed with pole weapons such as pollaxes and bills) in the centre.

- Longbowmen were usually deployed primarily on the flanks, sometimes to the front.

- Cavalry was rarely used but, where deployed, either on the flanks (to make or protect against flank attacks), or in the centre in reserve, to be deployed as needed (for example, to counter any breakthroughs).

In the 16th century, these formations evolved in line with new technologies and techniques from the continent. Formations with a central core of pikes and bills were flanked by companies of "shot" made up of a mixture of archers and arquebusiers, sometimes with a skirmish screen of archers and arquebusiers in front.*[66]

1.7.5 Surviving bows and arrows

More than 3,500 arrows and 137 whole longbows were recovered from the *Mary Rose*, a ship of Henry VIII's navy that capsized and sank at Portsmouth in 1545. It is an important source for the history of the longbow, as the bows, archery implements and the skeletons of archers have been preserved. The bows range in length from 1.87 to 2.11 m (6 ft 2 in to 6 ft 11 in) with an average length of 1.98 m (6 ft 6 in).*[8] The majority of the arrows were made of poplar, others were made of beech, ash and hazel. Draw lengths of the arrows varied between 61 and 81 centimetres (24 and 32 in) with the majority having a draw length of 76 centimetres (30 in).*[21] The head would add 5–15 cm depending on type, though some 2–4.5 cm must be allowed for the insertion of the shaft into the socket.*[67]

The longbows on the *Mary Rose* were in excellent finished condition. There were enough bows to test some to destruction which resulted in draw forces of 450 N (100 lbf) on average. However, analysis of the wood indicated that they had degraded significantly in the seawater and mud, which had weakened their draw forces. Replicas were made and when tested had draw forces of from 445 N to 823 N (100 to 185 lbf).[9]

In 1980, before the finds from the *Mary Rose*, Robert E. Kaiser published a paper stating that there were five known surviving longbows:[2]

- The first bow comes from the Battle of Hedgeley Moor in 1464, during the Wars of the Roses. A family who lived at the castle since the battle had preserved it to modern times. It is 1.66 m (65 in) and a 270 N (60 lbf) draw force.[68]

- The second dates to the Battle of Flodden in 1513 ("a landmark in the history of archery, as the last battle on English soil to be fought with the longbow as the principal weapon..." [56]). It hung in the rafters at the headquarters of the Royal Scottish Archers in Edinburgh.[2] It has a draw force of 360 to 410 N (80 to 90 lbf).

- The third and fourth were recovered in 1836 by John Deane from the *Mary Rose*.[69] Both weapons are in the Tower of London Armoury and Horace Ford writing in 1887 estimated them to have a draw force of 280 to 320 N (65 to 70 lbf).[70] A modern replica made in the early 1970s of these bows has a draw force of 460 N (102 lbf).[71]

- The fifth surviving longbow comes from the armoury of the church in the village of Mendlesham in Suffolk, and is believed to date either from the period of Henry VIII or Queen Elizabeth I. The Mendlesham Bow is broken but has an estimated length of 1.73 to 1.75 m (68 to 69 in) and draw force of 350 N (80 lbf).[72]

1.7.6 Social importance

The importance of the longbow in English culture can be seen in the legends of Robin Hood, which increasingly depicted him as a master archer, and also in the "Song of the Bow", a poem from *The White Company* by Sir Arthur Conan Doyle.[73]

During the reign of Henry III the Assize of Arms of 1252 required that all "citizens, burgesses, free tenants, villeins and others from 15 to 60 years of age" should be armed.[74] The poorest of them were expected to have a halberd and a knife, and a bow if they owned land worth more than £2.[75] This made it easier for the King to raise an army, but also meant that the bow was a weapon commonly used by rebels during the Peasants' Revolt. From the time that the yeoman class of England became proficient with the longbow, the nobility in England had to be careful not to push them into open rebellion.[76][77]

It has been conjectured that yew trees were commonly planted in English churchyards to have readily available longbow wood.[78]

1.7.7 See also

- Archery
- Infantry in the Middle Ages

1.7.8 Notes

[1] Bacon 1971, p. 16.

[2] Kaiser 1980.

[3] Levick 1992

[4] Kaiser 1980 footnote 5, citing "The Berkhamsted Bow", Antiquaries Journal 11 (London), p. 423

[5] Kaiser 1980 footnote 6, citing Major Richard G. Bartelot, Assistant Historical Secretary, Royal Artillery Institution, Old Military Academy, Woolwich, England. Letter, 16 February 1976

[6] Longman & Walrond 1967, p. 132.

[7] Bradbury 1985

[8] Staff 2007, p. 6.

[9] Strickland & Hardy 2005, p. 17

[10] Strickland & Hardy 2005, pp. 13,18.

[11] A review of *The Great Warbow* "The power of a bow is measured in its draw-weight, and these days few men can pull a bow above 80lb... and skeletons retrieved from the wreck show spinal distortions, indicating just what it took to be a proper archer" (Cohu 2005).

[12] In the English language there is the expression that someone "was not pulling their weight". This is thought to infer that someone was using a longbow that had a draw weight that was less than that person's body weight.

[13] Trevelyan 2008, pp. 18,88.

[14] Trevelyan 2008, p. 18 quoting W. Gilpin (1791) *Forest Scenery*

[15] Oakeshott 1960, p. 294.

[16] *Statutes at Large*, **3**, 1762, p. 408, ...because that our sovereign lord the King, by a petition delivered to him in the said parliament, by the commons of the same, hath perceived That the great scarcity of bowstaves is now in this realm, and the bowstaves that be in this realm be sold as an excessive price...

[17] Hageneder 2007, p. .

[18] Strickland & Hardy 2005, p. 42.

[19] War arrows were often described as being a "cloth yard" in length - the cloth yard being the slightly longer physical measure from the finger tips to the nose, but with the head turned away from the finger tips. At the time of the Hundred Years' War archers drew the arrow back to the ear rather than to the chin.

[20] Wadge 2007, pp. 160–161.

[21] Staff 2007, p. 7.

[22] Jessop, Oliver. "A New Artefact Typology for the Study of Medieval Arrowheads" (PDF).

[23] Wadge 2007, pp. 184–185.

[24] Dr. A.J. Stirland. Raising the Dead: the Skeleton Crew of Henry VIII's Great Ship the Mary Rose. (Chichester 2002) As cited in Strickland & Hardy 2005, p.

[25] Oakeshott 1960, p. 297.

[26] Loades 2013, p. 32.

[27] Loades 2013, p. 33.

[28] Strickland & Hardy 2005, p. 18, Appendix 408–418

[29] Loades 2013, p. 65.

[30] *A right exelent and pleasaunt dialogue, betwene Mercury and an English souldier contayning his supplication to Mars: bevvtified with sundry worthy histories, rare inuentions, and politike deuises.* wrytten by B. Rich: gen. 1574. Published 1574 by J. Day. These bookes are to be sold [by H. Disle] at the corner shop, at the South west doore of Paules church in London. https://bowvsmusket.com/2015/07/14/barnabe-rich-a-right-exelent-and-pleasaunt-dialouge-1574/ accessed 21 April 2016

[31] Pope 2003, Chapter IV.--Archery in general, p.30.

[32] "Royal Armouries: 6. Armour-piercing arrowheads".

[33] Bane 2006.

[34] Soar et al. 2010, pp. 127–151.

[35] Loades 2013, pp. 72-73.

[36] Kaiser 2003.

[37] *Itinerarium Cambriae*, (1191)

[38] *Weapon 030 - The Longbow*, Osprey, p. 66, 12 At the time, 1191, this would be mail chausses, and the story is that having had one leg shot through and pinned to the saddle by an arrow, the knight wheeled his horse around, only to receive a second arrow, which nailed the other leg in the same fashion.

[39] "The Efficacy of the Medieval Longbow: A Reply to Kelly DeVries," *War in History* 5, no. 2 (1998): 233-42; idem, "The Battle of Agincourt", *The Hundred Years War (Part II): Different Vistas*, ed. L. J. Andrew Villalon and Donald J. Kagay (Leiden: Brill, 2008): 37–132.

[40] Strickland & Hardy 2005, pp. 272–278.

[41] Loades 2013, p. 10.

[42] Strickland & Hardy 2005, p. 31.

[43] The statistics on rates of shot are taken from *Agincourt: Henry V and the Battle That Made England* (Barker 2006).

[44] "The mean depth of arrow wounds, for example, was an inch and a half, that of gunshot wounds six inches, not counting balls that went right through the body or head" (Gunn & Gromelski 2012, pp. 1222–1223).

[45] Wilson, Thomas (1901). "Arrow Wounds". *American Anthropologist* (3 ed.). **3**. ISSN 1548-1433. JSTOR 659204.

[46] Israili, ZH. "Antimicrobial Properties of Honey". *Am J Ther*. **21**: 304–23. PMID 23782759. doi:10.1097/MJT.0b013e318293b09b.

[47] Cummins 2006.

[48] Strickland & Hardy 2005, pp. 34-48.

[49] Bradbury 1985, pp. 14-15.

[50] Strickland & Hardy 2005, pp. 37-38, 48.

[51] Rogers 2011.

[52] Wadge 2012, pp. 211–212.

[53] Rothero 1984, 4:The Welsh Wars 1277–1282 "one arrow could pierce a mail hauberk, breeches and saddle of an armoured knight and pin him by the thigh to his horse's flank. The Welsh fought [in] a well-planned ambush".

[54] Conan Doyle 1997.

[55] Gunn 2010, pp. 53–81.

[56] Heath n.d., p. 134

[57] John Norton, letter dated 5 October 1642. As printed in The Garrisons of Shropshire during the Civil War, Leake and Evans publishers, Shrewsbury, 1867, page 32. "every man from 16 to 50 and upwards, gott himself into such armes as they could presently attaine, or could imagine be conduceable for the defence of the towne". "some companies of foote.. with their musketts... began to wade foarde, which being descried, we, with our bowes and arrows did so gaule them (being unarmed men) that with their utmost speed they did retreate" https://play.google.com/store/books/details?id=4HBMAAAAMAAJ&rdid=book-4HBMAAAAMAAJ&rdot=1 accessed 7 August 2012

[58] http://www.historic-uk.com/HistoryUK/HistoryofEngland/The-Longbow/

[59] Heath 1980, pp. 208-9.

[60] Featherstone 1973, p. 154.

[61] Featherstone 1973, pp. 157–158.

[62] Heath 1980, pp. 215-216.

[63] Burne 1991, pp. 37–39.

[64] Bradbury 1985, pp. 95–98.

[65] Bennett 1994, p. 1–20.

[66] Strickland & Hardy 2005, p. 403.

[67] Strickland & Hardy 2005, p. 6.

[68] Kaiser 1980 cites: Gordon, Henry; Webb, Alf (1972). "The Hedgeley Moor Bow at Alnwick Castle". *Journal of the Society of Archer-Antiquaries.* **15**: 8, 9.

[69] Kaiser 1980 cites: Gordon, Paul H. (1939). *The New Archery*. New York: D. Appleton-Century Co. p. 183.

[70] Kaiser 1980 cites: Ford, Horace (1887). *The Theory and Practice of Archery*. London: Longman Green and Co. p. 3..

[71] Kaiser 1980 cites: McKee, Alexander (1974). *King Henry VIII's Mary Rose*. New York: Stein and Day. p. 103.

[72] Kaiser 1980 cites: W.F. Paterson, Chairman, Society of Archer-Antiquaries. Letters, 5 May 1976.

[73] Conan Doyle 1997

[74] Kruschke 1985, p. 31

[75] *The right to keep and bear arms: report of the Subcommittee on the Constitution of the Committee on the Judiciary, United States Senate, Ninety-seventh Congress, second session*, U.S. G.P.O., 1982 p. 46 (see also: David T. Hardy, Partner in the Law Firm Sando & Hardy *Historical Bases of the Right To Keep and Bear Arms*)

[76] Andrzejewski 2003, p. 65 "It is surely not accidental that the only peasant revolt in England which succeeded took place at the time of the predominance of the long bow".

[77] Trevelyan 2008, p. 18 "The good yeoman archer 'whose limbs were made in England' was not a retrospective fancy of Shakespeare, but an unpleasant reality for French and Scots, and a formidable consideration for bailiffs and Justices trying to enforce servile dues or statutory rates of wages in the name of Law, which no one high or low, regarded with any great respect".

[78] "Yew Trees in Churchyards". *Internet Sacred Texts Archive*. Retrieved 17 August 2014.

1.7.9 References

- Andrzejewski, Stanislaw (2003) [1954]. *Military organization and society*. ISBN 978-0-415-17680-4.

- Bacon, Edward (1971). *Archaeology: Discoveries in the 1960s*. New York: Praeger. ISBN 0-304-93635-9.

- Bennett, Matthew (1994). "The Development of Battle Tactics in the Hundred Years War". In Curry, Anne; Hughes, Michael L. *Arms, armies, and fortifications in the Hundred Years War*. Woodbridge, England: Boydell Press. pp. 1–20. ISBN 0-85115-365-8.

- Bradbury, Jim (1985). *The Medieval Archer*. The Boydell Press. ISBN 0-85115-194-9.

- Barker, Juliet (2006). *Agincourt: Henry V and the Battle That Made England*. Little, Brown and Co. ISBN 0-316-01503-2.

- Burne, A.H. (1991) [1955]. *The Crecy War*. London: Greenhill Books. pp. 37–39. ISBN 1-85367-081-2.

- Conan Doyle, Arthur (1 May 1997). *The White Company*. Project Gutenberg.

- Featherstone, Donald (1973) [1967]. *Bowmen of England*. London: New English Library. ISBN 9780450016264.

- Gunn, Steven (2010). "Archery Practice in Early Tudor England". *Past and Present.* **209** (1): 53–81. doi:10.1093/pastj/gtq029.

- Gunn, Steven; Gromelski, Tomasz (2012). "For whom the bell tolls: accidental deaths in Tudor England". *The Lancet.* **380** (9849): 1222–1223. doi:10.1016/S0140-6736(12)61702-4.

- Hageneder, F. (2007). *Yew: A History*. Sutton Publishing. ISBN 978-0-7509-4597-4.

- Heath, E.G. (1980). *Archery : A Military History*. London: Osprey. ISBN 0850453534.

- Heath, E.G. (n.d.) [1972]. *The Grey Goose Wing*. p. 134.

- Kruschke, Earl Roger (1985). *The right to keep and bear arms: a continuing American dilemma*. C.C. Thomas Publishing Co. ISBN 0-398-05141-0.

- Loades, Mike (2013). *The Longbow*. Botley, Oxford: Osprey Publishing. ISBN 9781782000853.

- Longman, C.J.; Walrond, H. (1967). *Archery*. New York: Fiederick Ungar Publishing Co.

- Oakeshott, R. Ewart (1960). *The Archaeology of Weapons*. London: Lutterworth Press.

- Pope, Saxton (2003). *Hunting with the Bow and Arrow*. Project Gutenberg EBook.

- Rothero, Christopher (1984). *The Scottish and Welsh wars, 1250–1400*. Men at Arms. London: Osprey. ISBN 0-85045-542-1.

- Soar, Hugh; Gibbs, Joseph; Jury, Christopher; Stretton, Mark (2010). *Secrets of the English War Bow*. Westholme. pp. 127–151. ISBN 9781594161261.

- Strickland, Matthew; Hardy, Robert (2005). *The Great Warbow: From Hastings to the Mary Rose*. Sutton Publishing. ISBN 0-7509-3167-1.

- Trevelyan, G. M. (2008). *English Social History – A Survey of Six Centuries – Chaucer to Queen Victoria*. Longman. ISBN 978-1-4437-2095-3.

- Wadge, Richard (2007). *Arrowstorm*. Stroud: Spellmount. pp. 160–1. ISBN 978-1-86227-388-7.

- Wadge, Richard (2012). *Archery in Medieval England: Who Were the Bowmen of Crecy?*. Stroud, Gloucestershire: History Press Limited. pp. 211–212. ISBN 9780752465876.

Journals

- Cummins, Josephine (November 2006). "Saving Prince Hal: maxillo-facial surgery, 1403" (PDF). *Dental History Magazine*. Glasgow, Scotland: History of Dentistry Research Group, University of Glasgow (19). ISSN 1756-1728. Archived from the original (PDF) on 1 February 2013. Retrieved 19 August 2012.

- Kaiser, Robert E. (December 2003). "Medieval Military Surgery". *Medieval History Magazine*. **1** (4).

- Kaiser, Robert E. (1980). "The Medieval English Longbow". *Journal of the Society of Archer-Antiquaries*. **23**.

- Rogers, Clifford J. (2011). "The development of the longbow in late medieval England and "technological determinism"". *Journal of Medieval History*. **37** (3): 321–341. doi:10.1016/j.jmedhist.2011.06.002.

Other

- Bane, Matheus (2006). "English Longbow Testing against various armor circa 1400" (PDF). Retrieved 8 November 2016.

- Cohu, Will (3 April 2005). "How they did affright the air at Agincourt". Daily Telegraph.

- Levick, Ben (1992). "They Didn't Have Bows, Did They?". Regia Anglorum Publications.

- Staff (2007). "The Ship – Armament – Bows" (10 pages ed.). The Mary Rose Trust. pp. 6, 7. Archived from the original on 25 February 2008.

1.7.10 Further reading

Books

- Auden, Thomas (2008). *Memorials of Old Shropshire*. Read Books. ISBN 1-4097-6478-8.

- Allely, Steve; et al. (2000) [1992]. Hamm, Jim, ed. *The Traditional Bowyers Bible*. **1**. The Lyons Press. ISBN 1-59921-453-9.

- Aspel, G. Fred; et al. (2000) [1993]. Hamm, Jim, ed. *The Traditional Bowyers Bible*. **2**. The Lyons Press. ISBN 1-58574-086-1.

- Baker, Tim; et al. (2000) [1994]. Hamm, Jim, ed. *The Traditional Bowyers Bible*. **3**. The Lyons Press. ISBN 1-58574-087-X.

- Allely, Steve; et al. (2008). Hamm, Jim, ed. *The Traditional Bowyers Bible*. **4**. The Lyons Press. ISBN 978-1-59921-453-5.

- Hardy, Robert (1992). *Longbow: A Social and Military History*. Patrick Stephens. ISBN 1-85260-412-3.

- Soar, Hugh David Hewitt (2004). *The Crooked Stick: A History of the Longbow (Weapons in History S.)*. Westholme U.S. ISBN 1-59416-002-3.

    - A review by Bernard Cornwell in The Times

- Sellman, Roger (1964). *Mediaeval English Warfare*. London: Methuen. ISBN 978-0-416-63620-8.

Journals

- Thomas Esper *The Replacement of the Longbow by Firearms in the English Army*, Technology and Culture, Vol. VI, No. 3, 1965.

- B.W. Kooi C.A. Bergman. *PDF:An Approach to the Study of Ancient Archery using Mathematical Modelling*, Antiquity 71:(271) 124–134 (1979)

Other

- Rulon l. Hancock. *PDF: United States National Archery Association Flight committee modern longbow flight rules*, U.S. National Archery Association. September 2002.

- Paul Lalonde. *A Bundle of Tudor War Arrows*, An article about the arrows found on the Mary Rose.

- Liesl Wilhelmstochter. *Ealdormere Archery Handbook: Section 11: Towards a more medieval archer*

- Staff. *Mary Rose historical ship*, The Mary Rose Trust – {note: BACK of bow faces enemy.}

- The Great Northwood Bowmen Medieval Longbow Archery and re-enactment Society, re-enacting the 15th century, based in London.

1.8 Gorytos

For the racehorse, see Gorytus (horse).

A **gorytos** (Greek: γωρυτός, Latin: gorytus) designated

Scythian warrior with gorytos and other equipment

in Antiquity a bow-case for a short recurve, or Scythian, bow. Usually, the gorytos would allow to store the full quiver, with bow and arrows. Many gorytos were highly decorated. Some have been found in Macedonian tombs, such as the so-called "Tomb of Philip" in Vergina of the 2nd half of the 4th century BCE. They were also used by the Persians. Indo-Greeks adopted the recurve bow and the gorytos as part of their horse-fighting equipment from around 100 BCE, as can be seen on their coins.

1.8.1 External links

- Gold gorytos from the tomb of Philip

1.9 History of crossbows

Late medieval crossbowman from ca. 1480

It is not clear exactly where and when the crossbow originated, however it is believed to have been invented in Europe and China around 6th to 5th century BC. The current archaeological evidence points to the common usage of crossbows in China for military purposes during the Warring States period from at the very latest, the second half of the 4th century BC onwards.

Ancient Chinese crossbow (2nd century BC). Guimet Museum, Paris.

1.9.1 China and South East Asia

The earliest evidence of crossbows (Chinese: 弩; pinyin: *nǔ*) in ancient China and neighboring peoples dates back to at least the 6th century BC. According to Sir Joseph Needham in his Science and Civilisation in China, it is not possible to pinpoint exactly which of the East Asian peoples invented the crossbow. Linguistically, it derives from non-Chinese languages of China's then neighbors, who were often hired as marksmen mercenaries, while the first records and examples of representations as well as specimens are from China. However, there is unquestionable evidence that the crossbow was used for military purposes at least as far back as the Warring States period from the second half of the 4th century BC onwards.*[1]

In terms of archaeological evidence, bronze crossbow bolts dating from as early as the mid-5th century BC have been found at a Chu burial site in Yutaishan, Jiangling County, Hubei Province.*[2] The earliest handheld crossbow stocks with a bronze trigger, dating from the 6th century BC, were found in Tombs 3 and 12 at Qufu, Shandong, previously the capital of Lu.*[3]*[4] Other early finds of crossbows were discovered in Tomb 138 at Saobatang, Hunan Province and dated to the mid-4th century BC.*[5]*[6] However, ammunition for crossbows could have apparently also been shaped as spherical bullets. Jing Fang (78-37 BC), a Western-Han era Chinese mathematician and music theorist, discussed astronomical topics such as solar and lunar eclipses.*[7] He wrote that the moon, shaped like a ball, produced no light, yet instead acted like a mirror in reflecting the light illuminated only by the sun, which he compared to the shape of a round crossbow bullet.*[7]

Repeating crossbows, first mentioned in the *Records of the Three Kingdoms*, were discovered in 1986 in Tomb 47 at Qinjiazui, Hubei Province, and were dated to around the 4th century BC.*[8] The earliest Chinese documents mentioning a crossbow were texts from the 4th to 3rd centuries BC attributed to the followers of Mozi. This source refers to the use of a giant crossbow catapult between the 6th and 5th centuries BC, corresponding to the late Spring and Autumn Period. Sun Tzu's influential book *The Art of War* (first appearance dated between 500 BC to 300 BC*[9]) refers to the characteristics and use of crossbows in chapters 5 and 12 respectively.*[10] One of the earliest reliable descriptions of this weapon in warfare is of an ambush which took place at the Battle of Maling in 341 BC. Crossbow remains have also been found amongst the soldiers of the Terracotta Army near the mausoleum of China's first emperor Qin Shi Huang (260-210 BC).*[11]

The repeating crossbow and multiple bow arcuballista were both developed in China.*[12] When discussing the advantages and disadvantages of the nomadic Xiongnu and Han dynasty armies in a memorandum to the throne in 169 BC, official Chao Cuo deemed the crossbow and repeating crossbow of the Han armies superior to the Xiongnu bow, even though the latter were trained to shoot behind themselves while riding.*[13] According to one authority, the crossbow had become "nothing less than the standard weapon of the Han armies," by the second century BC.*[14]

In Vietnamese historical legend, the ruler and general Thục Phán who ruled over the ancient kingdom of Âu Lạc from 257 to 207 BC is said to have owed his power to a magic crossbow, capable of shooting thousands of arrows at once.

Crossbows were given to the Chams by China with instruction in crossbows and mounted archery being given by a Chinese official in 1171.*[16]*[17] In 1177 the transfer of crossbow technology by the Chinese was used by the Champa in their invasion and sacking of Angkor, the Khmer Empire's capital.*[18]*[19]*[20]

According to the Chinese *Wujing Zongyao* military manuscript of 1044, the crossbow used *en masse* was the most effective weapon against northern nomadic cavalry charges.*[21] Elite crossbowmen were also valued as long-range snipers as was the case when the Liao Dynasty general Xiao Talin was picked off by a Song crossbowman at the Battle of Shanzhou in 1004.*[21] Crossbows were mass-produced in state armories with designs improving as time went on, such as the use of a mulberry wood stock and brass;

a crossbow in 1068 could pierce a tree at 140 paces.*[22]

- 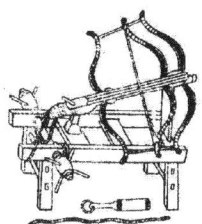 Chinese *Chuangzi Nu* stationary windlass device with triple-bow arcuballista

-  Chinese repeating crossbow with pull lever and automatic reload magazine

-  Chinese Lian Nu (連弩), multiple shot crossbow without a visible nut or cocking aid

1.9.2 Europe

The earliest evidence for a form of the crossbow in Europe dates to the 5th century BC when the *gastraphetes*, an ancient Greek crossbow type, appeared. The device was described by the Greek author Heron of Alexandria in his work *Belopoeica* ("On Catapult-making"), which draws on an earlier account of his famous compatriot engineer Ctesibius (fl. 285–222 BC). Heron identifies the gastraphetes as the forerunner of the later catapult, which places its invention some unknown time prior to 420 BC.*[23]

The gastraphetes was a large artillery crossbow mounted on a heavy stock with a lower and upper section, the lower being the case fixed to the bow and the upper being the slider which had the same dimensions as the case.*[24] Meaning "belly-bow",*[24] it was called as such because the concave withdrawal rest at one end of the stock was placed against the stomach of the operator, which he could press to withdraw the slider before attaching a string to the trigger and loading the bolt; this could thus store more energy than regular Greek bows.*[25] It was used in the Siege of Motya in 397 BC. This was a key Carthaginian stronghold in Sicily, as described in the 1st century AD by Heron of Alexandria in his book *Belopoeica*.*[26] Alexander the Great's 332 BC siege of Tyre provides reliable sources for the use of these weapons by the Greek besiegers.*[27]

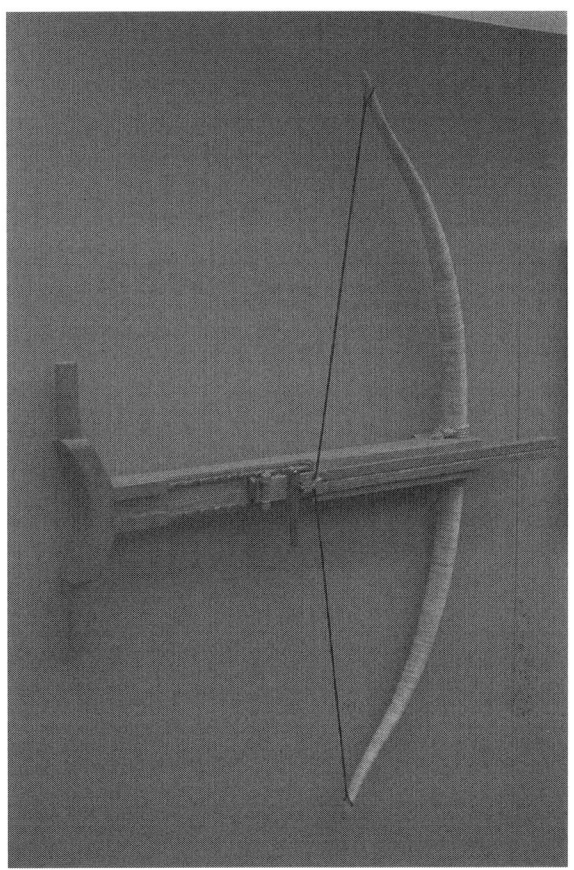

Greek gastraphetes

Arsenal of ancient mechanical artillery: Catapults (standing), chain drive of Polybolos (bottom center), Gastraphetes (on wall)

The efficiency of the gastraphetes was improved by introducing the ballista. Its application in sieges and against rigid infantry formations featured more and more powerful projectiles, leading to technical improvements and larger ballistae. The smaller sniper version was often called *Scor-*

pio.[28] An example for the importance of ballistae in Hellenistic warfare is the *Helepolis*, a siege tower employed by Demetrius during the siege of Rhodes in 305 BC. At each level of the moveable tower were several ballistae. The large ballistae at the bottom level were designed to destroy the parapet and clear it of any hostile troop concentrations while the small armorbreaking scorpios at the top level sniped at the besieged. This suppressive shooting would allow them to mount the wall with ladders more safely.*[29]

A medieval crossbowman drawing his bow behind his pavise

The use of the modern crossbow in European warfare dates back to Roman times. According to R. Ernest Dupuy and Trevor N. Dupuy, in 36 BC a Han empire expedition into central Asia encountered and defeated a contingent of Roman legionaries. The Romans were suggested to have been part of Antony's campaign against Parthia. Chinese victory was based on their crossbows, whose bolts and darts seem to "have penetrated Roman shields and armor." The theory is that the Chinese crossbow was transmitted to the Roman world through this encounter.*[30]

The crossbow was particularly prominent in European warfare from the battle of Hastings (1066) until about 1525.*[31] In the armies of Europe,*[32] mounted and unmounted crossbowmen, often mixed with slingers, javeliners and archers, occupied a central position in battle formations. Usually they engaged the enemy in offensive skirmishes before an assault of mounted knights. Crossbowmen were also valuable in counterattacks to protect their infantry. Crossbowmen were held in high esteem as professional soldiers, often commanding higher rates of pay than other foot soldiers.*[33] The rank of commanding officer of the crossbowmen corps was one of the highest positions in many medieval armies, including those of Spain, France, and Italy. Crossbowmen were held in such high regard in Spain that they were granted status on par with the knightly class.*[31] Along with polearm weapons made from farming equipment, the crossbow was also a weapon of choice for insurgent peasants such as the Taborites. Genoese crossbowmen were famous mercenaries hired throughout medieval Europe, while the crossbow also played an important role in anti-personnel defense of ships.*[34] Mounted knights armed with lances proved ineffective against formations of pikemen combined with crossbowmen whose weapons could penetrate most knights' armor. The invention of pushlever and ratchet drawing mechanisms enabled the use of crossbows on horseback, leading to the development of new cavalry tactics. Knights and mercenaries deployed in triangular formations, with the most heavily armored knights at the front. Some of these riders would carry small, powerful all-metal crossbows of their own.

The crossbow almost completely superseded hand bows in many European armies in the twelfth century for a number of reasons (England, where the longbow was more popular, being a rare exception). Although a longbow had greater range, and could achieve comparable accuracy and faster shooting rate than a wooden or composite crossbow, the latter can be used effectively after a week of training, while a comparable single-shot skill with a longbow could take years of practice. Later crossbows (sometimes referred to as arbalests), utilizing all-steel prods, were able to achieve power close (and sometime superior) to longbows, but were more expensive to produce and slower to reload because they required the aid of mechanical devices such as the cranequin or windlass to draw back their extremely heavy bows. Usually these could only shoot two bolts per minute versus twelve or more with a skilled archer, often necessitating the use of a pavise to protect the operator from enemy fire.*[35] Crossbowmen among the Flemish citizens, in the army of Richard Lionheart, and others, could have up to two servants, two crossbows and a pavise to protect the men. Then one of the servants had the task of reloading the weapons, while the second subordinate would carry and hold the pavise (the archer himself also wore protective armor). Such a three-man team could shoot eight shots per minute, compared to a single crossbowman's three shots per minute. The archer was the leader of the team, the one who owned the equipment, and the one who received payment for their services.*[32]

The payment for a crossbow mercenary was higher than for

16th century French mounted crossbowman ("cranequinier")

a longbow mercenary, but the longbowman did not have to pay a team of assistants and his equipment was cheaper. Thus the crossbow team was twelve percent less efficient than the longbowman since three of the latter could be part of the army in place of one crossbow team. Furthermore, the prod and bow string of a composite crossbow were subject to damage in rain whereas the longbowman could simply unstring his bow to protect the string. French forces employing the composite crossbow were outmatched by English longbowmen at Crécy in 1346, at Poitiers in 1356 and at Agincourt in 1415. As a result, use of the crossbow declined sharply in France,[35] and the French authorities made attempts to train longbowmen of their own. After the conclusion of the Hundred Years' War, however, the French largely abandoned the use of the longbow, and consequently the military crossbow saw a resurgence in popularity. The crossbow continued to see use in French armies by both infantry and mounted troops until as late as 1520 when, as with elsewhere in continental Europe, the crossbow would be largely eclipsed by the handgun. Spanish forces in the New World would make extensive use of the crossbow, even after it had largely fallen out of use in Europe. Crossbowmen participated in Hernán Cortés' conquest of Mexico and accompanied Francisco Pizarro on his initial expedition to Peru, though by the time of the conquest of Peru in 1532-1523 he would have only a dozen such men remaining in his service.[31]

Crossbows were eventually replaced in warfare by gunpowder weapons, although early guns had slower rates of fire and much worse accuracy than contemporary crossbows. The Battle of Cerignola in 1503 was largely won by Spain through the use of matchlock firearms, marking the first time a major battle was won through the use of firearms. Later, similar competing tactics would feature harquebusiers or musketeers in formation with pikemen, pitted against cavalry firing pistols or carbines. While the military crossbow had largely been supplanted by firearms on the battlefield by 1525, the sporting crossbow in various forms remained a popular hunting weapon in Europe until the eighteenth century.[36] Up until the seventeenth century most beekeepers in Europe kept their hives spread across the woods and had to defend them against bears. Therefore, their guild was granted the right to bear arms and is commonly depicted carrying heavy crossbows.

French soldiers with a Sauterelle *bomb-throwing crossbow in 1915.*

A bomb-throwing crossbow called the *Sauterelle* was used by the French and British armies on the Western Front during World War I. It could throw an F1 grenade or Mills bomb 110–140 m (120–150 yd).[37]

1.9.3 Islamic World

The Saracens called the crossbow *qaws Ferengi*, or "Frankish bow", as the Crusaders used the crossbow against the Arab and Turkoman horsemen with remarkable success. The adapted crossbow was used by the Islamic armies in defence of their castles. Later footstrapped version become very popular among the Muslim armies in Iberia. During the Crusades, Europeans were exposed to Saracen composite bows, made from layers of different material—often wood, horn and sinew—glued together and bound with animal tendon. These composite bows could be made smaller and handier than wooden self-bows while retaining the pull, and were adopted for crossbow prods across Europe. Crossbow prods could be more easily waterproofed than hand bows, which was essential in the humid European climate.

1.9.4 Africa and in the Americas

In Central Africa simple crossbows were used for hunting and as a scout weapon, previously thought to have been first introduced by the Portuguese. Until recently they were especially in use by different tribes of the pygmy-people, usually with poisoned and relatively small arrows. This silent technique of hunting in the tropical forest is quite similar to that of the South American indigenous hunting method with blow pipe and poisoned arrows. It makes sure not to startle up the prey, for example if a first shot goes astray. Since the small arrow is rarely deadly itself, the animal will drop from the trees after some time because of the poisoning. In the American South, the crossbow was used by the conquistadors for hunting and warfare when firearms or gunpowder were unavailable because of economic hardships or isolation.*[34] Light hunting crossbows were traditionally used by the Inuit in Northern America.

1.9.5 Use of crossbows today

A whale shot by a modified crossbow bolt

Crossbows are mostly used for target shooting in modern archery. In some countries they are still used for hunting, such as in most of states within the USA, parts of Asia, Europe, Australia and Africa. Crossbows with special projectiles are used in whale research to take blubber biopsy samples without harming the whales or other marine big "game".*[38]

Modern military and paramilitary usage

The crossbow is still used in modern times by various militaries,*[39]*[40]*[41]*[42] tribal forces*[43] and in China even by the police forces.*[44] As their worldwide distribution is not restricted by regulations on arms, they are used as silent weapons and for their psychological effect,*[45] even reportedly using poisoned projectiles.*[46] Crossbows are used for ambush and anti-sniper*[47] operations or in conjunction with ropes to establish zip-lines in difficult terrain.*[48]

1.9.6 See also

- Medieval warfare

1.9.7 References

[1] Needham, Joseph (2004), *Science and Civilisation in China, Vol 5 Part 6*, Cambridge University Press, p. 135, ISBN 0-521-08732-5

[2] Wagner, Donald B. (1993). *Iron and Steel in Ancient China: Second Impression, With Corrections*. Leiden: E.J. Brill. ISBN 90-04-09632-9. pp. 153, 157–158.

[3] You (1994), 80.

[4] A Crossbow Mechanism with Some Unique Features from Shandong, China. Asian Traditional Archery Research Network. Retrieved on 2008-08-20.

[5] Mao (1998), 109–110.

[6] Wright (2001), 159.

[7] Needham, Joseph (1986). *Science and Civilization in China: Volume 3, Mathematics and the Sciences of the Heavens and the Earth*. Taipei: Caves Books Ltd, p. 227.

[8] Lin (1993), 36.

[9] James Clavell, *The Art of War*, prelude

[10] https://www.gutenberg.org/files/132/132.txt

[11] Weapons of the terracotta army

[12] "A look at crossbows in China".

[13] Di Cosmo, Nicola. (2002). Ancient China and Its Enemies: The Rise of Nomadic Power in East Asian History. Cambridge: Cambridge University Press. ISBN 0-521-77064-5. Page 203.

[14] Graff 2002, p. 22.

[15] Needham, Joseph (2004). *Science and Civilisation in China, Vol 5 Part 6*. Cambridge University Press. p. 135. ISBN 0-521-08732-5.

[16] Joseph Needham; Ling Wang; Robin D. S. Yates; Gwei-Djen Lu; Ping-Yü Ho (1994). *Science and Civilisation in China: Vol. 5, Chemistry and chemical technology ; Pt. 6, Military technology : missiles and sieges*. Cambridge University Press. pp. 145–. ISBN 978-0-521-32727-5.

[17] Stephen Turnbull (20 August 2012). *Siege Weapons of the Far East (1): AD 612–1300*. Bloomsbury Publishing. pp. –. ISBN 978-1-78200-225-3.

[18] R. G. Grant (2005). *Battle: A Visual Journey Through 5,000 Years of Combat*. DK Pub. p. 100. ISBN 978-0-7566-1360-0.

[19] Stephen Turnbull (20 August 2012). *Siege Weapons of the Far East (1): AD 612-1300*. Osprey Publishing Limited. pp. 42–. ISBN 978-1-78200-225-3.

[20] Stephen Turnbull (20 August 2012). *Siege Weapons of the Far East (1): AD 612–1300*. Bloomsbury Publishing. pp. –. ISBN 978-1-78200-225-3.

[21] Peers, 130.

[22] Peers, 130–131.

[23] Campbell 2003, pp. 3ff.; Schellenberg 2006, pp. 18f.

[24] DeVries, Kelly Robert. (2003). *Medieval Military Technology*. Petersborough: Broadview Press. ISBN 0-921149-74-3. Page 127.

[25] DeVries, Kelly Robert. (2003). *Medieval Military Technology*. Petersborough: Broadview Press. ISBN 0-921149-74-3. Page 128.

[26] Stanley M. Burstein, Walter Donlan, Sarah B. Pomeroy, and Jennifer Tolbert Roberts (1999). *Ancient Greece: A Political, Social, and Cultural History*. Oxford University Press. ISBN 0-19-509742-4, p. 366

[27] John Warry, *Warfare in the Classical World*, p. 79

[28] Duncan B Campbell, *Ancient Siege Warfare* 2005 Osprey Publishing ISBN 1-84176-770-0, p. 26-56

[29] John Warry, *Warfare in the Classical World*, University of Oklahoma Press, ISBN 0-8061-2794-5, p.90

[30] R. Ernest Dupuy and Trevor N. Dupuy, *The Harper Encyclopedia of Military History from 3500 B.C. to the Present*, Fourth Edition (New York: HarperCollins Publishers, 1993), 133, apparently relying on Homer H. Dubs, "A Roman City in Ancient China", in *Greece and Rome*, Second Series, Vol. 4, No. 2 (Oct., 1957), pp. 139–148

[31] Sir Ralph Payne-Gallwey (1995). "The Book of the Crossbow". Dover. ISBN 0-486-28720-3, p. 48

[32] Verbruggen, J.F (1997). *The Art of Warfare in Western Europe during the Middle Ages, second revised and enlarged edition (English translation)*. Boydell&Brewer. ISBN 0-85115-570-7.

[33] Robert Hardy (1992). "Longbow: A Social and Military History". Lyons & Burford. ISBN 1-85260-412-3, p. 44

[34] Notes On West African Crossbow Technology

[35] Robert Hardy (1992). "Longbow: A Social and Military History". Lyons & Burford. ISBN 1-85260-412-3, p. 75

[36] Sir Ralph Payne-Gallwey (1995). "The Book of the Crossbow". Dover. ISBN 0-486-28720-3, p. 48-53

[37] *The Royal Engineers Journal*. The Institution of Royal Engineers. **39**: 79. 1925. Missing or empty |title= (help)

[38] The St. Lawrence

[39] Chinese news report on crossbows.

[40] Chinese special forces with crossbows.

[41] Greek soldiers uses crossbow.

[42] Turkish special ops.

[43] <<Antique Montagnard crossbow>>

[44] Chinese traffic police using crossbows.

[45] Day Life Serbia report Archived 12 January 2009 at the Wayback Machine.

[46] bharat-rakshak article on Marine Commandos Archived 25 October 2007 at the Wayback Machine.

[47] The Guardian.

[48] Ejercito prepare for deployment.

1.9.8 Sources

- Campbell, Duncan (2003), *Greek and Roman Artillery 399 BCE-CE 363*, Oxford: Osprey Publishing, ISBN 1-84176-634-8

- Graff, David A. (2002), *Medieval Chinese Warfare, 300-900*, Warfare and History, London: Routledge, ISBN 0415239559

- Schellenberg, Hans Michael (2006), "Diodor von Sizilien 14,42,1 und die Erfindung der Artillerie im Mittelmeerraum" (PDF), *Frankfurter Elektronische Rundschau zur Altertumskunde*, **3**: 14–23

- Crombie, Laura (2016), *Archery and Crossbow Guilds in Medieval Flanders*, Woodbridge: Boydell and Brewer, ISBN 9781783271047

1.9.9 Further reading

- Nickel, H, ed. (1982). The Art of Chivalry : European arms and armor from the Metropolitan Museum of Art : an exhibition . New York: The Metropolitan Museum of Art and The American Federation of Arts.

1.10 Mary Rose

For later ships with the same name, see HMS Mary Rose. For the play by J.M. Barrie, see Mary Rose (play). For the American scientist and educator, see Mary Swartz Rose.

The *Mary Rose* is a carrack-type warship of the English Tudor navy of King Henry VIII. After serving for 33 years in several wars against France, Scotland, and Brittany and after being substantially rebuilt in 1536, she saw her last action on 19 July 1545. While leading the attack on the galleys of a French invasion fleet, she sank in the Solent, the straits north of the Isle of Wight.

The wreck of the *Mary Rose* was rediscovered in 1971. It was raised in 1982 by the Mary Rose Trust, in one of the most complex and expensive projects in the history of maritime archaeology. The surviving section of the ship and thousands of recovered artefacts are of immeasurable value as a Tudor-era time capsule. The excavation and raising of the *Mary Rose* was a milestone in the field of maritime archaeology, comparable in complexity and cost only to the raising of the Swedish 17th-century warship *Vasa* in 1961.

The finds include weapons, sailing equipment, naval supplies and a wide array of objects used by the crew. Many of the artefacts are unique to the *Mary Rose* and have provided insights into topics ranging from naval warfare to the history of musical instruments. Since the mid-1980s, while undergoing conservation, the remains of the hull have been on display at the Portsmouth Historic Dockyard. An extensive collection of well-preserved artefacts is on display at the nearby Mary Rose Museum, built to display the reconstructed ship and its artefacts.

The *Mary Rose* was one of the largest ships in the English navy through more than three decades of intermittent war and was one of the earliest examples of a purpose-built sailing warship. She was armed with new types of heavy guns that could fire through the recently invented gun-ports. After being substantially rebuilt in 1536, she was also one of the earliest ships that could fire a broadside, although the line of battle tactics that employed it had not yet been developed. Several theories have sought to explain the demise of the *Mary Rose*, based on historical records, knowledge of 16th-century shipbuilding, and modern experiments. The precise cause of her sinking is still unclear, because of conflicting testimonies and a lack of conclusive physical evidence.

1.10.1 Historical context

Painting of Henry VIII in 1509, the year he became king; oil on panel by unknown artist

In the late 15th century, England was a relatively insignificant state on the periphery of Europe. The great victories against France in the Hundred Years' War were in the past; only the small enclave of Calais in northern France remained of the vast continental holdings of the English kings. The War of the Roses—the civil war between the houses of York and Lancaster—had ended with Henry VII's establishment of the House of Tudor, the new ruling dynasty of England. The ambitious naval policies of Henry V were not continued by his successors, and from 1422 to 1509 only six ships were built for the crown. The marriage alliance between Anne of Brittany and Charles VIII of France in 1491, and his successor Louis XII in 1499, left England with a weakened strategic position on its southern flank. Despite this, Henry VII managed to maintain a comparatively long period of peace and a small but powerful core of

1.10. MARY ROSE

a navy.*[1]

At the onset of the early modern period, the great European powers were France, the Holy Roman Empire and Spain. All three became involved in the War of the League of Cambrai in 1508. The conflict was initially aimed at the Republic of Venice but eventually turned against France. Through the Spanish possessions in the Low Countries, England had close economic ties with the Spanish Habsburgs, and it was the young Henry VIII's ambition to repeat the glorious martial endeavours of his predecessors. In 1509, six weeks into his reign, Henry married the Spanish princess Catherine of Aragon and joined the League, intent on certifying his historical claim as king of both England and France. By 1511 Henry was part of an anti-French alliance that included Ferdinand II of Aragon, Pope Julius II and Holy Roman emperor Maximilian.*[2]

The small navy that Henry VIII inherited from his father had only two sizeable ships, the carracks *Regent* and *Sovereign*. Just months after his accession, two large ships were ordered: the *Mary Rose* and the *Peter Pomegranate* (later known as the *Peter* after being rebuilt in 1536) of about 500 and 450 tons respectively. Which king ordered the building of the *Mary Rose* is unclear; although construction began during Henry VIII's reign, the plans for naval expansion could have been in the making earlier. Henry VIII oversaw the project and he ordered additional large ships to be built, most notably the *Henry Grace à Dieu* ("Henry by the Grace of God"), or *Great Harry* at more than 1000 tons burthen.*[3] By the 1520s the English state had established a *de facto* permanent "Navy Royal", the organizational ancestor of the modern Royal Navy.*[4]

1.10.2 Construction

The Embarkation of Henry VIII at Dover, *a painting that commemorated King Henry's voyage to the Field of the Cloth of Gold in 1520, painted in 1540. The vessels in the painting are shown decorated with wooden panels similar to those that would have been used on the* Mary Rose *on special occasions.*

The construction of the *Mary Rose* began in 1510 in Portsmouth and she was launched in July 1511. She was then towed to London and fitted with rigging and decking, and supplied with armaments. Other than the structural details needed to sail, stock and arm the *Mary Rose*, she was also equipped with flags, banners and streamers (extremely elongated flags that were flown from the top of the masts) that were either painted or gilded.*[5]

Constructing a warship of the size of the *Mary Rose* was a major undertaking, requiring vast quantities of high-quality material. In the case of building a state-of-the-art warship, these materials were primarily oak. The total amount of timber needed for the construction can only be roughly calculated since only about one third of the ship still exists.*[6] One estimate for the number of trees is around 600 mostly large oaks, representing about 16 hectares (40 acres) of woodland. The huge trees that had been common in Europe and the British Isles in previous centuries were by the 16th century quite rare, which meant that timbers were brought in from all over southern England. The largest timbers used in the construction were of roughly the same size as those used in the roofs of the largest cathedrals in the high Middle Ages. An unworked hull plank would have weighed over 300 kg (660 lb), and one of the main deck beams would have weighed close to three-quarters of a tonne.*[7]

Naming

The common explanation for the ship's name was that it was inspired by Henry VIII's favourite sister, Mary Tudor, and the rose as the emblem of the Tudors.*[8] According to historians David Childs, David Loades and Peter Marsden, no direct evidence of naming the ship after the King's sister exists. It was far more common at the time to give ships pious Christian names, a long-standing tradition in Western Europe, or to associate them with their royal patrons. Names like *Grace Dieu* (Thank God) and *Holighost* (Holy Spirit) had been common since the 15th century and other Tudor navy ships had names like the *Regent* and *Three Ostrich Feathers* (referring to the crest of the Prince of Wales). The Virgin Mary is a more likely candidate for a namesake, and she was also associated with the Rosa Mystica (mystic rose). The name of the sister ship of the *Mary Rose*, the *Peter Pomegranate*, is believed to have been named in honour of Saint Peter, and the badge of the Queen Catharine of Aragon, a pomegranate. According to Childs, Loades and Marsden, the two ships, which were built around the same time, were named in honour of the king and queen, respectively.*[9]

1.10.3 Design

The *Mary Rose* was substantially rebuilt in 1536. The 1536 rebuilding turned a ship of 500 tons into one of 700 tons, and added an entire extra tier of broadside guns to the old

The Mary Rose *as depicted in the Anthony Roll. The distinct carrack profile with high "castles" fore and aft can clearly be seen. Although the number of guns and gun ports is not entirely accurate, the picture is overall an accurate illustration of the ship.*

The remains of the Mary Rose's *hull. All deck levels can be made out clearly, including the minor remnants of the sterncastle deck.*

carrack-style structure. By consequence, modern research is based mostly on interpretations of the concrete physical evidence of this version of the *Mary Rose*. The construction of the original design from 1509 is less known.

The *Mary Rose* was built according to the carrack-style with high "castles" in the bow and stern with a low waist of open decking in the middle. The shape of the hull has a so-called tumblehome form and reflected the use of the ship as a platform for heavy guns. Above the waterline, the hull gradually narrows to compensate for the weight of the guns and to make boarding more difficult.*[10] Since only part of the hull has survived, it is not possible to determine many of the basic dimensions with any great accuracy. The moulded breadth, the widest point of the ship roughly above the waterline, was about 12 metres (39 ft) and the keel about 32 metres (105 ft), although the ship's overall length is uncertain.*[11]

The hull had four levels separated by three decks. The terminology for these in the 16th century was still not standardised so the terms used here are those that were applied by the Mary Rose Trust. The *hold* lay furthest down in the ship, right above the bottom planking below the waterline. This is where the kitchen, or galley, was situated and the food was cooked. Directly aft of the galley was the mast step, a rebate in the centre-most timber of the keelson, right above the keel, which supported the main mast, and next to it the main bilge pump. To increase the stability of the ship, the hold was where the ballast was placed and much of the supplies were kept. Right above the hold was the *orlop*, the lowest deck. Like the hold it was partitioned and was also used as a storage area for everything from food to spare sails.*[12]

Above the orlop lay the *main deck* which housed the heaviest guns. The side of the hull on the main deck level had seven gunports on each side fitted with heavy lids that would have been watertight when closed. This was also the highest deck that was caulked and waterproof. Along the sides of the main deck there were cabins under the forecastle and sterncastle which have been identified as belonging to the carpenter, barber-surgeon, pilot and possibly also the master gunner and some of the officers. The top deck in the hull structure was the *upper deck* (or weather deck) which was exposed to the elements in the waist. It was a dedicated fighting deck without any known partitions and a mix of heavy and light guns. Over the open waist the upper deck was entirely covered with a coarse netting as a defence measure against boarding.*[13] Though very little of the upper deck has survived, it has been suggested that it housed the main living quarters of the crew underneath the sterncastle. A drainage located in this area has been identified as a possible "piss-dale", a general urinal to complement the regular toilets that would probably have been located in the bow.*[14]

The castles of the *Mary Rose* had additional decks, but since virtually nothing of them survives, their design has had to be reconstructed from historical records. Contemporary ships of equal size were consistently listed as having three decks in both castles. Although speculative, this layout is supported by the illustration in the Anthony Roll and the gun inventories.*[15]

During the early stages of excavation of the wreck, it was believed that the ship had originally been built with clinker (or clench) planking, a technique where the hull consisted of overlapping planks that bore the structural strength of the ship. Cutting gunports into a clinker-built hull would have meant weakening the ship's structural integrity, and it was assumed that she was later rebuilt to accommodate a hull with carvel edge-to-edge planking with a skeletal structure to support a hull perforated with gunports.*[16] Later examination indicates that the clinker planking is not present throughout the ship; only the outer structure of the sterncastle is built with overlapping planking, though not with a true clinker technique.*[17]

Sails and rigging

A small selection of the many rigging blocks raised from the Mary Rose

Although only the lower fittings of the rigging survives, a 1514 inventory and the only known contemporary depiction of the ship from the Anthony Roll have been used to determine how the propulsion system of the *Mary Rose* was designed. Nine, or possibly ten, sails were flown from four masts and a bowsprit: the foremast and mainmast had two and three square sails respectively; the mizzen mast had a lateen sail and a small square sail and the bonaventure mizzen had at least one lateen sail, and possibly also a square sail, and the bowsprit flew a small square spritsail.*[18] According to the Anthony Roll illustration (see top of this section), the yards (the spars from which the sails were set) on the foremast and mainmast were also equipped with sheerhooks, twin curved blades sharpened on the inside, that were intended to cut an enemy ship's rigging during boarding actions.*[19]

The sailing capabilities of the *Mary Rose* were commented on by her contemporaries and were once even put to the test. In March 1513 a contest was arranged off The Downs, west of Kent, in which she raced against nine other ships. She won the contest, and Admiral Edward Howard described her enthusiastically as "the noblest ship of sayle [of any] gret ship, at this howr, that I trow [believe] be in Cristendom".*[20] Several years later, while sailing between Dover and The Downs, Vice-Admiral William Fitzwilliam noted that both the *Henry Grace à Dieu* and the *Mary Rose* performed very well, riding steadily in rough seas and that it would have been a "hard chose" between the two.*[21] Modern experts have been more sceptical to her sailing qualities, believing that ships at this time were almost incapable of sailing close against the wind, and describing the handling of the *Mary Rose* as being like "a wet haystack".*[22]

Armament

An illustration from a French edition of the Froissart Chronicle depicting the battle of Sluys in 1340. The picture clearly shows how medieval naval tactics focused on close combat fighting and boarding.

The *Mary Rose* represented a transitional ship design in naval warfare. Since ancient times, war at sea had been fought much like that on land: with melee weapons and bows and arrows, but on floating wooden platforms rather than battlefields. Though the introduction of guns was a significant change, it only slowly changed the dynamics of ship-to-ship combat.*[23] As guns became heavier and able to take more powerful gunpowder charges, they needed to be placed lower in the ship, closer to the water line. Gunports cut in the hull of ships had been introduced as early as 1501, only about a decade before the *Mary Rose* was built.*[24] This made broadsides,*[25] coordinated volleys from all the guns on one side of a ship, possible for the first time in history, at least in theory. Naval tactics throughout the 16th century and well into the 17th century focused on countering the oar-powered galleys that were armed with heavy guns in the bow, facing forwards, which were aimed by turning the entire ship against its target. Combined with inefficient gunpowder and the difficulties inherent in firing accurately from moving platforms, this meant that boarding remained the primary tactic for decisive victory throughout the 16th century.*[26]

Two culverins and two demi-cannons from the Mary Rose *on display at the Mary Rose Museum*

Bronze and iron guns As the *Mary Rose* was built and served during a period of rapid development of heavy artillery, her armament was a mix of old designs and innovations. The heavy armament was a mix of older-type wrought iron and cast bronze guns, which differed considerably in size, range and design. The large iron guns were made up of staves or bars welded into cylinders and then reinforced by shrinking iron hoops and breech loaded, from the back, and equipped with simpler gun-carriages made from hollowed-out elm logs with only one pair of wheels, or without wheels entirely. The bronze guns were cast in one piece and rested on four-wheel carriages which were essentially the same as those used until the 19th century. The breech-loaders were cheaper to produce and both easier and faster to reload, but could take less powerful charges than cast bronze guns. Generally, the bronze guns used cast iron shot and were more suited to penetrate hull sides while the iron guns used stone shot that would shatter on impact and leave large, jagged holes, but both could also fire a variety of ammunition intended to destroy rigging and light structure or injure enemy personnel.*[27]

The majority of the guns were small iron guns with short range that could be aimed and fired by a single person. The two most common are the *bases*, breech-loading swivel guns, most likely placed in the castles, and *hailshot pieces*, small muzzle-loaders with rectangular bores and fin-like protrusions that were used to support the guns against the railing and allow the ship structure to take the force of the recoil. Though the design is unknown, there were two *top pieces* in a 1546 inventory (finished after the sinking) which was probably similar to a base, but placed in one or more of the fighting tops.*[28]

A cast bronze culverin (front) and a wrought iron port piece (back), modern reproductions of two of the guns that were on board the Mary Rose *when she sank, on display at Fort Nelson near Portsmouth*

The ship went through several changes in her armament throughout her career, most significantly accompanying her "rebuilding" in 1536 (see below), when the number of antipersonnel guns was reduced and a second tier of carriage-mounted long guns fitted. There are three inventories that list her guns, dating to 1514, 1540 and 1546.*[30] Together with records from the armoury at the Tower of London, these show how the configuration of guns changed as gun-making technology evolved and new classifications were invented. In 1514, the armament consisted mostly of antipersonnel guns like the larger breech-loading iron *murderers* and the small *serpentines*, *demi-slings* and stone guns. Only a handful of guns in the first inventory were powerful enough to hole enemy ships, and most would have been supported by the ship's structure rather than resting on carriages. The inventories of both the *Mary Rose* and the Tower had changed radically by 1540. There were now the new cast bronze *cannons*, *demi-cannons*, *culverins* and *sakers* and the wrought iron *port pieces* (a name that indicated they fired through ports), all of which required carriages, had longer range and were capable of doing serious damage to other ships. The analysis of the 1514 inventory combined with hints of structural changes in the ship both indicate that the gunports on the main deck were indeed a later addition.*[31]

Various types of ammunition could be used for different purposes: plain spherical shot of stone or iron smashed hulls, spiked bar shot and shot linked with chains would tear sails or damage rigging, and canister shot packed with sharp flints produced a devastating shotgun effect.*[33] Trials made with replicas of culverins and port pieces showed that they could penetrate wood the same thickness of the *Mary Rose's* hull planking, indicating a stand-off range of at least 90 m (295 ft). The port pieces proved particularly efficient at smashing large holes in wood when firing stone shot and were a devastating anti-personnel weapon when loaded with flakes or pebbles.*[34]

Some of the bollock daggers found on board the Mary Rose*; for most of the daggers, only the handles have remained while the blades have either rusted away or have been preserved only as concretions.*

Hand-held weapons To defend against being boarded, *Mary Rose* carried large stocks of melee weapons, including pikes and bills; 150 of each kind were stocked on the ship according to the Anthony Roll, a figure confirmed roughly by the excavations. Swords and daggers were personal possessions and not listed in the inventories, but the remains of both have been found in great quantities, including the earliest dated example of a British basket-hilted sword.*[35]

A total of 250 longbows were carried on board, and 172 of these have so far been found, as well as almost 4,000 arrows, bracers (arm guards) and other archery-related equipment.*[36] Longbow archery in Tudor England was mandatory for all able adult men, and despite the introduction of field artillery and handguns, they were used alongside new missile weapons in great quantities. On the *Mary Rose*, the longbows could only have been drawn and shot properly from behind protective panels in the open waist or from the top of the castles as the lower decks lacked sufficient headroom. There were several types of bows of various size and range. Lighter bows would have been used as "sniper" bows, while the heavier design could possibly have been used to shoot fire arrows.*[37]

The inventories of both 1514 and 1546*[30] also list several hundred heavy darts and lime pots that were designed to be thrown onto the deck of enemy ships from the fighting tops, although no physical evidence of either of these weapon types has been identified. Of the 50 handguns listed in the Anthony Roll, the complete stocks of five matchlock muskets and fragments of another eleven have been found. They had been manufactured mainly in Italy, with some originating from Germany. Found in storage were several *gunshields*, a rare type of firearm consisting of a wooden shield with a small gun fixed in the middle.*[38]

Crew

Throughout her 33-year career, the crew of the *Mary Rose* changed several times and varied considerably in size. It would have a minimal skeleton crew of 17 men or fewer in peace time and when she was "laid up in ordinary" (in reserve).*[39] The average wartime manning would have been about 185 soldiers, 200 sailors, 20–30 gunners and an assortment of other specialists such as surgeons, trumpeters and members of the admiral's staff, for a total of 400–450 men. When taking part in land invasions or raids, such as in the summer of 1512, the number of soldiers could have swelled to just over 400 for a combined total of more than 700. Even with the normal crew size of around 400, the ship was quite crowded, and with additional soldiers would have been extremely cramped.*[40]

Little is known of the identities of the men who served on the *Mary Rose*, even when it comes to the names of the officers, who would have belonged to the gentry. Two admirals and four captains (including Edward and Thomas Howard, who served both positions) are known through records, as well as a few ship masters, pursers, master gunners and other specialists.*[41] Forensic science has been used by artists to create reconstructions of faces of eight crew members, and the results were publicized in May 2013. In addition, researchers have extracted DNA from remains in the

Vice-Admiral George Carew, who perished with the Mary Rose; *contemporary miniature by Hans Holbein the Younger*

hopes of identifying origins of crew, and potentially living descendants.*[42]

Of the vast majority of the crewmen, soldiers, sailors and gunners alike, nothing has been recorded. The only source of information for these men has been through osteological analysis of the human bones found at the wrecksite. An approximate composition of some of the crew has been conjectured based on contemporary records. The *Mary Rose* would have carried a captain, a master responsible for navigation, and deck crew. There would also have been a purser responsible for handling payments, a boatswain, the captain's second in command, at least one carpenter, a pilot in charge of navigation, and a cook, all of whom had one or more assistants (mates). The ship was also staffed by a barber-surgeon who tended to the sick and wounded, along with an apprentice or mate and possibly also a junior surgeon.*[43] The only positively identified person who went down with the ship was Vice-Admiral George Carew. McKee, Stirland and several other authors have also named Roger Grenville, father of Richard Grenville of the Elizabethan-era *Revenge*, captain during the final battle, although the accuracy of the sourcing for this has been disputed by maritime archaeologist Peter Marsden.*[44]

The bones of a total of 179 people were found during the excavations of the *Mary Rose*, including 92 "fairly complete skeletons", more or less complete collections of bones associated with specific individuals.*[47] Analysis of these has shown that crew members were all male, most of them young adults. Some were no more than 11–13 years old, and the majority (81%) under 30. They were mainly of English origin and, according to archaeologist Julie Gardiner, they most likely came from the West Country; many following their aristocratic masters into maritime service.*[43] There were also a few people from continental Europe. An eyewitness testimony right after the sinking refers to a survivor who was a Fleming, and the pilot may very well have been French. Analysis of oxygen isotopes in teeth indicates that some were also of southern European origin.*[48] In general they were strong, well-fed men, but many of the bones also reveal tell-tale signs of childhood diseases and a life of grinding toil. The bones also showed traces of numerous healed fractures, probably the result of on-board accidents.*[49]

There are no extant written records of the make-up of the broader categories of soldiers and sailors, but since the *Mary Rose* carried some 300 longbows and several thousand arrows there had to be a considerable proportion of longbow archers. Examination of the skeletal remains has found that there was a disproportionate number of men with a condition known as *os acromiale*, affecting their shoulder blades. This condition is known among modern elite archery athletes and is caused by placing considerable stress on the arm and shoulder muscles, particularly of the left arm that is used to hold the bow to brace against the pull on the bowstring. Among the men who died on the ship it was likely that some had practised using the longbow since childhood, and served on board as specialist archers.*[50]

A group of six skeletons was found grouped close to one of the 2-tonne bronze culverins on the main deck near the bow. Fusing of parts of the spine and ossification, the growth of new bone, on several vertebrae evidenced all but one of these crewmen to have been strong, well-muscled men who had been engaged in heavy pulling and pushing, the exception possibly being a "powder monkey" not involved in heavy work. These have been tentatively classified as members of a complete gun crew, all having died at their battle station.*[51]

1.10.4 Military career

First French war

Main article: War of the League of Cambrai
The *Mary Rose* first saw battle in 1512, in a joint naval operation with the Spanish against the French. The English were to meet the French and Breton fleets in the English Channel while the Spanish attacked them in the Bay of Biscay and then attack Gascony. The 35-year-old Sir Edward Howard was appointed Lord High Admiral in April and chose the *Mary Rose* as his flagship. His first mission was to clear the seas of French naval forces between England to the northern coast of Spain to allow for the landing of supporting troops

1.10. MARY ROSE

A contemporary illustration of Germain de Brie's poem Chordigerae navis conflagratio *depicting the* Cordelière *and* Regent *ablaze after the explosion on board the former*

near the French border at Fuenterrabia. The fleet consisted of 18 ships, among them the large ships the *Regent* and the *Peter Pomegranate*, carrying over 5,000 men. Howard's expedition led to the capture of twelve Breton ships and a four-day raiding tour of Brittany where English forces successfully fought against local forces and burned numerous settlements.*[52]

The fleet returned to Southampton in June where it was visited by King Henry. In August the fleet sailed for Brest where it encountered a joint, but ill-coordinated, French-Breton fleet at the battle of St. Mathieu. The English with one of the great ships in the lead (according to Marsden the *Mary Rose*) battered the French ships with heavy gunfire and forced them to retreat. The Breton flagship *Cordelière* put up a fight and was boarded by the 1,000-ton *Regent*. By accident or through the unwillingness of the Breton crew to surrender, the powder magazine of the *Cordelière* caught fire and blew up in a violent explosion, setting fire to the *Regent* and eventually sinking her. About 180 English crew members saved themselves by throwing themselves into the sea and only a handful of Bretons survived, only to be captured. The captain of the *Regent*, 600 soldiers and sailors,

the High Admiral of France and the steward of the town of Morlaix were killed in the incident, making it the focal point of several contemporary chronicles and reports.*[53] On 11 August, the English burnt 27 French ships, captured another five and landed forces near Brest to raid and take prisoners, but storms forced the fleet back to Dartmouth in Devon and then to Southampton for repairs.*[54]

Carracks, similar to the Mary Rose, *attacked by highly manoeuvrable galleys; engraving by Frans Huys after a design by Pieter Bruegel the Elder, c. 1561*

In the spring of 1513, the *Mary Rose* was once more chosen by Howard as the flagship for an expedition against the French. Before seeing action, she took part in a race against other ships where she was deemed to be one of the most nimble and the fastest of the great ships in the fleet (see details under "Sails and rigging"). On 11 April, Howard's force arrived off Brest only to see a small enemy force join with the larger force in the safety of Brest harbour and its fortifications.*[55] The French had recently been reinforced by a force of galleys from the Mediterranean, which sank one English ship and seriously damaged another. Howard landed forces near Brest, but made no headway against the town and was by now getting low on supplies. Attempting to force a victory, he took a small force of small oared vessels on a daring frontal attack on the French galleys on 25 April. Howard himself managed to reach the ship of French admiral, Prégent de Bidoux, and led a small party to board it. The French fought back fiercely and cut the cables that attached the two ships, separating Howard from his men. It left him at the mercy of the soldiers aboard the galley, who instantly killed him.*[56]

Demoralised by the loss of its admiral and seriously short of food, the fleet returned to Plymouth. Thomas Howard, elder brother of Edward, was assigned the new Lord Admiral, and was set to the task of arranging another attack on

Brittany. The fleet was not able to mount the planned attack because of adverse winds and great difficulties in supplying the ships adequately and the *Mary Rose* took up winter quarters in Southampton. In August the Scots joined France in war against England, but were dealt a crushing defeat at the Battle of Flodden on 9 September 1513. A follow-up attack in early 1514 was supported by a naval force that included the *Mary Rose*, but without any known engagements.*[57] The French and English mounted raids on each other throughout that summer, but achieved little, and both sides were by then exhausted. By autumn the war was over and a peace treaty was sealed by the marriage of Henry's sister, Mary, to French king Louis XII.*[58]

After the peace *Mary Rose* was placed in the reserves, "in ordinary". She was laid up for maintenance along with her sister ship the *Peter Pomegranate* in July 1514. In 1518 she received a routine repair and caulking, waterproofing with tar and oakum (old rope fibres) and was then assigned a small skeleton crew who lived on board the ship until 1522. She served briefly on a mission with other warships to "scour the seas" in preparation for Henry VIII's journey across the Channel to the summit with the French king Francis I at the Field of the Cloth of Gold in June 1520.*[59]

Second French war

Main article: Italian War of 1521–1526

In 1522, England was once again at war with France because of a treaty with the Holy Roman Emperor Charles V. The plan was for an attack on two fronts with an English thrust in northern France. The *Mary Rose* participated in the escort transport of troops in June 1522, and by 1 July the Breton port of Morlaix was captured. The fleet sailed home and the *Mary Rose* berthed for the winter in Dartmouth.*[60] The war raged on until 1525 and saw the Scots join the French side. Though Charles Brandon came close to capturing Paris in 1523, there was little gained either against France or Scotland throughout the war. With the defeat of the French army and capture of Francis I by Charles V's forces at the Battle of Pavia on 24 February 1525, the war was effectively over without any major gains or major victories for the English side.*[61]

Maintenance and "in ordinary"

The *Mary Rose* was kept in reserve from 1522 to 1545. She was once more caulked and repaired in 1527 in a newly dug dock at Portsmouth and her longboat was repaired and trimmed. Little documentation about the *Mary Rose* between 1528 and 1539 exists. A document written by Thomas Cromwell in 1536 specifies that the *Mary Rose* and six other ships were "made new" during his service under the king, though it is unclear which years he was referring to and what "made new" actually meant. A later document from January 1536 by an anonymous author states that the *Mary Rose* and other ships were "new made", and dating of timbers from the ship confirms some type of repair being done in 1535 or 1536. This would have coincided with the controversial dissolution of the monasteries that resulted in a major influx of funds into the royal treasury.*[62] The nature and extent of this repair is unknown. Many experts, including Margaret Rule, the project leader for the raising of the *Mary Rose*, have assumed that it meant a complete rebuilding from clinker planking to carvel planking, and that it was only after 1536 that the ship took on the form that it had when it sank and that was eventually recovered in the 20th century. Marsden has speculated that it could even mean that the *Mary Rose* was originally built in a style that was closer to 15th-century ships, with a rounded, rather than square, stern and without the main deck gunports.*[63]

Third French war

Main article: Italian War of 1542–1546
 Henry's complicated marital situation and his high-handed dissolution of the monasteries angered the Pope and Catholic rulers throughout Europe, which increased England's diplomatic isolation. In 1544 Henry had agreed to attack France together with Emperor Charles V, and English forces captured Boulogne at great cost in September, but soon England was left in the lurch after Charles had achieved his objectives and brokered a separate peace.*[64]

In May 1545, the French had assembled a large fleet in the estuary of the Seine with the intent to land troops on English soil. The estimates of the size of the fleet varied considerably; between 123 and 300 vessels according to French sources; and up to 226 sailing ships and galleys according to the chronicler Edward Hall. In addition to the massive fleet, 50,000 troops were assembled at Havre de Grâce (modern-day Le Havre). An English force of 160 ships and 12,000 troops under Viscount Lisle was ready at Portsmouth by early June, before the French were ready to set sail, and an ineffective pre-emptive strike was made in the middle of the month. In early July the huge French force under the command of Admiral Claude d'Annebault set sail for England and entered the Solent unopposed with 128 ships on 16 July. The English had around 80 ships with which to oppose the French, including the flagship *Mary Rose*. But since they had virtually no heavy galleys, the vessels that were at their best in sheltered waters like the Solent, the English fleet promptly retreated into Portsmouth harbour.*[65]

Drawing of the French admiral, Claude d'Annebault, commander of the French naval force that launched the attack on the Isle of Wight; François Clouet, January 1535

Mary Rose - Oven & Cauldron

Battle of the Solent

Main article: Battle of the Solent

The English were becalmed in port and unable to manoeuvre. On 19 July 1545, the French galleys advanced on the immobilised English fleet, and initially threatened to destroy a force of 13 small galleys, or "rowbarges", the only ships that were able to move against them without a wind. The wind picked up and the sailing ships were able to go on the offensive before the oared vessels were overwhelmed.*[66] Two of the largest ships, the *Henry Grace à Dieu* and the *Mary Rose*, led the attack on the French galleys in the Solent.

Early in the battle something went wrong. While engaging the French galleys the *Mary Rose* suddenly heeled (leaned) heavily over to her starboard (right) side and water rushed in through the open gunports.*[67] The crew was powerless to correct the sudden imbalance, and could only scramble for the safety of the upper deck as the ship began to sink rapidly. As she leaned over, equipment, ammunition, supplies and storage containers shifted and came loose, adding to the general chaos. The massive port side brick oven in the galley collapsed completely and the huge 360-litre (90 gallon) copper cauldron was thrown onto the orlop deck above.*[68] Heavy guns came free and slammed into the opposite side, impeding escape or crushing men beneath them.

For those who were not injured or killed outright by moving objects, there was little time to reach safety, especially for the men who were manning the guns on the main deck or fetching ammunition and supplies in the hold. The companionways that connected the decks with one another would have become bottlenecks for fleeing men, something indicated by the positioning of many of the skeletons recovered from the wreck. What turned the sinking into a major tragedy in terms of lives lost was the anti-boarding netting that covered the upper decks in the waist (the midsection of the ship) and the sterncastle. With the exception of the men who were stationed in the tops in the masts, most of those who managed to get up from below deck were trapped under the netting; they would have been in view of the surface, and their colleagues above, but with little or no chance to break through, and were dragged down with the ship. Out of a crew of at least 400, fewer than 35 escaped, a catastrophic casualty rate of over 90%.*[69]

The Cowdray Engraving, depicting the Battle of the Solent. The main and foremasts of the recently sunken Mary Rose *are in the middle; bodies, debris and rigging float in the water and men are clinging to the fighting tops.*

1.10.5 Causes of sinking

Southsea Castle, from where Henry VIII witnessed the last battle and demise of the Mary Rose. *The castle has been heavily altered since that time.*[*][70]

Contemporary accounts

Several accounts of the sinking have been preserved that describe the incident, but the only confirmed eyewitness account is the testimony of a surviving Flemish crewman written down by the Holy Roman Emperor's ambassador François van der Delft in a letter dated 24 July. According to the unnamed Fleming, the ship had fired all of its guns of one side and was turning to present the guns on the other side to the enemy ship, when she was caught in a strong gust of wind, heeled and took in water through the open gunports.[*][71] In a letter to William Paget dated 23 July, former Lord High Admiral John Russel claimed that the ship had been lost because of "rechenes and great negligence".[*][72] Three years after the sinking, the Hall's Chronicle gave the reason for the sinking as being caused by "to[o] much foly ... for she was laden with much ordinaunce, and the portes left open, which were low, & the great ordinaunce unbreached, so that when the ship should turne, the water entered, and sodainly she sanke." [*][73]

Later accounts repeat the explanation that the ship heeled over while going about and that the ship was brought down because of the open gunports. A biography of Peter Carew, brother of George Carew, written by John Hooker sometime after 1575, gives the same reason for the sinking, but adds that insubordination among the crew was to blame. The biography claims that George Carew noted that the *Mary Rose* showed signs of instability as soon as her sails were raised. George's uncle Gawen Carew had passed by with his own ship the *Matthew Gonson* during the battle to inquire about the situation of his nephew's ship. In reply he was told "that he had a sorte of knaves whom he could not rule".[*][74] Contrary to all other accounts, Martin du Bellay, a French cavalry officer who was present at the battle, stated that the *Mary Rose* had been sunk by French guns.[*][75]

Modern theories

The most common explanation for the sinking among modern historians is that the ship was unstable for a number of reasons. When a strong gust of wind hit the sails at a critical moment, the open gunports proved fatal, the ship flooded and quickly foundered.[*][76] Coates offered a variant of this hypothesis, which explains why a ship which served for several decades without sinking, and which even fought in actions in the rough seas off Brittany, unexpectedly foundered: the ship had accumulated additional weight over the years in service and finally become unseaworthy.[*][77] That the ship was turning after firing all the cannons on one side has been questioned by Marsden after examination of guns recovered in both the 19th and 20th centuries; guns from both sides were found still loaded. This has been interpreted to mean that something else could have gone wrong since it is assumed that an experienced crew would not have failed to secure the gunports before making a potentially risky turn.[*][78]

The most recent surveys of the ship indicate that the ship was modified late in her career and have lent support to the idea that the *Mary Rose* was altered too much to be properly seaworthy. Marsden has suggested that the weight of additional heavy guns would have increased her draught so much that the waterline was less than one metre (c. 3 feet) from the gunports on the main deck.[*][79]

Peter Carew's claim of insubordination has been given support by James Watt, former Medical Director-General of the Royal Navy, based on records of an epidemic of dysentery in Portsmouth which could have rendered the crew incapable of handling the ship properly,[*][80] while historian Richard Barker has suggested that the crew actually knew that the ship was an accident waiting to happen, at which they balked and refused to follow orders.[*][81] Marsden has noted that the Carew biography is in some details inconsistent with the sequence of events reported by both French and English eyewitnesses. It also reports that there were 700 men on board, an unusually high number. The distance in time to the event it describes may mean that it was embellished to add a dramatic touch.[*][82] The report of French galleys sinking the *Mary Rose* as stated by Martin du Bellay has been described as "the account of a courtesan" by naval historian Maurice de Brossard. Du Bellay and his two brothers were close to king Francis I and du Bellay had much to gain from portraying the sinking as a French victory. English sources, even if biased, would have nothing to gain from portraying the sinking as the result of crew incompetence rather than conceding to a victory to the much-feared gun galleys.*[83]

Dominic Fontana, a geographer at the University of Portsmouth, has voiced support for du Bellay's version of the sinking based on the battle as it is depicted in the Cowdray Engraving, and modern GIS analysis of the modern scene of the battle. By plotting the fleets and calculating the conjectured final manoeuvres of the *Mary Rose*, Fontana reached the conclusion that the ship had been hit low in the hull by the galleys and was destabilised after taking in water. He has interpreted the final heading of the ship straight due north as a failed attempt to reach the shallows at Spitbank only a few hundred metres away. This theory has been given partial support by Alexzandra Hildred, one of the experts who has worked with the *Mary Rose*, though she has suggested that the close proximity to Spitbank could also indicate that the sinking occurred while trying to make a hard turn to avoid running aground.*[84]

Experiments

In 2000, the Channel 4 television programme *What Sank the Mary Rose?* attempted to investigate the causes suggested for her sinking by means of experiments with scale models of the ship and metal weights to simulate the presence of troops on the upper decks. Initial tests showed that the ship was able to make the turn described by eyewitnesses without capsizing. In later tests, a fan was used to create a breeze similar to the one reported to have suddenly sprung up on the day of the sinking as the real *Mary Rose* went to make the turn. As the model made the turn, the breeze in the upper works forced it to heel more than at calm, forcing the main deck gun ports below the waterline and foundering the model within a few seconds. The sequence of events closely followed what eyewitnesses had reported, particularly the suddenness with which the ship sank.*[85]

1.10.6 History as a shipwreck

A salvage attempt was ordered by Secretary of State William Paget only days after the sinking, and Charles Brandon, the king's brother-in-law, took charge of practical details. The operation followed the standard procedure for raising ships in shallow waters: strong cables were attached to the sunken ship and fastened to two empty ships, or hulks. At low tide, the ropes were pulled taut with capstans. When the high tide came in, the hulks rose and with them the wreck. It would then be towed into shallower water and the procedure repeated until the whole ship could be raised completely.*[86]

A list of necessary equipment was compiled by 1 August and included, among other things, massive cables, cap-

Charles Brandon, brother-in-law of King Henry VIII through marriage with Mary Tudor, who took charge of the failed salvage operation in 1545

stans, pulleys, and 40 pounds of tallow for lubrication. The proposed salvage team comprised 30 Venetian mariners and a Venetian carpenter with 60 English sailors to serve them.*[87] The two ships to be used as hulks were *Jesus of Lübeck* and *Samson*, each of 700 tons burthen and similar in size to the *Mary Rose*. Brandon was so confident of success that he reassured the king that it would only be a matter of days before they could raise the *Mary Rose*. The optimism proved unfounded. Since the ship had settled at a 60-degree angle to starboard much of it was stuck deep into the clay of the seabed. This made it virtually impossible to pass cables under the hull and required far more lifting power than if the ship had settled on a hard seabed. An attempt to secure cables to the main mast appears only to have resulted in its being snapped off.*[88]

The project was only successful in raising rigging, some guns and other items. At least two other salvage teams in 1547 and 1549 received payment for raising more guns from the wreck.*[89] Despite the failure of the first salvage operation, there was still lingering belief in the possibility of retrieving the *Mary Rose* at least until 1546, when she was presented as part of the illustrated list of English warships called the Anthony Roll. When all hope of raising the complete ship was finally abandoned is not known. It could have been after Henry VIII's death in January 1547 or even as late as 1549, when the last guns were brought up.*[90] The *Mary Rose* was remembered well into the reign of Elizabeth

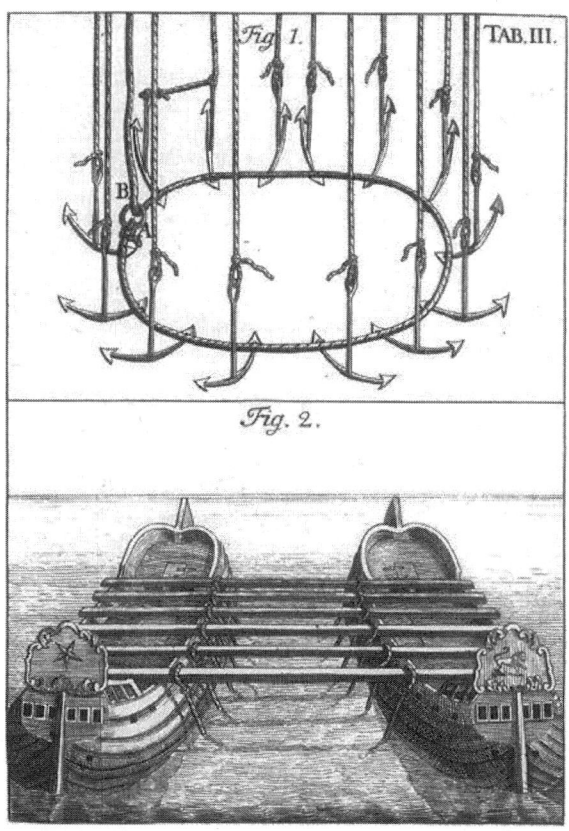

Illustration from a treatise on salvaging from 1734, showing the traditional method of raising a wreck with the help of anchors and ships or hulks as pontoons, the same method that was attempted by the Tudor era salvors

I, and according to one of the queen's admirals, William Monson (1569–1643), the wreck was visible from the surface at low tide in the late 16th century.[*][91]

Deterioration

After the sinking, the partially buried wreck created a barrier at a right angle against the currents of the Solent. Two scour pits, large underwater ditches, formed on either side of the wreck while silt and seaweed was deposited inside the ship. A deep but narrow pit formed on the upward tilting port side, while a shallower, broader pit formed on the starboard side, which had mostly been buried by the force of the impact. The abrasive actions of sand and silt carried by the currents and the activity of fungi, bacteria and wood-boring crustaceans and molluscs, such as the *teredo* "shipworm", began to break down the structure of the ship. Eventually the exposed wooden structure was weakened and gradually collapsed. The timbers and contents of the port side were deposited in the scour pits and the remaining ship structure, or else carried off by the currents. Following the collapse of the exposed parts of the ship the site was levelled with the seabed and was gradually covered by layers of sediment, concealing most of the remaining structure. During the 16th century a hard layer of compacted clay and crushed shells formed over the ship, stabilising the site and sealing the Tudor-era deposits. Further layers of soft silt covered the site during the 18th and 19th centuries, but frequent changes in the tidal patterns and currents in the Solent occasionally exposed some of the timbers, leading to its accidental rediscovery in 1836 and aided in locating the wreck in 1971.[*][92] After the ship had been raised it was determined that about 40% of the original structure had survived.[*][93]

Rediscovery in 19th century

In the summer of 1836, a group of five fishermen caught their nets on timbers protruding from the bottom of the Solent. They contacted a diver to help them remove the hindrance, and on 10 June, Henry Abbinett became the first person to see the *Mary Rose* in almost 300 years. Later, two other professional divers, John Deane and William Edwards, were employed. Using a recently invented rubber suit and metal diving helmet, Deane and Edwards began to examine the wreck and salvage items from it. Along with an assortment of timbers and wooden objects, including several longbows, they brought up several bronze and iron guns, which were sold to the Board of Ordnance for over £220. Initially, this caused a dispute between Deane (who had also brought in his brother Charles into the project), Abbinett and the fishermen who had hired them. The matter was eventually settled by allowing the fishermen a share of the proceeds from the sale of the first salvaged guns, while Deane received exclusive salvage rights at the expense of Abbinett. The wreck was soon identified as the *Mary Rose* from the inscriptions of one of the bronze guns manufactured in 1537.[*][94]

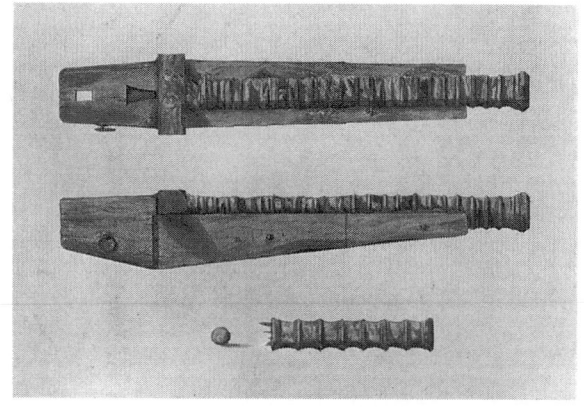

Watercolour painting of two perspectives of a sling, a wrought iron gun, complete with two-wheeled gun carriage (wheels missing) and part of another iron sling. The paintings were made to record some of the finds raised by the Deane brothers 1836–40.

The identification of the ship led to significant public interest in the salvage operation, and caused a great demand for the objects which were brought up. Though many of the objects could not be properly conserved at the time and subsequently deteriorated, many were documented with pencil sketches and watercolour drawings which survive to this day. John Deane ceased working on the wreck in 1836, but returned in 1840 with new, more destructive methods. With the help of condemned bomb shells filled with gunpowder acquired from the Ordnance Board he blasted his way into parts of the wreck. Fragments of bombs and traces of blasting craters were found during the modern excavations, but there was no evidence that Deane managed to penetrate the hard layer that had sealed off the Tudor levels. Deane reported retrieving a bilge pump and the lower part of the main mast, both of which would have been located inside the ship. The recovery of small wooden objects like longbows suggests that Deane did manage to penetrate the Tudor levels at some point, though this has been disputed by the excavation project leader Margaret Rule. Newspaper reports on Deane's diving operations in October 1840 report that the ship was clinker built, but since the sterncastle is the only part of the ship with this feature, an alternative explanation has been suggested: Deane did not penetrate the hard shelly layer that covered most of the ship, but only managed to get into remains of the sterncastle that today no longer exist. Despite the rough handling by Deane the *Mary Rose* escaped the wholesale destruction by giant rakes and explosives that was the fate of other wrecks in the Solent.*[95]

Modern rediscovery

The modern search for the *Mary Rose* was initiated by the Southsea branch of the British Sub-Aqua Club in 1965 as part of a project to locate shipwrecks in the Solent. The project was under the leadership of historian, journalist and amateur diver Alexander McKee. Another group led by Lieutenant-Commander Alan Bax of the Royal Navy, sponsored by the Committee for Nautical Archaeology in London, also formed a search team. Initially the two teams had differing views on where to find the wreck, but eventually joined forces. In February 1966 a chart from 1841 was found that marked the positions of the *Mary Rose* and several other wrecks. The charted position coincided with a trench (one of the scour pits) that had already been located by McKee's team, and a definite location was finally established at a position 3 km (1.9 mi) south of the entrance to Portsmouth Harbour (50°46′0″N 1°06′0″W / 50.76667°N 1.10000°W) in water with a depth of 11 m (36 feet) at low tide.*[96] Diving on the site began in 1966 and a sonar scan by Harold Edgerton in 1967–68 revealed some type of buried feature. In 1970 a loose timber was located and on 5 May 1971, the first structural details of the buried hull were identified after they were partially uncovered by winter storms.*[97]

A major problem for the team from the start was that wreck sites in the UK lacked any legal protection from plunderers and treasure hunters. Sunken ships, once being moving objects, were legally treated as chattel and were awarded to those who could first raise them. The Merchant Shipping Act of 1894 also stipulated that any objects raised from a wreck should be auctioned off to finance the salvage operations, and there was nothing preventing anyone from "stealing" the wreck and making a profit. The problem was handled by forming an organisation, the Mary Rose Committee, aiming "to find, excavate, raise and preserve for all time such remains of the ship *Mary Rose* as may be of historical or archaeological interest".*[98]

To keep intruders at bay, the Committee arranged a lease of the seabed where the wreck lay from the Portsmouth authorities, thereby discouraging anyone from trespassing on the underwater property. In hindsight this was only a legalistic charade which had little chance of holding up in a court of law. In combination with secrecy as to the exact location of the wreck, it saved the project from interference. It was not until the passing of the Protection of Wrecks Act on 5 February 1973 that the *Mary Rose* was declared to be of national historic interest that enjoyed full legal protection from any disturbance by commercial salvage teams. Despite this, years after the passing of the 1973 act and the excavation of the ship, lingering conflicts with salvage legislation remained a threat to the *Mary Rose* project as "personal" finds such as chests, clothing and cooking utensils risked being confiscated and auctioned off.*[99]

Survey and excavation Following the discovery of the wreck in 1971, the project became known to the general public and received increasing media attention. This helped bring in more donations and equipment, primarily from private sources. By 1974 the Committee had representatives from the National Maritime Museum, the Royal Navy, the BBC and local organisations. In 1974 the project received royal patronage from Prince Charles, who participated in dives on the site. This attracted yet more publicity, and also more funding and assistance.*[100] The initial aims of the Mary Rose Committee were now more officially and definitely confirmed. The Committee had become a registered charity in 1974, which made it easier to raise funds, and the application for excavation and raising of the ship had been officially approved by the UK government.*[101]

By 1978 the initial excavation work had uncovered a complete and coherent site with an intact ship structure and the orientation of the hull had been positively identified as being on an almost straight northerly heading with a 60-degree heel to starboard and a slight downward tilt towards the bow. As no records of English shipbuilding techniques used in vessels like the *Mary Rose* survive, excavation of the ship would allow for a detailed survey of her design and shed new light on the construction of ships of the era.*[102] A full excavation also meant removing the protective layers of silt that prevented the remaining ship structure from being destroyed through biological decay and the scouring of the currents; the operation had to be completed within a pre-determined timespan of a few years or it risked irreversible damage. It was also considered desirable to recover and preserve the remains of the hull if possible. For the first time, the project was faced with the practical difficulties of actually raising, conserving and preparing the hull for public display.*[103]

To handle this new, considerably more complex and expensive task, it was decided that a new organisation was needed. The Mary Rose Trust, a limited charitable trust,*[104] with representatives from many organisations would handle the need for a larger operation and a large infusion of funds. In 1979 a new diving vessel was purchased to replace the previous 12 m (40 ft) catamaran *Roger Greenville* which had been used from 1971. The choice fell on the salvage vessel *Sleipner*, the same craft that had been used as a platform for diving operations on the *Vasa*. The project went from a team of only twelve volunteers working four months a year to over 50 individuals working almost around the clock nine months a year. In addition there were over 500 volunteer divers and a laboratory staff of about 70 that ran the shore base and conservation facilities.*[105] During the four diving seasons from 1979 to 1982 over 22,000 diving hours was spent on the site, an effort that amounted to 11.8 man-years.*[106]

People viewing the salvage cage holding the Mary Rose *1982*

Raising the Ship Raising the *Mary Rose* meant overcoming a number of delicate problems that had never been encountered before. The raising of the Swedish warship *Vasa* 1959–61 was the only comparable precedent, but it had been a relatively straightforward operation since the hull was completely intact and rested upright on the seabed. It had been raised with basically the same methods as were in use in Tudor England: cables were slung under the hull and attached to two pontoons on either side of the ship which was then gradually raised and towed into shallower waters. Only one third of the *Mary Rose* was intact and she lay deeply embedded in mud. If the hull were raised in the traditional way, there was no guarantee that it would have enough structural strength to hold together out of water. Many suggestions for raising the ship were discarded, including the construction of a cofferdam around the wreck site, filling the ship with small buoyant objects (such as ping pong balls) or even pumping brine into the seabed and freezing it so that it would float and take the hull with it. After lengthy discussions it was decided in February 1980 that the hull would first be emptied of all its contents and strengthened with steel braces and frames. It would then be lifted to the surface with floating sheerlegs attached to nylon strops passing under the hull and transferred to a cradle. It was also decided that the ship would be recovered before the end of the diving season in 1982. If the wreck stayed uncovered any longer it risked irreversible damage from biological decay and tidal scouring.*[107]

During the last year of the operation, the massive scope of full excavation and raising was beginning to take its toll on those closely involved in the project. In May 1981, Alexander McKee voiced concerns about the method chosen for raising the timbers and openly questioned Margaret Rule's position as excavation leader. McKee felt ignored in what he viewed as a project where he had always played a central role, both as the initiator of the search for the *Mary Rose* and other ships in the Solent, and as an active member throughout the diving operations. He had several supporters who all pointed to the risk of the project's turning into an embarrassing failure if the ship were damaged during raising operations. To address these concerns it was suggested that the hull should be placed on top of a supporting steel cradle underwater. This would avoid the inherent risks of damaging the wooden structure if it were lifted out of the water without appropriate support. The idea of using nylon strops was also discarded in favour of drilling holes through the hull at 170 points and passing iron bolts through them to allow the attachment of wires connected to a lifting frame.*[108]

In the spring of 1982, after three intense seasons of archaeological underwater work, preparations began for raising the ship. The operation soon ran into problems: early on there were difficulties with the custom-made lifting equipment; divers on the project belonging to the Royal Engineers had to be pulled because of the outbreak of the Falklands War; and the method of lifting the hull had to be considerably altered as late as June. After the frame

The wreck of the Mary Rose *clear of the water on 11 October 1982*

was properly attached to the hull it was slowly jacked up on four legs straddling the wreck site to pull the ship off the seabed. The massive crane of the barge *Tog Mor* was then used to lift the frame and hull on to the specially designed cradle which was padded with water-filled bags. On the morning of 11 October 1982, the final lift of the entire package of cradle, hull and lifting frame began. At 9:03 the first timbers of the *Mary Rose* broke the surface in the presence of the team, Prince Charles and curious spectators on boats circling the site. A second set of bags under the hull was inflated with air to cushion the waterlogged wood and finally the whole package was transferred to the barge that would take the hull ashore. Though eventually successful, the operation was close to floundering on two occasions; first when one of the supporting legs of the lifting frame was bent and had to be removed and later when a corner of the frame, with "an unforgettable crunch",*[109] slipped more than a metre (3 feet) and came close to crushing part of the hull.*[110]

1.10.7 Archaeology

As one of the most ambitious and expensive projects in the history of maritime archaeology, the *Mary Rose* project broke new ground within this field in the UK.*[111] Besides becoming one of the first wrecks to be protected under the new Protection of Wrecks Act in 1973 it also created several new precedents. It was the first time that a British privately funded project was able to apply modern scientific standards fully and without having to auction off part of the findings to finance its activities; where previous projects often had to settle for just a partial recovery of finds, everything found in connection with the *Mary Rose* was recovered and recorded. The raising of the vessel made it possible to establish the first historic shipwreck museum in the UK to receive governmental accreditation and funding. The excavation of the *Mary Rose* wreck site proved that it was possible to achieve a level of exactness in underwater excavations comparable to those on dry land.*[112]

Throughout the 1970s, the *Mary Rose* was meticulously surveyed, excavated and recorded with the latest methods within the field of maritime archaeology. Working in an underwater environment meant that principles of land-based archaeology did not always apply. Mechanical excavators, airlifts and suction dredges were used in the process of locating the wreck, but as soon as it began to be uncovered in earnest, more delicate techniques were employed.*[113] Many objects from the *Mary Rose* had been well preserved in form and shape, but many were quite delicate, requiring careful handling. Artefacts of all sizes were supported with soft packing material, such as old plastic ice cream containers, and some of the arrows that were "soft like cream cheese" had to be brought up in special styrofoam containers.*[114] The airlifts that sucked up clay, sand and dirt offsite or to the surface were still used, but with much greater precision since they could potentially disrupt the site. The many layers of sediment that had accumulated on the site could be used to date artefacts in which they were found, and had to be recorded properly. The various types of accretions and remnants of chemicals with artefacts were essential clues to objects that had long since broken down and disappeared, and needed to be treated with considerable care.*[115]

The excavation and raising of the ship in the 1970s and early '80s meant that diving operations ceased, even though modern scaffolding and part of the bow were left on the seabed. The pressure on conservators to treat tens of thousands of artefacts and the high costs of conserving, storing and displaying the finds and the ship meant that there were no funds available for diving. In 2002, the UK Ministry of Defence announced plans to build two new aircraft carriers. Because of the massive size of the new vessels, the outlet from Portsmouth needed to be surveyed to make sure that they could sail no matter the tide. The planned route for the underwater channel ran close to the *Mary Rose* wrecksite, which meant that funding was supplied to survey and excavate the site once more. Even though the planned carriers were down-sized enough to not require alteration of Portsmouth outlet, the excavations had already exposed timbers and were completed in 2005. Among the most important finds was the ten-metre (32 feet) stem, the forward continuation of the keel, which provided more exact details about the original profile of the ship.*[116]

Finds

Over 26,000 artefacts and pieces of timber were raised along with remains of about half the crew members,*[117] The faces of some crew members have been reconstructed. Analysis of the crew skeletons shows many had suffered

A mallet, drill handle, plane, ruler, and various other carpentry tools, most of which were found in chests stowed in one of the main deck cabins

One of the many rosaries found on the Mary Rose *that once belonged to one of the lower-ranking crew members*

objects related to mundane everyday tasks such as personal hygiene, fishing and sewing.[120] The master carpenter's chest, for example, contained a backgammon set, a book, three plates, a sundial, and a tankard, goods suggesting he was relatively wealthy.[118]

The ship carried several skilled craftsmen and was equipped for handling both routine maintenance and repairing extensive battle damage. In and around one of the cabins on the main deck under the sterncastle, archaeologists found a "collection of woodworking tools ... unprecedented in its range and size", consisting of eight chests of carpentry tools. Along with loose mallets and tar pots used for caulking, this variety of tools belonged to one or several of the carpenters employed on the *Mary Rose*.[121]

Many of the cannons and other weapons from the *Mary Rose* have provided invaluable physical evidence about 16th-century weapon technology. The surviving gunshields are almost all from the *Mary Rose*, and the four small cast iron hailshot pieces are the only known examples of this type of weapon.[122]

Animal remains have been found in the wreck of the *Mary Rose*. These include the skeletons of a rat, a frog and a dog.[123] The dog, a mongrel between eighteen months and two years in age, was found near the hatch to the ship's carpenter's cabin and is thought to have been brought aboard as a ratter.[124] Nine barrels have been found to contain bones of cattle, indicating that they contained pieces of beef butchered and stored as ship's rations.[125] In addition, the bones of pigs and fish, stored in baskets, have also been found.[125]

malnutrition, and had evidence of rickets, scurvy, and other deficiency diseases was found. Crew members also developed arthritis through the stresses on their joints from heavy lifting and maritime life generally, and suffered bone fractures.[118] As the ship was intended to function as a floating, self-contained community, it was stocked with victuals (food and drink) that could sustain its inhabitants for extended periods of time. The casks used for storage on the *Mary Rose* have been compared with those from a wreck of a trade vessel from the 1560s and have revealed that they were of better quality, more robust and reliable, an indication that supplies for the Tudor navy were given high priority, and their requirements set a high standard for cask manufacturing at the time.[119] As a miniature society at sea, the wreck of the *Mary Rose* held personal objects belonging to individual crew members. This included clothing, games, various items for spiritual or recreation use, or

Musical instruments Two fiddles, a bow, a still shawm or *doucaine*, three three-hole pipes, and a tabor drum with a drumstick were found throughout the wreck. These would have been used for the personal enjoyment of the crew and to provide a rhythm to work on the rigging and turning the capstans on the upper decks. The tabor drum is the earliest known example of its kind and the drumstick of a previously unknown design. The tabor pipes are considerably longer than any known examples from the period. Their discovery proved that contemporary illustrations, previously viewed with some suspicion, were in fact accurate depictions of the instruments. Before the discovery of the *Mary Rose* shawm, an early predecessor to the oboe, instrument historians had been puzzled by reference to "still shawms", or "soft" shawms, that were said to have a sound that was less shrill than earlier shawms.[126] The still shawm disappeared from the musical scene some time in the 16th century, and the instrument found on the *Mary Rose* is the only surviving example. A reproduction has been made and played. Combined with a pipe and tabor, it provides a "very effective bass part" that would have produced "rich and full sound, which would have provided excellent music for dancing on board ship".*[127] Only a few other fiddle-type instruments from the 16th century exist, but none of them of the type found on the *Mary Rose*. Reproductions of both fiddles have been made, though less is known of their design than the shawm since the neck and strings were missing.*[128]

Navigation tools In the remains of a small cabin in the bow of the ship and in a few other locations around the wreck was found the earliest dated set of navigation instruments in Europe found so far: compasses, divider calipers, a stick used for charting, protractors, sounding leads, tide calculators and a logreel, an instrument for calculating speed. Several of these objects are not only unique in having such an early, definite dating, but also because they pre-date written records of their use; protractors would have reasonably been used to measure distance on maps, but sea charts are not known to have been used by English navigators during the first half of the 16th century, compasses were not depicted on English ships until the 1560s, and the first mention of a logreel is from 1574.*[129]

Along with the medical equipment were also personal items belonging to the barber-surgeon, including an expensive silk velvet coif identical to those worn by the members of the Worshipful Company of Barbers in this painting by Hans Holbein the Younger from 1540.[130]

Barber-surgeon's cabin The cabin located on the main deck underneath the sterncastle is thought to have belonged to the barber-surgeon. He was a trained professional who saw to the health and welfare of the crew and acted as the medical expert on board. The most important of these finds were found in an intact wooden chest which contained over 60 objects relating to the barber-surgeon's medical practice: the wooden handles of a complete set of surgical tools and several shaving razors (although none of the steel blades had survived), a copper syringe for wound irrigation and treatment of gonorrhoea, and even a skilfully crafted feeding bottle for feeding incapacitated patients. More objects were found around the cabin, such as earscoops, shaving bowls and combs. With this wide selection of tools and medicaments the barber-surgeon, along with one or more assistants, could set bone fractures, perform amputations and deal with other acute injuries, treat a number of diseases and provide crew members with a minimal standard of personal hygiene.*[131]

Conservation

The Mary Rose *being sprayed with water at the facility in Portsmouth in March 1984. Between December 1984 and July 1985 the steel cradle was gradually rotated to stand with the keel in an almost upright position.*[132]

Preservation of the *Mary Rose* and her contents was an essential part of the project from the start. Though many artefacts, especially those that were buried in silt, had been preserved, the long exposure to an underwater environment had rendered most of them sensitive to exposure to air after recovery. Archaeologists and conservators had to work in tandem from the start to prevent deterioration of the artefacts.*[133] After recovery, finds were placed in so-called passive storage, which would prevent any immediate deterioration before the active conservation which would allow them to be stored in an open-air environment. Passive storage depended on the type of material that the object was made of, and could vary considerably. Smaller objects from the most common material, wood, were sealed in polyethylene bags to preserve moisture. Timbers and other objects that were too large to be wrapped were stored in unsealed water tanks. Growth of fungi and microbes that could degrade wood were controlled by various techniques, including low-temperature storage, chemicals, and in the case of large objects, common pond snails that consumed wood-degrading organisms but not the wood itself.*[134]

Other organic materials such as leather, skin and textiles were treated similarly, by keeping them moist in tanks or sealed plastic containers. Bone and ivory was desalinated to prevent damage from salt crystallisation, as was glass, ceramic and stone. Iron, copper and copper alloy objects were kept moist in a sodium sesquicarbonate solution to prevent oxidisation and reaction with the chlorides that had penetrated the surface. Alloys of lead and pewter are inherently stable in the atmosphere and generally require no special treatment. Silver and gold were the only materials that required no special passive storage.*[135]

The hull of the Mary Rose *being sprayed at the facility in Portsmouth while a technician is servicing the system*

Conserving the hull of the *Mary Rose* was the most complicated and expensive task for the project. In 2002 a donation of £4.8 million from the Heritage Lottery Fund and equivalent monetary support from the Portsmouth City and Hampshire County Councils was needed to keep the work with conservation on schedule.*[136] During passive conservation, the ship structure could for practical reasons not be completely sealed, so instead it was regularly sprayed with filtered, recycled water that was kept at a temperature of 2 to 5 °C (35 to 41 °F) to keep it from drying out.*[137] Drying waterlogged wood that has been submerged for several centuries without appropriate conservation causes considerable shrinkage (20–50%) and leads to severe warping and cracking as water evaporates from the cellular structure of the wood. The substance polyethylene glycol (PEG) had been used before on archaeological wood, and was during the 1980s being used to conserve the *Vasa*. After almost ten years of small-scale trials on timbers, an active three-phase conservation programme of the hull of the *Mary Rose* began in 1994. During the first phase, which lasted from 1994 to 2003, the wood was sprayed with low-molecular-weight PEG to replace the water in the cellular structure of the wood. From 2003 to 2010, a higher-molecular-weight PEG was used to strengthen the mechanical properties of the outer surface layers. The third phase consisted of a controlled air drying ending in 2016.*[138]

1.10.8 Display

Concept plan of the new Mary Rose Museum by Wilkinson Eyre Architects.

Main article: Mary Rose Museum

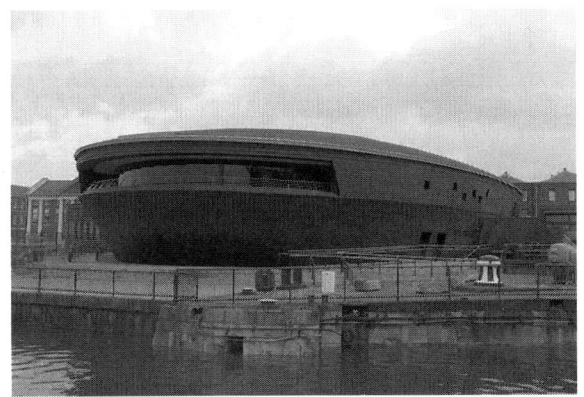

The Mary Rose Museum

After the decision to raise the *Mary Rose*, discussions ensued as to where she would eventually go on permanent display. The east end of Portsea Island at Eastney emerged as an early alternative, but was rejected because of parking problems and the distance from the dockyard where she was originally built. Placing the ship next to the famous flagship of Horatio Nelson, HMS *Victory*, at Portsmouth Historic Dockyard was proposed in July 1981. A group called the Maritime Preservation Society even suggested Southsea Castle, where Henry VIII had witnessed the sinking, as a final resting place and there was widespread scepticism to the dockyard location. At one point a county councillor even threatened to withdraw promised funds if the dockyard site became more than an interim solution. As costs for the project mounted, there was a debate in the Council chamber and in the local paper *The News* as to whether the money could be spent more appropriately. Although author David Childs writes that in the early 1980s "the debate was as a fiery one", the project was never seriously threatened because of the great symbolic importance of the *Mary Rose* to the naval history of both Portsmouth and England.*[139]

Since the mid-1980s, the hull of the *Mary Rose* has been kept in a covered dry dock while undergoing conservation. Although the hull has been open to the public for viewing, the need for keeping the ship saturated first with water and later a polyethylene glycol (PEG) solution has meant that visitors have been separated from the hull by a glass barrier. The specially built ship hall had been visited by over seven million visitors as of 2007, since it first opened on 4 October 1983, just under a year after it was successfully raised.*[140]

A separate Mary Rose Museum was housed in a structure called No. 5 Boathouse near the ship hall and was opened to the public on 9 July 1984.*[141] containing displays explaining the history of the ship and a small number of conserved artefacts, from entire bronze cannons to household items. In September 2009 the temporary Mary Rose display hall was closed to visitors to facilitate construction of the new £35 million museum building, which opened to the public on 31 May 2013.*[142]

The new Mary Rose Museum was designed by architects Wilkinson Eyre, Perkins+Will and built by construction firm Warings. The construction has been challenging because the museum has been built over the ship in the dry dock which is a listed monument. During construction of the museum, conservation of the hull continued inside a sealed "hotbox". In April 2013 the polyethylene glycol sprays were turned off and the process of controlled airdrying began. By 2016 the "hotbox" will be removed and for the first time since 1545, the ship will be revealed dry. This new museum displays most of the artefacts recovered from within the ship in context with the conserved hull. Since opening it has been visited by over 500,000 people.*[143]

1.10.9 See also

- Archaeology of shipwrecks
- *Batavia*
- *Mars*
- *Kronan*
- HMS *Royal George*
- List of world's largest wooden ships

1.10.10 Notes

[1] Rodger (1997), pp. 153–56.

[2] Marsden (2003), p. 1; Rodger (1997), pp. 164–65

[3] Marsden (2003), pp. 1–2; Rodger (1997), pp. 165–6.

[4] Rodger (1997), p. 221.

[5] Marsden (2003), pp. 2–5; see Maria Hayward, "The Flags, Fabric" in Knighton and Loades (2000), pp. 31–33 for a more detailed account of the making of the flags.

[6] Marsden (2003), p. 51.

[7] Damian Goodburn, "Woodworking Aspects of the *Mary Rose*" in Marsden (2009), pp. 66–68, 71.

[8] See for example McKee (1974), p. 4; Rodger (1997), p. 172; Rule (1983), p. 15; Weightman (1957), p. 286.

[9] Childs (2007), p. 17; David Loades, "The *Mary Rose* and Fighting Ships" in Marsden (2009), p. 5; Peter Marsden, "Reconstruction of the *Mary Rose*: her Design and Use" in Marsden (2009), p. 379.

[10] Marsden (2003), p. 90.

[11] Richard Barker, Brad Loewen and Christopher Dobbs, "Hull Design of the *Mary Rose*" in Marsden (2009), p. 36.

[12] For details of the construction, see especially Marsden (2009)

[13] Rule (1983), pp. 117–133; see Marsden (2009) for a detailed survey of deck design and construction.

[14] Peter Marsden, "The Upper Deck" in Marsden (2009), p. 216.

[15] Peter Marsden, "Reconstruction of the *Mary Rose*: her Design and Use" in Marsden (2009), pp. 371–78; Alexzandra Hildred, "The Fighting Ship" in Marsden (2009), pp. 340–41.

[16] See for example Rule (1983).

[17] Marsden (2003), pp. 94, 96

[18] Peter Marsden, "Propulsion, Masts and rigging" in Marsden (2009), pp. 242–49.

[19] Richard Endsor, "Propulsion, The rigging" in Marsden (2009), p. 261.

[20] Marsden (2003), pp. 7–8.

[21] Marsden (2003), p. 14.

[22] Loades (1992), pp. 94–95.

[23] Rodger (1997), pp. 205–6.

[24] Rodger (1997), p. 207.

[25] It was not until the 1590s that the word "broadside" in English was commonly used to refer to gunfire from the side of a ship rather than the ship's side itself; Rodger (1996), pp. 312, 316.

[26] Rodger (1996); Rodger (1997), pp. 206–8, 215.

[27] Alexzandra Hildred, "The Fighting Ship" in Marsden (2009), pp. 297–344.

[28] Alexzandra Hildred, "The Fighting Ship" in Marsden (2009), pp. 313–16.

[29] Based on tables in Marsden (2009), pp. 318, 332, 338, 341.

[30] The last record is the illustrated Anthony Roll, which was compiled after the sinking, when it was apparently still believed that the *Mary Rose* could be raised and restored.

[31] Alexzandra Hildred, "The Fighting Ship" in Marsden (2009), pp. 298–303.

[32] Based on table in Marsden (2009), p. 302.

[33] Rule (1983), pp. 149–68; David. Loades, "II: The Ordnance" in Knighton and Loades (2000), pp. 12–14; Alexandra Hildred, "(ii) Munitions" in Knighton and Loades (2000), pp. 16–19.

[34] Alexzandra Hildred, "The Fighting Ship" in Marsden (2009), pp. 311–12, 341.

[35] Childs (2007), p. 57; see also BBC News, "Sword from Mary Rose on display", 26 July 2007.

[36] Rule (1983), p. 172; Stirland (2000), p. 21.

[37] Rule (1983), pp. 181–82.

[38] Alexzandra Hildred, "The Fighting Ship" in Marsden (2009), pp. 324–25; see also Balfour, Metcalf & North, "A Gun-Shield from the Armoury of Henry VIII:Decorative Oddity or Important Discovery? Archived 20 January 2010 at the Wayback Machine." in *V&A Online Journal* No. 39 for more information.

[39] Marsden (2003), p. 13.

[40] Julie Gardiner, "The 'Good Shippe' *Mary Rose*: an Introduction" in Gardiner (2005), pp. 11–12; Marsden (2003), pp. 9–10; Stirland (2000), pp 53–54.

[41] For a detailed list of officers and other named people who served on the ship 1513–1545, see Marsden (2003), p. 9.

[42] Richard Gray, "Living relatives of Mary Rose crew may be identified through DNA", *The Telegraph*, 30 May 2013, accessed 27 April 2015

[43] Julie Gardiner, "The 'Good Shippe' *Mary Rose*: an Introduction" in Gardiner (2005), pp. 11–12.

[44] Marsden (2003), pp. 9–10; Stirland (2000), pp. 53–54.

[45] Based on table from Marsden (2003), p. 10.

[46] Dating uncertain since the Anthony Roll was made over a longer period of time that extended beyond the sinking of the *Mary Rose*.

[47] Stirland (2000), pp. 74–76

[48] Gardiner (2005), p. 12; Stirland (2000), p. 149.

[49] Stirland (2000), pp. 113–14

[50] Stirland (2000), pp. 118–30.

[51] Stirland (2000), pp. 139–42.

[52] Marsden (2003), p. 10.

[53] Loades (1992), p. 60; for estimates of losses see Marsden (2003) pp. 10–11.

[54] Marsden (2003), p. 11.

[55] Marsden (2003) pp. 11–12.

[56] Loades (1992), pp. 62–64; Rodger (1997), pp. 170–71.

[57] Marsden (2003), pp. 12–13

[58] Rodger (1997), p. 172.

1.10. MARY ROSE

[59] Marsden (2003) p. 13.

[60] Marsden (2003) pp. 13–15.

[61] Rodger (1997), pp. 174–75.

[62] Marsden (2003), pp. 15–16.

[63] Marsden (2003), p. 142; for examples of authors that have stated that the ship went through considerable alterations in 1536, see also p. 16.

[64] Rodger (1997), pp. 176–82.

[65] Loades (1992), pp. 131–32.

[66] Loades (1992), p. 133.

[67] Marsden (2003), pp. 18–19.

[68] Christopher Dobbs, "The Galley" in Marsden (2009), p. 133.

[69] Gardiner (2005), pp. 16–17; Marsden (2003), pp. 133–34. For more discussion supporting the suddenness and violent nature of the sinking, see also Julie Gardiner, "The 'Good Shippe' *Mary Rose*: an Introduction" in Gardiner (2005), pp. 16–17 and Colin McKewan, "The Ship's Carpenters and Their Tools" in Gardiner (2005), p. 297.

[70] Corney, Arthur (1968). *Southsea Castle*. Portsmouth City Council.

[71] Marsden (2003), p. 19.

[72] Marsden (2003), p. 178.

[73] Marsden (2003), pp. 19, 179.

[74] Marsden (2003), pp. 20, 181–82.

[75] For summaries and comments on the various accounts see Marsden (2003), pp. 18–20, 130–34, 178–79 and Rule (1983) pp. 36–38 and Stirland (2000), pp. 22–23.

[76] Rodger (1997); Rule (1983); Stirland (2000).

[77] Stirland (2000), pp. 22–23.

[78] Marsden (2003), pp. 132–33.

[79] Peter Marsden, "The Loss of the *Mary Rose*, 1545" in Marsden (2009), pp. 391–92.

[80] Watt (1983), p. 17.

[81] Barker (1992), p. 439.

[82] Marsden (2003), p. 130.

[83] de Brossard (1983).

[84] Alexzandra Hildred, "The Fighting Ship", pp. 307–8 in Marsden (2009). For a detailed account of Dominic Fontana's theory on the sinking see "The Cowdray engravings and the loss of the Mary Rose".

[85] Channel 4, "What Sank the *Mary Rose*?", 2000.

[86] For a detailed account of the raising operations, see Rule (1983), pp. 39–41; Marsden (2003), pp. 20; Peter Marsden, "Salvage, Saving and Surveying the *Mary Rose*" in Marsden (2009), pp. 12–14.

[87] *State Papers Henry VIII*, vol.1, (1830), pp.796–797 note, Suffolk to Paget, 1 August 1545: *Letters & Papers, Henry VIII*, vol.20 part 2 (1907), nos. 2, 3, 14, 16, 38, 39, 81, abbreviated

[88] Peter Marsden, "Salvage, Saving and Surveying the *Mary Rose*" in Marsden (2009), pp. 12–14; see Marsden (2003), p. 28 for a discussion of the possible salvage of part of the main mast during the 19th century salvage.

[89] Marsden (2003), p. 20.

[90] Marsden (2003), p. 20; Ann Payne, "An Artistic Survey", p .23 in Knighton and Loades (2000).

[91] Rule (1983), p. 41.

[92] Jones (2003), pp. 12–24; Rule (1983), pp. 69–71; see Marsden (2003), pp. 76–86 for a detailed stratigraphy of the wrecksite.

[93] Peter Marsden, "Understanding the *Mary Rose*" in Marsden (2009), p. 20.

[94] Marsden (2003), pp. 21–25.

[95] Marsden (2003), pp. 26–29; Rule (1983), p. 47. For a detailed account of the Deanes see John Bevan, *The Infernal Diver: the lives of John and Charles Deane, their invention of the diving helmet, and its first application to salvage, treasure hunting, civil engineering and military uses*. Submex, London. 1996. ISBN 978-0-9508242-1-5.

[96] Wille (2005) p. 388

[97] Marsden (2003), pp. 30–34; Rule (1983), pp. 47–56.

[98] Marsden (2003), pp. 32–33; quote from Rule (1983), p. 54.

[99] Rule (1983), pp. 54–56.

[100] Marsden (2003), p. 35.

[101] Rule (1983), p. 67.

[102] Rule (1983), p. 108.

[103] Rule (1983), p. 72.

[104] See The Mary Rose Trust, Registered Charity no. 277503 at the Charity Commission.

[105] Marsden (2003), pp. 40–41; Rule (1983), pp. 59, 73–76.

[106] Rule (1983), p. 220.

[107] Wendell Lewis, "Raising the *Mary Rose*" in Marsden (2003), pp. 51–53.

[108] Childs (2007), pp. 197–98.

[109] Rule (1983), p. 227.

[110] Wendell Lewis, "Raising the *Mary Rose*" in Marsden (2003), pp. 53–59; Rule (1983), pp. 206–27.

[111] Marsden (2003), p. 143.

[112] Marsden (2003), pp. 143–46.

[113] Rule (1983), p. 61.

[114] Rule (1983), p. 89.

[115] Marsden (2003), pp. 44–47.

[116] Childs (2007), pp. 208–10.

[117] Marsden (2003), xi.

[118] "The Mary Rose: A Tudor ship's secrets revealed", BBC

[119] Jen Rodrigues, "Staved containers (casks)" in Gardiner (2005), p. 421.

[120] Childs (2007), pp. 79–88.

[121] Colin McKewan, "The Ships' Carpenters and Their Tools", in Gardiner (2005), p. 297.

[122] Alexzandra Hildred, "The Fighting Ship" in Marsden (2009), p. 313; Rosemary Weinstein, Julie Gardiner and Robin Wood, "Official issue or personal possession?" in Gardiner (2005), pp. 494–95.

[123] Roseanna Cawthorne (5 October 2012). "10 things you might not know about the Mary Rose". *Current Archeology*. Current Publishing. Retrieved 11 March 2013.

[124] Uncreditted (12 March 2010). "Dog skeleton from Mary Rose displayed in Portsmouth". *BBC News*. British Broadcasting Corporation. Retrieved 11 March 2013.

[125] Anonymous (n.d.). "Life on Board the Mary Rose". *The Mary Rose*. Retrieved 11 March 2013.

[126] Jermy Montagu "Music on Board the *Mary Rose*," in Gardiner (2005), pp. 226–30

[127] Charles Foster "Wind Instruments," in Gardiner (2005), pp. 240–41.

[128] Mary Anne Alburger, "Bowed String Instruments," in Gardiner (2005), pp. 242–49.

[129] Robert Hicks, "Navigation and Ship's Communication" in Gardiner (2005), p. 264; Alan Stimson, "The Navigation Instruments" in Gardiner (2005), pp. 267–81.

[130] Kirstie Buckland, "Silk Hats to Woolly Socks: Clothing Remains from the *Mary Rose*, Silk caps or coifs" in Gardiner (2005), pp. 35–37.

[131] Jo Castle and several others, "Septicaemia, Scurvy and the Spanish Pox: Provisions for the Sickness and Injury at Sea" in Gardiner (2005), pp. 171–225.

[132] Richard Harrison, "Creating the *Mary Rose* Tudor Ship Museum" in Marsden (2003), p. 64.

[133] Marsden (2003), p. 145.

[134] Jones (2003), pp. 35–43.

[135] Jones (2003), pp. 47–49.

[136] Childs (2007), 204–5.

[137] Jones (2003), pp. 40–41.

[138] BBC News, Mary Rose warship: Full view revealed after museum revamp

[139] Childs (2007), p. 199.

[140] Richard Harrison, "Creating the *Mary Rose* Tudor Ship Museum" in Marsden (2003), pp. 64-66; Childs (2007), p. 210.

[141] Richard Harrison, "Creating the *Mary Rose* Tudor Ship Museum" in Marsden (2003), p. 66.

[142] Official website Archived 22 October 2012 at the Wayback Machine.. Mary Rose Trust. Retrieved 21 July 2013.

[143]

1.10.11 References

- Barker, Richard, "Shipshape for Discoveries, and Return", *Mariner's Mirror* 78 (1992), pp. 433–47

- de Brossard, M., "The French and English Versions of the Loss of the *Mary Rose* in 1545", *Mariner's Mirror* 70 (1984), p. 387.

- Childs, David, *The Warship Mary Rose: The Life and Times of King Henry VIII's Flagship* Chatham Publishing, London. 2007. ISBN 978-1-86176-267-2

- Gardiner, Julie (editor), *Before the Mast: Life and Death aboard the Mary Rose* /The Archaeology of the *Mary Rose*, Volume 4. The Mary Rose Trust, Portsmouth. 2005. ISBN 0-9544029-4-4

- Jones, Mark (editor), *For Future Generations: Conservation of a Tudor Maritime Collection* The Archaeology of the *Mary Rose*, Volume 5. The Mary Rose Trust, Portsmouth. 2003. ISBN 0-9544029-5-2

- Knighton, C. S. and Loades, David M., *The Anthony Roll of Henry VIII's Navy: Pepys Library 2991 and British Library Additional MS 22047 with related documents*. Ashgate Publishing, Aldershot. 2000. ISBN 0-7546-0094-7

- Loades, David, *The Tudor Navy: An administrative, political and military history*. Scolar Press, Aldershot. 1992. ISBN 0-85967-922-5

- McKee, Alexander, *King Henry VIII's Mary Rose*. Stein and Day, New York. 1974.

- Marsden, Peter, *Sealed by Time: The Loss and Recovery of the Mary Rose*. The Archaeology of the *Mary Rose*, Volume 1. The Mary Rose Trust, Portsmouth. 2003. ISBN 0-9544029-0-1

- Marsden, Peter (editor), *Your Noblest Shippe: Anatomy of a Tudor Warship*. The Archaeology of the *Mary Rose*, Volume 2. The Mary Rose Trust, Portsmouth. 2009. ISBN 978-0-9544029-2-1

- Rodger, Nicholas A. M., *The Safeguard of the Sea: A Naval History of Britain 660–1649*. W.W. Norton & Company, New York. 1997. ISBN 0-393-04579-X

- Rodger, Nicholas A. M., "The Development of Broadside Gunnery, 1450–1650." *Mariner's Mirror* 82 (1996), pp. 301–24.

- Rule, Margaret, *The Mary Rose: The Excavation and Raising of Henry VIII's Flagship*. (2nd edition) Conway Maritime Press, London. 1983. ISBN 0-85177-289-7

- Stirland, Ann J., *Raising the Dead: The Skeleton Crew of Henry VIII's Great Ship, the* Mary Rose. John Wiley & Sons, Chichester. 2000. ISBN 0-471-98485-X

- Watt, James, "The Surgeons of the *Mary Rose*: the practice of surgery in Tudor England", *Mariner's Mirror* 69 (1983), pp. 3–19.

- Weightman, Alfred Edwin, *Heraldry in the Royal Navy: Crests and Badges of H.M. ships* Gale & Polden, Aldershot. 1957.

- Wille, Peter, *Sound Images of the Ocean in Research and Monitoring*. Berlin: Springer 2005. ISBN 3-540-24122-1

1.10.12 Further reading

- Hildred, Alexzandra (editor), *Weapons of Warre: The Armaments of the Mary Rose*. The Archaeology of the *Mary Rose*, Volume 3. Mary Rose Trust, Portsmouth. 2011. ISBN 978-0-9544029-3-8

- Miller, Peter (May 1983). "Henry VIII's Lost Warship". *National Geographic*. Vol. 163 no. 5. pp. 646–675. ISSN 0027-9358. OCLC 643483454.

1.10.13 External links

- Official website
- Official website of the *Mary Rose* 500 Appeal
- The *Mary Rose* National Historic Ships
- Thee *Mary Rose* at Portsmouth Historic Dockyard
- Press association, "Divers may have found more of *Mary Rose*", *The Guardian*, 18 August 2003
- The raising of the *Mary Rose*
- *Mary Rose* Excavation 2003–2005
- UNESCO Convention on the Protection of the Underwater Cultural Heritage

Coordinates: 50°47′59″N 1°06′24″W / 50.79972°N 1.10667°W

1.11 Medieval archery

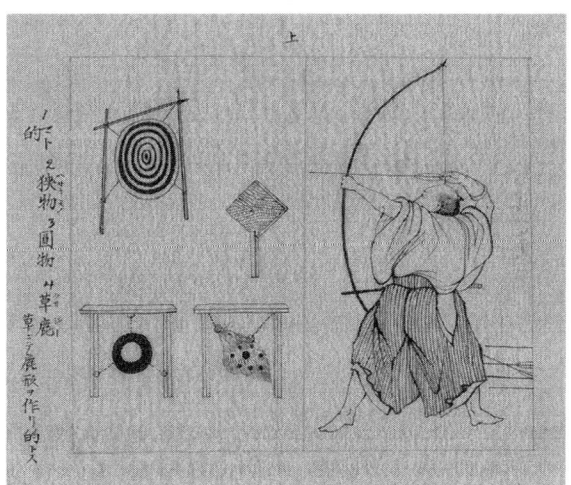

A Japanese archer with targets. Ink on paper, 1878.

The bow and arrow are known to have been invented by the end of the Upper Paleolithic, and for at least 10,000 years archery was an important military and hunting skill, and features prominently in the mythologies of many cultures.

Archers, whether on foot, in chariots and on horseback were a major part of most militaries until about 1500 when they began to be replaced by firearms, first in Europe, and then progressively elsewhere.

Archery continues to be a popular sport; most commonly in the form of target archery, but in some places also for hunting.

1.11.1 Prehistory

Epipaleolithic

Based on indirect evidence, the bow seems to have been invented near the transition from the Upper Paleolithic to the Mesolithic, some 10,000 years ago. The oldest direct evidence dates to 8,000 years ago. The discovery of stone points in Sibudu Cave, South Africa, has prompted the proposal that bow and arrow technology existed as early as 64,000 years ago.*[1]

In the Levant, artifacts which may be arrow-shaft straighteners are known from the Natufian culture, (ca. 12,800-10,300 BP) onwards. The Khiamian and PPN A shouldered Khiam-points may well be arrowheads.

The oldest indication for archery in Europe comes from Stellmoor in the Ahrensburg valley north of Hamburg, Germany. They were associated with artifacts of the late Paleolithic (11,000-9,000 BP). The arrows were made of pine and consisted of a mainshaft and a 15-20 centimetre (6-8 inches) long foreshaft with a flint point. They had shallow grooves on the base, indicating that they were shot from a bow.*[2]

The oldest definite bows known so far come from the Holmegård swamp in Denmark. In the 1940s, two bows were found there, dated to about 8,000 BP.*[3] The Holmegaard bows are made of elm and have flat arms and a D-shaped midsection. The center section is biconvex. The complete bow is 1.50 m (5 ft) long. Bows of Holmegaard-type were in use until the Bronze Age; the convexity of the midsection has decreased with time.

Mesolithic pointed shafts have been found in England, Germany, Denmark, and Sweden. They were often rather long, up to 120 cm (4 ft) and made of European hazel (*Corylus avellana*), wayfaring tree (*Viburnum lantana*) and other small woody shoots. Some still have flint arrow-heads preserved; others have blunt wooden ends for hunting birds and small game. The ends show traces of fletching, which was fastened on with birch-tar.

The oldest depictions of combat, found in Iberian cave art of the Mesolithic, show battles between archers.*[4] A group of three archers encircled by a group of four is found in Cueva del Roure, Morella la Vella, Castellón, Valencia. A depiction of a larger battle (which may, however, date to the early Neolithic), in which eleven archers are attacked by seventeen running archers, is found in Les Dogue, Ares del Maestrat, Castellón, Valencia.*[5] At Val del Charco del Agua Amarga, Alcañiz, Aragon, seven archers with plumes on their heads are fleeing a group of eight archers running in pursuit.*[6]

Archery seems to have arrived in the Americas via Alaska,

Cave painting of a battle between archers, Morella la Vella, Valencia, Spain.

as early as 6000 BCE,*[7] with the Arctic small tool tradition, about 2,500 BCE, spreading south into the temperate zones as early as 2,000 BCE, and was widely known among the indigenous peoples of North America from about 500 CE.*[8]

Neolithic

The oldest Neolithic bow known from Europe was found in anaerobic layers dating between 7,400-7,200 BP, the earliest layer of settlement at the lake settlement at La Draga, Banyoles, Girona, Spain. The intact specimen is short at 1.08m, has a D-shaped cross-section, and is made of yew wood.*[9] European Neolithic fortifications, arrow-heads, injuries, and representations indicate that, in Neolithic and Early Bronze Age Europe, archery was a major form of interpersonal violence.*[10] Stone wrist-guards, interpreted as display versions of bracers, form a defining part of the Beaker culture and arrowheads are also commonly found in Beaker graves.

Bronze Age

Chariot-borne archers became a defining feature of Middle Bronze Age warfare, from Europe to Eastern Asia and India. However, in the Middle Bronze Age, with the development of massed infantry tactics, and with the use of chariots for shock tactics or as prestigious command vehicles, archery seems to have lessened in importance in European warfare.*[10] In approximately the same period, with the Seima-Turbino Phenomenon and the spread of

1.11. MEDIEVAL ARCHERY

the Andronovo culture, mounted archery became a defining feature of Eurasian nomad cultures and a foundation of their military success, until the massed use of guns. In China, crossbows were developed, and Han Dynasty writers attributed Chinese success in battles against nomad invaders to the massed use of crossbows, first definitely attested at the Battle of Ma-Ling in 341 BCE.*[11]

1.11.2 Ancient history

Further information: Mounted archery, Composite bow, Perso-Parthian bow, Parthian shot, Sassanid army, Rashidun army, Mongol military tactics and organization, Mongol bow, Turkish archery, Turkish bow, and English longbow

Ancient civilizations, notably the Persians, Parthians,

Archers with recurve bows and short spears, detail from the archers' frieze in Darius' palace in Susa. Siliceous glazed bricks, c. 510 BC.

Indians, Koreans, Chinese, and Japanese fielded large numbers of archers in their armies. Arrows were destructive against massed formations, and the use of archers often proved decisive. The Sanskrit term for archery, dhanurveda, came to refer to martial arts in general. Mounted archers were used as the main military force for many of the equestrian nomads, including the Cimmerians and the Mongols.

Ancient Near East

The ancient Egyptian people took to archery as early as 5,000 years ago. Archery was widespread by the time of the earliest pharaohs and was practiced both for hunting and use in warfare. Legendary figures from the tombs of Thebes are depicted giving "lessons in archery".*[12] Some Egyptian deities are also connected to archery.*[13] The "Nine bows" were a conventional representation of Egypt's external enemies. One of the oldest representations of the Nine bows is on the seated statue of Pharaoh Djoser (3rd Dynasty, 27th century BCE).*[14]

Archer wearing feather headdress. Alabaster. From Nineveh, Iraq. Reign of Ashurbanipal II, 668-627 BCE. The Burrell Collection, Glasgow, UK

The Assyrians and Babylonians extensively used the bow and arrow; the Old Testament has multiple references to archery as a skill identified with the ancient Hebrews. Xenophon describes long bows used to great effect in Corduene.

The Chariot warriors of the Kassites relied heavily on the bow. The Nuzi texts detail the bows and the number of arrows assigned to the chariot crew. Archery was essential to the role of the light horse-drawn chariot as a vehicle of warfare.*[15]

Female acrobat shooting an arrow with a bow in her feet; Gnathia style pelikai *pottery; 4th century BC*

Three-bladed (trilobate) arrowheads have been found in the United Arab Emirates, dated to 100BCE-150CE.*[16]

Greco-Roman antiquity

Apollo and Artemis. Tondo of an Attic red-figure cup, ca. 470 BC.

The people of Crete practiced archery and Cretan mercenary archers were in great demand.*[17] Crete was known

Scythian bowmen on gold plaque from Kul Oba kurgan, in Crimea, 4th century BC.

for its unbroken tradition of archery.*[18]

The Greek god Apollo is the god of archery, also of plague and the sun, metaphorically perceived as shooting invisible arrows, Artemis the goddess of hunting. Heracles and Odysseus and other mythological figures are often depicted with a bow.

During the invasion of India, Alexander the Great personally took command of the shield-bearing guards, foot-companions, archers, Agrianians and horse-javelin-men and led them against the Kamboja clans—the Aspasios of Kunar valleys, the Guraeans of the Guraeus (Panjkora) valley, and the Assakenois of the Swat and Buner valleys.*[19]

The early Romans had very few archers, if any. As their empire grew, they recruited auxiliary archers from other nations. Julius Caesar's armies in Gaul included Cretan archers, and Vercingetorix his enemy ordered "all the archers, of whom there was a very great number in Gaul, to be collected".*[20] By the 4th century, archers with powerful composite bows were a regular part of Roman armies throughout the empire. After the fall of the western empire, the Romans came under severe pressure from the highly skilled mounted archers belonging to the Hun invaders, and later Eastern Roman armies relied heavily on mounted archery.*[21]

East Asia

Main articles: Chinese archery, Gungdo, Kyudo, and Yabusame

For millennia, archery has played a pivotal role in Chinese history.*[22] In particular, archery featured prominently in ancient Chinese culture and philosophy: archery

1.11. MEDIEVAL ARCHERY

was one of the Six Noble Arts of the Zhou dynasty (1146–256 BCE); archery skill was a virtue for Chinese emperors; Confucius himself was an archery teacher; and Lie Zi (a Daoist philosopher) was an avid archer.*[23]*[24] Because the cultures associated with Chinese society spanned a wide geography and time range, the techniques and equipment associated with Chinese archery are diverse.*[25]

In East Asia Joseon Korea adopted a military-service examination system from China,*[26] and South Korea remains a particularly strong performer at Olympic archery competitions even to this day.*[27]*[28]

India

The bow and arrow constituted the classical Indian weapon of warfare, from the Vedic period, until the advent of Islam.*[29]*[30] Some Rigvedic hymns lay emphasis on the use of the bow and arrow.*[31]

Detailed accounts of training methodologies in early India concern archery, considered to be an essential martial skill in early India.*[32] Legendary figures like Drona, are depicted as masters in the art of archery.*[33] Arjuna, Eklavya, Karna, Rama, Lakshmana, Bharata and Shatrughna the great warrior are also associated with archery.

1.11.3 Middle Ages

A complete arrow of 75 cm*[34] (along with other fragments and arrow heads) dated back to 1283 CE, was discovered inside a cave*[35] situated in the Qadisha Valley,*[36] Lebanon.

A treatise on Saracen archery was written in 1368. This was a didactic poem on archery dedicated to a Mameluke sultan by ṬAIBUGHĀ, al-Ashrafī.*[37]

A 14th century treatise on Arab archery was written by Hussain bin Abd al-Rahman.*[38]

A treatise on Arab archery by Ibn Qayyim Al-Jawziyya, Muḥammad ibn Abī Bakr (1292AD-1350AD) comes from the 14th century.*[39] Another treatise, *A book on the excellence of the bow & arrow* of c. 1500 details the practices and techniques of archery among the Arabs of that time.*[40] An online copy of the text is available.*[41]

Skilled archers were prized in Europe throughout the Middle Ages. The Assize of Arms of 1252 tells us that English yeomen were required by law, in an early version of a militia, to practice archery and maintain their skills. We are told that 6,000 English archers launched 42,000 arrows per minute at the Battle of Crecy in 1346.*[42] The Battle of Agincourt in 1415 is notable for Henry V's introduction of the English longbow into military lore. Henry VIII was so concerned about the state of his archers that he enjoined tennis and other frivolous pursuits in his Unlawful Games Act 1541.

1.11.4 Decline of archery

Panels depicting Archery in England from Joseph Strutt's 1801 book, The sports and pastimes of the people of England from the earliest period. *The date of the top image is unknown; the middle image is from 1496 and the bottom panel is circa fourteenth century.*

The advent of firearms eventually rendered bows obsolete in warfare. Despite the high social status, ongoing utility, and widespread pleasure of archery, almost every culture that gained access to even early firearms used them widely, to the relative neglect of archery.

"Have them bring as many guns as possible, for no other equipment is needed. Give strict orders that all men, even the samurai, carry

Archery game outside the town. Jan Lamsvelt in Van Heemskerk: Batavische Arcadia, 1708.

guns."
—Asano Yukinaga, 1598*[43]

In Ireland, Geoffrey Keating (c. 1569 - c. 1644) mentions archery as having been practiced "down to a recent period within our own memory" *[44]

Early firearms were inferior in rate-of-fire (a Tudor English author expects eight shots from the English longbow in the time needed for a "ready shooter" to give five from the musket),*[45] and François Bernier reports that well-trained mounted archers at the Battle of Samugarh in 1658 were "shooting six times before a musketeer can fire twice" .*[46] Firearms were also very susceptible to wet weather. However, they had a longer effective range (up to 200 yards for the longbow, up to 600 yards for the musket),*[45]*[47] greater penetration,*[48] and were tactically superior in the common situation of soldiers shooting at each other from behind obstructions. They also penetrated steel armour without any need to develop special musculature. Armies equipped with guns could thus provide superior firepower, and highly trained archers became obsolete on the battlefield. The Battle of Cerignola in 1503 was won by Spain mainly by the use of matchlock firearms, marking the first time a major battle was won through the use of firearms.

The last regular unit armed with bows was the Archers' Company of the Honourable Artillery Company, ironically a part of the oldest regular unit in England to be armed with gunpowder weapons. The last recorded use of bows in battle in Britain seems to have been a skirmish at Bridgnorth; in October 1642, during the English Civil War, an impromptu militia, armed with bows, was effective against unarmoured musketmen.*[49] (A more recent use of archery in war was in 1940, on the retreat to Dunkirk, when Jack Churchill, who had brought his bows on active service, "was delighted to see his arrow strike the centre German in the left of the chest and penetrate his body").*[50]

Archery continued in some areas that were subject to limitations on the ownership of arms, such as the Scottish Highlands during the repression that followed the decline of the Jacobite cause, and the Cherokees after the Trail of Tears. The Tokugawa shogunate severely limited the import and manufacture of guns, and encouraged traditional martial skills among the samurai; towards the end of the Satsuma Rebellion in 1877, some rebels fell back on the use of bows and arrows. Archery remained an important part of the military examinations until 1894 in Korea and 1904 in China.

Within the steppe of Eurasia, archery continued to play an important part in warfare, although now restricted to mounted archery. The Ottoman Empire still fielded auxiliary cavalry which was noted for its use of bows from horseback. This practice was continued by the Ottoman subject nations, despite the Empire itself being a proponent of early firearms. The practice declined after the Crimean Khanate was absorbed by Russia; however mounted archers remained in the Ottoman order of battle until the post 1826 reforms to the Ottoman Army. The art of traditional archery remained in minority use for sport and for hunting in Turkey up until the 1820s, but the knowledge of constructing composite bows, fell out of use with the death of the last bowyer in the 1930s. The rest of the Middle East also lost the continuity of its archery tradition at this time.

An exception to this trend was the Comanche culture of North America, where mounted archery remained competitive with muzzle-loading guns. "After... about 1800, most Comanches began to discard muskets and pistols and to rely on their older weapons." *[51] Repeating firearms, however, were superior in turn, and the Comanches adopted them when they could. Bows remained effective hunting weapons for skilled horse archers, used to some extent by all Native Americans on the Great Plains to hunt buffalo as long as there were buffalo to hunt. The last Comanche hunt was in 1878, and it failed for lack of buffalo, not lack of appropriate weapons.*[52]

Ongoing use of bows and arrows was maintained in isolated cultures with little or no contact with the outside world. The use of traditional archery in some African conflicts has been reported in the 21st century, and the Sentinelese still use bows as part of a lifestyle scarcely touched by outside contact. A remote group in Brazil, recently photographed from the air, aimed bows at the aeroplane.*[53] Bows and arrows saw considerable use in the 2007–2008 Kenyan crisis.

1.11.5 Recreational revival

A print of the 1822 meeting of the "Royal British Bowmen" archery club.

The British initiated a major revival of archery as an upper-class pursuit from about 1780-1840.*[54] Early recreational archery societies included the Finsbury Archers and the Kilwinning Papingo, established in 1688. The latter held competitions in which the archers had to dislodge a wooden parrot from the top of an abbey tower. The Company of Scottish Archers was formed in 1676 and is one of the oldest sporting bodies in the world. It remained a small and scattered pastime, however, until the late 18th century when it experienced a fashionable revival among the aristocracy. Sir Ashton Lever, an antiquarian and collector, formed the Toxophilite Society in London in 1781, with the patronage of George, the Prince of Wales.

Archery societies were set up across the country, each with its own strict entry criteria and outlandish costumes. Recreational archery soon became extravagant social and ceremonial events for the nobility, complete with flags, music and 21 gun salutes for the competitors. The clubs were "the drawing rooms of the great country houses placed outside" and thus came to play an important role in the social networks of local elites. As well as its emphasis on display and status, the sport was notable for its popularity with females. Young women could not only compete in the contests but retain and show off their sexuality while doing so.

Thus, archery came to act as a forum for introductions, flirtation and romance.*[54] It was often consciously styled in the manner of a Medieval tournament with titles and laurel wreaths being presented as a reward to the victor. General meetings were held from 1789, in which local lodges convened together to standardise the rules and ceremonies. Archery was also co-opted as a distinctively British tradition, dating back to the lore of Robin Hood and it served as a patriotic form of entertainment at a time of political tension in Europe. The societies were also elitist, and the new middle class bourgeoisie were excluded from the clubs due to their lack of social status.

After the Napoleonic Wars, the sport became increasingly popular among all classes, and it was framed as a nostalgic reimagining of the preindustrial rural Britain. Particularly influential was Sir Walter Scott's 1819 novel, *Ivanhoe* that depicted the heroic character Lockseley winning an archery tournament.*[55]

1.11.6 A modern sport

The 1840s saw the first attempts at turning the recreation into a modern sport. The first Grand National Archery Society meeting was held in York in 1844 and over the next decade the extravagant and festive practices of the past were gradually whittled away and the rules were standardised as the 'York Round' - a series of shoots at 60, 80, and 100 yards. Horace A. Ford helped to improve archery standards and pioneered new archery techniques. He won the Grand National 11 times in a row and published a highly influential guide to the sport in 1856.

Towards the end of the 19th century, the sport experienced declining participation as alternative sports such as croquet and tennis became more popular among the middle class. By 1889, just 50 archery clubs were left in Britain, but it was still included as a sport at the 1900 Paris Olympics.

In the United States, primitive archery was revived in the early 20th century. The last of the Yahi Indian tribe, a native known as Ishi, came out of hiding in California in 1911.*[56]*[57] His doctor, Saxton Pope, learned many of Ishi's traditional archery skills, and popularized them.*[58]*[59] The Pope and Young Club, founded in 1961 and named in honor of Pope and his friend, Arthur Young, became one of North America's leading bowhunting and conservation organizations. Founded as a nonprofit scientific organization, the Club was patterned after the prestigious Boone and Crockett Club and advocated responsible bowhunting by promoting quality, fair chase hunting, and sound conservation practices.

In Korea, the transformation of archery to a healthy pastime was led by Emperor Gojong, and is the basis of a popular

Picture of Pope taken while grizzly hunting at Yellowstone

modern sport. The Japanese continue to make and use their unique traditional equipment. Among the Cherokees, popular use of their traditional longbows never died out.*[60]

In China, at the beginning of the 21st century, there has been revival in interest among craftsmen looking to construct bows and arrows, as well as in practicing technique in the traditional Chinese style.*[61]*[62]

In modern times, mounted archery continues to be practiced as a popular competitive sport in modern Hungary and in some Asian countries but it is not recognized as an international competition.*[63] Archery is the national sport of the Kingdom of Bhutan.*[64]

From the 1920s, professional engineers took an interest in archery, previously the exclusive field of traditional craft experts.*[65] They led the commercial development of new forms of bow including the modern recurve and compound bow. These modern forms are now dominant in modern Western archery; traditional bows are in a minority. In the 1980s, the skills of traditional archery were revived by American enthusiasts, and combined with the new scientific understanding. Much of this expertise is available in the *Traditional Bowyer's Bibles* (see Additional reading). Modern game archery owes much of its success to Fred Bear, an American bow hunter and bow manufacturer.*[66]

1.11.7 See also

- Archery
- Kyūdō, Japanese archery
- Yabusame, Japanese horseback archery
- Gungdo, Korean archery
- Turkish archery
- Chinese archery
- Archery in India

1.11.8 References

[1] Backwell, Lucinda; d'Errico, Francesco; Wadley, Lyn (2008). "Middle Stone Age bone tools from the Howiesons Poort layers, Sibudu Cave, South Africa". *Journal of Archaeological Science*. **35** (6): 1566–1580. doi:10.1016/j.jas.2007.11.006. "Explicit tests for distinctions between thrown spears and projected arrows have not yet been conducted, and many of the segments could have been employed equally successfully as insets for spears or arrows (Lombard & Pargeter 2008)." Lombard, Marlize; Phillipson, Laurel (2010). "Indications of bow and stone-tipped arrow use 64 000 years ago in KwaZulu-Natal, South Africa". *Antiquity*. **84**: 635–648. doi:10.1017/s0003598x00100134.

[2] McEwen E, Bergman R, Miller C. Early bow design and construction. Scientific American 1991 vol. 264 pp76-82.

[3] Charles E. Grayson, Mary French, Michael J. O'Brien. Traditional Archery from Six Continents: The Charles E. Grayson Collection. University of Missouri Press 2007. ISBN 978-0-8262-1751-6 p=1

[4] Keith F. Otterbein, *How War Began* (2004), p. 72.

[5] Christensen J. 2004. "Warfare in the European Neolithic", *Acta Archaeologica* 75, 129–156.

[6] S.L. Washburn, *Social Life of Early Man* (1962), p. 207.

[7] Blitz, John. "Adoption of the Bow in Prehistoric North America. *North American Archaeologist*, vol 9 no 2, 1988" (PDF).

[8] Brian Fagan. The first North Americans. Thames and Hudson, London, 2011. ISBN 978-0-500-02120-0 Hodge, Frederick Webb (1907). *Handbook of American Indians North of Mexico, Vol 1* pg 485. Government Printing Office

[9] accessed The oldest Neolithic Bow discovered in Europe, Universitat Autònoma de Barcelona 2012. 1 July 2012

[10] Bronze Age Warfare. Richard Osgood and Sarah Monks with Judith Toms. The History Press 2000. pp.139-142

[11] Needham (1986), Volume 5, Part 6, 124–128.

[12] Wilson, John (1956). *The Culture of Ancient Egypt* pg 186. University of Chicago Press

[13] Traunecker, Claude (2001). *The Gods of Egypt* pg 29. Cornell University Press

[14] "Enemies of Civilization: Attitudes toward Foreigners in Ancient Mesopotamia, Egypt, and China", Mu-chou Poo, Mu-chou Poo Muzhou Pu. SUNY Press, Feb 1, 2012. p. 43. Retrieved 7 jan 2017

[15] Drews, Roberts (1993). *The End of the Bronze Age: Changes in Warfare and the Catastrophe Ca. 1200 B.C.* pg 119. Princeton University Press

[16] "A trilobate arrowhead can be defined as an arrowhead that has three wings or blades that are usually placed at equal angles (i.e. c. 120°) around the imaginary longitudinal axis extending from the centre of the socket or tang. Since this type of arrowhead is rare in southeastern Arabia, we must investigate its origin and the reasons behind its presence at ed-Dur."Delrue, Parsival (2007). "Trilobate Arrowheads at Ed-Dur (U.A.E, Emirate of Umm Al-Qaiwain)"." . *Arabian Archaeology and Epigraphy*. **18** (2): 239–250. doi:10.1111/j.1600-0471.2007.00281.x.

[17] Cambridge University Press (2000). *Cambridge Ancient History* pg 174.

[18] Kirk, Geoffrey etc (1993). *The Iliad: a commentary* pg 136. Cambridge University Press

[19] The Ashvayanas living on river Guraeus (modern river Panjkora), which are the Gauri of Mahabharata, were also known as Gorys or Guraios, modern Ghori or Gori, a wide spread tribe, branches of which are still to be found on the Panjkora and on both sides of the Kabul at the point of its confluence with Landai (See: *History of Punjab*, Vol I, 1997, p 227, Publication Bureau, Punjabi University, Patiala (Editors) Dr L. M. Joshi, Dr Fauja Singh). The clan name Gore or Gaure is also found among the modern Kamboj people of Punjab and it is stated that the Punjab Kamboj Gaure/Gore came from the Kunar valley to Punjab at some point in time in the past (Ref: These Kamboja People, 1979, 122; Kambojas Through the Ages, 2005, p 131, Kirpal Singh).

[20] gutenberg.org Caius Julius Caesar. *Caesar's Commentaries*. Translated by W. A. Macdevitt.

[21] *Greece and Rome at War*, Peter Connolly, Adrian Keith Goldsworthy. Greenhill Books 1998 ISBN 1-85367-303-X ISBN 978-1853673030

[22] "Archived copy". Archived from the original on 31 January 2011. Retrieved 26 December 2010.

[23] Six Arts of Ancient China

[24] Chinese Archery (Paperback). Stephen Selby. Hong Kong University Press 2000. ISBN 962-209-501-1 ISBN 978-962-209-501-4

[25] The Bows of China. Stephen Selby. Journal of Chinese Martial Studies, Winter 2010 Issue 2. Three-In-One Press, 2010.

[26] Korea archery at anthromuseum.missouri.edu "During the Choson period (1392-1910), Korea adopted a military-service examination system from China that included a focus on archery skills and that contributed to the development of Korean archery as a practical martial art."

[27] Archery in South Korea at lycos.com/info/archery

[28] "South sweep," 28 September 2000 at sportsillustrated.cnn.com

[29] Zimmer, Heinrich and Campbell, Joseph (1969). *Philosophies of India* pg 140. Princeton University Press.

[30] Drews, Robert (1993). *The End of the Bronze Age: Changes in Warfare and the Catastrophe Ca. 1200 B.C.* pg 119. Princeton University Press

[31] *With the bow let us win cows, with the bow let us win the contest and violent battles with the bow. The bow ruins the enemy's pleasure; with the bow let us conquer all corners of the world.* -- Drews, Roberts (1993). *The End of the Bronze Age: Changes in Warfare and the Catastrophe Ca. 1200 B.C.* pg 125. Princeton University Press

[32] Scharfe, Hartmut (2002). *Education in Ancient India* pg 271. Brill Academic Publishers

[33] Van Buitenen, J. A. B. (1980). *The Mahabharata: The Book of the Beginning* pg 153. University of Chicago Press

[34] Abi Aoun B., Baroudy F., Ghaouch A. Khawaja P and alias Momies du Liban: Rapport préliminaire sur la découverte archaéologique de 'Asi-al-Hadat (XIIIe siècle), France, Éd-ifra, 1994

[35] http://www.cavinglebanon.com/asi-l-hadath-fortified-cave

[36] http://www.whc.unesco.org/en/list/850

[37] Boudot-Lamotte, A. 1972. "J. D. Latham et Lt. Cdr. W. F. PATERSON, Saracen Archery, An English version and exposition of a mameluke work on Archery (ca. A.D. 1368), with Introduction, Glossary, and Illustrations, London (The Holland Press) 1970, XL + 219 pp". Arabica. 19, no. 1: 98-99.

[38] Jallon, A.D. Kitab Fi Ma "Rifat "Ilm Ramy Al-Siham, a Treatise on Archery by Husayn B. "Abd Al-Rahman B. Muhammad B. Muhammad B. "Abdallah Al-Yunini AH 647 (?) - 724, AH 1249-50 (?) - 1324: A Critical Edition of the Arabic Text Together with a Study of the Work in English. University of Manchester, 1980. OCLC: 499854155.

[39] Ibn Qayyim al-Jawzīyah, Muḥammad ibn Abī Bakr. kitab ʿuniyat al-ṭullāb fī maʿrifat al-rāmī bil-nushshāb. [Cairo?]: [s.n.], 1932. OCLC: 643468400.

[40] Faris, Nabih Amin, and Robert Potter Elmer. Arab archery. An Arabic manuscript of about A.D. 1500, "A book on the excellence of the bow & arrow" and the description thereof. Princeton, N.J.: Princeton University Press, 1945. Translation of "Kitāb fī bayān fadl al-qaws w-al-sahm wa-awsāfihima," no. 793 in Descriptive catalog of the Garrett collection of Arabic manuscripts in the Princeton university library.

[41] [tuba-archery.com/article/arab-archery.pdf Arab Archery].

[42] Rhoten, R.: "Trebuchet Energy Efficiency - Experimental Results" AIAA 2006-775

[43] Asano Yukinaga, 1598 CE, letter to his father, quoted in The Samurai, by S.R. Turnbull, Osprey, London 1977. ISBN 0-85045-097-7

[44] Geoffrey Keating. The History of Ireland, translated into English and preface by David Comyn, Patrick S. Dinneen. Accessed 9 December 2007

[45] A right exelent and pleasaunt dialogue, betwene Mercury and an English souldier contayning his supplication to Mars: bevvtified with sundry worthy histories, rare inuentions, and politike deuises. wrytten by B. Rich: gen. 1574. Published 1574 by J. Day. These bookes are to be sold [by H. Disle] at the corner shop, at the South west doore of Paules church in London. https://bowvsmusket.com/2015/07/14/barnabe-rich-a-right-exelent-and-pleasaunt-dialouge-1574/ accessed 21 April 2016

[46] as attributed to Bernier by Dirk H.A. Kolff. Naukar, Rajput, & Sepoy. The ethnohistory of the military labour market in Hindustan, 1450-1860. University of Cambridge Oriental Publications no. 43. Cambridge University Press 1990., p.23

[47] Korean Traditional Archery. Duvernay TA, Duvernay NY. Handong Global University, 2007

[48] Gunn, Steven; Gromelski, Tomasz (2012). "For whom the bell tolls: accidental deaths in Tudor England". *The Lancet.* **380** (9849): 1222–1223. doi:10.1016/S0140-6736(12)61702-4. "The mean depth of arrow wounds, for example, was an inch and a half, that of gunshot wounds six inches, not counting balls that went right through the body or head"

[49] John Norton, letter dated 5 October 1642. As printed in The Garrisons of Shropshire during the Civil War, Leake and Evans publishers, Shrewsbury, 1867, page 32. "every man from 16 to 50 and upwards, gott himself into such armes as they could presently attaine, or could imagine be conduceable for the defence of the towne". "some companies of foote.. with their musketts... began to wade foarde, which being descried, we, with our bowes and arrows did so gaule them (being unarmed men) that with their utmost speed they did retreate" accessed 7 August 2012

[50] The archer's craft: A sheaf of notes on certain matters concerning archers and archery, the making of archers' tackle and the art of hunting with the bow. Adrian Eliot Hodgkin. Faber 1951

[51] T.R. Fehrenbach. Comanches, the history of a people. Vintage Books. London, 2007. ISBN 978-0-09-952055-9. First published in the USA by Alfred Knopf, 1974. Page 125.

[52] T.R. Fehrenbach. Comanches, the history of a people. Vintage Books. London, 2007. ISBN 978-0-09-952055-9. First published in the USA by Alfred Knopf, 1974. Page 553.

[53] "Amazonian archers". *BBC News.* 2008-05-30. Retrieved 2010-01-05.

[54] Johnes, Martin. "Archery—Romance-and-Elite-Culture-in-England-and-Wales —c-1780-1840 Martin Johnes. Archery, Romance and Elite Culture in England and Wales, c. 1780–1840". Swansea.academia.edu. Retrieved 2013-03-26.

[55] "The Royal Company of Archers". Retrieved 2012-12-17.

[56] Allely, Steve; et al. (2008), *The Traditional Bowyer's Bible, Volume 4*, The Lyons Press, ISBN 978-0-9645741-6-8

[57] Kroeber, Theodora (2004), *Ishi in Two Worlds: a biography of the last wild Indian in North America*, Berkeley: University of California Press, ISBN 978-0-520-24037-7

[58] Pope, Saxton (1925), *Hunting with the Bow and Arrow*, New York: G. P. Putnam's Sons

[59] Pope, Saxton (1926), *Adventurous Bowmen: field notes on African archery*, New York: G. P. Putnam's Sons

[60] Cherokee Bows and Arrows: How to Make and Shoot Primitive Bows and Arrows. Al Herrin. White Bear Pub (Nov 1989). ISBN 978-0962360138

[61] Article about the 2009 Chinese Traditional Archery Seminar

[62] News coverage of the 2010 Chinese Traditional Archery Seminar

[63] "Magyar index".

[64] "Bhutanese Traditional Archery".

[65] Hickman, C. N.; Nagler, Forrest; Klopsteg, Paul E. (1947), *Archery: The Technical Side. A compilation of scientific and technical articles on theory, construction, use and performance of bows and arrows, reprinted from journals of science and of archery*, National Field Archery Association

[66] Bertalan, Dan. *Traditional Bowyers Encyclopedia: The Bowhunting and Bowmaking World of the Nation's Top Crafters of Longbows and Recurves*, 2007. p. 73.

- uiowa.edu

*[1]

1.11.9 Further reading

- *The Traditional Bowyers Bible Volume 1.* The Lyons Press, 1992. ISBN 1-58574-085-3
- *The Traditional Bowyers Bible Volume 2.* The Lyons Press, 1992. ISBN 1-58574-086-1
- *The Traditional Bowyers Bible Volume 3.* The Lyons Press, 1994. ISBN 1-58574-087-X
- *The Traditional Bowyers Bible Volume 4.* The Lyons Press, 2008. ISBN 978-0-9645741-6-8

1.11.10 External links

- Archery Library Online Archery Books with historical content

[1] Crombie, Laura (2016). *Archery and Crossbow Guilds in Medieval Flanders.* Woodbridge: Boydell and Brewer.

1.12 Mongol bow

The **Mongol bow** is a type of recurved composite bow used in Mongolia. "Mongol bow" can refer to two types of bow. From the 17th century onward, most of the traditional bows in Mongolia were replaced with the similar Manchu Bow which is primarily distinguished by larger siyahs and the presence of prominent string bridges.

1.12.1 Pre-Qing Mongol Bow

The old Mongolian bows that were used during the rule of Genghis Khan were smaller than the modern Manchu derived weapons used at most Naadam. Paintings as well as at least one surviving example of a 13th century Mongol bow from Cagaan Chad demonstrate that the medieval Mongolian bows had smaller siyahs and much less prominent leather string bridges.*[1]

1.12.2 Influence of the Qing Dynasty

From the 17th-20th century, horseback archery in Mongolia (and around the world) declined in prominence in proportion to the availability of firearms. Contemporary depictions of the 1768 Battle of Khorgos between the Qing Dynasty and the Western Mongolian Dzungars show the mounted Dzungars primarily armed with muskets. Despite changes in bow construction over time, the Mongolian archery tradition has been continuous. The traditions of Mongolian archery were partially kept alive by

This c. 1280 painting depicts an archer shooting a traditional Mongol bow from horseback in the upper left corner

By the 18th century, although the Qing Dynasty maintained archery for military purposes, many Mongol groups had traded their bows for firearms. This print depicts the majority of Western Mongolian Dzungars (right hand side) as being armed with muskets while their Qing foes are primarily armed with the Manchu Bow.

the Qing Imperial court which maintained a cohort Mongolian Imperial Bodyguards specifically trained in archery with Manchurian bows. Gradually, construction of composite bows in Mongolia, China, and Tibet largely shifted to Manchu derived designs to the point where the traditional "Mongolian bow" used in the Nandaam festival actually derives from the Manchu popularized design *[2]

1.12.3 Construction

Hulagu Khan with the older composite bow used during the time of the Mongol conquest. It is smaller in size and has no string bridges

Main article: Composite bow

Ancient and modern Mongol bows are part of the Asian composite bow tradition. The core is bamboo, with horn on the belly (facing towards the archer) and sinew on the back, bound together with animal glue.*[3] As animal glue is dissolved by water, composite bows may be ruined by rain or excess humidity; a wrapper of (waterproof) birch bark may give limited protection from moisture and from mechanical damage. The bow is usually stored in a leather case for protection when not in use.

1.12.4 The arrows

Birch is a typical material for arrows. The normal length of an arrow is between 80 and 100 cm, and the shaft's diameter is around 1 cm.

As for fletchings, tail feathers of crane are favored, but tail feathers of all birds are usable. Eagle feathers make a particularly exclusive arrow, but since eagles are rare most arrows obviously cannot have fletchings from eagle's tail feathers. Feathers taken from the wings are said to flow less smoothly through the air, so if given the choice tail feathers are picked. The Mongols characteristically pay close attention to minutest of detail; the placement of the fletchings in relation to their size, and what part of the bird they were taken from, is of great importance for correct rotation and good balance in the air. Consequently, these factors are painstakingly considered when making arrows after the Old Mongol standard.

The arrowheads, or points, could be everything from wide metal blades used for big game (or in war) to bone and wooden points, which are used for hunting birds and small animals. The high impact of this bow ensures that a bony point will be lethal when hitting the body of a smaller animal or a bird. In addition to these kinds of arrows, whistling arrows are useful during hunting, because the effect on animals of an arrow whistling away high above the ground is often to make it stop, curious to see what is in the air. This gives the hunter time to launch a second arrow, this time with a game head to kill the animal. These whistling arrows made by inserting an arrowhead of bone in which air channels have been created. When shot, such arrowheads make a very audible sound through the air.

A Timurid depiction of a Mongol archer. (Signed (lower right): Muhammad ibn Mahmudshah al-Khayyam, early 15th century).

1.12.5 Range

An inscription thought to be from 1226 was found on a stone stele in Nerchinsk, Siberia. It may have said: "While Chinggis Khan was holding an assembly of Mongolian dignitaries, after his conquest of Sartaul (East Turkestan), [Chinggis's nephew] Esungge shot a target at 335 alds (536m)." *[4]

In the historical novel "Khökh Sudar" Injinashi, the Mongolian philosopher, historian and writer, imagines the competition amongst all Mongolian men in about 1194-1195: five archers each hit the target three times from a distance of 500 bows (1 bow = at least 1 metre).

1.12. MONGOL BOW

Mongol cavalrymen during the time of the Mongol conquest used a smaller bow suitable for horse archery.

1.12.6 Mongolian draw and release

Main article: Bow draw

The Mongolian draw, or thumb draw, uses only the thumb,

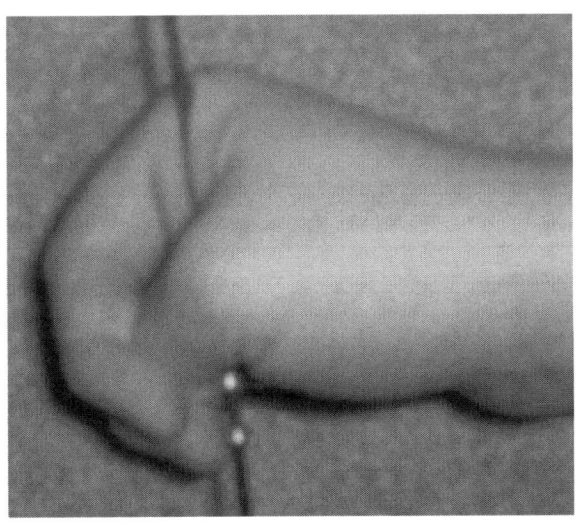

A Mongolian draw

the strongest single digit, to grasp the string. Around the back of the thumb, the index and/or middle fingers reinforce the grip. This is traditional across the Asian steppes, as well as in Korea,[5] Japan, Tibet, China, Turkey, India and recent Persia.[6] It was also used by Ishi, the last of the Yana, with his short bows.

It gives a narrower grip on the string, as only one digit is used, and this may help to avoid "string pinch" with shorter bows, such as the composite bows normally used from horseback. Mongol archers would wear a thumb ring made from leather, bone, horn, and in some cases silver to protect the thumb.[7] It may also avoid a problem occasionally faced by archers using the Mediterranean release, when the three fingers do not release at exactly the same time and thus foul the draw. This release is normally used with the arrow on the right side of the bow for a right-handed archer, and on the left side of the bow for a left-handed archer.

1.12.7 See also

- Composite bow
- Turkish bow
- Korean bow
- Bow draw
- Bow string
- Mounted archery

1.12.8 References

[1] Dekker, Peter. "Evolution of the Manchu Bow".

[2] Dekker, Peter. "Did the Manchu's Really Ban Archery in Mongolia.". *Fe Doro Archery*. Retrieved 23 August 2016.

[3] John C Halpin, Halpin C Halpin, *Primer on Composite Materials Analysis*, CRC Press, Apr 15, 1992, ISBN 0-87762-754-1

[4] WHAT IS THE SCRIPT ON THE CHINGGIS KHAN'S STELE ABOUT?, Gongor LHAGVASUREN

[5] "Korea Horseback Archery History".

[6] Archery Traditions of Asia. Stephen Selby. Hong Kong Museum of Coastal Defence, 2003. ISBN 962-7039-47-0

[7] "Mongolian Draw and Releas".

1.12.9 External links

- Asian Traditional Archery Research Network

[1] "CSEN Home Page". Center for the Study of Eurasian Nomads. Retrieved 2008-03-04.

1.13 Mounted archery

Horse archer presentation in Hungary

A **horse archer** is a cavalryman armed with a bow, able to shoot while riding from horseback. Archery has occasionally been used from the backs of other riding animals. In large open areas, it was a highly successful technique for hunting, for protecting the herds, and for war. It was a defining characteristic of the Eurasian nomads during antiquity and the medieval period, as well as the Iranian peoples (Scythians, Sarmatians, Parthians, Sassanid Persians) and Indians in antiquity, and by the Mongols and the Turkic peoples during the Middle Ages. By the expansion of these peoples, the practice also spread to Eastern Europe (via the Sarmatians and the Huns), to Mesopotamia, and to East Asia. In East Asia, horse archery came to be particularly honoured in the samurai tradition of Japan, where horse archery is called Yabusame.

The term **mounted archer** occurs in medieval English sources to describe a soldier who rode to battle but who dismounted to shoot. In the modern English usage, however, "mounted archer" and "horse archer" are essentially interchangeable terms

Horse archery developed separately among the peoples of the South American pampas and the North American prairies; the Comanches were especially skilled.*[1]

1.13.1 Basic features

Since using a bow requires the rider to let go of the reins with both hands, horse archers need superb equestrian skills if they are to shoot on the move. The natives of large grassland areas used mounted archery for hunting, for protecting their herds, and for war. Horse archery was for many groups a basic survival skill, and additionally made each ablebodied man, at need, a highly-mobile warrior. The buf-

Young prince (later Holy Roman Emperor Maximilian I) hunting for birds as a horsed archer. Woodcut by Albrecht Dürer.

A Timurid drawing of an Ilkhanid horse archer. Signed (lower right) Muhammad ibn Mahmudshah al-Khayyam Iran, early 15th century. Ink and gold on paper

falo hunts of the North American prairies may be the best-recorded examples of bowhunting by mounted archers.*[2]

In battle, light horse archers were typically skirmishers, lightly armed missile troops capable of moving swiftly to avoid close combat or to deliver a rapid blow to the flanks or rear of the foe. Captain Robert G. Carter described the experience of facing Quanah Parker's forces: "an irregular line of swirling warriors, all rapidly moving in right and left hand circles.. while advancing, to the right or left, and as rapidly concentrating... in the centre... and their falling back in the same manner...all was most puzzling to our... veterans who had never witnessed such tactical maneuvers, or such a flexible line of skirmishers" *[3]

In the tactic of the Parthian shot the rider would retreat from the enemy while turning his upper body and shooting backwards. Due to the superior speed of mounted archers, troops under attack from horse archers were unable to respond to the threat if they did not have ranged weapons of their own. Constant harassment would result in casualties, morale drop and disruption of the formation. Any attempts to charge the archers would also slow the entire army down.

An example of these tactics comes from an attack on Comanche horse archers by a group of Texas Rangers, who were saved by their muzzle-loading firearms and by a convenient terrain feature. Fifty Rangers armed with guns met about 20 Comanche hunters who were hunting buffalo, and attacked them. The Comanches fled, easily keeping clear of the Rangers, for several miles across the open prairie. They led the Rangers into a stronger force of two hundred. The Rangers immediately retreated, only to discover they had committed a classic error in fighting mounted archers: the Comanches pursued in turn, able to shoot what seemed like clouds of arrows. The Rangers found a ravine where they could shoot at the Comanche from cover. The horse archers did not charge, but kept the Rangers under siege until seven of them were dead or dying, whereupon the Rangers retreated but claimed victory.*[4]

Heavy horse archers

Horse archers may be either light, such as Scythian, Hun, Parthian, Cuman or Pecheneg horsemen, or heavy, such as Byzantine kavallarioi, Turkish timariots, Russian druzhina and Japanese samurai. Heavy horse archers typically fought as disciplined units. Instead of harassing without ever making contact, they shot in volleys, weakening the enemy before they charged. In addition to bows, they often also carried close combat weapons, such as lances or spears. Some nations, like medieval Mongols, Hungarians and Cumans fielded both light and heavy horse archers. In some armies, such as those of the Parthians, Palmyrans, and the Teutonic Order of Knights, the mounted troops consisted of both super-heavy troops (cataphracts, knights) without bows, and light horse archers.

1.13.2 Appearance in history

Mounted archery first developed during the Iron Age, gradually replacing the Bronze Age chariot.

The earliest depictions of mounted archers are found in artwork of the Neo-Assyrian Empire of about the 9th century

Assyrian relief of a mounted archer

Parthian horse archer, undated relief at the Palazzo Madama, Turin.

BC and reflects the incursions of the early Iranian peoples. Early horse archery, depicted on the Assyrian carvings, involved two riders, one controlling both horses while the second shot.

Skirmishing requires vast areas of free space to run, manoeuvre and flee, and if the terrain is close, light horse archers can be charged and defeated easily. Light horse archers are also very vulnerable to foot archers and crossbowmen, who are smaller targets and can outshoot horsemen. Large armies very seldom relied solely on skirmishing mounted archers, but there are many examples of victories in which horse archers played a leading part. The Roman general Crassus led a large army, with inadequate cavalry and missile troops, to catastrophe against Parthian horse archers and cataphracts at the Battle of Carrhae. The

Persian king Darius the Great led a campaign against the mounted Scythians, who refused to engage in pitched battle; Darius conquered and occupied land but lost enough troops and supplies that he was compelled to retreat. Darius, however, kept the lands he had conquered.

According to the Greek historian Herodotus, the Persian general Mardonius used horse archers to attack and harass his opponents during the Battle of Plataea,*[5] which was won by the Greeks. Philip of Macedon scored an epic victory against the Scythians residing north of the Danube, killing their king, Ateas, and causing their kingdom to fall apart thereafter. Alexander the Great defeated Scythians/Sakas in 329 BC at the Battle of Jaxartes, at the Syr Darya river. Later on, Alexander himself used mounted archers recruited among the Scythians and Dahae, during the Greek invasion of India.*[6]

The Roman Empire and its military also had an extensive use of horse archers after their conflict with eastern armies that relied heavily on mounted archery in the 1st century BC. They had regiments such as the Equites Sagittarii, who acted as Rome's mounted horse archers in combat.*[7] The Crusaders used conscripted cavalry and horse archers known as the Turcopole, made up of mostly Greek and Turks.*[8]

Heavy horse archers first appeared in the Assyrian army in the 7th century BC after abandoning chariot warfare and formed a link between light skirmishing cavalrymen and heavy cataphract cavalry. The heavy horse archers usually had mail or lamellar armour and helmets, and sometimes even their horses were armoured. Heavy horse archers, instead of skirmishing and hit-and-run tactics, formed in disciplined formations and units, sometimes intermixed with lancers as in Byzantine and Turkish armies, and shot as volleys instead of shooting as individuals. The usual tactic was to first shoot five or six volleys at the enemy to weaken him and to disorganise them, and then charge. Heavy horse archers often carried spears or lances for close combat, or formed mixed units with lancers. The Mongol armies and others included both heavy and light horse archers.

Heavy horse archers could usually outshoot their light counterparts, and wearing armour, could stand their shooting. The Russian druzhina cavalry developed as a countermeasure to the Tatar light troops. Likewise, the Turkish timariots and qapikulu were often as heavily armoured as Western knights, and could stand the Hungarian, Albanian and Mongol horse archers.

The German and Scandinavian Medieval armies made extensive use of mounted crossbowmen. They would act not only as scouts and skirmishers, but also protecting the flanks of the knights and infantry, and chasing away the enemy light cavalry. When the battle was fully engaged, they would charge at the enemy flank, shoot a single devastating volley

16th-century Muscovite cavalry.

at point-blank range and then attack the enemy with swords, without reloading. In some instances, mounted crossbowmen can also reload and fire continuously on horseback if they use specific "weak" crossbows that can be reloaded easily with the hand, such as the 13th century Speculum Regale,*[9] and the invention of the goat's foot lever and the ratchet cranequin allowed the mounted crossbowmen to reload and fire heavy crossbows on horseback.*[10]*[11]

Decline

Mounted archery was usually ineffective against massed foot archery. The foot archers or crossbowmen could outshoot the horse archers and a man alone is a smaller target than a man and a horse. The Crusaders countered the Turkoman horse archery with their crossbowmen, and Genoese crossbowmen were favoured mercenaries in both Mamluk and Mongol armies. Likewise the Chinese armies consisted of massed crossbowmen to counter the nomad armies. A nomad army that wanted to engage in an archery exchange with foot archers would itself normally dismount. The typical Mongol archer shot from a sitting position when dismounted.

Another example of combined troops winning against armies mostly of horse archers is the highly successful Han campaign against the mounted Xiongnu nomads. Well-led Roman troops managed to score crushing defeats against the Parthians, including the Roman–Parthian War of 161–66 and Trajan's war against Parthia, they even sacked the Parthian capital on three occasions.

1.13. MOUNTED ARCHERY

Horse archers were eventually rendered obsolete by the maturity of firearm technology. In the 16th and subsequent centuries, various cavalry forces armed with firearms gradually started appearing. Because the conventional arquebus and musket were too awkward for a cavalryman to use, lighter weapons such as the carbine had to be developed, that could be effectively used from horseback, much in the same manner as the composite recurve bow presumably developed from earlier bows. 16th-century Dragoons and Carabiniers were heavier cavalry equipped only with firearms, but pistols coexisted with the composite bow, often used by the same rider, well into the 17th century in Eastern European cavalry such as Muscovites, Kalmyks, Turks and Cossacks. Mounted archery remained an effective tactical system in open country until the introduction of repeating firearms. It has been proposed that firearms began to replace bows in Europe and Russia not because firearms were superior but because they were easier to use and required less practice.*[12] The Comanches of North America found their bows more effective than muzzle loading guns. "After... about 1800, most Comanches began to discard muskets and pistols and to rely on their older weapons."*[13] Bows were still used in the fighting that ended the freedom of Native Americans in the United States, but almost all warriors who had immediate access to modern repeating firearms used these guns instead.

1.13.3 Technology

See also: Composite bow and Domestication of the horse

The weapon of choice for Eurasian horse archers was most commonly a composite recurve bow, because it was compact enough to shoot conveniently from a horse while retaining sufficient range and penetrating power. North Americans used short wooden bows often backed with sinew, but never developed the full three-layer composite bow.

1.13.4 Modern revival of mounted archery

Mounted archery and associated skills were revived in Mongolia after independence in 1921 and are displayed at festivals, in particular the Naadam.*[14] Despite the formidable history of Mongolian horse archers, the sport is very limited in Mongolia itself today and at most Naadam festivals the archery and horse-riding competitions are conducted independently; the horses are raced with one another, and the archery is traditionally practiced from a standing position rather than mounted. In the past five years a desire to revive the tradition seems to have been addressed with the foundation of the Mongolian Horseback Archery Association whose members have competed in South Korea and Europe.

1.13.5 Chinese mounted archery

Main article: Chinese_archery § Modern_reconstruction_and_revival

Mathematics, calligraphy, literature, equestrianism,

Wall fragment from a Chinese tomb, with an incised relief decoration showing a hunting scene with mounted archery, Han dynasty (202 BC - 220 AD) National Museum of Oriental Art, Rome

archery, music, and rites were the Six Arts.*[15]

At the Guozijian, law, mathematics, calligraphy, equestrianism, and archery were emphasized by the Ming dynasty Hongwu Emperor in addition to Confucian classics and also required in the Imperial Examinations.*[16]*[17]*[18]*[19]*[20]*[21] Archery and equestrianism were added to the exam by Hongwu in 1370 like how archery and equestrianism were required for non-military officials at the 武舉 College of War in 1162 by the Song Emperor Xiaozong.*[22] The area around the Meridian Gate of Nanjing was used for archery by guards and generals under Hongwu.*[23]

The Imperial exam included archery. Archery on horseback was practiced by Chinese living near the frontier. Wang Ju's writings on archery were followed during the Ming and Yuan and the Ming developed new methods of archery.*[17] Jinling Tuyong showed archery in Nanjing during the Ming.*[24] Contests in archery were held in the capital for Garrison of Guard soldiers who were handpicked.*[25]

Equestrianism and archery were favored activities of Zhu Di (the Yongle Emperor).*[26]

Archery and equestrianism were frequent pastimes by the Zhengde Emperor.*[27] He practiced archery and horseriding with eunuchs.*[28] Tibetan Buddhist monks, Muslim women and musicians were obtained and provided to

Zhengde by his guard Ch'ien Ning, who acquainted him with the ambidextrous archer and military officer Chiang Pin.*[29] An accomplished military commander and archer was demoted to commoner status on a wrongful charge of treason was the Prince of Lu's grandson in 1514.*[30]

He was disinterested in military matters but had prowess in archery (Hongxi Emperor).*[31]

Archery competitions, equestrianism and calligraphy were some of the pastimes of Wanli Emperor.*[32]

Football and archery were practiced by the Ming Emperors.*[33]*[34]

1.13.6 Traditional Korean school

Korea has a tradition of horseback archery. In 2007, the Korean government passed a law to preserve and encourage development of traditional Korean martial arts, including horseback archery.

In Korean archery competitions there are five disciplines that are competed separately. The major difference in Korean archery is that all arrows must be stowed somewhere on the archer or horse, unlike Hungarian style where the archer can take the arrows from the bow hand. Traditionally this is a quiver on the right thigh, but it may also be through a belt, a sash, a saddle quiver or even held in a boot or arm quiver.

The first competition is a single shot to the side. The track is 90 metres (300 ft) long (as in the Hungarian method) but carries only one target set back around 5–10m from the track. This has a unique fascia that consists of five square concentric rings which increase in point score from the outer to inner; the inner (often decorated with a 'Tiger' face) is worth the maximum five points. Each archer has two passes to complete, and each run has to be completed within 16 seconds (or penalty points are incurred).

The next competition is very similar but is known as the *double shot* which features one target in the first 30m, slightly angled forwards, and a second target in the last 30m, slightly angled backwards.

The final competition for the static targets is the *serial shot* which consists of five targets evenly spaced along a 110 metres (360 ft) track, approximately one target every 20 metres (66 ft) or so. In all three static target competitions, additional bonus points are awarded for style and form.*[35]

Another major difference in Korean archery style is the *Mogu*, or moving target competition. This consists of one rider towing a large cotton-and-bamboo ball behind their horse while another archer attempts to shoot the ball (with special turnip-headed arrows which have been dipped in ink). The archer attempts to hit the ball as many times as possible. A second *Mo Gu* event consists of a team of two trying to hit the target towed by a third rider. Points are awarded for how many arrows strike the ball (verified by the ink stains on the Mogu).

1.13.7 Traditional Japanese horseback archery

Main article: Yabusame

The history of Japanese horseback archery dates back to

Yabusame archer on horseback

the 4th century.*[36] It became popular in Japan, attracting crowds. The emperor found that the crowds were not appropriate to the solemn and sacred nature of the occasion, and banned public displays in 698.*[37] Horseback archery was a widely used combat technique from the Heian Period to the Warring States Period.*[38] Nasu no Yoichi, a samurai of the Kamakura Period is the most famous horseback archer in Japan. Three kinds of Japanese horseback archery (Kasagake, Yabusame, and Inuoumono (dog shooting)) were defined.

When the arquebus was introduced by the Portuguese to Japan in the 16th century, archery became outdated. To maintain traditional Japanese horseback archery, Tokugawa Yoshimune, the shogun, ordered the Ogasawara clan to found a school. Current Japanese horseback archery succeeds to the technique reformed by the Ogasawara clan.

Traditionally, women were barred from performing in yabusame, but in 1963 female archers participated in a yabusame demonstration for the first time.*[39]

The Yabusame school of horseback archery has found a following in Australia, with the setting up of the Australian Horse Archery School which today conducts public shows in various parts of the world.

1.13.8 Mounted archery in the United States

Mounted archery is a growing sport in the United States, as well. Through the efforts of The Mounted Archery Association of the Americas, there are horseback archery clubs around the country. Competitive courses one might find in the U.S. incorporate the Korean, Hungarian and Persian Styles (i.e., the Qabaq). Participants combine the skills of an archer with the skills of a good rider to create this beautiful equestrian sport. Emphasis on care and training of the horse is evident as riders run reinless down a 90-meter course while loosing arrows at various target arrangements. Surprisingly, as challenging as the sport appears to be, many who have never picked up a bow can achieve great success with some courage and a little practice. MA3 Clubs around the country offer members the opportunity to learn the sport by providing ranges, a ranking system, and competitions.

1.13.9 Horseback Archery in the United Kingdom

The National Horseback Archery Society*[40] is based at The Centre of Horseback Combat in Gaddesden in Hertfordshire. It is the governing body of horseback archery in the U.K.*[41]*[42]

The British Horseback Archery Association was established in 2007, and its first national competition took place in 2010.*[43]*[44] Since 2013, members have represented Great Britain in international team competitions*[45]*[46] Postal matches are also held with participants from across the UK. Categories for disabled riders and for juniors have also been introduced.

1.13.10 See also

- Archery
- Camel archer
- Cataphract
- Composite bow
- Eurasian nomads
- Horse people
- Horses in East Asian warfare
- Hungarian bow
- Mongol bow
- Nomadic empires
- Parthian shot
- Recurve bow
- Sagittarii
- Turkish bow
- Yabusame

1.13.11 References

[1] T. R. Fehrenbach. Comanches, the history of a people. Vintage Books. London, 2007. ISBN 978-0-09-952055-9. First published in the USA by Alfred Knopf, 1974. Page 124.

[2] Comanche Indians Chasing Buffalo with Lances and Bows. George Catlin 1846-1848. Western Landscape

[3] Carter, Captain R. G. On the border with Mackenzie, or Winning West Texas from the Comanches. p 289-290. New York, Antiquarian Press, 1961 (First published 1935). As quoted in Los Comanches. The Horse People, 1751-1845. Stanley Noyes. University of New Mexico Press, Albuquerque. 1993 ISBN 0-82631459-7 p. 221-222.

[4] T.R. Fehrenbach. Comanches, the history of a people. Vintage Books. London, 2007. ISBN 978-0-09-952055-9. First published in the USA by Alfred Knopf, 1974.

[5] http://www.luc.edu/faculty/ldossey/Herodotus.htm

[6] Ashley. p. 35.

[7] Jeffrey L. Davies: *Roman Arrowheads from Dinorben and the 'Sagittarii' of the Roman Army*, Britannia, Vol. 8. (1977), pp. 257-270

[8] R.C. Small: Crusading Warfare 1097-1193, pp. 111-112, ISBN 978-0-521-48029-1

[9] Heath, Ian. *Armies of Feudal Europe 1066-1300*. Wargames Research Group; 2nd Revised edition edition (Sept. 1989). p. 165. ISBN 978-0904417432

[10] Payne-Gallwey, Ralph. *The Crossbow: Its Military and Sporting History, Construction and Use.* Skyhorse Publishing; First Edition edition (April 1, 2007). ISBN 978-1602390102

[11] Dezobry and Bachelet, *Dictionary of Biography*, t.1, Ch.Delagrave, 1876, p. 704

[12] Donald Ostrowski, "The Replacement of the Composite Reflex Bow by Firearms in the Muscovite Cavalry," Kritika: Explorations in Russian and Eurasian History 11, no. 3 (2010): 513-534

[13] T.R. Fehrenbach. Comanches, the history of a people. Vintage Books. London, 2007. ISBN 978-0-09-952055-9. First published in the USA by Alfred Knopf, 1974. Page 125.

[14] http://www.atarn.org/mongolian/mn_nat_arch/mn_nat_arch.htm Mongolian National Archery by Munkhtsetseg.

[15] Zhidong Hao (1 February 2012). *Intellectuals at a Crossroads: The Changing Politics of China's Knowledge Workers.* SUNY Press. pp. 37–. ISBN 978-0-7914-8757-0.

[16] Frederick W. Mote; Denis Twitchett (26 February 1988). *The Cambridge History of China: Volume 7, The Ming Dynasty, 1368-1644.* Cambridge University Press. pp. 122–. ISBN 978-0-521-24332-2.

[17] Stephen Selby (1 January 2000). *Chinese Archery.* Hong Kong University Press. pp. 267–. ISBN 978-962-209-501-4.

[18] Edward L. Farmer (1995). *Zhu Yuanzhang and Early Ming Legislation: The Reordering of Chinese Society Following the Era of Mongol Rule.* BRILL. pp. 59–. ISBN 90-04-10391-0.

[19] Sarah Schneewind (2006). *Community Schools and the State in Ming China.* Stanford University Press. pp. 54–. ISBN 978-0-8047-5174-2.

[20] http://www.san.beck.org/3-7-MingEmpire.html

[21] http://www.atarn.org/training/chinese_archery_bckgrnd.htm

[22] Lo Jung-pang (1 January 2012). *China as a Sea Power, 1127-1368: A Preliminary Survey of the Maritime Expansion and Naval Exploits of the Chinese People During the Southern Song and Yuan Periods.* NUS Press. pp. 103–. ISBN 978-9971-69-505-7.

[23] http://en.dpm.org.cn/EXPLORE/ming-qing/

[24] Si-yen Fei (2009). *Negotiating Urban Space: Urbanization and Late Ming Nanjing.* Harvard University Press. pp. x–. ISBN 978-0-674-03561-4.

[25] Foon Ming Liew (1 January 1998). *The Treatises on Military Affairs of the Ming Dynastic History (1368-1644): An Annotated Translation of the Treatises on Military Affairs, Chapter 89 and Chapter 90: Supplemented by the Treatises on Military Affairs of the Draft of the Ming Dynastic History: A Documentation of Ming-Qing Historiography and the Decline and Fall of.* Ges.f. Natur-e.V. p. 243. ISBN 978-3-928463-64-5.

[26] Shih-shan Henry Tsai (1 July 2011). *Perpetual happiness: the Ming emperor Yongle.* University of Washington Press. pp. 23–. ISBN 978-0-295-80022-6.

[27] Frederick W. Mote; Denis Twitchett (26 February 1988). *The Cambridge History of China: Volume 7, The Ming Dynasty, 1368-1644.* Cambridge University Press. pp. 403–. ISBN 978-0-521-24332-2.

[28] Frederick W. Mote; Denis Twitchett (26 February 1988). *The Cambridge History of China: Volume 7, The Ming Dynasty, 1368-1644.* Cambridge University Press. pp. 404–. ISBN 978-0-521-24332-2.

[29] Frederick W. Mote; Denis Twitchett (26 February 1988). *The Cambridge History of China: Volume 7, The Ming Dynasty, 1368-1644.* Cambridge University Press. pp. 414–. ISBN 978-0-521-24332-2.

[30] Frederick W. Mote; Denis Twitchett (26 February 1988). *The Cambridge History of China: Volume 7, The Ming Dynasty, 1368-1644.* Cambridge University Press. pp. 425–. ISBN 978-0-521-24332-2.

[31] Frederick W. Mote; Denis Twitchett (26 February 1988). *The Cambridge History of China: Volume 7, The Ming Dynasty, 1368-1644.* Cambridge University Press. pp. 277–. ISBN 978-0-521-24332-2.

[32] Frederick W. Mote; Denis Twitchett (26 February 1988). *The Cambridge History of China: Volume 7, The Ming Dynasty, 1368-1644.* Cambridge University Press. pp. 514–. ISBN 978-0-521-24332-2.

[33] https://blog.britishmuseum.org/category/exhibitions/ming-50-years-that-changed-china/

[34] https://www.theguardian.com/artanddesign/2014/aug/24/ming-british-museum-empire-strikes-back-50-years-changed-china

[35] For a pictorial presentation, see: Korean track

[36] Nihon Shoki volume 14 "大泊瀬天皇 彎弓驟馬 (horseback archery) 而陽呼日猪有即射殺市邊押磐皇子皇子帳内佐伯部賣輪"

[37] Shoku Nihongi volume 1 " 禁山背國賀茂祭日會衆騎射 (horseback archery)"

[38] Turnbull S. The samurai, a military history. Page 19 "At this time [about 1000 CE] the bow was the most important weapon and the mark of the samurai... The samurai was essentially a mounted archer."

[39] Kishagasa, by Alice Gordenker. Japan Times Tuesday, May 16, 2006. http://search.japantimes.co.jp/cgi-bin/ek20060516wh.html

[40] "NHAS". *www.horsebackcombat.co.uk*. Retrieved 2017-06-14.

[41] "Gaddesden Estate: equestrian centre of Hertfordshire". *Hertfordshire*. Retrieved 2017-06-14.

[42] "NHAS". *www.horsebackcombat.co.uk*. Retrieved 2017-06-14.

[43] "The 2010 BHAA Championships". 2011-05-13. Retrieved 2017-06-14.

[44] Sawyer, Claire. "BHAA championships". *www.bhaa.org.uk*. Retrieved 2016-09-20.

[45] Sawyer, Claire. "international match report 13". *www.bhaa.org.uk*. Retrieved 2016-09-20.

[46] "horseback archery competition | Cotteswold Mounted Archers". *www.mountedarchery.org.uk*. Retrieved 2016-09-20.

1.13.12 Further reading

- Schreiner, Robert. "Horseback Archery New Zealand". Retrieved 2005-04-30.

1.13.13 External links

- Australian Horse Archery Association
- Horseback Archery in Belgium
- Chinese Horseback archery
- Finnish horseback archery union - Suomen Ratsastusjousiampujain Liitto ry
- German mounted Archery Site
- Polish Horseback Archery Association
- United Kingdom national horseback combat society
- British Horseback Archery Association
- Mounted Archery in USA
- Mounted Archery Of The Americas

Rahotep, a superintendent of the military, and military supplies, including archers–(Note Archer hieroglyph, and quiver hieroglyph). (Superintendent-(overseer): is 'Emir', represented by the Owl above mouth hieroglyphs, for "m-r", 'emeer'.)

1.14 Pítati

The ***Pítati*** (*pí-ta-ti*) were a contingent of archers of ancient Egypt that were often requested and dispatched to support Egyptian vassals in Canaan. They are recorded in the correspondence of the 1350 BC Amarna letters, and were often requested to defend against the Habiru, also rogue vassal-kings and foreign troops of neighboring kingdoms (for example, Hatti), who were on the attack.

The vassal cities and "city-states" were constantly requesting the services-(protection) of the Pharaoh's armies, by means of this "archer-army" force, basically garrison forces. A request for lodging, and preparations of food, drink, straw, and other supplies required,[*][1] is often demanded by the pharaoh, for a small, or a large contingent.

The pítati archer force were mercenaries from the southern Egyptian "land of Kush"-(named *Kaša*, or *Kaši* in the letters).

The first use of Nubian mercenaries was by Weni of the Sixth Dynasty of Egypt during the Old Kingdom of Egypt, about 2300 BC.

1.14.1 A letter example--no. 337

A vassal–state letter example from Hiziru, a "mayor", often referred to as the "Man (Lugal) of the City", in ancient Palestine is EA 337, entitled "Abundant supplies ready". The letter is short and undamaged:

> Say to the king, my lord, my Sun, my god: Message of Hiziru, your servant. I fall at the feet of the king, my lord, 7 times and 7 times. The

king, my lord, wrote to me, "Prepare the supplies before the arrival of a large army of *pí-ta-ti* of the king, [m]y l[ord]." May the god of the king, my lord, grant that the king, my lord, come forth along with his large army and learn about his lands. I have indeed prepared accordingly abundant supplies before the arrival of a large army of the king, my lord.

The king, my lord, wrote to me, "Guard Maya," the commissioner of the king, my lord. Truly. I guard Maya very carefully. -EA 337, lines 1-30 (complete)

1.14.2 "Archers and myrrh"

Letter no. 3 of 5 by Milkilu of Gazru (modern Gezer):

Say to the god, my king, my lord, my Sun: Message of Milkilu, your servant, the dirt at your feet. I fall at the feet of the god, my king, my lord, my Sun, 7 times and 7 times. I have heard what the king, my lord, wrote to me, and so may the king, my lord, send the *archers* to his servants, and may the king, my lord send myrrh for medication. -EA 269, lines 1-17 (complete)

1.14.3 Analysis

Part of the debate in analyzing the army-archer-force is whether the army just annually accompanied the pharaoh's commissioner or envoy and were then extracting tribute, or whether the archer-force duty was strictly military, and in support of the Egyptian borderlands control and influence. The short time period of the Amarna letters, 15–20 years, (17?), may give an answer to the influence of the archer-forces.

1.14.4 See also

- Letters from Yidya, (EA 325)

1.14.5 References

[1] Moran, William L., 1992. *The Amarna Letters*, p. 352-353. *EA 325*: Title: (from, Man of the City: Yidya): *Preparations completed, (2),*
"...indeed prepared absolutely everything —food, strong drink, oxen, 'sheep and goats', grain, straw, absolutely everything that the king, my lord, commanded."

- Moran, William L., 1992. *The Amarna Letters.* Johns Hopkins University Press, 1987, 1992. (softcover, ISBN 0-8018-6715-0)

1.15 Scorton Arrow

The **Antient Scorton Silver Arrow**[1] is an archery tournament that was incepted on Sunday 14 May 1673 in the village of Scorton in Yorkshire, England. Twenty-two archers competed in the first event for the prize of a silver arrow. This was won by Henry Calverley of Eryholme on Tees, who had provided the trophy. The event proved so successful that a new organisation, the Society of Archers, was formed to hold the event on an annual basis.

Participants shoot at targets at a range of 100 yards. The target face is a standard four-foot (122 cm) five-colour face, with the addition of a three-inch black spot at the centre. The winner is the first person to hit the black spot. The winner is appointed Captain of the Arrow. The first person to hit the red zone is appointed Lieutenant of the Arrow.

The winner is presented with a replica of the original silver arrow, which he keeps for a year. The original silver arrow is held at the Royal Armouries Museum in Leeds.

The event is open to men aged 21 years or over, using hand bows other than compound bows. A similar event for women, the Ascham Silver Arrow, was introduced in 1976.[2]

The event normally takes place annually, but postponements and cancellations have occurred. In the 336 years to 2008, 300 meetings have taken place.[3]

The event has been held at many places in Yorkshire, since the organising of the event for one year is the responsibility of the person who became Captain of the Arrow in the previous year (assisted by the Lieutenant of the Arrow). The first event was held at the village of Scorton in Yorkshire, and the event has returned to Scorton on 14 occasions. The 2008 event, which was the 300th meeting, was also held in Scorton.

The Antient Scorton Silver Arrow claims to be the oldest sporting event still running. Several other sporting events claim to have been running for longer than the Antient Scorton Silver Arrow, notably the Papingo shoot at Kilwinning[4] and the Kiplingcotes Derby Horserace.[5] They may well be correct, but reliable records of these events do not go back as far as those of the Scorton Arrow.

1.15.1 References

[1] Scorton Arrow

[2] Ascham Silver Arrow

[3] "Aim of the game". The Harrogate Advertiser. 23 May 2008. Retrieved 2008-08-08.

[4] Ancient Society of Kilwinning Archers

[5] The Kiplingcotes Derby

1.16 Shooting an apple off one's child's head

William Tell's apple-shot as depicted in Sebastian Münster's Cosmographia *(1554 edition).*

Shooting an apple off one's child's head, also known as **apple-shot** (from German *Apfelschuss*) is a feat of marksmanship with a bow or crossbow that occurs as a motif in a number of legends in Germanic folklore (and has been connected with non-European folklore). In the Stith Thompson Motif Index it is F661.3, described as "Skillful marksman shoots apple from man's head" or "apple shot from man's head",*[1] though it always occurs in the form of the marksman being ordered to shoot an apple (or occasionally another smaller object) off his own son's head. It is best known as William Tell's feat.*[2]

1.16.1 Examples

Palnatoki

The earliest known occurrence of the motif is from the 12th century, in Saxo Grammaticus' version of the story of Palnatoki, whom he calls *Toko* (*Gesta Danorum* Book 10, chapter 7).

> Toko, who had been for some time in the service of the king [Harald Bluetooth], had, by the deeds in which he surpassed his fellow-soldiers, made several enemies of his virtues. One day, when he had drunk rather much, he boasted to those who were at table with him, that his skill in archery was such that he could hit, with the first shot of an arrow, ever so small an apple set on the top of a wand at a considerable distance. His detractors hearing these words, lost no time in conveying them to the ears of the king. But the wickedness of the prince speedily conveyed the confidence of the father to the peril of the son, ordering the sweetest pledge of his life to stand instead of the wand, from whom, if the utterer of the boast did not strike down the apple which was placed on him at the first shot of his arrow, he should with his own head pay the penalty of his idle boast. . . . When the youth was led forth, Toko carefully admonished him to receive the whiz of the coming arrow as steadily as possible, with attentive ears, and without moving his head, lest by a slight motion of his body he should frustrate the experience of his well-tried skill. He made him also, as a means of diminishing his apprehension, stand with his back to him, lest he should be terrified at the sight of the arrow. He then drew three arrows from his quiver, and the first he shot struck the proposed mark. Toko then being asked by the king why he had taken so many arrows out of his quiver, when he was to make but one trial with the bow, "That I might avenge on thee," said he, "the error of the first by the points of the others, lest my innocence might hap to be afflicted and thy injustice to go unpunished!"*[3]

Palnatoki later kills the king.

Þiðrekssaga

In the 13th-century *Þiðrekssaga*,*[4] chapter 128, Egill, brother of Völund, is commanded by King Nidung to shoot an apple off his three-year-old son's head:

> Now the king wished to try whether Egill shot so well as was said or not, so he let Egill's son, a

boy of three years old, be taken, and made them put an apple on his head, and bade Egill shoot so that the shaft struck neither above the head nor to the left nor the right.[*][5]

Like Palnatoki, he keeps two more arrows to kill the king in case he fails, but the king does not punish him for saying so, but rather praises him: "The king took that well from him, and all thought it was boldly spoken."

William Tell

The best-known version of the story is in the legend of William Tell, told first in the 15th-century *White Book of Sarnen*, then in Aegidius Tschudi's 16th-century *Chronicon Helveticum*, and later the basis for Friedrich Schiller's 1804 play. Tell is arrested for failing to bow in respect to the hat that the newly appointed Austrian *Vogt*, Albrecht Gessler, has placed on a pole, and Gessler commands him to shoot an apple off his son's head with a single bolt from his crossbow. After splitting the apple with the single shot (supposedly on November 18, 1307), Tell is asked why he took more than one bolt out; at first he responds that it was out of habit, but when assured he will not be killed for answering honestly, says the second bolt was meant for Gessler's heart should he fail. In Schiller's play, the demand to shoot the apple off the boy's head motivates Gessler's murder.

Malleus Maleficarum

In Heinrich Kramer's 1486 *Malleus Maleficarum* (Book 2, chapter 16), a related story occurs: Punker of Rohrbach (also spelled Puncker or Puncher) in the Upper Rhineland is said to have been ordered by "a very eminent person" in about 1430 to prove his extraordinary marksmanship (regarded by Kramer as a sign of consorting with the devil) by shooting a penny off the cap on his young son's head without disturbing the cap. He, too, kept a second arrow in reserve to kill the prince in case he failed.[*][6][*][7]

Henning Wulf

Henning Wulf, or von Wulfen, of Wewelsfleth in Holstein sided with Count Gerhard in 1472 and was banished by King Christian I of Denmark. In a folk tale, the king had him shoot an apple off his son's head, and a window in the Wewelsfleth church depicted the boy with an apple on his head, pierced through by the arrow, while Henning's bow was undrawn but there was another arrow between his teeth. Between archer and boy there was a wolf.[*][8][*][9][*][10]

William of Cloudeslee

In the Northumbrian ballad of *Adam Bell, Clym of the Clough, and Wyllyam of Cloudeslee*, which was a source of Walter Scott's *Ivanhoe*, William of Cloudeslee tells the king he will put an apple on his seven-year-old son's head and shoot it off at 120 paces:[*][11]

> I have a sonne seven years old;
>
> Hee is to me full deere;
> I will tye him to a stake—
> All shall see him that bee here—
> And lay an apple upon his head,
> And goe six [score] paces him froe,
> And I myself with a broad arrowe
>
> Shall cleave the apple in towe.[*][12][*][13]

1.16.2 Related stories

Hemingr Áslákson

In *Hemings þáttr Áslákssonar* in the *Orkneyinga saga* (about 1200), Harald Hardrada challenges the archer Hemingr to shoot a hazelnut off his younger brother Björn's head, which he does.[*][11][*][14] There are two versions of this *þáttr*, one set in the Faroes, and in one Hemingr uses a spear to achieve the feat, rather than an arrow.[*][15] Hemingr later takes revenge by shooting the king dead at the Battle of Stamford Bridge.[*][16] There are also Norwegian and Faroese ballads on *Hemingen unge*.[*][9]

Eindriði Pansa

One related story turns the motif on its head: after matching him in swimming and in other shooting contests, King Olaf of Norway converted Eindriði Pansa (the Splay-Footed) from heathenry by shooting at either a chess piece or a writing tablet on Eindriði's son's head. The king's shot narrowly missed but the boy was unharmed; Eindriði gave in to his mother's and sister's pleas and did not try the feat himself.[*][17][*][18][*][19]

1.16.3 Scholarly study

The motif was studied and written about as early as 1760 by Gottlieb Emmanuel von Haller and the pastor Simeon Uriel Freudenberger in a pamphlet in French and German with the title *Der Wilhelm Tell, ein dänisches Mährgen* (William

Tell, a Danish Fable).*[20] During the 19th century, several scholars wrote about the internationalism of the motif. In 1834 Thomas Keightley noted the similarities between Palnatoki's and Tell's stories.*[21] There is a summary of the various versions in Jacob Grimm's *Teutonic Mythology*,*[22] and another in John Fiske's *Myths and Myth-Makers*.*[23] The most detailed precedes Child's edition of the ballad of "Adam Bell, Clim of the Clough, and William of Cloudesly." *[24]

In an 1877 book on the historicity of the William Tell legend, Ernst Ludwig Rochholz connects the similarity of the Tell legend to the stories of Egil and Palnatoki with legends of a migration from Sweden to Switzerland during the Middle Ages.*[25] He also adduces parallels in folktales among the Finns and the Lapps (Sami), and also from Norse mythology compares Ullr, called the "bow-god", Heimdall, and also Óðinn, who according to the *Gesta Danorum* Book 1, chapter 8.16, is said to have assisted Haddingus by shooting ten arrows from a crossbow in one shot, killing as many foes.*[26]*[27] Further comparing Indo-European and Oriental traditions, Rochholz concludes that the legend of the master marksman shooting an apple (or similar small target) was known outside the Germanic sphere and the adjacent regions (Finland and the Baltic) in India, Arabia, Persia and the Balkans (Serbia).*[28]

1.16.4 See also

- Freischutz
- Death of Joan Vollmer

1.16.5 References

[1] Stith Thompson, *Motif-Index of Folk-Literature: Index A-K : A Classification of Narrative Elements in Folktales, Ballads, Myths, Fables, Mediaeval Romances, Exempla, Fabliaux, Jest-Books, and Local Legends*, repr. Bloomington, Indiana: Indiana University Press, 2001, ISBN 0-253-34089-6, pp. 29, "apple," 368, "head".

[2] Stith Thompson, p. 783: "Tell shoots apple from son's head."

[3] Translation from Thomas Keightley, *Tales and Popular Fictions: Their Resemblance and Transmission from Country to Country*, London: Whittaker, 1834, OCLC 457836365, pp. 293–94. For a fuller version see George Webbe Dasent, *Popular Tales from the Norse*, 3rd ed. Edinburgh: Douglas, 1888, repr. BiblioBazaar 2005, ISBN 978-1-113-45357-0, pp. 403–04, note 5.

[4] Called *Vilkina saga* by many scholars writing on the motif

[5] Dasent, p. 404, note 5.

[6] pp. 150–51.

[7] Dasent, p. 404, note 5.

[8] Karl Müllenhoff, *Sagen, Märchen und Lieder der herzogtümer Schleswig, Holstein und Lauenburg*, revised ed. Otto Mensing, Schleswig: Bergas, 1921, OCLC 804563, p. 58. (in German)

[9] Francis James Child, *The English and Scottish Popular Ballads*, Volume 3, Boston: Houghton Mifflin, 1888, p. 17.

[10] Jacob Grimm, *Teutonic Mythology*, 4th ed. tr. James Steven Stallybrass, vol. 1, London: Bell, 1882, p. 381 calls him Hemming Wolf.

[11] Grimm, p. 382.

[12] John Fiske, *Myths and Myth-Makers: Old Tales and Superstitions Interpreted by Comparative Mythology*, London: Trübner, 1873; Boston: Houghton Mifflin, 1900, repr. BiblioLife, 2009, ISBN 1-110-87842-7, p. 5.

[13] Child, p. 29.

[14] Saxo Grammaticus, *Danorum regum heroumque historia books x–xvi: the text of the first edition with translation and commentary in three volumes*, ed. Eric Christiansen, Oxford: B.A.R., 1980–81, ISBN 0-86054-097-9, p. 172, note 43.

[15] Ebenezer Cobham Brewer and Marion Harland, *Character Sketches of Romance, Fiction and the Drama* volume 7, p. 84.

[16] *Orkneyinga saga and Magnus saga, with appendices*, ed. Gudbrand Vigfusson and Sir George Dasent, The Rolls Series Icelandic Sagas vol. 1, 1887, p. xvi: "The Tale of Heming . . . is a mixture of the legend of Tell-Egill and the traditional account of the battle of Stamford Bridge, derived from the Kings' Lives. . . . The link binding the Archer story to the other is the arrow with which Heming slays the king, his foe, in revenge for his wrongs." The þáttr is Appendix C, pp. 347–87, in this edition.

[17] Grimm, p. 381 – writing tablet.

[18] "Editor's Easy Chair," *Harper's new monthly magazine*, Volume 58, Issues 343–348, 1879, p. 461 – chess piece.

[19] Brewer and Harland, pp. 83–84, say that this was also an apple, and that Eindriði then shot himself, successfully hitting the apple without harming the boy.

[20] Jean-François Bergier, *Wilhelm Tell: Realität und Mythos*, Munich: List, 1990, pp. 80-81. (in German)

[21] Keightley, p. 295: "In the year 1307, among the mountains of Helvetia, an action similar to this of Toko is said to have been performed; and it has given immortality to the name of William Tell"; in note 1 he adds *Vilkina Saga* (*Þiðrekssaga*), which he theorizes got the story from Saxo.

[22] Grimm, pp. 380–83.

[23] Fiske, pp. 3–6.

[24] Child, pp. 14–22.

[25] Ernst Ludwig Rochholz, *Tell und Gessler in Sage und Geschichte. Nach urkundlichen Quellen*, Heilbronn: Henninger, 1877, OCLC 2846953; reprinted BiblioBazaar, 2010, ISBN 978-1-143-29279-8; online at the Internet Archive (in German). Rochholz had published an article on the topic in 1869, "Tell als Zauberschütze"; see the list of publications in Joachim Meyer, *Schillers Wilhelm Tell auf seine Quellen zurückgeführt und sprachlich erläutert*, Nuremberg: Barbeck, 1876, OCLC 614817741, p. 47.

[26] Saxo Grammaticus, *The History of the Danes: Books I-IX*, ed. Hilda Ellis Davidson, tr. Peter Fisher, Cambridge: Brewer, 1979–80, repr. 1996, 1999, ISBN 0-85991-502-6, p. 31.

[27] As early as 1845, Kuhn connected William Tell with Robin Hood and Óðinn: Felix Adolph Korn Nork, *Andeutungen eines System der Mythologie entwickelt aus der priesterlichen Mysteriosophie und Hierologie des alten Orients*, Leipzig: Dyck, 1850, OCLC 26330879, p. 93 (in German).

[28] Rochholz, pp. 35–41.

1.16.6 Sources

- Helmut de Boor. "Die nordischen, englischen und deutschen Darstellungen des Apfelschussmotivs." *Quellenwerk zur Entstehung der schweizerischen Eidgenossenschaft*. III *Chroniken* III *Anhang* pp. 1–53. Aarau: Sauerländer, 1947. (in German)

- Roger E. Mitchell and Joyce P. Mitchell. "Schiller's William Tell: A Folkloristic Perspective." *Journal of American Folklore* 83 (1970) 44–52.

- Alan Dundes. "The Apple-Shot: Interpreting the Legend of William Tell." *Western Folklore* 50 (October 1991) 327–60. JSTOR. Reprinted in *From Game to War and Other Psychoanalytic Essays on Folklore*. Lexington, Kentucky: University Press of Kentucky, 1997. ISBN 0-8131-2031-4. pp. 46–77.

- *Hemings þáttr Áslákssonar: An edition of texts from Flateyjarbók, Hrokkinskinna and Hauksbók*. Ed. Gillian Fellows Jensen. Editiones Arnamagnæanæ series B. volume 3. Copenhagen: Munksgaard, 1962. OCLC 559417993.

- Th. Alwin. *Henning Wulf, der ditmarsische Tell*. Bonn: Heidelsmann, 1904. OCLC 250589189. (in German)

1.16.7 External links

- Adam Bell, Clim of the Clough and William of Cloudesly ballad text

1.17 Society of Archers

The Society of Archers [1] is an English archery organisation that was formed on Sunday 14 May 1673.

The purpose of the Society is to continue the annual Antient Scorton Silver Arrow tournament and preserve details of its entrants and winners. The Society was formed immediately following the first Antient Scorton Silver Arrow tournament.

Membership is obtained by entering the tournament and agreeing to abide by its rules. Entry to the tournament is restricted to men aged 21 years or over.

1.17.1 References

[1] The Society of Archers and the Antient Scorton Silver Arrow

1.18 St Mary's Butts

St Mary's Butts is a thoroughfare in the English town of Reading, Berkshire. On its west side is the Broad Street Mall. It is connected to the north with Broad Street, the pedestrianised primary high street of Reading. St Mary's Church and Butts are where the town of Reading originally grew from.[1]

To the south, St Mary's Butts reaches a cross-roads, where it meets Gun Street (the western continuation of Minster Street) to the east, Castle Street to the west, and Bridge Street to the south.

1.18.1 History

In the Middle Ages, Edward IV made it compulsory for all yeomen in England to learn archery. An archery butts was set up on the land in front of the Minster Church of St Mary the Virgin. It was used by the adult males of Reading to practice on Sundays. Some of the archers who fought at the Battle of Agincourt trained at St Mary's Butts. In 1631 the town paid £3 to have the archery grounds closed.[2][3] Located in the southern end is the Jubilee Fountain, erected in 1887 for Queen Victoria's Jubilee.[4]

1.18.2 References

[1] Phillips, Daphne (1980). *The Story of Reading*. Countryside Books. p. 32. ISBN 0-905392-07-8.

[2] "St Mary's Butts". Reading History Trail. Archived from the original on 17 January 2010. Retrieved 16 January 2015.

[3] Lambert, Tim. "A History of Reading, Berkshire". A World History Encyclopedia. Retrieved 20 April 2011.

[4] Phillips, Daphne (1980). *The Story of Reading*. Countryside Books. p. 136. ISBN 0-905392-07-8.

1.18.3 External links

Media related to St Mary's Butts at Wikimedia Commons

1.19 Stone wrist-guard

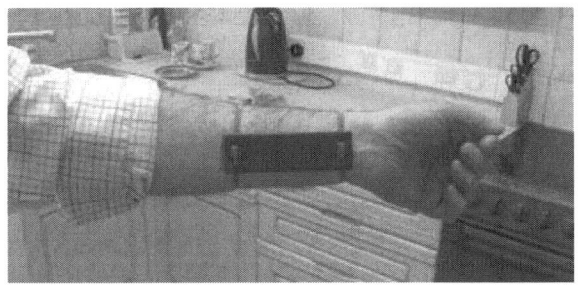

Replica of slate stone wrist-guard as it might have been worn.

Early Bronze Age **stone wrist-guards** are found across Europe from around 2400-1900 BC and are closely associated with the Beaker culture and Unetice culture. In the past they have been variously known as *stone bracers*, *stone arm-guards* and *armlets*, although "stone wrist-guard" is currently the favoured terminology;[1] and it's no longer thought that they were functional archer's bracers.[2]

1.19.1 Description

The wrist-guards are small rectangles of stone (often slate) with a number of perforations, typically between two and six, which might allow attachment to the arm with cord. One, from Hemp Knoll in Wiltshire, had markings which clearly indicate its attachment to the arm by two cords. The shapes of the wrist-guard are stereotyped and common forms exhibit a narrowed 'waist' and curved cross-section (presumably so they fit the arm better).

Stone wrist-guards are exclusively found in the graves of males, often lying next to the corpse's wrist. Rare examples - three in Great Britain - use rare imported greenstone and are decorated with gold-capped rivets or foil, clearly representing an elite form. The three British examples are from burials at Driffield, Barnack and Culduthel Mains in Scotland.

1.19.2 Original use

It was originally thought that these stone wrist-guards were bracers, used by archers to protect their bow arms from the string of the bow. However, recent research has highlighted that (in Britain at least) they do not commonly occur in graves in association with arrowheads (the Amesbury Archer being a notable exception), nor are they commonly found on the part of the arm that would need protection from the bowstring (on a right-handed archer, the inside left wrist).[3][4] They are usually found on the outside of the arm where they would have been more conspicuous. Many have only two holes which would make them difficult to fasten securely to the arm, and some have projecting rivets which would catch on the bowstring and make them unsuitable for use as a bracer.

When the objects occur in barrows, they always occur in the central primary grave, a place thought to be reserved for heads of family and other important people. Many show great skill in polishing and stone working, and few are found in areas from which their stone originates. It seems likely that, as found in graves, these objects were used as symbols of status within family groups. They may have been status symbols of prowess in hunting or war, possibly mounted as decorations on functional bracers. However, one at least (from Barnack in Cambridgeshire) had pressed foil caps in each of its 18 holes. These caps would have prohibited any form of rivet or cord being used as a means of attachment. A few prehistoric wrist-guards made of gold or amber have also been found; these are generally accepted not to be functional.[2]

Famous burials containing stone wrist-guards include the Amesbury Archer and Barnack Burial.

1.19.3 Terminology

The wrist-guards are commonly classified following either the 1970 Atkinson classification (cited in Clarke 1970) or the 2006 Smith classification. Of the two it is the 2006 Smith classification which is less rigid and more descriptive. It uses a three-character system to classify the objects on three simple characteristics:

Total number of perforations: (e.g. 2, 4, 6 etc.)

Shape in plan: described as-

- '**Waisted**', having a narrow midsection

- '**T**apered', having narrow ends
- '**S**traight-sided', having a rectangular plan

Shape in transverse cross-section: described as-

- '**C**urved', having a concavo-convex cross-section
- '**P**lano-**C**onvex', having a plano-convex cross-section, (i.e. one side flat and the other curved)
- '**F**lat', having a flat or slightly bi-convex cross-section

The most common types of wrist-guard are the 'tapered variety' consisting of **2TF**s, 'straight variety' consisting mainly of **4SF**s and **6SF**s and the 'waisted variety' consisting mainly of **4WC**s

This is how the 1970 Atkinson classification translates into the newer classificatory system:

A1 = 2TF

A2 = 2TF

B1 = 2SF

B2 = 4SF

B3 = 6SF

C1 = 4WC

C2 = 2WC

1.19.4 References

[1] Clarke, D.L. 1970. *Beaker Pottery of Great Britain and Ireland* (two volumes). Cambridge: Cambridge University Press

[2] "Bracers or Bracelets? About the Functionality and Meaning of Bell Beaker Wrist-guards", Harry Fokkens, Yvonne Achterkamp, and Maikel Kuijpers. Proceedings of the Prehistoric Society 2008 vol. 74 pp.109-149

[3] "Early Bronze Age Stone Wrist-Guards in Britain: archer's bracer or social symbol?", Smith, J. 2006

[4] Woodward, A., Hunter, J., Ixer, R., Roe, F., Potts, P.J., Webb, P.C., Watson, J.S. and Jones, M.C. 2006. "Beaker age bracers in England: sources, function and use" in *Antiquity* 80, p 530-543

1.20 The Archer's Craft

The Archer's Craft (ISBN 1-897853-80-7, first published in 1951) by A. E. Hodgkin is a book on the making and use of traditional English and Welsh bows. The book describes

First edition (publ. Faber)

how to make both longbows and short hunting bows and arrows. It also describes hunting with the bow and on its history and place in English culture of the yeoman class and royal mandates. It draws inspiration and often quotes from the 16th century *Toxophilus* written by Roger Ascham.

1.21 The Witchery of Archery

The Witchery of Archery, written by Maurice Thompson in 1878, was the first book in English about hunting with a bow ever published.*[1] Its full title is **The Witchery of Archery: A Complete Manual of Archery. With Many Chapters of Adventures by Field and Flood, and an Appendix Containing Practical Directions for the Manufacture and Use of Archery Implements**.*[2] It was the first important book about archery written in English since *Toxophilus*, which was written in 1545.*[3] It was said that *Witchery* "...has as much effect on archery as *Uncle Tom's Cabin* had on the Civil War.*[4]

1.21.1 Background

When Thompson wrote *The Witchery of Archery*, he filled it with various stories, many of which were humorous. However, it also gave practical advice on the sport, such as the

Front cover of The Witchery of Archery

manufacturing of archery paraphernalia and how to use the equipment while hunting.*[5]

The Witchery of Archery was accredited for returning the sport of archery to public interest. Some of this was due to rifles bringing back bad memories of the American Civil War.*[6] However, the revival also served some larger, pragmatic purpose: ex-Confederate soldiers were not allowed guns, but needed hunting to survive; archery became a convenient substitution. In addition, the late 1800s saw the last of the American Indian Wars, thus romanticizing the Native Americans and their cultures, which, in most accounts, included expert archery. In 1880, with the book less than two years old, patents relating to archery items greatly increased. More than any other book, *The Witchery of Archery* led to the increased interest in archery for the next half-century.*[7]

A year after *The Witchery of Archery* was published, Thompson was selected as the first president of the National Archery Association, largely due to the book.*[8]

A writer of several books, Thompson seemed to show little pride in writing *The Witchery of Archery*. On the title pages of his various works, he would list several titles he authored, but never did he list '"*The Witchery of Archery'.*[9]

1.21.2 See also

- History of archery

1.21.3 Notes

[1] Wegner p.227

[2] Thompson (front cover)

[3] Grayson p.239

[4] Allely p.13

[5] Wegner p.227

[6] Wegner p.227

[7] Wegner p.227

[8] Wegner p.227

[9] Flower p.717

1.21.4 References

- Allely, Steve (2007). *The Traditional Bowyer's Bible*. Globe Pequot. ISBN 1-58574-087-X.

- Flower, Benjamin (1897). *The Arena*. Arena.

- Grayson, Charles E. (2000). *Traditional Archery from Six Continents: The Charles E. Grayson Collection*. University of Missouri Press. ISBN 0-8262-1751-6.

- Thompson, Maurice (1878). *The Witchery of Archery*. C. Scribner's sons.

- *The Witchery of Archery*

- Wegner, Robert (1992). *Deer and Deer Hunting: The Serious Hunter's Guide*. Stackpole Books. ISBN 0-8117-2585-5.

1.22 Thumb ring

This article is about the protective archery equipment. For the ordinary jewelry items worn on the thumb, see Ring (jewelry).

A **thumb ring** is a piece of equipment designed to protect the thumb during archery. This is a ring of leather, stone, horn, wood, bone, antler, ivory, metal, ceramics, plastic, or glass which fits over the end of the thumb, coming to rest at the outer edge of the outer joint. Typically a flat area extends from the ring to protect the pad of the thumb from the bowstring; this may be supplemented by a leather extension.

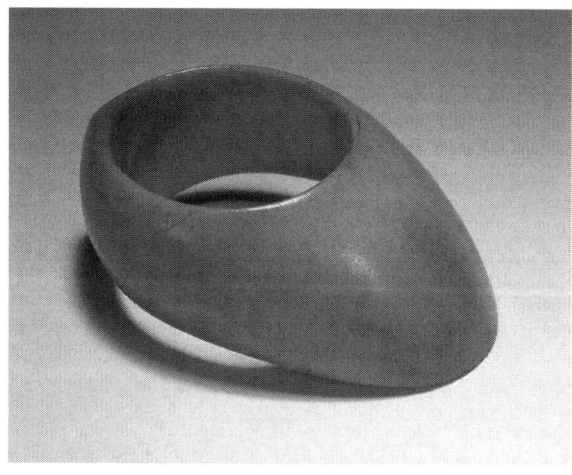

17th century Mughal thumb ring

1.22.1 Use

Tibetan archer using a cylindrical thumb ring, 1938

When drawing a bow using a thumb draw, the thumb is hooked around the bowstring just beneath the arrow and its grip reinforced with the first (sometimes second) finger. The bowstring rests against the inner pad of the archer's thumb and the thumb ring protects the skin. The bowstring rests against the flat of the ring when the bow is drawn. Today, thumb rings are used by archers practicing styles from most of Asia and some regions of northern Africa. Ishi, the "last wild American Indian", used a thumb draw, but no skin protection.

1.22.2 Historic specimens

Thumb rings have been in use in Asia since the Neolithic period. The first examples were likely made of leather, but artifacts made entirely of leather do not last thousands of years. Surviving artifact rings are made of bone, horn, or stone; presumably most would have incorporated a leather guard. Comparison with historical and modern rings shows little functional change over the millennia.*[1] In the cemetery of the small Rui state at Liangdaicun near Hancheng on the Yellow River (where it flows south between the provinces of Shaanxi and Shanxi), a Lord of Rui was interred in a tomb, M 27, dated to the eighth century BCE. His grave goods included two thumb rings, made of gold but of an entirely modern pattern.*[2]

The author of "Arab Archery" refers to rings as being usually made of leather.*[3] A "thumb tip" or "thumb ring" which is called "kustubān" by the Persian and "khayta 'ah" by the Arabs, consists of a ring or leather or some other material. It is worn over the right thumb, leaving the nail and knuckle exposed, and is use for the protection of the thumb against injuries which are usually caused by the string when it is drawn and released." *[4] Possibly, most ordinary archers historically used tabs of leather, much cheaper and easier to make, but such rings are not likely to survive. Metal thumb rings of silver or bronze were thought to be too inflexible in use, and thus were less accurate.

Many surviving historic thumbrings are hardstone carvings in jade and other gemstones, or are made of precious metal. Most are very practical but some have the release surface so ornamented as to be unusable. The rings could be displayed on a cord from the belt, or, in China, in a special box. In the 16th century court of the Ottoman Empire they had the extra function of being "used when executing disgraced officials to tighten a handkerchief wound round the throat" .*[5]

1.22.3 Variants

In territories of the Qing dynasty, Manchurian cylindrical thumb rings gradually displaced more thumb pad shaped thumb rings. These cylindrical thumb rings would go over the primary thumb joint, hooking the draw string around the base of the cylinder.

A cylindrical manchu thumbring. The thumb hole is typically round.

1.22.4 Gallery

-  Jade thumb ring, Mughal Empire, 17th century

- 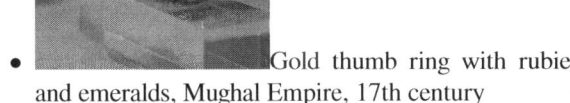 Gold thumb ring with rubies and emeralds, Mughal Empire, 17th century

- Three Indian thumb rings in agate and jade, 17th-19th century

- 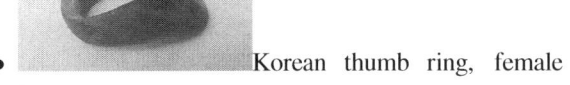 Korean thumb ring, female type

-  Korean thumb ring, male type

1.22.5 References

[1] http://www.atarn.org/chinese/thumbrings/archers_rings.htm

[2] Rawson, Jessica. *Steppe Weapons in Ancient China and the Role of Hand-to-hand Combat*. School of Archaeology. University of Oxford. p. 58 and fig. 18 page 91. Retrieved 7 February 2016.

[3] "Arab Archery. An Arabic manuscript of about A.D. 1500 "A book on the excellence of the bow & arrow" and the description thereof. Translated and edited by Nabih Amin Faris and Robert Potter Elmer" (PDF). Princeton University Press. 1945.

[4] "Chapter XLII. On thumb-tips and the various kind thereof."

[5] Rogers, J.M.; Ward, R.M. (1988). *Süleyman the Magnificent*. British Museum Publications. p. 152. ISBN 0-7141-1440-5.

1.22.6 External links

Media related to Archer's rings at Wikimedia Commons

- A collection of thumbrings at the University of Missouri Museum of Anthropology
- How do I use a Thumb-ring with a Mongolian Draw?
- Making a thumbring from a billiard ball
- Ancient Chinese thumb rings, Shang Dynasty to Han Dynasty
- On using cylindrical Chinese / Manchu style thumb rings
- - German language chinese archery site: Containing the kind, form, material and use of chinese / manchuraian thumb rings

1.23 Toxophilus

Toxophilus is a book about longbow archery by Roger Ascham, first published in London in 1545. Dedicated to King Henry VIII, it is the first book on archery written in English.

Henry VIII, the dedicatee of Toxophilus

Ascham was a keen archer and a lecturer at St John's College, Cambridge, and wrote *Toxophilus or the Schole or Partitions of Shooting* to defend archery against claims that it was a sport unbefitting a scholar.[*][1]

Toxophilus is written in the form of a dialogue between two characters, Philologus ("a lover of study") and Toxophilus ("a lover of the bow"), who is also a scholar and defends archery as a noble pastime.

Ascham prefixed his work with an elaborate dedication to Henry VIII, who approved of the book and granted Ascham a pension of £10 a year, which was confirmed and augmented by Edward VI.

1.23.1 Influence on English

As well as being the earliest printed book in English about archery, *Toxophilus* is also important as a model for how books of instruction could be written in English (rather than Latin) and how English could be written in a clear style, for as he remarks in his preface "To All Gentle Men and Yeomen of England": "Many English writers have not done so, but using strange words, as Latin, French, and Italian, do make all things dark and hard."

So, unlike other scholars writing in English at the time, such as Thomas Elyot and John Cheke, he avoided neologisms and flowery classical terms, and "succeeded in making his English work as a vehicle of wide communication ... Some of the passages describing the environment (for example, the way in which the wind could interfere with the aim of an expert archer) were vivid and at the time unparalleled in English writing."[*][2]

The word "Toxophilus" was invented by Ascham. The noun "toxophilite", meaning "a lover or devotee of archery, an archer", is derived from it.[*][3]

1.23.2 History of archery

The next major work on archery in English was *The Art of Archerie* by Gervase Markham, published in London in 1634.

Toxophilus has served as a source book for many subsequent works on the history of archery, for example *The Archer's Craft* by A. E. Hodgkin.[*][4]

1.23.3 Editions

- Ascham, Roger; ed. Arber, Edward (1868). *English Reprints: Toxophilus, 1545*. London: Murray.

- Ascham, Roger; ed. Wright, William Aldis (1904). *English Works: Toxophilus, Report of the Affaires and State of Germany, The Scholemaster*. Cambridge: Cambridge University Press.

1.23.4 See also

- 16th century in literature

1.23.5 References

[1] Rosemary O'Day, 'Ascham, Roger (1514/15–1568)', *Oxford Dictionary of National Biography*, Oxford University Press, 2004 accessed 8 March 2011

[2] Rosemary O'Day, 'Ascham, Roger (1514/15–1568)', *Oxford Dictionary of National Biography*, Oxford University Press, 2004 accessed 8 March 2011

[3] "imaginary proper name invented by Ascham, and hence title of his book (1545), intended to mean 'lover of the bow'." "toxophilite, n." *Oxford English Dictionary*. Second edition, 1989; online version November 2010. <http://www.oed.com:80/Entry/204131>; accessed 10 March 2011. Earlier version first published in *New English Dictionary*, 1913.

[4] Hodgkin, Adrian Eliot (1951). *The Archer's Craft*. London: Faber & Faber. ISBN 1-897853-80-7.

1.23.6 Further reading

- Hardy, Robert (2006). *Longbow: A Social and Military History*. Patrick Stephens Ltd. ISBN 978-1-85260-620-6.

- Ryan, L. V. (1963). *Roger Ascham*. Stanford University Press. ISBN 978-0-8047-0149-5.

1.23.7 External links

- *Toxophilus* - online text at the Archery Library

- Society of Archer-Antiquaries

1.24 Turkish archery

Turkish archery is a tradition of archery which became highly developed in the Ottoman Empire, although its origins date back to the Eurasian Steppe in the second millennium BC.

1.24.1 History

From the decline of military archery after the battle of Lepanto, mainly flight archery was practiced, and Turkish bowyers specialized in weapons which were particularly good for imparting high velocity to very light arrows. The sport of archery declined gradually until the reign of Mahmud II who made great efforts to revive it. He also ordered his archery student, Mustafa Kani, to write a book about the history, construction, and use of these bows, from which comes most of what is now known of Turkish bowyery.*[1] After the death of Mahmud II in 1839, archery resumed its decline. *[2] The living art of Turkish bowyery was lost in the 1930s with the death of the last bowyer and famous calligrapher, Neçmeddin Okyay; it has since been revived.*[3]

1.24.2 Equipment

Ottoman Horse Archer

Turkish Bow

The **Turkish bow** is a recurved composite bow used in the Ottoman Empire. The construction is similar to that of other classic Asiatic composite bows, with a wooden core (maple was most desirable), animal horn on the belly (the side facing the archer), and sinew on the front, with the layers secured together with Animal glue. However, several features of the Turkish bow are distinct. The curvature tends to be more extreme when the bow is unstrung, with the limbs curling forward into the shape of the letter "C" . With some bows, the rigid tips of the limbs ("kasan") even touch. The grip area is not recessed like other Asianic bows and is fairly flat on the belly, while the front of the grip bulges outwards.

The dramatic curvature of the bows makes stringing them very different from straighter bows found in Europe. There is an old saying in Turkey that there are "120 ways to string a bow," though the most common methods involve sitting on ground with one's feet pressed against the grip. Heavier bows usually require the use of a long, looped strap called a "kemend" to pull the limbs back and hold them while the string is seated.*[4]

For many years the excellence of Turkish bows could be

seen from historical records. In 1910 an archery contest was held on the beach at Le Touquet, France, where Ingo Simon was able to shoot an arrow 434 m using an old Turkish composite bow requiring a force of 440N or 99 lb.*[5]

Zihgir

Main article: Thumb ring

Zihgir is the Turkish word for the thumb ring used to draw the bow in the Ottoman Empire. Turkish thumb rings were made of wood, metal, ivory, bone, horn or leather. These rings signified that the person wearing them was a warrior. In time they became a symbol of prestige in Ottoman society, and some later examples have so much ornamentation on the surface from which the bowstring slides that they could not be used to shoot with. Surviving examples are often made of precious metals and richly decorated. Some are carved from precious stones.

Siper and Majra

The *siper* and *majra* are devices used to draw arrows past the bow's front limb where the arrow would normally rest. The siper is a type of shelf strapped to the archer's bow hand, which allows the archer to pull the bow back to extreme lengths in order to get the maximum amount of force behind the arrow. They are most commonly used for Flight Archery, to achieve the greatest distance. The Majra is a thin piece of wood with a channel cut in it and small loop for the archer's draw hand. The device allows the archer to pull back arrows that are much shorter than were intended for the bow. There is some debate among historians if this device was designed to shoot arrows that were too short for the enemy to pick up and shoot back, or if it was a way to reuse bolts fired by Chinese crossbowmen. In modern times they are primarily used in Flight Archery to shoot shorter arrows to cut down on weight.

1.24.3 Technique

Like many other Eastern archery styles, Turkish archery uses a "thumb draw," employing a type of grip called "mandal." This grip prevents the arrow from moving if the archer is on a horse and/or firing at an unusual angle. The draw itself is relatively short, usually under the chin or by the cheek, compared to archery styles in China or Japan where the nock is pulled past the head. When the arrow is released, the draw arm is kept relatively steady rather than allowing the arm to swing backwards.

Turkish archers developed several unique techniques to aid in combat. One was the practice of holding several arrows in between the fingers of the draw hand, allowing fast repeat shots. Another was "Jarmakee" which involves drawing the bow with the draw arm going behind the head so as the fire at a steep downward angle. This was used to fire from atop walls down at enemy troops.

1.24.4 See also

- Composite bow
- Mongol bow
- Gungdo
- Mounted archery
- Arab archery
- Chinese archery
- English Longbow

1.24.5 External links

- *Türk Okçuluğu Ağı (Turkish Archery Network) - in Turkish* by Z. Metin Ateş
- *Turkish Traditional Archery* by Z. Metin Ateş
- "Turkish Traditional Archery Part 2: Technique and Tackle by Murat Özveri
- "Turkish Traditional Archery Part 1: History, Disciplines, Institutions, Mystic Aspects" by Murat Özveri

1.24.6 References

[1] Paul E Klopsteg. Turkish Archery and the Composite Bow. Chapter I, Background of Turkish Archery. Second edition, revised, 1947, published by the author, 2424 Lincolnwood Drive, Evanston, Ill.

[2] "Archery Guide". Sunday, 5 February 2017

[3] Ottoman Turkish bows, manufacture and design. Adam Karpowicz (author and publisher). ISBN 978-0-9811372-0-9

[4] Altinkulp, Gokmen (18 August 2011). "How to string a Turkish bow - Turkish Flight Archery Research And Practice". Retrieved 30 April 2013.

[5] "Invention and Evolution" by M. J. French (1988, Cambridge Univ. Press) (chapter 3.4.2)

1.25 Unlawful Games Act 1541

The Unlawful Games Act 1541 (33 Hen 8 c 9), sometimes referred to as the **Suppression of Unlawful Games Act 1541**,*[3] was an Act of the Parliament of England, designed to prohibit "Several new devised Games" that caused "the Decay of Archery".*[4] All Men under the Age of sixty Years "shall have Bows and Arrows for shooting". Men-Children between Seven "Years and Seventeen shall have a Bow and 2 Shafts". Men about Seventeen "Years of Age shall keep a Bow and 4 Arrows". The penalty for nonobservance was set at 6s.8d.

Archery, which had been the key to Henry V's victory at the 1415 Battle of Agincourt, had been required of the labourers, servants, artificers, or victuallers as early as 1388 (12 Ric 2, c.6) and 1409 (11 Hen IV, c.4), and again in An Act concerning shooting in Long Bows (3 Hen 8, c.3) and the Act for Maintenance of Archery (6 Hen 8, c.2), among others.*[5] In fact, the law of 1409 had as punishment six days' imprisonment; and reference is made herein to an act in the Parliament at Canterbury of Richard the Lionheart.

John Warleman of St Mary Magdalen Oxford was prosecuted for fixing a game of *Le Tenyse*. while the Tudor kings played on:*[6]

> *Item duodecim jurati presentant quod quidam Iohannes Warleman de parochia sancte Magdalene recepit diatim infra domum suam diversos homines ludentes ad pilam vocat le Tenyse & alia joca illicita.*

Section 1 of the Gaming Act 1845 repealed much of the Unlawful Games Act 1541.

The Statute Law Revision Act 1948 repealed Sections 11 to 13, part of Section 8, and the preambulatory words "by reason therof Archerie ys sore decayed, and dayly is lyke to be more mynished..." *[7] Archery could not compete with the nefarious pursuits of cricket, dicing, and carding.*[8]

The remainder of the whole Act was repealed by section 15 of, and Part I of Schedule 6 to, the Betting and Gaming Act 1960 (8 & 9 Eliz. 2, c.60).*[9]*[10]*[11]

The Act forbade all sport on Christmas Day with the exception of archery practice, meaning that footballers who played on Christmas Day before 1960, when the Football League routinely scheduled fixtures for 25 December, had technically broken the law.*[12]

1.25.1 Section 5

This is section 7 in Ruffhead's Edition. It was of a local character.*[13]

18th century dice players

1.25.2 See also

- List of Acts of the Parliament of England, 1485–1601
- Halsbury's Statutes,
- The Statutes: Revised Edition. Volume I. Eyre and Spottiswoode, Printers to the Queen. London. 1870. Pages lxxiv and 494 to 498.

1.25.3 References

[1] The citation of this Act by this short title was authorised by section 5 of, and Schedule 2 to, the Statute Law Revision Act 1948. Due to the repeal of those provisions, it is now authorised by section 19(2) of the Interpretation Act 1978.

[2] These words are printed against this Act in the second column of Schedule 2 to the Statute Law Revision Act 1948, which is headed "Title".

[3] (1950) 48 Knight's Local Government and Magisterial Reports 177, 180 and 681 , (1950) 85 Weekly Notes xvi

[4] duhaime.org: "Crazy Laws - English Style (1482-1541)" 9 Aug 2006

[5] forbes.com: "Britain's Archery Mandate" (Underhill) 16 Jun 2010

[6] *Did you know that tennis was once illegal?* St Luke's Church "Luke & Learn" 1 Jul 2004, Issue 5, p.2

[7] utexas.edu: "Statute Law Revision Act 1948" (11&12 Geo 6, c.62)

[8] spectator.co.uk: "LEGAL COBWEBS" 16 SEPTEMBER 1948, Page 12 (RH Cecil)

[9] lawcommission.justice.gov.uk: "Legal Curiosities: Fact or Fable?" March 2013

[10] "25 J. Crim. L. 149 (1961): The Betting and Gaming Act, 1960

[11] nationalarchives.gov.uk: "Discussions leading to Betting and Gaming Act, 1960"

[12] see e.g. 11 Hen 4, c.4; 12 Ric 2, c.6; and 7 Ric

[13] The Statutes: Revised Edition. Volume I. Eyre and Spottiswoode, Printers to the Queen. London. 1870. Page lxxiv.

1.26 William Tell

For other uses, see William Tell (disambiguation).

William Tell (in the four languages of Switzerland:

Tell is arrested for not saluting Gessler's hat (mosaic at the Swiss National Museum, Hans Sandreuter, 1901)

German: *Wilhelm Tell*; French: *Guillaume Tell*; Italian: *Guglielmo Tell*; Romansh: *Guglielm Tell*) is a folk hero of Switzerland. His legend is recorded in a late 15th-century Swiss illustrated chronicle. It is set in the time of the original foundation of the Old Swiss Confederacy in the early 14th century. According to the legend, Tell—an expert marksman with the crossbow—assassinated Gessler, a tyrannical reeve of Habsburg Austria positioned in Altdorf, Uri.

Along with Arnold von Winkelried, Tell is a central figure in Swiss patriotism as it was constructed during the Restoration of the Confederacy after the Napoleonic era.

1.26.1 Legend

*Tell's leap (*Tellensprung*) from the boat of his captors at the Axen cliffs. Study by Ernst Stückelberg (1879) for his fresco at the Tellskapelle.*

Several accounts of the Tell legend exist. The earliest sources give an account of the apple shot, Tell's escape, and the ensuing rebellion. The assassination of Gessler is not mentioned in the *Tellenlied* but is already present in the *White Book of Sarnen* account.

The legend as told by Tschudi (ca. 1570) essentially follows the account in the *White Book,* but adds further detail, such as Tell's given name Wilhelm, his being from Bürglen in the Schächental, and the precise date of the apple-shot of 18 November 1307.

William Tell was known as a strong man, a mountain climber, and an expert shot with the crossbow. In his time, the Habsburg emperors of Austria were seeking to dominate Uri, and Tell became one of the conspirators of Werner Stauffacher, vowing to resist Habsburg rule. Gessler, the newly appointed Austrian *Vogt* of Altdorf, raised a pole under the village lindentree, hung his hat on top of it, and demanded that all the townsfolk bow before the hat.

On 18 November 1307, Tell visited Altdorf with his young son and passed by the hat, publicly refusing to bow to it, and was arrested. Gessler—intrigued by Tell's famed marksmanship but resentful of his defiance—devised a cruel punishment. Tell and his son were to be executed. However, he could redeem his life by shooting an apple off the head of his son Robert in a single attempt. Tell split the apple with a bolt from his crossbow. Gessler then noticed that Tell had removed *two* crossbow bolts from his quiver. Before releasing him, he asked why. Tell was reluctant to answer, but after Gessler promised he would not kill him, he replied that had he killed his son, he would have killed Gessler with the second bolt. Gessler was furious and ordered Tell to be bound, saying that he had promised to spare his life, but instead would imprison him for the remainder of his life.

1.26. WILLIAM TELL

Tell was brought to Gessler's boat to be taken to the dungeon in the castle at Küssnacht. A storm broke on Lake Lucerne, and the guards were afraid that their boat would sink. They begged Gessler to remove Tell's shackles so he could take the helm and save them. Gessler gave in, but once freed, Tell led the boat to a rocky place and leapt from the boat. The site is already known in the "White Book" as the "Tellsplatte" ("Tell's slab"). Since the 16th century the site has been marked by a memorial chapel.

The Hohle Gasse *between Immensee and Küssnacht.*

Tell ran cross-country to Küssnacht. As Gessler arrived, Tell assassinated him, using the second crossbow bolt, along a stretch of the road cut through the rock between Immensee and Küssnacht, now known as the *Hohle Gasse*.*[1] Tell's blow for liberty sparked a rebellion in which he played a leading part, leading to the formation of the Old Swiss Confederacy.*[2]

According to Tschudi, Tell fought again against Austria in the 1315 Battle of Morgarten. Tschudi also has an account of Tell's death in 1354, according to which he was killed trying to save a child from drowning in the Schächenbach River in Uri.*[2]

1.26.2 Earliest mentions (15th century)

Page of the White Book of Sarnen *(p. 447, first page of the Tell legend, pp. 447–449).*

The first reference to William Tell appears in the *White Book of Sarnen* (German: *Weisses Buch von Sarnen*). This volume was written in c. 1474 by a country scribe named Hans Schreiber. It mentions the Rütli oath (German: *Rütlischwur*) and names Tell as one of the conspirators of the Rütli, whose heroic tyrannicide triggered the Burgenbruch rebellion.*[3]

An equally early account of Tell is found in the *Tellenlied*, a song composed in the 1470s, with its oldest extant manuscript copy dating to 1501. The song begins with the Tell legend, which it presents as the origin of the Confederacy, calling Tell the "first confederate". The narrative includes Tell's apple-shot, his preparation of a second arrow to shoot Gessler, and his escape, but it does not mention any assassination of Gessler.*[4]

The text then enumerates the cantons of the Confederacy, and says was expanded with "current events" during the course of the Burgundy Wars, ending with the death of Charles the Bold in 1477.*[4]

1.26.3 Early Modern period

Chronicles

A depiction of the apple-shot scene in Sebastian Münster's Cosmographia *(1554 edition).*

Der Apfelschuss. *Fresco by Ernst Stückelberg (1831–1903) in the Tellskapelle, Switzerland.*

Further reference to William Tell is found in Petermann Etterlin's *Chronicle of the Swiss Confederation* (German: *Kronika von der loblichen Eydtgenossenschaft*). Etterlin's 1507 chronicle is the earliest printed version of the Tell story.[5]

An account of William Tell's deeds is also given in the chronicle of Melchior Russ from Lucerne. This book, which its author dates to 1482, is an incoherent compilation of older writings, including the *Song of the Founding of the Confederation*, Conrad Justinger's *Bernese Chronicle*, and the *Chronicle of the State of Bern* (in German, *Chronik der Stadt Bern*).[6]

The version of the legend compiled by Aegidius Tschudi from Glarus in his monumental *Chronicon Helveticum* (ca. 1570) became the major model for later writers dealing with William Tell.[7] Not only did Tschudi's chronicle become the main source for Johannes von Müller's *History of the Swiss Confederation* (German: *Geschichte Schweizerischer Eidgenossenschaft*, 1780), it also served as a model for Friedrich Schiller's play *William Tell* (1804).[7] Tschudi is known to have manipulated documents.[8]

Popular veneration

A widespread veneration of Tell, including sight-seeing excursions to the scenes of his deeds, can be ascertained for the early 16th century. Heinrich Brennwald in the early 16th century mentions the chapel (*Tellskapelle*) on the site of Tell's leap from his captors' boat. Tschudi mentions a "holy cottage" (*heilig hüslin*) built on the site of Gessler's assassination. Peter Hagendorf, a soldier in the Thirty Years' War, mentions a visit to 'the chapel where William Tell escaped' in his diary.[9]

The first recorded Tell play (*Tellspiel*), known as the *Urner Tellspiel* ("Tell Play of Uri"),[10] was probably performed in the winter of either 1512 or 1513 in Altdorf.[6]

The church of Bürglen had a bell dedicated to Tell from 1581, and a nearby chapel has a fresco dated to 1582 showing Tell's death in the Schächenbach.[11]

The Three Tells

The Three Tells (*die Drei Tellen*, also *die Drei Telle*) were symbolic figures of the Swiss Peasant War of 1653. They expressed the hope of the subject population to repeat the success story of the rebellion against Habsburg in the early 14th century.

By the 18th century, the Drei Tellen had become associated with a sleeping hero legend. They were said to be asleep in a cave at the Rigi. The return of Tell in times of need was already foretold in the Tellenlied of 1653 and symbolically fulfilled in the impersonation of the Three Tells by costumed individuals, in one instance culminating in an actual assassination executed by these impersonators in historical costume.

Tell during the 16th century had become closely associated and eventually merged with the Rütlischwur legend, and the "Three Tells" represented the three conspirators or *Eidgenossen* Walter Fürst, Arnold von Melchtal and Werner Stauffacher.

In 1653, three men dressed in historical costume representing the Three Tells appeared in Schüpfheim. Other impersonations of the Three Tells also appeared in the Freie Ämter and in the Emmental.

The first impersonators of the Three Tells were Hans Zemp, Kaspar Unternährer of Schüpfheim and Ueli Dahinden of Hasle. They appeared at a number of important peasant conferences during the war, symbolizing the continuity of the present rebellion with the resistance movement against the Habsburg overlords at the origin of the Swiss Confederacy. Unternährer and Dahinden fled to the Entlebuch alps before the arrival of the troops of general Sebastian Peregrin Zwyers; Zemp escaped to the Alsace. After the suppression of the rebellion, the peasants voted for a tyrannicide, directly inspired by the Tell legend, attempting to kill the Lucerne Schultheiss Ulrich Dulliker.*[12]

Dahinden and Unternährer returned in their roles of Tells, joined by Hans Stadelmann replacing Zemp. In an ambush, they managed to injure Dulliker and killed a member of the Lucerne parliament, Caspar Studer. The assassination attempt—an exceptional act in the culture of the Old Swiss Confederacy—was widely recognized and welcomed among the peasant population, but its impact was not sufficient to rekindle the rebellion.*[12]

Even though it did not have any direct political effect, its symbolic value was considerable, placing the Lucerne authorities in the role of the tyrant (Habsburg and Gessler) and the peasant population in that of the freedom fighters (Tell). The Three Tells after the deed went to mass, still wearing their costumes, without being molested. Dahinden and Unternährer were eventually killed in October 1653 by Lucerne troops under Colonel Alphons von Sonnenberg. In July 1654, Zemp betrayed his successor Stadelmann in exchange for pardon and Stadelmann was executed on 15 July 1654.*[12]

The Three Tells appear in a 1672 comedy by Johann Caspar Weissenbach. The "sleeping hero" version of the Three Tells legend was published in *Deutsche Sagen* by the Brothers Grimm in 1816 (no. 298).*[13]

1.26.4 Reception 1789–1945

Throughout the long nineteenth century, and into the World War II period, Tell was perceived as a symbol of rebellion against tyranny both in Switzerland and in Europe.

Antoine-Marin Lemierre wrote a play inspired by Tell in 1766 and revived it in 1786. The success of this work established the association of Tell as a fighter against tyranny with the history of the French Revolution.

The French revolutionary fascination with Tell was reflected in Switzerland with the establishment of the Helvetic Re-

An allegorical Tell defeating the chimera of the French Revolution (1798).

Sketches of Gessler and Tell by Ernst Stückelberg (1880).

public. Tell became, as it were, the mascot of the short-lived republic, his figure being featured on its official seal. The French Navy also had a *Tonnant* class ship of the line named *Guillaume Tell,* which was captured by the British Royal Navy in 1800.

Johann Wolfgang von Goethe learned of the Tell saga during his travels through Switzerland between 1775 and 1795. He obtained a copy of Tschudi's chronicles and considered writing a play about Tell, but ultimately gave the idea to his friend Friedrich von Schiller, who in 1803–04 wrote the play *Wilhelm Tell,* first performed on March 17, 1804, in

Official seal of the Helvetic Republic.

Statue of William Tell and his son, City Hall, Tell City, Indiana

Weimar. Schiller's Tell is heavily inspired by the political events of the late 18th century, the French and American revolutions, in particular. Schiller's play was performed at Interlaken (the *Tellspiele*) in the summers of 1912 to 1914, 1931 to 1939 and every year since 1947. In 2004 it was first performed in Altdorf itself.

Gioachino Rossini used Schiller's play as the basis for his 1829 opera *William Tell*. The *William Tell Overture* is one of his best-known and most frequently imitated pieces of music; in the 20th Century, the "coda" of the *Overture* became the theme for the radio, television, and motion picture incarnations of The Lone Ranger, a fictional American Frontier hero.

In 1836 the first William Tell patterned playing cards were produced in Pest, Hungary. They were inspired by Schiller's play and made during tense relations with the ruling Habsburgs. The cards became popular throughout the Austrian Empire during the Revolution of 1848.

In 1858, the Swiss Colonization Society, a group of Swiss and German immigrants to the United States, founded its first (and only) planned city on the banks of the Ohio River in Perry County, Indiana. The town was originally dubbed Helvetia, but was quickly changed to Tell City to honor the legendary Swiss hero. The city became known for its manufacturing, especially of fine wood furniture. William Tell and symbols of an apple with an arrow through it are prominent in the town which includes a bronze statue of Tell and his son, based on the one in Altdorf, Switzerland. The statue was erected on a fountain in front of city hall in 1974. Tell City High School uses these symbols in its crest or logo, and the sports teams are called "The Marksmen." The William Tell Overture is often played by the school's pep band at high school games. Each August since 1958, Tell City's centennial year, the town has held "Schweizer Fest," a community festival of entertainment, stage productions, historical presentations, carnival rides, beer garden, sporting events and class reunions, to honor its Swiss-German heritage. Many of the activities occur on the grounds of City Hall and Main Street, at the feet of the Tell statue.

John Wilkes Booth, the assassin of Abraham Lincoln, was inspired by Tell. Lamenting the negative reaction to his action, Booth wrote in his journal on April 21, 1865 "with every man's hand against me, I am here in despair. And why; For doing what Brutus was honored for and what made Tell a Hero. And yet I for striking down a greater tyrant than they ever knew am looked upon as a common cutthroat." (He himself was shot to death, without standing trial, days later.)

Following a national competition, won by Richard Kissling, Altdorf in 1895 erected a monument to its hero. Kissling casts Tell as a peasant and man of the mountains, with strong features and muscular limbs. His powerful hand rests lovingly on the shoulder of little Walter, but the apple is not shown. The depiction is in marked contrast with that used by the Helvetic Republic, where Tell is shown as a landsknecht rather than a peasant, with a sword at his belt and a feathered hat, bending down to pick up his son who is still holding the apple.

The first film about Tell was made by French director Charles Pathé in 1900; only a short fragment survives.
A version of the legend was retold in P.G. Wodehouse's *William Tell Told Again* (1904), written in prose and verse with characteristic Wodehousian flair.

The design of the Federal 5 francs coin issued from 1922 features the bust of a generic "mountain shepherd" designed by Paul Burkard, but due to a similarity of the bust with Kissling's statue, in spite of the missing beard, it was immediately widely identified as Tell.

Adolf Hitler was enthusiastic about Schiller's play, quoting it in his *Mein Kampf,* and approving of a German/Swiss co-production of the play in which Hermann Göring's mistress Emmy Sonnemann appeared as Tell's wife. But on June 3, 1941, Hitler had the play banned. The reason for the ban is not known, but may have been related to the failed assassination attempt in 1938 by young Swiss Maurice Bavaud*[14] (executed on May 14, 1941, and later dubbed "a new William Tell" by Rolf Hochhuth), or the subversive nature of the play.*[15]*[16] Hitler is reported to have exclaimed at a banquet in 1942: "Why did Schiller have to immortalize that Swiss sniper!"*[15]

Salvador Dalí painted *The Old Age of William Tell* and *William Tell and Gradiva* in 1931, and *The Enigma of William Tell* in 1933.

Charlie Chaplin parodies William Tell in his famous 1928 silent movie *The Circus*.

Max Frisch in his "William Tell for Schools" deconstructed the legend, portraying the bailiff as a well-meaning administrator suffering from being placed in a barbaric back-corner of the empire, while Tell is a simpleton who stumbles into his adventure by a series of misunderstandings.

Spanish playwright Alfonso Sastre re-worked the legend in 1955 in his "Guillermo Tell tiene los ojos tristes" (William Tell has sad eyes); it was not performed until the Franco regime in Spain ended.

In *Schweizer Helden* (*Unlikely Heroes*), a 2014 Swiss film directed by Peter Luisi, a group of immigrant asylum seekers perform a play of Wilhelm Tell.*[17]*[18]*[19] *Schweizer Helden* received the Prix du Public UBS award at the 2014 Locarno Film Festival.*[20]

William Tell lives on as a hero in popular culture. He is still a powerful identification figure, and according to a 2004 survey, 60% of the Swiss people still believe that he actually existed.*[21]

1.26.5 Historicity debate

A 1782 depiction of Tell in the Schweizerisches Landesmuseum, Zürich.

The historicity of William Tell has been subject to debate. François Guillimann, a statesman of Fribourg and later historian and advisor of the Habsburg Emperor Rudolph II, wrote to Melchior Goldast in 1607: "I followed popular belief by reporting certain details in my *Swiss antiquities* [published in 1598], but when I examine them closely the whole story seems to me to be pure fable."

In 1760, Simeon Uriel Freudenberger from Luzern anonymously published a tract arguing that the legend of Tell in all likelihood was based on the Danish saga of Palnatoki. A French edition of his book, written by Gottlieb Emanuel von Haller (*Guillaume Tell, Fable danoise*), was burnt in Altdorf.*[22]

The skeptical view of Tell's existence remained very unpopular. Friedrich von Schiller used Tschudi's version as the basis for his play *Wilhelm Tell* in 1804, interpreting Tell as a glorified patriot assassin. This interpretation became very popular, especially in Switzerland, where the Tell figure was used in the early 19th century as a "national hero" and identification figure in the Helvetic Republic, and later in the beginnings of the *Schweizerische Eidgenossenschaft*, the modern democratic federal state that developed. When historian Joseph Eutych Kopp dared to question the legend in the 1830s, his effigy was burnt on the *Rütli*, a meadow above Lake Lucerne where—according to the legend—the oath was sworn that concluded the alliance between the founding cantons of the Swiss confederacy.

Historians continued to argue over the saga until well into the 20th century. In 1891 Wilhelm Öchsli published a scientific account of the founding of the confederacy (commissioned by the government for the celebration of the first National holiday of Switzerland on August 1, 1891), dismissing the story as fiction. Still, 50 years later in 1941, when Tell had again become a national identification figure, historian Karl Meyer tried to tie the saga's events to known places and events. Modern historians generally regard the saga to be fiction, since neither Tell's nor Gessler's existence can be proven. The legend also tells of a *Burgenbruch*, a coordinated uprising including the slighting of many forts; however, archeological evidence shows that many of these forts were abandoned and destroyed long before 1307–1308.

A possible historical basis of the legend was suggested by Arnold Schärer in 1986. He identified a Wilhelm Gorkeit of Tellikon (modern Dällikon in the Canton of Zürich) as the real William Tell. "Gorkeit", he claimed, was a version of the surname *Armbruster* (crossbow maker). Historians were not convinced, but the theory was once referred to by Rudolf Keller, at the time president of the nationalistic right Swiss Democrats, on 1 August 2004 in Basel.*[23]

1.26.6 Comparative mythology

Main article: Shooting an apple off one's child's head
The Tell legend has been compared to a number of other myths or legends, specifically in Norse mythology, involving a magical marksman coming to the aid of a suppressed people under the sway of a tyrant. The story of a great outlaw successfully shooting an apple from his child's head is an archetype present in the story of Egil in the Thidreks saga (associated with the god Ullr in Eddaic tradition) as well as in the stories of Adam Bell from England, Palnatoki from Denmark and a story from Holstein.

Such parallels were pointed out as early as 1760 by Gottlieb Emanuel von Haller and the pastor Simeon Uriel Freudenberger in a short leaflet with the title *William Tell, a Danish Fable* (German: *Der Wilhelm Tell, ein dänisches Mährgen*).*[24]

Rochholz (1877) connects the similarity of the Tell legend to the stories of Egil and Palnatoki with the legends of a migration from Sweden to Switzerland during the Middle

Detail from the Statue of William Tell and his son in Altdorf (Richard Kissling, 1895).

Ages. He also adduces parallels in folktales among the Finns and the Lapps (Sami). From pre-Christian Norse mythology, Rochholz compares Ullr, who bears the epithet of *Boga-As* ("bow-god"), Heimdall and also Odin himself, who according to the *Gesta Danorum* (Book 1, chapter 8.16) assisted Haddingus by shooting ten bolts from a crossbow in one shot, killing as many foes. Rochholz further compares Indo-European and oriental traditions and concludes (pp. 35–41) that the legend of the master marksman shooting an apple (or similar small target) was known outside the Germanic sphere (Germany, Scandinavia, England) and the adjacent regions (Finland and the Baltic) in India, Arabia, Persia and the Balkans (Serbia).

The Danish legend of Palnatoki, first attested in the twelfth-century *Gesta Danorum* by Saxo Grammaticus.*[25] is the earliest known parallel to the Tell legend. As with William Tell, Palnatoki is forced by the ruler, (in this case King Harald Bluetooth), to shoot an apple off his son's head as proof of his marksmanship.*[26] A striking similarity between William Tell and Palnatoki is that both heroes take more than one arrow out of their quiver.*[25] When asked why he pulled several arrows out of his quiver, Palnatoki, too, replies that if he had struck his son with the first arrow, he would have shot King Harald with the remaining two arrows.*[25] According to Saxo, Palnatoki later joins Harald's son Swein Forkbeard in a rebellion and kills Harald with an arrow.*[27]

1.26.7 See also

- Arnold Winkelried, Swiss cultural hero

William Tell. Plastic Toy Soldier of Reamsa (1965)

Non-Swiss figures:

- Punker of Rohrbach
- Robin Hood
- William Wallace

General:

- Historiography of Switzerland

1.26.8 Notes and references

[1] *Hohle Gasse* in German, French and Italian in the online *Historical Dictionary of Switzerland*.

[2] Meyers Konversations-Lexikon, Verlag des Bibliographischen Instituts, Leipzig und Wien, Fourth edition, 1885–1892, entry on "Tell, Wilhelm," pp. 576–77 in volume 15. In German.

[3] Bergier, p 63.

[4] Rochus von Liliencron, *Historische Volkslieder der Deutschen*, vol. 2 (1866), no. 147, cited by Rochholz (1877), p. 187; c.f. Bergier, p. 70–71.

[5] Bergier, p. 77.

[6] Bergier, p. 76.

[7] Bergier, p. 16.

[8] Chrisholm, Hugh (Ed.): *Encyclopædia Britannica Eleventh Edition*, 1911. Article "Tschudi". URL last accessed 2011-08-26.

[9] Helfferich, Tryntje, The Thirty Years War: A Documentary History (Cambridge, 2009), p. 279.

[10] Head, p. 528.

[11] Kaiser, P.: *Liberation myths* in German, French and Italian in the online *Historical Dictionary of Switzerland*, 2002-05-20. URL last accessed 6 November 2006.

[12] *Drei Tellen* in German, French and Italian in the online *Historical Dictionary of Switzerland*.

[13] Germany, SPIEGEL ONLINE, Hamburg,. "von - Text im Projekt Gutenberg".

[14] dpa: *Hitler verbot Schillers "Tell"*, news agency announcement of a speech by Rolf Hochhuth, May 11, 2004. In German. URL last accessed 11 February 2008.

[15] Ruppelt, G.: *Hitler gegen Tell*, Hannover, 2004. In German. URL last accessed 11 February 2008.

[16] Sapan, A.: *Wilhelm Tell (Friedrich von Schiller)*. In German. URL last accessed 11 February 2008.

[17] "*Schweizer Helden (Unlikely Heroes)*". IMDb. Retrieved December 3, 2015.

[18] "Peter Luisi". *IMDb*. Retrieved December 3, 2015.

[19] "*Schweizer Helden*". Schweizer Helden *official website*. Retrieved December 3, 2015.

[20] "Past winners of Prix du Public UBS". *Festival del Film Locarno official website*. Retrieved December 3, 2015.

[21] According to a 2004 survey of 620 participants performed by the *LINK-Institut* of Lucerne for *Coopzeitung*. 58% of those asked held that Tell was historical, compared to 29% who held that Tell was unhistorical.

[22] Troxler, J. *et al.*: *Guillaume Tell*, pp. 43–46; Ketty & Alexandre, Chapelle-sur-Moudon, 1985, ISBN 2-88114-001-7. See also "Le pamphlet de von Haller" (in French).

[23] Keller, R.: Speech held on August 1, 2004.

[24] Bergier, p. 80f.

[25] Bergier, p. 82.

[26] Keightley, p. 293.

[27] Zeeberg, Peter (2000). *Saxos Danmarkshistorie*. Denmark: Gads Forlag. p. 909. ISBN 978-87-12-04745-2.

1.26.9 Bibliography

- Bergier, Jean-François. *Wilhelm Tell: Realität und Mythos.* München: Paul List Verlag, 1990.

- Fiske, John. *Myths and Myth-Makers: Old Tales and Superstitions Interpreted by Comparative Mythology,* 1877. Ch. 1: (On-line) Quotes Saxo Grammaticus, the ballad of William of Cloudeslee, and instances other independent occurrences.

- Head, Randolph C. "William Tell and His Comrades: Association and Fraternity in the Propaganda of Fifteenth- and Sixteenth-Century Switzerland." in *The Journal of Modern History* 67.3 (1995): 527–557.

- Keightley, Thomas. *Tales and Popular Fictions: Their Resemblance and Transmission from Country to Country.* London: Whittaker, 1834.

- Öchsli, W. *Die Anfänge der Schweizerischen Eidgenossenschaft.* Zürich, 1891.

- Rochholz, Ernst Ludwig, *Tell und Gessler in Sage und Geschichte. Nach urkundlichen Quellen,* Heilbronn, 1877 (online copy).

- Salis, J.-R. v.: *Ursprung, Gestalt, und Wirkung des schweizerischen Mythos von Tell;* Bern, 1973.

- Schärer, Arnold Claudio, *Und es gab Tell doch,* Lucerne, 1986, ISBN 3-85725-106-9, OCLC 19264018.

1.26.10 External links

- Wilhelm Tell Festival, New Glarus

- William Tell, Swissinfo special

- *The Legend of William Tell* by Markus Jud.

- *The birth of the Swiss Confederation.*

- William Tell is a lie; Coopzeitung 28/2004, interview with historian Roger Sablonier, Zurich, translated

- Translation of Grimm's Saga No. 298 "The Three Tells"

- Tell City, Indiana

- Translation of Grimm's Saga No. 517 "Wilhelm Tell"

Yabusame archer on horseback

1.27 Yabusame

Yabusame (流鏑馬) is a type of mounted archery in traditional Japanese archery. An archer on a running horse shoots three special "turnip-headed" arrows successively at three wooden targets.

This style of archery has its origins at the beginning of the Kamakura period. Minamoto no Yoritomo became alarmed at the lack of archery skills his samurai had. He organized yabusame as a form of practice.

Nowadays, the best places to see yabusame performed are at the Tsurugaoka Hachiman-gū in Kamakura and Shimogamo Shrine in Kyoto (during Aoi Matsuri in early May). It is also performed in Samukawa and on the beach at Zushi, as well as other locations.

1.27.1 History

Japanese bows date back to prehistoric times —the Jōmon Period. The long, unique asymmetrical bow style with the grip below the center emerged under the Yayoi culture (300 BC – 300 AD). Bows became the symbol of authority and

Yabusame archer takes aim on the second target

power. The legendary first emperor of Japan, Emperor Jimmu, is always depicted carrying a bow.

The use of the bow had been on foot until around the 4th century when elite soldiers took to fighting on horseback with bows and swords. In the 10th century, samurai would have archery duels on horseback. They would ride at each other and try to shoot at least three arrows. These duels did not necessarily have to end in death, as long as honor was satisfied. One of the most famous and celebrated incidents of Japanese mounted archery occurred during the Genpei War (1180–1185), an epic struggle for power between the Minamoto and Taira clans that was to have a major impact on Japanese culture, society, and politics.

At the Battle of Yashima, the Heike, having been defeated in battle, fled to Yashima and took to their boats. They were fiercely pursued by the Genji on horseback, but the Genji were halted by the sea.

As the Heike waited for the winds to be right, they presented a fan hung from a mast as a target for any Genji archer to shoot at in a gesture of chivalrous rivalry between enemies.

One of the Genji samurai, Nasu no Yoichi, accepted the challenge. He rode his horse into the sea and shot the fan cleanly through. Nasu won much fame and his feat is still celebrated to this day.

During the Kamakura Period (1192–1334), mounted archery was used as a military training exercise to keep samurai prepared for war. Those archers who did poorly might find themselves commanded to commit seppuku, or ritualistic suicide.

One style of mounted archery was inuoumono —shooting at dogs.*[1] Buddhist priests were able to prevail upon the samurai to have the arrows padded so that the dogs were only annoyed and bruised rather than killed. This sport is no longer practiced.

1.27.2 Ritual

A mounted samurai with bow & arrows, wearing a horned helmet. Circa 1878.

Yabusame was designed as a way to please and entertain the myriad of gods that watch over Japan, thus encouraging their blessings for the prosperity of the land, the people, and the harvest.

A yabusame archer gallops down a 255-meter-long track at high speed. The archer mainly controls his horse with his knees, as he needs both hands to draw and shoot his bow. As he approaches a target, he brings his bow up and draws the arrow past his ear before letting the arrow fly with a deep shout of In-Yo-In-Yo (darkness and light). The arrow is blunt and round-shaped in order to make a louder sound when it strikes the board.

Experienced archers are allowed to use arrows with a V-shaped prong. If the board is struck, it will splinter with a confetti-like material and fall to the ground. To hit all three targets is considered an admirable accomplishment. Yabusame targets and their placement are designed to ritually replicate the optimum target for a lethal blow on an opponent wearing full traditional samurai armor (O-Yoroi) which left the space just beneath the helmet visor bare.

Yabusame is characterized as a ritual rather than a sport because of its solemn style and religious aspects, and is often performed for special ceremonies or official events, such as entertaining foreign dignitaries and heads of state. Yabusame demonstrations have been given for the formal visits of US Presidents Ronald Reagan and George W. Bush. A yabusame demonstration was given in the United Kingdom for Prince Charles, who reportedly was fascinated and pleased with the performance.

To be selected as a yabusame archer is a great honor. In the past, they were chosen from only the best warriors. The archer who performs the best is awarded a white cloth, signifying divine favor.

1.27.3 Famous schools

Yabusame Archer wearing traditional 13th Century clothing

There are two famous schools of mounted archery that perform yabusame. One is the Ogasawara school. The founder, Ogasawara Nagakiyo, was instructed by the shogun Minamoto Yoritomo (1147–1199) to start a school for archery. Yoritomo wanted his warriors to be highly skilled and disciplined. Archery was seen as a good way for instilling the necessary principles for a samurai warrior.

Zen became a major element in both foot and mounted archery as it also became popular among the samurai in every aspect of their life during the Kamakura Period.

Yabusame as a martial art helped a samurai learn concentration, discipline, and refinement. Zen taught breathing techniques to stabilize the mind and body, giving clarity and focus. To be able to calmly draw one's bow, aim, and shoot in the heat of battle, and then repeat, was the mark of a true samurai who had mastered his training and his fear.

The other archery school was begun earlier by Minamoto Yoshiari in the 9th century at the command of Emperor Uda. This school became known as the Takeda school of archery. The Takeda style has been featured in classic samurai films such as Akira Kurosawa's "Seven Samurai" (1954) and "Kagemusha" (1980). The famed actor of many samurai films, Toshiro Mifune, was a noted student of the Takeda school.

1.27.4 Decline and revival

Yabusame demonstrated for the president George W. Bush (at Meiji Jingu shrine).

With the arrival of the Portuguese and their guns in the mid-16th century, the bow began to lose its importance on the battlefield. At the Battle of Nagashino in 1575, well-placed groups of musketeers serving Oda Nobunaga and Tokugawa shot in volleys and practically annihilated the cavalry charges of the Takeda clan.

Mounted archery was revived in the Edo Period (1600–1867) by Ogasawara Heibei Tsuneharu (1666–1747) under the command of the shogun Tokugawa Yoshimune (1684–1751). Given that the nation was at peace, archery as well as other military martial arts became more of a method of personal development rather than military training.

1.27.5 Contemporary practice

Yabusame at Tsurugaoka Hachiman-gū

Yabusame is held at various times of the year, generally near Shinto shrines. In May, the Aoi Matsuri (Hollyhock festival) in Kyoto includes yabusame.*[2] Other locations include Tsurugaoka Hachiman-gū in Kamakura, together with Samukawa and on the beach at Zushi.

1.27.6 See also

- Horses in East Asian warfare
- Horses in warfare
- Jinba ittai

1.27.7 Notes

[1] Doris G. Bargen. *Suicidal honor: General Nogi and the writings of Mori Ōgai and Natsume Sōseki*. University of Hawaii Press, 2006. ISBN 0-8248-2998-0, ISBN 978-0-8248-2998-8. Pg 107

[2] "Aoi matsuri". Kyoto City Tourism and Culture Information System.

1.27.8 External links

- Takeda school Kyubadou Yabusame
- Short Video of the Takeda School Performing Yabusame at Meiji Shrine
- Japan Times article

- Encyclopedia of Shinto entry
- JAANUS, *Kamo no keiba*

1.28 Yeoman

For other uses, see Yeoman (disambiguation).

A **yeoman** /ˈjoʊmən/ was a member of a social class in

A Yeoman Warder at the Tower of London in England

late medieval to early modern England. In early recorded uses, a yeoman was an attendant in a noble household; hence titles such as "Yeoman of the Chamber", "Yeoman of the Crown", "Yeoman Usher", "King's Yeoman", Yeomen Warders, Yeomen of the Guard. The later sense of yeoman as "a commoner who cultivates his own land" is recorded from the 15th century; in military context, yeoman was the rank of the third order of "fighting men", below knights and squires, but above knaves. A specialized meaning in naval terminology, "petty officer in charge of supplies", arose in the 1660s.

1.28.1 Etymology

The term is first recorded c. 1300. Its etymology is unclear. It may be a contraction of Old English *iunge man*, meaning "young man" (compare knave, meaning "boy"), but there are alternative suggestions, such as derivations from an unattested **geaman* (a hypothetical cognate of Old Frisian *gaman*, from *gea-* "province") meaning "villager; rustic". The Canon's Yeoman's Prologue and Tale appears in Geoffrey Chaucer's *Canterbury Tales*, written between 1387 and 1400.

1.28.2 History of Yeomen

During the late 14th to 18th centuries, yeomen were farmers who owned land (freehold, leasehold or copyhold). Their wealth and the size of their landholding varied. Sir Anthony Richard Wagner, Garter Principal King of Arms, wrote that "a Yeoman would not normally have less than 100 acres" (40 hectares) "and in social status is one step down from the Landed gentry, but above, say, a husbandman".[1] Often it was hard to distinguish minor landed gentry from the wealthier yeomen, and wealthier husbandmen from the poorer yeomen.

The *Concise Oxford Dictionary* (edited by H.W. & F.G. Fowler, Clarendon Press, Oxford, 1972 reprint, p. 1516) states that a yeoman was "a person qualified by possessing free land of 40/- (shillings) annual [feudal] value, and who can serve on juries and vote for a Knight of the Shire. He is sometimes described as a small landowner, a farmer of the middle classes".

The term had a military sense as in the Yeomanry Cavalry of the late 18th century and Imperial Yeomanry of the late 1890s. The 'yeoman archer' was unique to England and Wales (in particular, the south Wales areas of Monmouthshire with the famed archers of Gwent; and Glamorgan, Crickhowell, and Abergavenny; and South West England with the Royal Forest of Dean, Kingswood Royal Forest near Bristol, and the New Forest). Though Kentish Weald and Cheshire archers were noted for their skills, it appears that the bulk of the 'yeomanry' was from the English and Welsh Marches (border regions).

The original Yeomen of the Guard (originally archers) chartered in 1485 were most likely of Brittonic descent, including Welshmen and Bretons. They were established by King Henry VII, himself a Briton who was exiled in Brittany during the Wars of the Roses. He recruited his forces mostly from Wales and the West Midlands of England on his journey to victory at Bosworth Field.

Yeomen were often constables of their parish, and sometimes chief constables of the district, shire or hundred. Many yeomen held the positions of bailiffs for the High Sheriff or for the shire or hundred. Other civic duties would include churchwarden, bridge warden, and other warden duties. It was also common for a yeoman to be an overseer for his parish. Yeomen, whether working for a lord, king, shire, knight, district or parish served in localised or municipal police forces raised by or led by the landed gentry.

Some of these roles, in particular those of constable and bailiff were carried down through families. Yeomen often filled ranging, roaming, surveying, and policing roles. In Chaucer's Friar's Tale, a yeoman who is a bailiff of the forest who tricks the Summoner turns out to be the devil ready to grant wishes already made.

The earlier class of franklins (freemen or French or Norman freeholders) were similar to yeomen: wealthy peasant landowners, freeholders or village officials. They were typically village leaders (aldermen), constables or mayors. Franklin militias were similar to later yeomanries. Yeomen took over those roles in the 14th century as many of them became leaders, constables, sheriffs, justices of the peace, mayors and significant leaders of their country districts.[2] It was too much, for even 'valets' known as 'yeoman archers' were forbidden to be returned to parliament, indicating they even held power at a level never before held by the upper class of commoners. In districts remoter from landed gentry and burgesses, yeomen held more official power: this is attested in statutes of the reign of Henry VIII indicating yeomen along with knights and squires as leaders for certain purposes.

The yeoman also comprised a military class or status (usually known as in the third order of the fighting class, between squire and page). By contrast, in contemporary feudal continental Europe, the divide between commoners and gentry was far wider: though a middle class existed, it was less esteemed than the yeoman of England of that time.

1.28.3 United States

Main article: Plain Folk of the Old South

In the United States, yeomen were identified in the 18th and 19th centuries as non-slaveholding, small landowning, family farmers. In Southern areas where land was poor, like East Tennessee,[3] the landowning yeomen were typically subsistence farmers, but some managed to grow some crops for market. Whether they engaged in subsistence or commercial agriculture, they controlled far more modest landholdings than those of the planters, typically in the range of 50–200 acres. In the North, practically all the farms were operated by yeoman farmers as family farms.

Coat of arms of Wisconsin during the Civil War, with yeoman on the right

Thomas Jefferson was a leading advocate of the yeomen, arguing that the independent farmers formed the basis of republican values.*[4] Indeed, Jeffersonian Democracy as a political force was largely built around the yeomen.*[5] After the Civil War, organizations of farmers, especially the Grange, formed to organize and enhance the status of the yeoman farmers.*[6]

U.S. Navy and U.S. Coast Guard

Main article: Yeoman (United States Navy)

In the U.S. Navy and the U.S. Coast Guard, the enlisted rating of yeoman describes an enlisted service member who performs administrative and clerical work ashore and embarked aboard vessels at sea. They deal with protocol, naval instructions, enlisted evaluations, commissioned officer fitness reports, naval messages, visitors, telephone calls and mail (both conventional and electronic). They organize files and operate office equipment and order and distribute office supplies. They write and type business and social letters, notices, directives, forms and reports.

1.28.4 Other references

In popular culture

- In William Caxton's printing of *The Canterbury Tales*, there is a woodcut engraving of the knight's yeoman.

- In William Shakespeare's *Hamlet*, Prince Hamlet states his under-appreciated ability to write elegantly in a particular situation had done him "yeoman's service".

- In the oldest stories of Robin Hood, such as *A Gest of Robyn Hode*, Robin Hood is a yeoman, although later retellings make him a knight. According to Sir Walter Scott's *Ivanhoe*, Robin Hood's Band of Merry Men is composed largely of yeomen.

- In Thomas Malory's tale of Arthurian legend *Le Morte d'Arthur*, Sir Gawain states that he was made a yeoman at Yule.

- *The Yeomen of the Guard* (1888) is a Savoy Opera by Gilbert and Sullivan.

- In The Magician's Nephew by C.S.Lewis, part of the Narnia cycle,(1955) the magician Uncle Andrew complained about Jadis' behavior and mentioned a cousin Edward who frequented pawn shops and was in the yeomanry.

- The Dr. Seuss book *The 500 Hats of Bartholomew Cubbins* includes a "Yeoman of the Bowmen", a master archer who shoots a hat off the title character's head.

- In Elizabeth Moon's *The Deed of Paksenarrion* fantasy novels, the followers of St. Gird (many of whom are farmers) call themselves the "Yeomen of Gird".

- In Hunter S. Thompson's *The Rum Diary*, one of the two characters Thompson had based on himself was named Yeoman.*[7]

- In the American TV series *The Love Boat* (1977–1987), former actor Fred Grandy's character, Burl "Gopher" Smith, is introduced at the start of each episode as "Your Yeoman Purser".

- In *Star Trek*, following U.S. Navy usage, as a role in the TV series held by mainly female (although sometimes male) enlisted personnel in assistance to higher-ranking officers. Notably, Yeoman Janice Rand. The same is true in the *Mass Effect* video game series, with Yeoman Kelly Chambers (female Cerberus crewman in *Mass Effect 2*) and Yeoman Copeland (male Alliance Ensign in *Mass Effect 3*).

Other

- In falconry, the bird for the yeoman is the goshawk, a forest bird.

- In computer and information technologies, Yeoman is an open-source web scaffolding tool announced at Google I/O in 2012 by Paul Irish.*[8]*[9]

1.28.5 See also

- Yeomanry (military)
- Social history of England
- Franklin (class)

1.28.6 Notes

[1] Wagner, Sir Anthony R., *English Genealogy*, Oxford University Press, 1960, pp. 125–130.

[2] Cerasano, S. P.; Hirschfeld, Heather Anne (2006-10-01). *Medieval and Renaissance Drama in England*. Fairleigh Dickinson Univ Press. p. 159. ISBN 9780838641194.

[3] The difficulty yeoman farmers faced in this region was notorious enough that it inspired the lyrics "Corn don't grow at all on Rocky Top; dirt's too rocky by far" in Rocky Top, now one of Tennessee's state songs.

[4] Samuel C. Hyde Jr., "Plain Folk Yeomanry in the Antebellum South", in John Boles, Jr., ed., *Companion to the American South*, (2004) pp 139–155

[5] Steven Hahn, *The Roots of Southern Populism: Yeoman Farmers and the Transformation of the Georgia Upcountry, 1850–1890* (1983)

[6] Thomas A. Woods, *Knights of the Plow: Oliver H. Kelley and the Origins of the Grange in Republican Ideology* (2002)

[7] DeSaulnier, Jordan. "Johnny Depp Talks 'The Rum Diary'". *iamrogue.com*. Retrieved 17 February 2015.

[8] Osmani, Addy. "Improved Developer Tooling and Yeoman". Retrieved 16 August 2014.

[9] "The Web's Scaffolding Tool for Modern Webapps". Retrieved 16 August 2014.

1.28.7 Further reading

- Allen, Robert C. *Enclosure and the Yeoman* (1992) Oxford U. Press 376p.
- Broad, John. "The Fate of the Midland Yeoman: Tenants, Copyholders, and Freeholders as Farmers in North Buckinghamshire, 1620–1800", *Continuity & Change* 1999 14(3): 325–347.
- Campbell, Mildred. *The English Yeoman*
- Genovese, Eugene D. "Yeomen Farmers in a Slaveholders' Democracy", *Agricultural History* Vol. 49, No. 2 (April 1975), pp. 331–342 in JSTOR, antebellum U.S.
- Hallas, Christine S. "Yeomen and Peasants? Landownership Patterns in the North Yorkshire Pennines c. 1770–1900", *Rural History* 1998 9(2): 157–176.

1.28.8 External links

- Yeomen of the Guard
- Official Yeomen of the Guard
- Yeoman Board Game
- Knight's Yeoman
- The Yeoman Warders
- Worcester Yeomanry Cavalry

Chapter 2

Medieval Archery

2.1 Arbalest

Not to be confused with Arbalist (crossbowman).

The **arbalest** (also **arblast**) was a late variation of the crossbow coming into use in Europe during the 12th century. A large weapon, the arbalest had a steel prod ("bow"). Since the arbalest was much larger than earlier crossbows, and because of the greater tensile strength of steel, it had a greater force. However, the greater draw weight was offset by the smaller powerstroke, which limited its potential in fully transferring the energy into the crossbow bolt. The strongest windlass-pulled arbalests could have up to 22 kN (5000 lbf) of force and be accurate up to 100 m. A skilled arbalestier (arbalester) could loose two bolts per minute.

2.1.1 Nomenclature

The term "arbalest" is sometimes used interchangeably with "crossbow". *Arbalest* is a Medieval French word originating from the Roman name *arcuballista* (from *arcus* 'bow' + *ballista* 'missile-throwing engine'),[1] which was then used for crossbows, although originally used for types of artillery. Modern French uses the word *arbalète*, which is linguistically one step further from the stem (disappearance of the *s* phoneme in the last syllable, before *t*).

The word applies to both crossbow and arbalest (the latter may be referred to as a *heavy crossbow*, but an actual heavy crossbow may not be the same as an arbalest). In some cases, the word has been used to refer to arbalists, the people who actually used the weapon.

2.1.2 References

- Tanner, Norman P. (1990). *Decrees of the Ecumenical Councils, Vol. 1. Nicaea 1 to Lateran V.* London / Washington, D.C.: Sheed & Ward. Georgetown University Press. ISBN 0-87840-490-2.

- Bellamy, Alex J. (2006). *Just Wars: From Cicero to Iraq*. Polity. Page 32. ISBN 0-7456-3282-3.

[1] "arbalest". *Oxford English Dictionary* (3rd ed.). Oxford University Press. September 2005. (Subscription or UK public library membership required.) (arbalist, arblast)

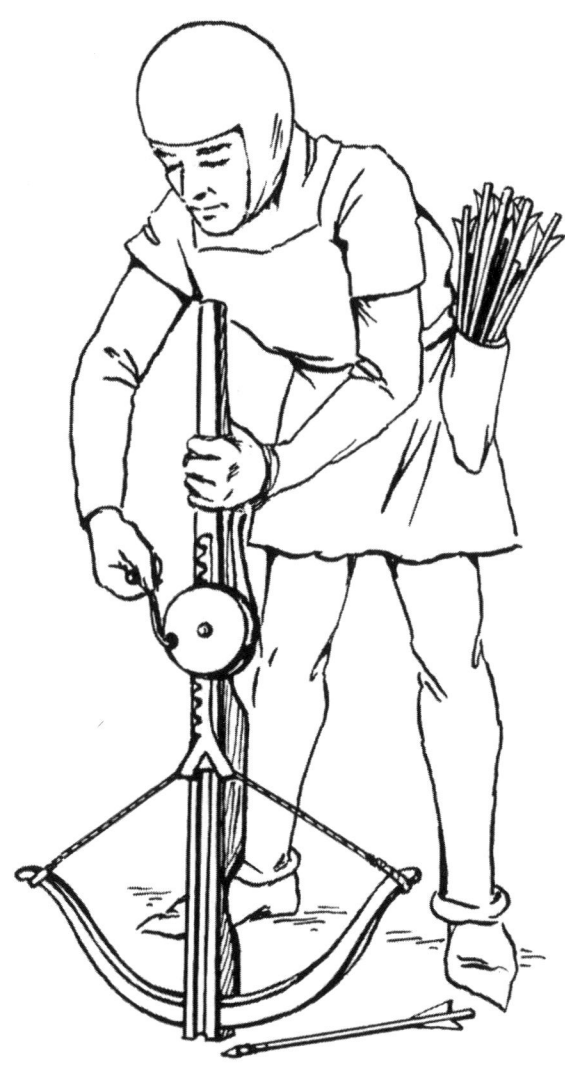

Crossbowman cocking an arbalest

2.2 Archer's stake

Archer's stakes in the Battle of Nicopolis (painting from the 15th century)

An **archer's stake** was an anti-cavalry defence used by longbowmen in the 15th and 16th centuries.

2.2.1 Origins

At the Battle of Nicopolis in 1396 Turkish archers were stationed behind a barrier of stakes. This may have inspired Henry V when he instructed his men to provide themselves with six foot stakes, which were to be planted in front of them at an angle to impale horses of attacking French men-at-arms prior to the Battle of Agincourt.[1]

2.2.2 Deployment

There are three schools of thought about the deployment of stakes. The traditional view is that all the stakes were placed in front of the front rank to create a fence.[2] In 1976, John Keegan proposed that each archer placed his stake in front of him where he stood in the ranks, thus creating a defensive belt of stakes several yards wide within which the archers operated.[3] Keegan's proposal has been challenged by Clifford J. Rogers, who argues that most stakes were placed in a fence arrangement, with staggered gaps for archers to move through, in combination with a band of more widely spaced stakes.[4]

2.2.3 Usage

After the Agincourt campaign, stakes became a common piece of equipment for the English longbowman fighting in France. After the end of the Hundred Years War, stakes continued to be used, for example at the Battle of Blore Heath during the Wars of the Roses[5] and by the English mercenaries at the Battle of Montlhéry during the War of the Public Weal.[6] Tudor archers also used stakes in the early 16th century. Henry VIII's army which invaded France in 1513 carried 5000 stakes in wagons[7] and iron-bound archers' stakes are mentioned on several occasions thereafter.[8]

2.2.4 References

[1] Strickland, Matthew; Hardy,Robert (2005). *The Great Warbow*. Stroud: Sutton. pp. 326–7. ISBN 0-7509-3167-1.

[2] Burne, A.H. (1991) [1956]. *The Agincourt War*. London: Greenhill Books. p. 81. ISBN 1-85367-087-1.

[3] Keegan, John (1976). *The Face of Battle: A Study of Agincourt, Waterloo, and the Somme*. Penguin Classics. ISBN 978-0-14-004897-1.

[4] Rogers, Clifford J. (2008). "The Battle of Agincourt". In Villalon, L. J. Andrew; Kagay, Donald J. *The Hundred Years War (Part II): Different Vistas*. Leiden: Brill. pp. 53–6. ISBN 978-90-04-16821-3.

[5] Strickland and Hardy (2005), p.371

[6] Strickland and Hardy (2005), p.362

[7] Cruikshank, Charles (1990). *Henry VIII and the Invasion of France*. Stroud: Alan Sutton. p. 71. ISBN 0-86299-768-2.

[8] Cornish, Paul (1987). *Henry VIII's Army*. London: Osprey. p. 22. ISBN 0-85045-798-X.

2.3 Franc-archer

The *Francs-archers* (*Free archers*) militia were the first attempt at the formation of regular infantry in France. They were created by the *ordonnance* of Montil-lès-Tours on 28 April 1448, which prescribed that in each parish an archer should be chosen from among the most apt in the use of arms; who was to be exempt from the *taille* and certain obligations, to practise shooting with the bow on Sundays and feast-days, and to hold himself ready to march fully equipped at the first signal. Under Charles VII the *francs-archers* distinguished themselves in numerous battles with the English, and assisted the king in driving them from France.

The *Francs-archers* deficient combat performance, indiscipline and unreliability led Louis XI in 1480 to train a professional army under Marshal Philippe de Crèvecœur d'Esquerdes and abolish the militia a year later, ordering their equipment to be put in store in the parishes.*[1] The cost of this permanent force was too great for the kingdom's finances, with the standing army being disbanded in 1483–1484 after Louis XI's death.*[1] In 1485 the *franc-archer* system was re-established and they were employed again in the Flanders campaign of the Mad War under Esquerdes.

During the Italian Wars, the *francs-archers* were primarily used for frontier defense. In May 1513 Louis XII raised 22,000 of them for such a purpose. They occasionally served in the field during campaigns such as in 1522 and 1523. They were levied for the last time after the French defeat at Pavia. The *francs-archers* were definitively disbanded in 1535.*[2]*[3]

2.3.1 Recruitment and composition

A *Franc-archer* was recruited in every parish of France. The parish was obligated to choose an archer and supply him with the specified equipment. The archer would train himself on feast-days and holidays. They were free from all taxes (hence the name) and were paid four francs for every month of service. The *Francs-archers* were predominantly older men, with the average age being 32.*[2] They often had to be re-equipped after service, breeding resentment among the villagers. They would also misuse their position to oppress the peasantry, while pretending to be simply obeying the king's will.*[2]

2.3.2 Organization and equipment

During the Hundred Years' War the *francs-archers* fought in companies of 200–300 men.*[2] The companies were led by nobles and were later put under the command of 4 captains-general.*[2] The 1448 *ordonnance* specified the equipment of the archer as a sallet helmet, dagger, sword, a bow, a sheath of arrows, a jerkin and a coat of mail.*[2] In 1466 they used the pike for the first time and by the late 1470s some companies were employing Swiss-style pikemen.*[2] During the Mad War in 1488, Esquerdes took 12,000 *francs-archers* for his campaign in Flanders.

In 1513, the 22,000-strong *francs-archers* levy was raised for 18 months and was organised into 44 ensigns of 500 men, each led by five *centeniers*. In 1510 Machiavelli noted that each *franc-archer* was required to have a horse.*[1] The Decree of 17 January 1522 listed the updated equipment of the *franc-archer* as comprising a corselet, a mail gorget, arm-pieces, a mail skirt and a helmet. Two-thirds were to be pikemen and the rest would be armed with halberds, crossbows and arquebuses.*[1]

2.3.3 Service

The *Francs-archers* were primarily used for frontier defense against foreign enemies and against bandits in the interior such as the *aventuriers*.*[4] They were also used in field battles, though their combat effectiveness against professional troops was low, such as against the Germans at Guinegate. In addition, they were prone to desertion, treason and capitulation.*[1]

During the reign of Louis XI the *francs-archers* performed poorly at the battle of Guinegate while under the command of Marshal Joachim Rouault. Lacking any unit training or discipline, they lost 6,000 men killed in action and many of them looted the enemy camp instead of fighting.*[1]

2.3.4 Franc-archers in literature

The franc-archers was a stock figure of fun in literary satire as early as the late 15th century. In these satires the franc-archer is portrayed as vainglorious, cowardly and militarily useless.*[5] François Rabelais mocked the *francs-archers* as cowards in his 1542 edition of Pantagruel.*[6] The *francs-archers* were nicknamed *francs-taupins*, meaning either "free-moles" *[7] or "free-beetles" .*[8]

2.3.5 References

[1] Potter 2008, p. 103.

[2] Potter 2008, p. 102.

[3] Arthur Augustus Tilley, Medieval France: A Companion to French Studies, Volume 5 (CUP Archive, 1964), pp. 159-61.

[4] Potter 2008, pp. 102-103.

[5] Potter 2008, pp. 324-327.

[6] Potter 2008, p. 324.

[7] William Duane (1810): A Military Dictionary

[8] Dr Faustroll (2007):Pataphysica 4: Pataphysica E Alchimia 2,pub iUniverse,ISBN 9780595426102, p.61

2.3.6 Bibliography

- Potter, D. (2008). *Renaissance France at War: Armies, Culture and Society, c.1480–1560*. Woodbridge, Suffolk: Boydell Press. ISBN 978-1-84383-405-2.

This article incorporates text from a publication now in the public domain: Chisholm, Hugh, ed. (1911). "Francs-archers". *Encyclopædia Britannica*. **11** (11th ed.). Cambridge University Press. p. 15.

2.4 Gakgung

The **Korean Bow** (Korean: 각궁, Gak-gung hanja: 角弓, or *horn bow*) is a water buffalo horn-based composite reflex bow, standardized about centuries ago from a variety of similar weapons in earlier use. Due to its long use by Koreans, it is also known as Guk Gung (Korean: 국궁 hanja: 國弓, or *national bow*). The Korean bow utilizes a thumb draw and therefore employing the use of a thumb ring is quite common. The Korean thumb ring is somewhat different from the Manchu, Mongol, or the Turkish Thumb Ring, as it comes in two styles, male and female. Male thumb rings are shaped with a small protrusion that sticks out that the bowstring hooks behind (similar to a release aid), while the female thumb ring simply covers the front joint of the thumb as protection from getting blisters (pulling heavy bows repetitively with only the thumb can easily cause blisters to form on the pad of the thumb).*[1] Also, the arrow is laid on the right side of the bow, unlike the western bow, where the arrow is laid on the left side of the bow.

Gungsul, Korean: 궁술, hanja: 弓術, sometimes also romanized as *goong sool*, literally means "techniques of the bow" or "skill with the bow." It is also referred to as Korean traditional archery. **Gungdo**, Korean: 궁도, hanja: 弓道, is another epithet for *traditional Korean archery*, as used by Koreans.

2.4.1 History of Military Origin and Usage

Korean Horse Back Archery in 5th-century

Oracle bone script version of the yi character

The reflex bow had been the most important weapon in Korean wars with Chinese dynasties and nomadic peoples, recorded from the 1st century BC.*[2] Legend says the first king and founder of the Goguryeo, Go Jumong, was a master of archery, able to catch 5 flies with one arrow. Bak Hyeokgeose, the first king of the Silla, was also said to be a skilled archer. The ancient Chinese gave the people of the north east, Siberia, Manchuria and the Korean Peninsula, the name of Dongyi (東夷) (Eastern part of the Four Barbarians (四夷)), the latter character (夷) being a combination of the two characters for "large" (大) and "bow" (弓).

However, the word 夷 was first used in Chinese history referring to the people South of Yellow River over 5,000 years ago. Later, when Yi 夷 people joined the tribes of Hua Xia [華夏] Chinese, 夷 meant outsider (in foreigner meanings) or *exterminate*. By that time, DongYi refers to Manchurian, Tunguistic tribes in Manchuria or Korean Peninsula, Korean and Japanese as in Outsiders from the East.*[3]

Yi Seonggye, the founding king of Joseon was known to have been a master archer. In a battle against Japanese pirates, Seonggye, assisted by Yi Bangsil, killed the young samurai commander "Agibaldo" with two successive arrows, one arrow knocking out his helmet, with the second arrow entering his mouth. In his letter to General Choi Young, Seonggye lists as one of five reasons not to invade Ming China as during the monsoon season, glue holding together the composite bow weakens, reducing the effectiveness of the bow.

The founding of Joseon dynasty saw the retention of the composite bow as the mainstay of the Joseon military.

2.4. GAKGUNG

Archery was the main martial event tested during the military portion of the national service exam held annually from 1392 to 1894. Under Joseon, archery reached its zenith, resulting in the invention of pyeonjeon, which saw great service against the Japanese in 1592 and against the Manchus in early 1600s.

Until the Imjin wars, archery was the main long-range weapon system. During those wars, the tactical superiority of the matchlock arquebus became apparent, despite its slow rate of fire and susceptibility to wet weather.*[4] However, it was the *gakgung*, referred to as the "half bow" by the Japanese, that halted the Japanese at the Battle of Haengju as well as at the Battle of Ulsan. Although Joseon adopted the arquebus during the Imjin War, the *gakgung* retained its position of importance in the military until the reforms of 1894. Under King Hyojong's military reforms, an attempt was made to revive horse archery as a significant element of the military. It was also practiced for pleasure and for health, and many young males - including the king - and a some many females would spend their free time practicing it.

2.4.2 Transition to Recreational Sport

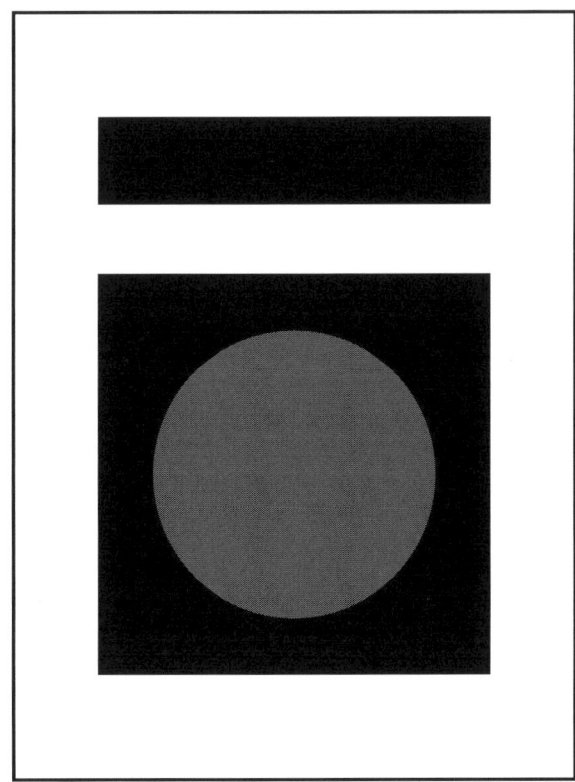

Standard gungdo target

In 1899, the visiting Prince Heinrich of Prussia expressed his astonishment to Emperor Gojong at a traditional archery demonstration. The Prince, hailing from a militarized Prussian culture, sought out demonstrations of Korean martial arts, and Archery was the most impressive among the arts demonstrated. He was familiar with Turkish and Hungarian Archery of Europe, which were similar to Korean Archery. Prince Heinrich suggested making the art into a national sport. The emperor, convinced by the Prince, decreed "let people enjoy archery to develop their physical strength" and established an archery club. In the subsequent standardization of Korean archery, the nature of the bow and the arrow was standardized, as was the range of the targets. Korean traditional archery now uses one specific type of composite bow, bamboo arrows, and a standard target at a standard distance of 120 bo (about 145 meters). Korean Archery as a sport developed under the Japanese Occupation, its textbook, "Joseon eui Goongdo" being published in 1920.

2.4.3 Construction and competition

Master Heon Kim

The *Gakgung* is a highly reflexed version of the classic Eurasian composite bow. The core is bamboo with sinew backed to prevent the bow breaking and to add a pulling strength to the limbs, with oak at the handle. On the belly is water buffalo horn which significantly increases the power by pushing the limbs. This combination of horn which pushes from the belly and sinew that pulls from the back is the defining strength of the bow. The siyahs, the stiffened outer ends of the limbs, are made of either mulberry or black locust spliced (v-splice) onto the bamboo. The glue is made from isinglass. Over the sinew backing is a special birch bark that is imported from Northeast China. It is soaked in sea water (possibly for one year). It is applied to the back using diluted rubber cement (using benzene as the solvent). No sights or other modern attachments are used.

The draw weights vary, but most are above twenty kilograms. The cost for this type of bow is in the US$800 range. For a similar modern version made of laminated fiberglass, the cost is US$200–300. For most competitions, either bow may be used, with carbon-fiber arrows, but for national competitions, only the composite bow and bamboo arrows may be used. Korean archers have also been very successful in Olympic and other competitions with more modern types of bow.[5]

The sukgung, a kind of crossbow, and the Gak-gung are a small but very powerful bow. A sukgung can shoot up to 400 meters while a Gak-gung can shoot up to 350 meters.

The art of constructing traditional Korean bows was designated an Important Intangible Cultural Property in 1971.[6]

2.4.4 See also

- Composite bow
- Hungarian bow
- Turkish bow
- Mongol bow
- Pyeonjeon
- Singijeon

2.4.5 References

[1] http://www.koreanarchery.org/classic/thumbrng.html

[2] Korean Traditional Archery

[3] (in Chinese) *Records of the Three Kingdoms* on the Chinese Text Project page

[4] Korean Traditional Archery. Duvernay TA, Duvernay NY. Handong Global University, 2007

[5] "South sweep". Sports Illustrated. 2000-09-28. Retrieved 2008-03-16.

[6] "Gungsi". UNESCO Intangible Cultural Heritage Centre. Retrieved 8 April 2013.

Further reading

- Korean Traditional Archery. Duvernay TA, Duvernay NY. Handong Global University, 2007.

2.4.6 External links

- Korean Traditional Archery
- The Way of the Bow
- Korean Archery News (Korean)
- Korean Traditional Archery Documentary

2.5 Newington Butts

The north end terminates at a roundabout of the Elephant and Castle junction, where the Elizabethan theatre stood.

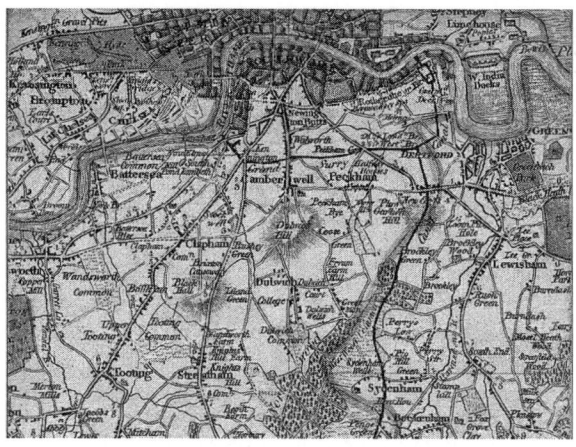

In 1800, Newington Butts was still part of rural Surrey.

Newington Butts is a former hamlet, now an area of the London Borough of Southwark, that gives its name to a segment of the A3 road running south-west from the Elephant and Castle junction. The road continues as Kennington Park Road leading to Kennington; a fork right is Kennington Lane, leading to Vauxhall Bridge.

It is believed to take its name from an archery butts, or practice field.[1][2] The area gave its name to an Elizabethan

2.5. NEWINGTON BUTTS

The playground in St Mary's churchyard has mounds that can be thought of as archery butts.

More mounds in the field of St Mary's churchyard.

theatre which saw the earliest recorded performances of some Shakespearean plays.[*][2]

2.5.1 Toponymy

The Middle English word "butt" referred to an abutting strip of land, and is often associated with medieval field systems.[*][3] The 1955 *Survey of London* published by London County Council could find no historical reference to archery butts in Newington[*][4] although the connection is mentioned elsewhere (e.g., in 1792[*][1]). The name may have alternatively derived from the triangle of land between the roads, as the word "butts" is used elsewhere in Surrey to refer to odd corners or ends of land.[*][4]

2.5.2 History

Newington was a rural village that grew up on the Walworth Road at its junction with the Portsmouth Road, about a mile south of London Bridge. Being outside the jurisdiction of the City of London it became home to activities such as plays that were banned near London during hot weather, for fear of spreading infection.

In the 17th and 18th centuries, the triangle of ground between the roads was known as the Three Falcons and was copyhold of the manor of Walworth.[*][4] In 1791 the leading scientist Michael Faraday was born at Newington Butts. In 1802, Thomas Hardwick reported that the estate consisted of a number of small tenements in bad condition.[*][4]

In the spring of 2008, St Mary's Churchyard, the green open space on the northern border of Newington Butts, was given a face lift. The largely grassy area now contains a children's playground. Dotted about within the playground and on the grass elsewhere are concrete mounds with rubber (safety) surfaces which were designed to add interest and topography to the developed area. These mounds might recall archery butts but this has been denied by the Elephant and Castle Regeneration Team.

In Cockney rhyming slang, 'Newington Butts' means 'guts'.[*][5]

2.5.3 Theatre

The Newington Butts Theatre was one of the earliest Elizabethan theatres, possibly predating even The Theatre of 1576 and the Curtain Theatre, which are usually regarded as the first dedicated playhouses in London.

2.5.4 See also

- English Renaissance theatre

- Newington, London

- Newington Causeway

2.5.5 Notes and references

[1] Lysons, Daniel (1792). *Newington Butts*. Volume 1. British History Online. pp. 389–398. Retrieved 21 August 2013. External link in |publisher= (help)

[2] "Newington Butts Playhouse". *PastScape*. UK: English Heritage. Retrieved 21 August 2013. External link in |work= (help)

[3] "Archery butts – 3 General description". English Heritage. Archived from the original on 2012-03-01. Retrieved 2010-08-22.

[4] Darlington, Ida (1955), *Survey of London Volume 25 – St George's Fields, the Parishes of St. George the Martyr Southwark and St. Mary, Newington*, London County Council, pp. 83–84

[5] "Newington Butts". Retrieved 15 May 2014.

2.5.6 Further reading

- Gladstone Wickham, Glynne William; Berry, Herbert; Ingram, William (2000), *English professional theatre, 1530–1660*, Cambridge University Press, pp. 320–329, ISBN 978-0-521-23012-4 transcribes the original manuscripts relating to Newington Butts playhouse.

- *Shakespearean Playhouses*, by Joseph Quincy Adams, Jr. from Project Gutenberg

2.5.7 External links

- Newington Butts, Kennington photograph, c. 1870.

Coordinates: 51°29′34″N 0°6′4″W / 51.49278°N 0.10111°W

2.6 Yumi

This article is about the Japanese bow. For other uses, see Yumi (disambiguation).

Yumi (弓) is the Japanese term for a bow. As used in English, *yumi* refers more specifically to traditional Japanese asymmetrical bows, and includes the longer **daikyū** (大弓) and the shorter **hankyū** (半弓) used in the practice of kyūdō and kyūjutsu, or Japanese archery. The *yumi* was an important weapon of the samurai warrior during the feudal period of Japan.

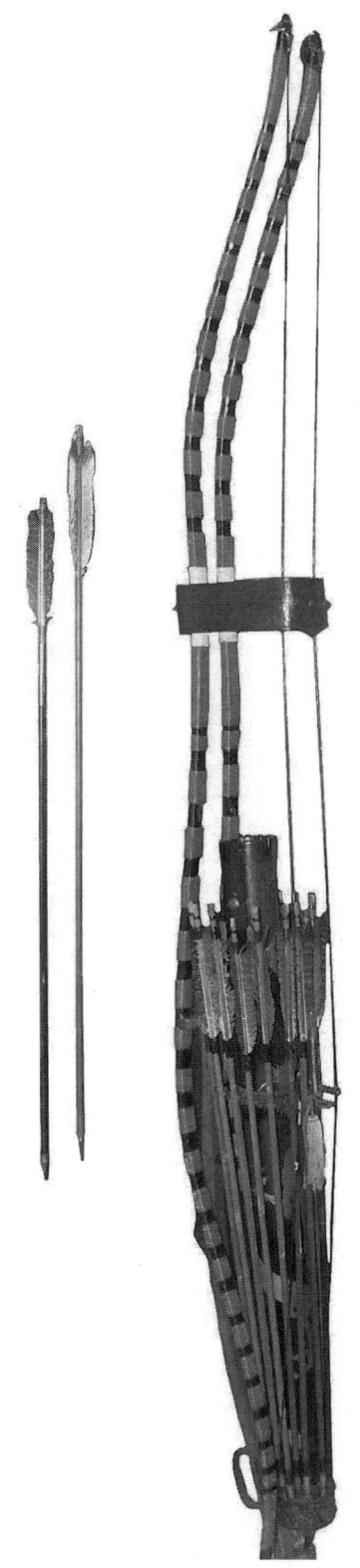

Japanese bows, arrows, and arrow-stand

2.6. YUMI

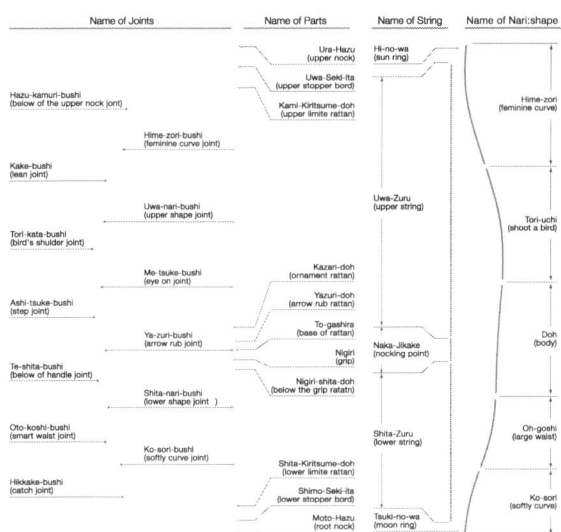

Yumi bow names

2.6.1 History

Early Japanese used bows of various sizes but the majority were short with a center grip. By the 3rd century BC, the bow length had grown to nearly 2 meters. This bow was called the *maruki yumi* and was constructed from a small sapling or tree limb. It is unknown when the asymmetrical *yumi* came into use, but the first written record is in the *Book of Wei*, a Chinese historical manuscript from the 3rd century AD, which describes the people of the Japanese islands using "spears, shields, and wooden bows for arms; the wooden bows are made with the lower limbs short and the upper limbs long; and bamboo arrows with points of either iron or bone."*[1] The oldest asymmetrical yumi found to date was discovered in Nara and is estimated to be from the 5th century.*[2]

During the Heian period (794-1185) the length of the *yumi* was fixed at a little over two meters and the use of laminated construction was adopted from the Chinese. By the end of the 10th century the Japanese developed a two piece bamboo and wood laminated *yumi*. Over the next several hundred years the bow's construction evolved and by the 16th century the design was considered to be nearly perfect. The modern bamboo *yumi* is practically identical to the *yumi* of the 16th and 17th centuries.*[3]

2.6.2 Shape

The yumi is exceptionally tall, standing over two meters, and typically surpasses the height of the archer (*ite*, 射手).*[4] They are traditionally made by laminating bamboo, wood and leather, using techniques which have not changed for centuries, although some archers (particularly beginners) may use a synthetic yumi.

The yumi is asymmetric; According to the All Nippon Kyudo Federation, the grip (*nigiri*) has to be positioned at about two thirds of the distance from the upper tip.

Scale representation of a drawn yumi

The upper and lower curves also differ. Several hypotheses have been offered for this asymmetric shape. Some believe it was designed for use on a horse, where the yumi could be moved from one side of the horse to the other with ease, however there is evidence that the asymmetrical shape predates its use on horseback.*[5]

Others claim that asymmetry was needed to enable shooting from a kneeling position. Yet another explanation is the characteristics of the wood from a time before laminating techniques. In case the bow is made from a single piece of wood, its modulus of elasticity is different between the part taken from the treetop side and the other side. A lower grip balances it.

The hand holding the yumi may also experience less vibration due to the grip being on a vibration node of the bow. A perfectly uniform pole has nodes at 1/4 and 3/4 of the way from the ends, or 1/2 if held taut at the ends – these positions will change significantly with shape and consistency of the bow material.

2.6.3 String

The string of a yumi is traditionally made of hemp, although most modern archers will use strings made of synthetic materials such as Kevlar, which will last longer. Strings are usually not replaced until they break; this results in the yumi flexing in the direction opposite to the way it is drawn, and is considered beneficial to the health of the yumi. The nocking point on the string is built up through the application of hemp and glue to protect the string and to provide a thickness which helps hold the nock (*hazu*) of the arrow (*ya*) in place while drawing the yumi. But can also be made of strands of waxed bamboo.

2.6.4 Care and maintenance

A bamboo yumi requires careful attention. Left unattended, the yumi can become out-of-shape and may eventually become unusable. The shape of a yumi will change through normal use and can be re-formed when needed through manual application of pressure, through shaping blocks, or by leaving it strung or unstrung when not in use.

The shape of the curves of a yumi is greatly affected by whether it is left strung or unstrung when not in use. The decision to leave a yumi strung or unstrung depends upon the current shape of the yumi. A yumi that is relatively flat when unstrung will usually be left unstrung when not in use (a yumi in this state is sometimes referred to as being 'tired'). A yumi that has excessive curvature when unstrung is typically left strung for a period of time to 'tame' the yumi.

A well cared-for yumi can last many generations, while the usable life of a mistreated yumi can be very short.

2.6.5 Bow lengths

2.6.6 Yumi history

The Korekawa bow, from the late Jōmon period which ended about 400 BCE, is laminated.*[6]

2.6.7 Gallery

- 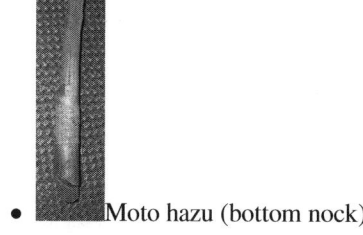Moto hazu (bottom nock)

- 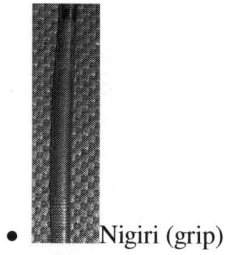Nigiri (grip)

- 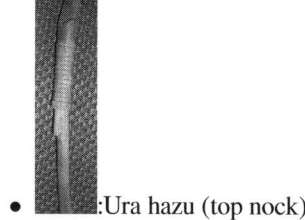:Ura hazu (top nock)

- 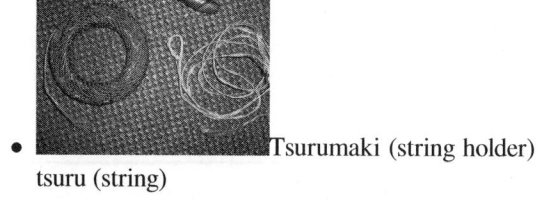Tsurumaki (string holder) and tsuru (string)

- Antique hankyū (shortbow)

- Antique daikyū (longbow) and hankyū (shortbow)

- Yumi bukuro (cloth cover)

2.6.8 See also

- Azusa Yumi—a "Catalpawood Bow"
- Hama Yumi—a "Evil Destroying Bow"
- Shigehto Yumi—a "Unity Bow"

2.6.9 References

[1] *Records of the Three Kingdoms*, Book of Wei: 兵用矛楯木弓木弓短下長上竹箭或鐵鏃或骨鏃

[2] *Kyudo: the essence and practice of Japanese archery*, Hideharu Onuma, Dan DeProspero, Jackie DeProspero, Kodansha International, 1993 P.37

[3] *Kyudo: the essence and practice of Japanese archery*, Hideharu Onuma, Dan DeProspero, Jackie DeProspero, Kodansha International, 1993 P.40

[4] Onuma, Hideharu (1993). *Kyudo: The Essence and Practice of Japanese Archery* (1 ed.). Tokyo: Kodansha International Ltd. p. 43. ISBN 4-7700-1734-0.

[5] Friday, Karl (2004). *Samurai, Warfare and the State in Early Medieval Japan*. New York NY: Routledge. p. 69. ISBN 0-415-32962-0.

[6] The Korekawa bow at Nara National Museum Accessed 2007-06-15 Archived September 27, 2007, at the Wayback Machine.

2.6.10 Further reading

- Herrigel, Eugen (1999). *Zen in the Art of Archery*. Vintage. ISBN 0-375-70509-0.

- Michael, Henry N. (1958). "The Neolithic Age in Eastern Siberia". *Transactions of the American Philosophical Society*. New Series. Philadelphia: The American Philosophical Society (published April 1958). **49** (2): 1–108. doi:10.2307/1005699. Retrieved 2008-02-13.

2.6.11 External links

Chapter 3

Text and image sources, contributors, and licenses

3.1 Text

- **History of archery** *Source:* https://en.wikipedia.org/wiki/History_of_archery?oldid=791291562 *Contributors:* Julesd, Michael Devore, Per Honor et Gloria, Chowbok, Mike Rosoft, D6, Xezbeth, Dbachmann, Bender235, Bendono, Smalljim, Bart133, ReyBrujo, Woohookitty, Spettro9, Kurzon, GregorB, BD2412, Rjwilmsi, Bedford, DVdm, Aaron Walden, JFD, Donald Albury, Dspradau, Katieh5584, SmackBot, Jagged 85, Gilliam, Hmains, Mr Barndoor, Durova, Snori, Kfroog, Freedom skies, Hibernian, Ncameron, Fuhghettaboutit, Attys, Gobonobo, Dl2000, Norm mit, Ken Gallager, Richard Keatinge, Cydebot, Max Ackerman, ChristTrekker, Ghostexorcist, Arwen4014, הסרפד, Headbomb, Nick Number, Northumbrian, Magioladitis, KConWiki, Philg88, Mattinbgn, Vamooom, Anaxial, R'n'B, Erik Springelkamp, Pal0165, Nwbeeson, Rosenknospe, DadaNeem, BrettAllen, KylieTastic, Philip Trueman, The Kings Yeomanry, Einar Ragnarsson, Master of the Oríchalcos, Insanity Incarnate, PericlesofAthens, Moerou toukon, StAnselm, WereSpielChequers, Flyer22 Reborn, Randy Kryn, ClueBot, GorillaWarfare, CounterVandalismBot, Excirial, Jusdafax, MartinFields, UltimateDestroyerOfWorlds, Audaciter, Berean Hunter, Heironymous Rowe, Blast Ulna, Addbot, Some jerk on the Internet, CL, Dcb1101, Lightbot, Сергей Олегович, Ben Ben, Yobot, KamikazeBot, AnomieBOT, Hadden, Jim1138, KRLS, E2eamon, SassoBot, Berylcloud, WebCiteBOT, Kak Dela?, Haploidavey, HamburgerRadio, Pinethicket, Koakhtzvigad, Cnwilliams, Readability, Lotje, RjwilmsiBot, Hello1107, GoingBatty, MikeyMouse10, Érico, CurtisKeim, Will-is-here, Noodleki, Donner60, Petrb, Mistbreeze, ClueBot NG, Jtma, Widr, Helpful Pixie Bot, BG19bot, Emayv, TheGeneralUser, Marcocapelle, Glacialfox, Rutebega, Neuroforever, ChrisGualtieri, Khazar2, Lugia2453, Krakkos, Juzumaru, Hillbillyholiday, Faizan, Bananasoldier, Captain-Fox501st, Hansmuller, Jackmcbarn, Wiloy22, 󠀀5, Monkbot, Filedelinkerbot, Vieque, Nitebradley, Kaitlyn153, Jason.nlw, Boehunter, BD2412bot, InternetArchiveBot, Unitatoisme, Bender the Bot, Home Lander, Magic links bot and Anonymous: 164

- **Arab archery** *Source:* https://en.wikipedia.org/wiki/Arab_archery?oldid=791483037 *Contributors:* Richard Keatinge, Cydebot, AnomieBOT, Hadden, John of Reading, BattyBot, KSFT and Anonymous: 4

- **Archery butt** *Source:* https://en.wikipedia.org/wiki/Archery_butt?oldid=789632586 *Contributors:* Varlaam, LindsayH, Bender235, Bobo192, RainbowOfLight, Sbp, NawlinWiki, Jpbowen, Mr Stephen, Aarktica, CmdrObot, WeggeBot, Aodhdubh, JamesAM, JustAGal, Hasek is the best, Waacstats, MartinBot, R'n'B, Chienlit, FlyingLeopard2014, ClueBot, Berean Hunter, Addbot, Kelly, Paul21455, Materialscientist, Le Deluge, Humpty18, BaldBoris, Mean as custard, RjwilmsiBot, ClueBot NG, Widr, YOURMOMASAURUS, Rawley Myers, SheaUK, Fyddlestix, Dickbutt12, InternetArchiveBot, Hhshjfjhs and Anonymous: 33

- **Assize of Arms of 1252** *Source:* https://en.wikipedia.org/wiki/Assize_of_Arms_of_1252?oldid=789608532 *Contributors:* Eastlaw, Int21h, Helpful Pixie Bot, Marcocapelle, Bender the Bot and Anonymous: 1

- **Battle of Crécy** *Source:* https://en.wikipedia.org/wiki/Battle_of_Cr%C3%A9cy?oldid=793687831 *Contributors:* AxelBoldt, BlckKnght, Sjc, Eclecticology, Gsl, Christian List, Deb, Maury Markowitz, Olivier, Leandrod, Kchishol1970, Infrogmation, Paul Barlow, Yann, Muriel Gottrop~enwiki, Plop, Darkwind, Djnjwd, Jiang, Raven in Orbit, JidGom, Charles Matthews, Adam Bishop, Molinari, Reddi, Dysprosia, Joy, Wetman, Qertis, ChrisO~enwiki, PBS, Kadin2048, Naddy, Securiger, Acegikmo1, SoLando, DocWatson42, Tom harrison, Gamaliel, Varlaam, Leonard G., Per Honor et Gloria, Kudz75, Neilc, Andycjp, Jasper Chua, Gdr, Albrecht, Antandrus, Mozgulek, PFHLai, Qui1che, Grstain, D6, Miborovsky, Discospinster, Rich Farmbrough, Ericamick, MeltBanana, Stbalbach, Bender235, ESkog, Kross, Jpgordon, Reuben, Masterchief~enwiki, Giraffedata, LtNOWIS, Jeltz, Feanaro, Ksnow, Velella, Fdewaele, A D Monroe III, Woohookitty, Woyzzeck~enwiki, Zivago, Merlinme, Greekmythfan, 󠀀, Dodiad, Turnsole80, Bkwillwm, Insomniac By Choice, GraemeLeggett, Mattmorgan, Palica, WBardwin, Deltabeignet, Ketiltrout, Rjwilmsi, Tim!, Jivecat, FayssalF, FlaBot, Old Moonraker, Harmil, Mark J, Choess, Nomadtales, Gdrbot, YurikBot, Wavelength, TexasAndroid, RobotE, Oldwindybear, NTBot~enwiki, Fabartus, EDM, Matt01, KevinOB, Witan, Kirill Lokshin, Lavenderbunny, Member, Wikimachine, NawlinWiki, Rjensen, Renata3, Denihilonihil, Tony1, Zwobot, Bota47, HLGallon, Mev532, Saukkomies, Garion96, Allens, Nick-D, Mhardcastle, Attilios, KnightRider~enwiki, Nathan Robinson, SmackBot, Dweller, Thedus, Hux, Lajbi, McGeddon, Davewild, Dpwkbw, Peter Isotalo, Gilliam, Durova, Chris the speller, Rex Germanus, Grimhelm, Cloj, L clausewitz, Jeff5102, Colonies Chris, Veggies, Writtenright, GrahameS, SpiderJon, Ohconfucius, RASAM, Akendall, Ergative rlt, Beetstra, Peyre, Clarityfiend, RekishiEJ, Balthamel, TriniSocialist, Revcasy, Mellery, Causantin, Nunquam Dormio, Eddiervc, Equendil, Cydebot, Jackyd101, Alphageekpa, Sdoradus,

3.1. TEXT

Christian75, DiScOrD tHe LuNaTiC, Wandalstouring, Epbr123, Biruitorul, Boubelium, Nonagonal Spider, Headbomb, Qp10qp, Liquid-aimbot, Brendandh, Mutt Lunker, GWhitewood, JAnDbot, MER-C, Arch dude, Andonic, Alastair Haines, Boleslaw, WolfmanSF, Secret Squïrrel, VoABot II, Jaakko Sivonen, JamesBWatson, Mclay1, Jllm06, Michael Goodyear, The Anomebot2, Eldumpo, Perebot~enwiki, Cpl Syx, Philg88, Amitchell125, R'n'B, CommonsDelinker, Lilac Soul, Nev1, Rrostrom, Tyman7, Troutsneeze, Skier Dude, AntiSpamBot, Gip213, Malerin, Student7, Ninanta, Trip Johnson, Segilla, Gpier66, Signalhead, Nikthestunned, Deor, VolkovBot, Nburden, Chienlit, TXiKiBoT, Sean D Martin, Karpatia~enwiki, Ironflange, Vaubin, Haerenia, Truthanado, Finnrind, SieBot, Tiddly Tom, Triwbe, Bentogoa, Flyer22 Reborn, Monegasque, KoshVorlon, Lord Phat, IdreamofJeanie, Rosiestep, Caedmon85, Epass, Denisarona, ClueBot, Deanlaw, XPTO, Mild Bill Hiccup, TheOldJacobite, The Red Guy, Prottos007, CounterVandalismBot, Piledhigheranddeeper, Alexbot, Socrates2008, Baseballbaker23, Friedliebend und tapfer, Bellroth, DumZiBoT, XLinkBot, Avmarle, Actam, Dubmill, Addbot, Tiggywinkle25, Some jerk on the Internet, Dunhere, Mabdul, Jeanne boleyn, Groundsquirrel13, Download, Knerlo, AndersBot, Chzz, Favonian, Jamesdowsett, Tassedethe, Ehrenkater, Ben Ben, Luckasbot, Yobot, Jan Arkesteijn, PMLawrence, Nallimbot, KamikazeBot, AnomieBOT, Rubinbot, Jonesboyinsydney, Ulric1313, Mugginsx, Ahusni, LilHelpa, Laurent7575, Sodacan, Anonymous from the 21st century, Secher nbiw, GrouchoBot, Coltsfan, Sabrebd, AustralianRupert, Mattis, DITWIN GRIM, FrescoBot, Tobby72, Daniel moar, Picosaur, D'ohBot, Ladril, Chenopodiaceous, Winterst, TexasTankMech, I dream of horses, Plucas58, Dragovit, Anaruna, JefferyBerry, Bierstein, Diannaa, Wilytilt, Sideways713, Jorwar, Snerfl, Flyingmonkey666, Mukogodo, Emaus-Bot, Pjposullivan, Littlebluedevil6, Eeesy, Tommy2010, Lobsterthermidor, Hazard-SJ, Kals1234, GenghisOwns, Darthkenobi0, Wingman4l7, Voyledd, JoeSperrazza, MedMil, Brandmeister, Donner60, Andercm, 19thPharaoh, TheCajun80, ClueBot NG, Wonmean, Omnisome, Zukertort, Helpful Pixie Bot, Mr. Credible, BG19bot, Trumpkinius, Tinynanorobots, Robert the Devil, Trevayne08, Gamershark15, Laodah, Only in death, Awesome335, TeriEmbrey, Migget2025, Marcusgee12345, Toxophilus, Nsteffel, Bobsy345, Jon M. Loose, Boldair, Padrianprice, Monkbot, DanKriedt, Agilulf2007, Gog the Mild, Skeletalclown, Captainiom, Jerodlycett, LITTOW1346, Ira Leviton, My Chemistry romantic, FriendoftheBHP, Berty688, Emelkaji, The oriflamme, Tjmarsh09, SirNoelRules, Lorenzo.piazzoli, Selrahcmattmonde, Droyselich, AirshipJungleman29, Zpov333, Dragon23330, MARX, Julius, Tamagosh, PrimeBOT, Eochadh, Magic links bot, Appah Rao, Qmbv and Anonymous: 375

- **Crossbow** *Source:* https://en.wikipedia.org/wiki/Crossbow?oldid=790584788 *Contributors:* Magnus Manske, TwoOneTwo, Tarquin, Kowloonese, XJaM, Rmhermen, Ktsquare, Youandme, Hephaestos, Frecklefoot, Edward, Patrick, JohnOwens, JakeVortex, Liftarn, Ixfd64, Ellywa, Glenn, Samw, Raven in Orbit, Agtx, David Latapie, Tjunier, Patrick0Moran, Furrykef, Nv8200pa, Taxman, AnonMoos, Wetman, Robbot, Cdang, Blades, Kizor, Tomchiukc, Modulatum, Bryce, Academic Challenger, Rasmus Faber, Bkell, Demerzel~enwiki, Guy Peters, Apol0gies, Kbahey, Tom harrison, Everyking, Varlaam, Maroux, Per Honor et Gloria, Mboverload, Jackol, Bobblewik, Utcursch, Antandrus, WhiteDragon, Hgfernan, Wikster E, Aerion, Mschlindwein, Bbpen, Avihu, DMG413, Abdull, Mike Rosoft, Miborovsky, Jpg, Discospinster, Rich Farmbrough, Rama, Dbachmann, Stbalbach, Bender235, ESkog, Kbh3rd, Appleboy, Kross, RoyBoy, Wareh, TMC1982, Jpgordon, Harald Hansen, Duk, .:Ajvol:., Elipongo, Mytildebang, Russ3Z, Idleguy, Pearle, Martin S Taylor, OGoncho, Alansohn, Anthony Appleyard, Sheehan, Trainik, Jeltz, Sjschen, Ashley Pomeroy, Garfield226, Cdc, Mysdaao, PeteVerdon, Snowolf, Wtmitchell, TaintedMustard, BRW, Rugxulo, Harej, Culix, Sciurinæ, LFaraone, BDD, Bookandcoffee, Postrach, A D Monroe III, Richard Arthur Norton (1958-), Simetrical, Woohookitty, PoccilScript, Daniel Case, Exxolon, Chris Buckey, Male1979, Tom W.M., Ashmoo, FreplySpang, Rjwilmsi, Astronaut, Vary, Matt Deres, FayssalF, Skyfiler, SchuminWeb, Klausner, MicroBio Hawk, Kri, Chobot, WriterHound, Gwernol, Siddhant, YurikBot, Hairy Dude, RussBot, Longbow4u, Anders.Warga, Hydrargyrum, Alyebard, Gaius Cornelius, Ksyrie, Prouddemocrat, NateDan, Wimt, NawlinWiki, -OOPSIE-, RL0919, Gerrymurphy, Sandman1142, DeadEyeArrow, Paaskynen, Candymonster, Nlu, Sandstein, Nikkimaria, Closedmouth, Josh3580, Reyk, GraemeL, Vicarious, Garion96, Darren Lee, Allens, Kungfuadam, Carlosguitar, Some guy, Groyolo, Attilios, SmackBot, Reedy, KnowledgeOfSelf, Olorin28, Lawrencekhoo, AndyZ, Stifle, RedSpruce, Arny, JimmyBlackwing, Yamaguchi 先生, Gilliam, Hmains, Durova, Chris the speller, Asclepius, JackyR, Thumperward, Jeekc, Apeloverage, Sadads, TheLeopard, Baa, Zachorious, Can't sleep, clown will eat me, Nick Levine, Cplakidas, Alphathon, Chlewbot, OrphanBot, Onorem, Gurps npc, Missinglincoln, Computerman45, Midnightcomm, Nakon, RandomP, Megalophias, DMacks, Ohconfucius, SashatoBot, Rory096, BrownHairedGirl, Markjeff, LWF, AllStarZ, Beerios, Maksim L., Intranetusa, RMHED, Galactor213, Yes0song, Twitchey, Iridescent, Shoeofdeath, Troy Frei, Tawkerbot2, LessHeard vanU, Eastlaw, Liam Skoda, CmdrObot, Causantin, Dycedarg, TheHerbalGerbil, Ninetyone, Rogerborg, Neelix, Ken Gallager, Richard Keatinge, Karenjc, Slazenger, =Axiom=, ChristTrekker, Gogo Dodo, Sullivan9211, DumbBOT, Custic, M.J.Stanham, Aldis90, Thijs!bot, Wandalstouring, Epbr123, Barticus88, Pajz, Interested2, Daniel, Nonagonal Spider, Sobreira, NigelR, Grayshi, The Hybrid, Mercutio.Wilder, Escarbot, Mentifisto, Hmrox, AntiVandalBot, WinBot, Seaphoto, Johnnydader, Doc Tropics, Paste, Aruffo, TimVickers, North Shoreman, Storkk, Qwerty Binary, Myanw, PresN, Ingolfson, JAnDbot, Dan D. Ric, MER-C, Seddon, Igodard, Sitethief, Hut 8.5, TAnthony, Barefact, PhilKnight, Acroterion, Bongwarrior, VoABot II, BigDukeSix, Fusionmix, Yandman, Froid, Fabrictramp, Allstarecho, Pikazilla, War wizard90, Gun Powder Ma, Yhinz17, Hdt83, MartinBot, Valthalas, Arjun01, Kiore, R'n'B, CommonsDelinker, Beit Or, Shellwood, J.delanoy, Nev1, Uncle Dick, Eliz81, Jerry, The Crying Orc, Acalamari, Rantir, Clerks, Cannibalicious!, Gurchzilla, Plasticup, NewEnglandYankee, Lygophile, Imawsome, Bklounge, Imnowei, KylieTastic, Juliancolton, STBotD, JavierMC, Davecrosby uk, Idioma-bot, Signalhead, Geosultan4, VolkovBot, Neverwake, Jeff G., Fw190a8, Nik Sage, Guardian Tiger, Kyle the bot, George Adam Horváth, Philip Trueman, Oshwah, MrZhuKeeper, Someguy1221, Amagase~enwiki, Martin451, Broadbot, LeaveSleaves, Assassinus, DesmondW, Doug, LanceBarber, Earl Marischal, Burntsauce, AgentCDE, Wikicake, Jvicarrow, Dhruvn, Master of the Oríchalcos, TinribsAndy, Monty845, AlleborgoBot, GavinTing, PericlesofAthens, SaltyBoatr, SieBot, Necronomicomedian, Nubiatech, Rfts, Canoescanoes, Lachrie, Happysailor, HkCaGu, Chukonu xbow, Mimihitam, Oxymoron83, Byrialbot, AngelOfSadness, Ealdgyth, Diablo52, IdreamofJeanie, Coldcreation, HighInBC, Pinkadelica, Escape Orbit, Explicit, Hoplon, ImageRemovalBot, Martarius, ClueBot, Snigbrook, Hgblob, Wysprgr2005, XPTO, Arakunem, Drmies, Wmgurst, SuperHamster, Foofbun, Alonades, PeteXor, Nick19thind, Haudcivitas, Excirial, Rhododendrites, Tyler, Dakovski, Ngebendi, Xianbataar, Frederik29, SchreiberBike, Gnip, AccursedOne, 7, Versus22, Berean Hunter, Vanished user uih38riiw4hjlsd, DumZiBoT, Mystery Correction, XLinkBot, Little Mountain 5, Ferics, NellieBly, Airplaneman, Liktnstein13, Addbot, Cxz111, Blanche of King's Lynn, Willking1979, SuperSmashBros.Brawl777, Ronhjones, Davis7, Jncraton, Ironholds, Mogrock1, Fluffernutter, Rchard2scout, LemmeyBOT, West.andrew.g, Alphacolony, Flappychappy, Martinac, Lightbot, OlEnglish, Pietrow, Zorrobot, Legobot, Luckasbot, Yobot, Fraggle81, TaBOT-zerem, Fenrir-of-the-Shadows, PMLawrence, Edfresh, Vibrantspirit, Dorieo, IW.HG, The Flying Spaghetti Monster, Pogonatos2, AnomieBOT, 1exec1, Jim1138, Piano non troppo, Ulric1313, Jpptgaiv, Bradybrady, Materialscientist, The High Fin Sperm Whale, Danno uk, Citation bot, Nicklol823, ArthurBot, LilHelpa, Xqbot, Narthring, Jeffrey Mall, Saracen86, Kurtdriver, SassoBot, Kobalt08, Governor Jerjerrod, SD5, Griffinofwales, FrescoBot, Surv1v4l1st, Ihateqwerty67, Benster1510, HJ Mitchell, HamburgerRadio, Citation bot 1, Rockends~enwiki, Pinethicket, I dream of horses, LittleWink, RoomTemperatureSeekingMissile, A8UDI, Jschnur, Serols, Meaghan, Monkeymanman, Miguel Escopeta, Orenburg1, Updatezz, Lotje, Vrenator, Clarkcj12, MrX, 564dude, Aston1238, Bakinblak111, MrTodo88, EmausBot, John of Reading, Immunize, Faceless Enemy, PhantomScott, Tommy2010, K6ka, Ranama181, Bravo Foxtrot, Josve05a, Imperial

Monarch, NicatronTg, Ebrambot, Wayne Slam, Lathdrinor, L1A1 FAL, Julierbutler, L Kensington, Donner60, Damirgraffiti, Peter Karlsen, Spykey808, Will Beback Auto, ClueBot NG, MelbourneStar, Joefromrandb, Frietjes, Elvonudinium, Mic5201, O.Koslowski, Newyorkadam, Jacob3211982, Italstenda, Helpful Pixie Bot, HMSSolent, J0ryj, Titodutta, BG19bot, MusikAnimal, Mifter Public, Frze, Amp71, Cold Season, Joydeep, Glevum, Dude1414, Nanobliss, Britehit23, Pratyya Ghosh, 希望, ChrisGualtieri, St-Margaret, Cwobeel, TheOneHonkingAntelope, Abdesk2008, Sigvit, Numbermaniac, Rajmaan, Robogetti56, Eyesnore, FunnyPika, Kogmaw, B14709, Vanished user 9oijnsdfknefijh3tjasfi34, Court Appointed Shrub, Wxzyn5168, FaperMcFapington, The Herald, D Eaketts, Snowsuit Wearer, LinkTheShadow, Ooaoaoao, Yoshi24517, Wandrative, Monkbot, Justin15w, Rajat Vij, Ivandabomb, Mysterypo, Nicolamack, Ironblacksmith, KH-1, Bigwilson77, Leokid2001, The Holm, DangerousJXD, Yprpyqp, JackAttackkk, Раціональне анархіст, Modernswordsmith, Tank6123, JJMC89, Yungdre007, My Chemistry romantic, Kanoro, BU Rob13, Csldigicol, Dilidor, Blorper234, InternetArchiveBot, GreenC bot, Egare123, Isaac Eyestone, ToxicReap, HazzaMcRazza, Alfie Gandon, Phuocnh2953, ProfesorKen, Bender the Bot, Heart of Destruction, 72, Nien Nunb, RichardBrower, Uptoniga, Ekpawel, Romanbrisk, Magic links bot and Anonymous: 765

- **English longbow** *Source:* https://en.wikipedia.org/wiki/English_longbow?oldid=784332819 *Contributors:* Sjc, -- April, Ed Poor, Gsl, William Avery, SimonP, Xlation, Leandrod, Kchishol1970, Egil, Ahoerstemeier, Julesd, Glenn, Marteau, Djnjwd, Csernica, Emperorbma, Revolver, Adam Bishop, Rbraunwa, Random832, David Latapie, Hyacinth, Taxman, Rls, AnonMoos, Wetman, Dale Arnett, Blades, PBS, Stephan Schulz, Babbage, Rholton, SoLando, GreatWhiteNortherner, Buster2058, DocWatson42, Wiglaf, Zigger, Yak, Ich, Everyking, TomViza, Varlaam, AlistairMcMillan, Dumbo1, Bobblewik, R. fiend, Kjetil r, Eregli bob, L353a1, Rwv37, Ruzulo, Sam Hocevar, Deewiant, GreenReaper, Kate, D6, Lehi, Rich Farmbrough, Loganberry, YUL89YYZ, Francis Davey, Dbachmann, Stbalbach, Bender235, CanisRufus, Cygnosis, Phiwum, Thuresson, Jonathan Drain, Bobo192, Ypacaraí, Ogress, Earendur, Ashley Pomeroy, MarkGallagher, Hohum, Verk, Pax~enwiki, Alfvaen, Gene Nygaard, Blaxthos, A D Monroe III, Stemonitis, Pekinensis, Qnonsense, Merlinme, CyrilleDunant, StradivariusTV, Pol098, 171046, AshishG, Bkwillwm, GregorB, Isnow, Trewornan, Grammarbot, Topsydog, Izaic3, Rjwilmsi, Quale, Jivecat, Zaak, Nneonneo, Stilgar135, Don-Siano, Ligulem, XR-CatD, Matt Deres, DirkvdM, Fish and karate, Wobble, Old Moonraker, Choess, Daycd, Dresdnhope, UkPaolo, Hairy Dude, Spleodrach, Wolfmankurd, Midgley, Witan, Gaius Cornelius, The Merciful, Tapir, Brian Crawford, Jpbowen, Kortoso, Thomas Esper, Sandstein, Mev532, Nae'blis, Validusername, Hitchhiker89, Kungfuadam, CrniBombarder!!!, SmackBot, Ariedartin, Mauls, Srnec, IstvanWolf, Ohnoitsjamie, Hmains, Durova, Chris the speller, Thumperward, Snori, Hibernian, Colonies Chris, Modest Genius, Gsp8181, Thomas Graves, Aldaron, Fuhghettaboutit, Nakon, Kukini, Andrei Stroe, Ceoil, Kuru, Waggers, Neddyseagoon, Vince In Milan, Iridescent, JoeBot, Native-Foreigner, TurabianNights, Rnb, Rdunn, Vaughnstull, CmdrObot, Causantin, Loganfong, 345Kai, Ballista, Richard Keatinge, Fordmadoxfraud, Cydebot, ChristTrekker, Dynaflow, DumbBOT, BenShade, BigShock, Malleus Fatuorum, Wandalstouring, Martin Hogbin, Zickzack, Nonagonal Spider, Headbomb, Son of Somebody, Uvaphdman, Brendandh, Farosdaughter, Paul1776, DuncanHill, WikipedianProlific, PhilKnight, Magioladitis, T@nn, Kokin, Avicennasis, Gun Powder Ma, Robek, Robin S, MartinBot, FlieGerFaUstMe262, Aviatora, Urselius, DrFrench, Gzkn, Acalamari, Mathglot, Chickenhawk2002, Joost de Kleine, Hugo999, Nik Sage, VasilievVV, FergusM1970, WOSlinker, Gwinva, Keddie, Don4of4, Jeremy Bolwell, Quindraco, Corvus coronoides, Gemilasultan, JF42, Bfpage, Tiddly Tom, SemperFideliS81, Flyer22 Reborn, Lightmouse, Int21h, Nosferatublue, ClueBot, Madpostie, Drmies, Mild Bill Hiccup, Auntof6, Excirial, Jusdafax, Jefflayman, ChrisHodgesUK, Bald Zebra, Agentel, Mearama, Berean Hunter, Dthomsen8, Ilikepie2221, Inchiquin, Emma 7979, Addbot, Jojhutton, Fyrael, Groundsquirrel13, Patton123, Gtlaxgoaliegirl, Lightbot, Willondon, Yobot, Fraggle81, Palamabron, AnomieBOT, 1exec1, LlywelynII, Bluerasberry, Materialscientist, Citation bot, LilHelpa, Bihco, Garrard munich, Owainglyndwr92, Dioxa, Pinethicket, Diomedea Exulans, FriedrichMILBarbarossa, Evan T Jones, Monstrelet, Serols, Trappist the monk, DARTH SIDIOUS 2, RjwilmsiBot, Emil.mckellar, Poneomenos, Hajatvrc, Faceless Enemy, Mobrun, RenamedUser01302013, Dcirovic, Azkm, Mz7, Wingman4l7, L1A1 FAL, Vogelabv, ClueBot NG, Griffy95, Frietjes, Delusion23, Breogan2008, Widr, Antiqueight, Helpful Pixie Bot, Calidum, DBigXray, Plantdrew, BG19bot, MusikAnimal, Carlstak, Richard Tennant, Achowat, BattyBot, Warsamer, Cyberbot II, ChrisGualtieri, Tech77, Arcandam, Dexbot, Abdesk2008, Cymraeg Warrior, Babitaarora, Correctrix, Xenxax, Monkbot, DynGlas, Cosmomopolis, Hannah da blondie, Starke Hathaway, Bobasdfjkl, Csldigicol, Ebookomane, Allthefoxes, InternetArchiveBot, Bender the Bot, James27031992, Sjm52, Cetacean Needed and Anonymous: 375

- **Gorytos** *Source:* https://en.wikipedia.org/wiki/Gorytos?oldid=704063264 *Contributors:* Skysmith, Per Honor et Gloria, Woohookitty, Jeff3000, Deucalionite, Bluebot, Picus viridis, Severo, Bcp67, ImageRemovalBot, Addbot, Dorieo, FrescoBot, Hmainsbot1 and Anonymous: 3

- **History of crossbows** *Source:* https://en.wikipedia.org/wiki/History_of_crossbows?oldid=785621152 *Contributors:* Edward, Quadell, Discospinster, Rich Farmbrough, Bender235, Smalljim, Sam Korn, GraemeLeggett, BD2412, Nihiltres, DVdm, Nikkimaria, Fram, SmackBot, Lawrencekhoo, Stifle, Gilliam, Skizzik, Chris the speller, Thumperward, PrimeHunter, Ohconfucius, Waggers, Intranetusa, Iridescent, Eastlaw, Hemlock Martinis, Alaibot, Wandalstouring, Epbr123, Magioladitis, Philg88, Gun Powder Ma, Ginsengbomb, KylieTastic, Davecrosby uk, Meiskam, MrZhuKeeper, Wiae, CharlesRClayton, Logan, PericlesofAthens, WereSpielChequers, ImageRemovalBot, ClueBot, Ndenison, Trilobite12, Wmgurst, Orthoepy, Haudcivitas, Frederik29, Palindromedairy, Gnip, Carriearchdale, Berean Hunter, DumZiBoT, Tealwisp, XLinkBot, Lstanley1979, Mifter, Blanche of King's Lynn, Yobot, AnomieBOT, Wayne Roberson, Austin, Texas, FrescoBot, Urgos, Igna, Trappist the monk, TangoFett, Polzisha, John of Reading, Demigord, Hikingherman, Dcirovic, ClueBot NG, Tadatsune, Widr, Helpful Pixie Bot, Rgarcia598, Thekillerpenguin, CitationCleanerBot, MrBill3, ChrisGualtieri, ZemplinTemplar, Rajmaan, JamieSc, King Philip V of Spain, Ilovesmallmgs, Aliensarereal123, HMSLavender, Yprpyqp, Dcmlibertadfinal, 3 of Diamonds, HeirOfSumer, BU Rob13, Csldigicol, 人族, InternetArchiveBot, Bender the Bot, Ellsworth Wiki, Magic links bot and Anonymous: 82

- **Mary Rose** *Source:* https://en.wikipedia.org/wiki/Mary_Rose?oldid=793317866 *Contributors:* Peter Winnberg, 0, WojPob, Deb, Imran, Isis~enwiki, Leandrod, Edward, Paul Barlow, Skysmith, Paul A, Stan Shebs, Dilgreen, IceKarma, Chris 73, Rholton, Mervyn, Seano1, Jooler, DocWatson42, Wizzy, Angmering, Obli, Yak, McPaul, Michael Devore, Mboverload, Solipsist, Brockert, Geni, Gdr, Antandrus, Eregli bob, Trelane, Icairns, Clemwang, Mtnerd, Mike Rosoft, Guanabot, MelBanana, SpookyMulder, ESkog, Jnestorius, Bluap, Susvolans, Art LaPella, Bobo192, Cmdrjameson, Vicarage, Zelda~enwiki, Anthony Appleyard, Couperman, Dinsdalepiranha, Andrewpmk, Denniss, Hu, Phyllis1753, Snowolf, Saga City, Gene Nygaard, Ghirlandajo, Pcpcpc, Richard Arthur Norton (1958-), Woohookitty, PatGallacher, TomTheHand, Pol098, Ardfern, Kralizec!, MarkusHagenlocher, Prashanthns, Mandarax, Graham87, Miq, Akubhai, Tabercil, Rjwilmsi, Coemgenus, Hiberniantears, Rillian, Mike Peel, Boatman, Ucucha, FlaBot, RobertG, Oliver Chettle, Old Moonraker, Nihiltres, NekoDaemon, No Swan So Fine, Jaraalbe, YurikBot, Butsuri, Daverocks, RussBot, Fabartus, Stephenb, Gaius Cornelius, CambridgeBayWeather, Shaddack, Tailpig, Sir48, Inhighspeed, Jpbowen, Pyroclastic, Raven4x4x, Tony1, EEMIV, AnnaKucsma, Mev532, Paul Magnussen, Jonthegeologist, Chase me ladies, I'm the Cavalry, Chaleur, Dspradau, Fram, Mais oui!, Mjroots, Nick-D, Attilios, SmackBot, YellowMonkey, Iacobus, Facius, Flamarande, Srnec, Ian Rose, Peter Isotalo, Binot~enwiki, Jimdpie, Chris the speller, KaragouniS, JackyR, Grimhelm, Roscelese, Hibernian, Sadads, Bluquail, Rcbutcher, Animal Mother~enwiki, Modest Genius, OrphanBot, Britmax, Rsm99833, Aldaron, Nakon, Bob Castle, Hunter2005, Henning Makholm,

3.1. TEXT

Ohconfucius, John, Jamestown, JonE, Minna Sora no Shita, Tlesher, Jxb311, Pfold, Ian Dalziel, A. Parrot, MarkSutton, Rock4arolla, Waggers, Viv Hamilton, Neddyseagoon, Hogyn Lleol, Peter Horn, Jrt989, Jc37, Haus, Beno1000, CapitalR, Hyperman 42, Drumlanrig, CmdrObot, The ed17, Erik Kennedy, Leevanjackson, Hollingsworth, AshLin, Cydebot, Jackyd101, JonEastham, Islander, Amandajm, Trident13, BenShade, PamD, Casliber, Malleus Fatuorum, Thijs!bot, Epbr123, Colin4C, Auror, WhiteCrane, Woody, Esemono, Arrowhead2006, Escarbot, Mentifisto, 49oxen, Fayenatic london, EP111, MortimerCat, Ericoides, Arch dude, QuantumEngineer, Leolaursen, PhilKnight, WolfmanSF, Secret Squïrrel, VoABot II, Ling.Nut, Kauko56, The Anomebot2, Catgut, Matt00055, Rif Winfield, Textorus, Martocticvs, SebastianMG, Laura1822, MartinBot, R'n'B, CommonsDelinker, Sege1701, J.delanoy, Pharaoh of the Wizards, Nev1, Bellagio99, Rose Palmer, Ncmvocalist, AntiSpamBot, M-le-mot-dit, NewEnglandYankee, SJP, Touch Of Light, Cometstyles, Gemini1980, RjCan, Daandyman, Richard New Forest, UnicornTapestry, Deor, Toddy1, Philip Trueman, TXiKiBoT, GimmeBot, Unoquha, Alan Rockefeller, Saber girl08, Dormskirk, Charlesdrakew, Una Smith, Don4of4, CanOfWorms, Natg 19, Persiana, Eubulides, Falcon8765, Tttom, Thunderbird2, Mfcayley, Nubiatech, Kingbird1, Oxymoron83, Jack1956, Benea, Lightmouse, Techman224, Ealdgyth, TriangleBelow, CharlesGillingham, StaticGull, Maralia, Dabomb87, Phil wink, Randy Kryn, Hasantosun, Explicit, Joao10000, Faithlessthewonderboy, Aandjnmr, Tanvir Ahmmed, MBK004, ClueBot, UrsusArctosL71, MIDI, Kendo70133, Gaia Octavia Agrippa, Mild Bill Hiccup, Ranger Steve, Niceguyedc, Parkwells, Lastenglishking, Pstaveley, Excirial, Anonymous101, Canis Lupus, Winston365, Shinkolobwe, Lartoven, Sun Creator, NuclearWarfare, Bonewah, Yeoni, Shem1805, Jtle515, Hannahtaylor, XLinkBot, Spitfire, Bilsonius, Little Mountain 5, Salam32, PL290, Spoonkymonkey, Lauren74irmo, CalumH93, Olyus, Addbot, Jojhutton, Groundsquirrel13, Proxima Centauri, CarsracBot, Chzz, Favonian, Tassedethe, Lightbot, II MusLiM HyBRiD II, Disillusioned-BitterAndKnackered, Baln101, Alexkin, Eric-Wester, AnomieBOT, Andrewrp, 1exec1, Jim1138, Piano non troppo, AdjustShift, LlywelynII, Crecy99, RandomAct, Chocolateyummyfatcake, Ifrit117, Xqbot, Capricorn4, 4twenty42o, Date delinker, Kieronoldham, Aa77zz, GrouchoBot, Auntieruth55, Brutaldeluxe, Miyagawa, Buchraeumer, Arco Scheepen, FrescoBot, D'ohBot, HJ Mitchell, Obituarist, AstaBOTh15, Metricmike, Aardvark32, December21st2012Freak, Lightlowemon, Trappist the monk, Jps 1001, Ale And Quail, SmartyBoots, Ridiculus mus, Nascar1996, Lwaioli, Difu Wu, Ineverheardofhim, Noommos, Charlesfjbarker, WinContro, Mukogodo, EmausBot, John of Reading, Immunize, Golfandme, GoingBatty, RA0808, 1Matt20, Wikipelli, Dcirovic, AvicBot, ZéroBot, Midas02, GrindtXX, UltimaRatio, L Kensington, 2001 Convention, Irrypride, Mx121fox, Palaeozoic99, ClueBot NG, Matthiaspaul, Hupaleju, Martin of Sheffield, Strike Eagle, Denovoid, Lowercase sigmabot, Cowdy001, Interchangeable, Marcocapelle, Tilly-jean, Willdude 132, BattyBot, Bricybricybricy, Khazar2, ÄDA - DÄP, Dexbot, Irondome, FoCuSandLeArN, Sminthopsis84, Sapperjack, Lugia2453, Jamesx12345, Corinne, The Anonymouse, Valetude, Literalman, Croinop, 49ersBelongInSanFrancisco, SMClabby-MR, XXXY syndrome, Gladamas, DiscantX, Saaj3105, 福田直樹, Morphdog, Forscher scs, CAPTAIN RAJU, InternetArchiveBot, Callum Watson Noooo, Ilovebenjibooboo, Bender the Bot, Jason Oberle, Magic links bot and Anonymous: 341

- **Medieval archery** *Source:* https://en.wikipedia.org/wiki/History_of_archery?oldid=791291562 *Contributors:* Julesd, Michael Devore, Per Honor et Gloria, Chowbok, Mike Rosoft, D6, Xezbeth, Dbachmann, Bender235, Bendono, Smalljim, Bart133, ReyBrujo, Woohookitty, Spettro9, Kurzon, GregorB, BD2412, Rjwilmsi, Bedford, DVdm, Aaron Walden, JFD, Donald Albury, Dspradau, Katieh5584, SmackBot, Jagged 85, Gilliam, Hmains, Mr Barndoor, Durova, Snori, Kfroog, Freedom skies, Hibernian, Ncameron, Fuhghettaboutit, Attys, Gobonobo, Dl2000, Norm mit, Ken Gallager, Richard Keatinge, Cydebot, Max Ackerman, ChristTrekker, Ghostexorcist, Arwen4014, הסרפד, Headbomb, Nick Number, Northumbrian, Magioladitis, KConWiki, Philg88, Mattinbgn, Vamooom, Anaxial, R'n'B, Erik Springelkamp, Pal0165, Nwbeeson, Rosenknospe, DadaNeem, BrettAllen, KylieTastic, Philip Trueman, The Kings Yeomanry, Einar Ragnarsson, Master of the Oríchalcos, Insanity Incarnate, PericlesofAthens, Moerou toukon, StAnselm, WereSpielChequers, Flyer22 Reborn, Randy Kryn, ClueBot, GorillaWarfare, CounterVandalismBot, Excirial, Jusdafax, MartinFields, UltimateDestroyerOfWorlds, Audaciter, Berean Hunter, Heironymous Rowe, Blast Ulna, Addbot, Some jerk on the Internet, CL, Dcb1101, Lightbot, Серей Олегович, Ben Ben, Yobot, KamikazeBot, AnomieBOT, Hadden, Jim1138, KRLS, E2eamon, SassoBot, Beryleloud, WebCiteBOT, Kak Dela?, Haploidavey, HamburgerRadio, Pinethicket, Koakhtzvigad, Cnwilliams, Readability, Lotje, RjwilmsiBot, Hello1107, GoingBatty, MikeyMouse10, Érico, CurtisKeim, Will-is-here, Noodleki, Donner60, Petrb, Mistbreeze, ClueBot NG, Jtma, Widr, Helpful Pixie Bot, BG19bot, Emayv, TheGeneralUser, Marcocapelle, Glacialfox, Rutebega, Neuroforever, ChrisGualtieri, Khazar2, Lugia2453, Krakkos, Juzumaru, Hillbillyholiday, Faizan, Bananasoldier, Captain-Fox501st, Hansmuller, Jackmcbarn, Wiloy22, 囗囗 5, Monkbot, Filedelinkerbot, Vieque, Nitebradley, Kaitlyn153, Jason.nlw, Boehunter, BD2412bot, InternetArchiveBot, Unitatoisme, Bender the Bot, Home Lander, Magic links bot and Anonymous: 164

- **Mongol bow** *Source:* https://en.wikipedia.org/wiki/Mongol_bow?oldid=787285866 *Contributors:* Hyacinth, GreatWhiteNortherner, Davidcannon, Punga~enwiki, ESkog, Smalljim, Chris huh, Optichan, Iolaire, Zaman, Bash, Cryptic, Kvn8907, Jpbowen, Durak, Groyolo, SmackBot, ScaldingHotSoup, OrphanBot, Latebird, Jfingers88, Statsone, Cold Water, Stwalkerster, Ka34, PaddyM, CmdrObot, Causantin, Andkore, Richard Keatinge, ChristTrekker, Wandalstouring, ColourBurst, Tigeroo, Andonic, Steveprutz, Bakilas, Albmont, Vito Genovese, Srice13, SquidSK, Boston, Knulclunk, Chinneeb, Nik Sage, TXiKiBoT, WikiReaderer, ParallelPain, Yaan, Synthebot, DEMENTED DAVE, Lightmouse, Porsenna1, ClueBot, MikeVitale, Niceguyedc, Eeekster, MacedonianBoy, Pqnelson, Berean Hunter, DumZiBoT, Hell Hawk, Classicbow, MystBot, Addbot, Chzz, Deathmonger855, Luckas-bot, Yobot, AnomieBOT, FrescoBot, OgreBot, Rackmasterh, Spicemix, Shadegan(goru), ClueBot NG, Jtma, Snotbot, Wrathkind, Helpful Pixie Bot, Jowilley9261996, BG19bot, MongolWiki, Glevum, Abdesk2008, Ibaclaan, Khanate General, Tigercompanion25, THemanRE$%S23, Prinsgezinde, Strapatch, Mergenjavuu2, Stonnefrety7777, CountryMusicMann, LehryDoo, PrimeBOT and Anonymous: 74

- **Mounted archery** *Source:* https://en.wikipedia.org/wiki/Mounted_archery?oldid=787979819 *Contributors:* Robbot, Fudoreaper, Grant65, Alex Cohn, Klemen Kocjancic, Dbachmann, Hajenso, Vanished user 19794758563875, TaintedMustard, Woohookitty, Mtloweman, Ninly, Owain.davies, Hardscarf, Scolaire, SmackBot, Jagged 85, Hmains, Chris the speller, Snori, Hibernian, Neo-Jay, Egsan Bacon, OrphanBot, Snowmanradio, Mr Bucket, Valenciano, Paul S, Keith-264, J Milburn, Richard Keatinge, Montanabw, Cydebot, Zickzack, KConWiki, Londubh, R'n'B, CommonsDelinker, Gamer112, Krysspana, Lovas, NinjaRobotPirate, PericlesofAthens, Enkyo2, SieBot, Rednbluearmy, Niceguyedc, Sun Creator, SchreiberBike, Staygyro, Lx 121, Berean Hunter, XLinkBot, Classicbow, Bilsonius, Ryebonfire, Dthomsen8, Addbot, Yobot, Ptbotgourou, AnomieBOT, Jim1138, W.stanovsky, Jun Kayama, Anotherclown, Jfischnaller, 超プロ住民, Лапоть, FrescoBot, 青鬼よし, I dream of horses, CandyRFI, Orenburg1, Frantic ferret, Dusty777, John of Reading, Samuraiantiqueworld, Fakirbakir, ZxxZxxZ, Lucas Thoms, Italia2006, RaptureBot, Co2gas, ClueBot NG, 0x44616e, Ptdtch, MerlIwBot, Helpful Pixie Bot, Smart Nomad, Wbm1058, BG19bot, Marcocapelle, Dainomite, Khazar2, Donostrowski2, Ayoo2, Kharadea, Juzumaru, Rajmaan, Bulls123, Crovata, Syncmaster913n, FactoProphyl, Filedelinkerbot, Mehdi khatibi, はぐれがらす, Urbanite79, Maximilianer48, Kepsır, Rjstcruzin, T.v.laaksonen, Bender the Bot, Magic links bot, Karl Greenwood and Anonymous: 78

- **Pítati** *Source:* https://en.wikipedia.org/wiki/P%C3%ADtati?oldid=782489490 *Contributors:* Dbachmann, Ogress, Woohookitty, Cuchullain, BD2412, Bgwhite, Mmcannis, Fusion7, Squids and Chips, SwordSmurf, AnnekeBart, Muhandes, Berean Hunter, Jncraton, J04n, FrescoBot,

DrilBot, The inconceivable ham, Magic links bot and Anonymous: 2

- **Scorton Arrow** *Source:* https://en.wikipedia.org/wiki/Scorton_Arrow?oldid=615876492 *Contributors:* Tim!, Jaraalbe, Irishguy, SmackBot, Mr Barndoor, Greenshed, GhostInTheMachine, WhaleyTim, Dantheman531, Just Chilling, Keith D, Dormskirk, Scortonarrow, The Thing That Should Not Be, Gerbilo, Mhockey, Addbot, VengeancePrime, DrilBot and Anonymous: 2

- **Shooting an apple off one's child's head** *Source:* https://en.wikipedia.org/wiki/Shooting_an_apple_off_one'{}s_child'{}s_head?oldid=788238999 *Contributors:* DavidBrooks, Now3d, Dbachmann, Jnestorius, Chris the speller, Albany NY, Cgingold, Maurice Carbonaro, Wilson44691, Piledhigheranddeeper, Addbot, Bermicourt, Yobot, Yngvadottir, GB fan, GreenC, Jfmantis, ClueBot NG, Helpful Pixie Bot, BG19bot, Memorial bench, Bender the Bot, Magic links bot and Anonymous: 8

- **Society of Archers** *Source:* https://en.wikipedia.org/wiki/Society_of_Archers?oldid=507190399 *Contributors:* Tim!, SmackBot, Mr Barndoor, JohnCD, WhaleyTim, Severo, Hugo999 and Ktr101

- **St Mary's Butts** *Source:* https://en.wikipedia.org/wiki/St_Mary'{}s_Butts?oldid=759284863 *Contributors:* Chris j wood, Rich Farmbrough, Cydebot, PKT, Severo, R'n'B, Hugo999, Icarusgeek, Ordishj, Redrose64, BaldBoris, Diannaa and GreenC bot

- **Stone wrist-guard** *Source:* https://en.wikipedia.org/wiki/Stone_wrist-guard?oldid=769895703 *Contributors:* Wetman, Lproven, Mboverload, Rich Farmbrough, Awiseman, Mmcannis, Hmains, Snori, Hibernian, Grumpy444grumpy~enwiki, Thefuguestate, CmdrObot, Richard Keatinge, Cydebot, Arch dude, Johnbod, Sahlqvist, Addbot, Carlog3, Throwaway85, Lotje, Khazar2 and Anonymous: 3

- **The Archer's Craft** *Source:* https://en.wikipedia.org/wiki/The_Archer'{}s_Craft?oldid=782489520 *Contributors:* Grstain, Antaeus Feldspar, Kappa, BDD, Jenblower, Jpbowen, Pegship, SmackBot, Gimme a reason to keep this, Ken Gallager, Severo, GrahamHardy, Addbot, Lightbot, Magic links bot and Anonymous: 2

- **The Witchery of Archery** *Source:* https://en.wikipedia.org/wiki/The_Witchery_of_Archery?oldid=728643481 *Contributors:* Delirium, Bender235, Bedford, John, Lampman, Julia Rossi, DOSGuy, Victuallers, GrahamHardy, EricSerge, Randy Kryn, Suntag, Helpful Pixie Bot, CitationCleanerBot and Anonymous: 4

- **Thumb ring** *Source:* https://en.wikipedia.org/wiki/Thumb_ring?oldid=780764731 *Contributors:* Ryuch, Architeuthis, Rob T Firefly, Thistledowne, SmackBot, Latebird, AndyBQ, Steel Rain, Nydas, Difference engine, Semper331fi, Richard Keatinge, Johnbod, BrettAllen, Calisun, Squids and Chips, Traumrune, Muzikislyf, Seraphim, Sarc37, Jdog73, Arqueira, Berean Hunter, Addbot, Jorghex, Yobot, AnomieBOT, Hadden, Surv1v4l1st, Lotje, Helpful Pixie Bot, Shakatark2, LehryDoo and Anonymous: 21

- **Toxophilus** *Source:* https://en.wikipedia.org/wiki/Toxophilus?oldid=788809126 *Contributors:* Mervyn, BDD, Crusoe8181, DexDor, Helpful Pixie Bot and Magic links bot

- **Turkish archery** *Source:* https://en.wikipedia.org/wiki/Turkish_archery?oldid=788536508 *Contributors:* Hyacinth, Dbachmann, CeeGee, Gertlex, Thiseye, PRehse, SmackBot, Hmains, Betacommand, Bluebot, Snori, Mukadderat, Shin00bi, Voceditenore, Slakr, Alessandro57, Drinibot, Richard Keatinge, Aldis90, Zickzack, Legitimus, WereSpielChequers, Trigaranus, Arjayay, Takabeg, Addbot, Twofistedcoffeedrinker, Yobot, Hadden, Mttll, Ellenois, Jansay, Chevymontecarlo, Mseren, Akocsg, WikitanvirBot, Dr.tolga, Mogism, DRHY, PrimeBOT and Anonymous: 16

- **Unlawful Games Act 1541** *Source:* https://en.wikipedia.org/wiki/Unlawful_Games_Act_1541?oldid=748291177 *Contributors:* RobinCarmody, Tim!, Hugo999, TutterMouse, AnomieBOT, James500, Cnwilliams, John of Reading, ClueBot NG, ASHaber, Qetuth, Nimetapoeg, Bender the Bot and Anonymous: 3

- **William Tell** *Source:* https://en.wikipedia.org/wiki/William_Tell?oldid=789294589 *Contributors:* Rjstott, Deb, Panairjdde~enwiki, Gabbe, Paul A, Docu, Haabet, Schneelocke, Gofreddo63, Cyrenaic, Jengod, Gestumblindi, Saltine, Itai, Wetman, Robbot, Fredrik, Sparky, Mirv, Academic Challenger, Smb1001, Carlj7, Lupo, Marc Venot, Clementi, Fennec, Omegium, Wiglaf, Merlante, Varlaam, BigHaz, Tristanreid, Chowbok, Ran, Antandrus, OwenBlacker, Gauss, Bodnotbod, Arcturus, JHCC, Thorwald, D6, Jake Wildstrom, Chris j wood, Rich Farmbrough, LindsayH, Dbachmann, Polynova, Snow steed~enwiki, Art LaPella, Smalljim, John Vandenberg, Sam Korn, Haham hanuka, Alansohn, Gary, PaulHanson, MrTree, Mo0, Ksnow, Aka, Sleigh, Nortonew, LOL, 25or6to4, Brunnock, PatGallacher, MattGiuca, Graham87, Magister Mathematicae, Cuchullain, BD2412, Opie, Schmendrick, Sjakkalle, Valentinejoesmith, BlueMoonlet, Wahkeenah, Ligulem, Bensin, JohnGH, Mark272, Ian Pitchford, RexNL, LeCire~enwiki, Chobot, DTOx, HarryCane, Satanael, YurikBot, Quentin X, RobotE, Vuvar1, Huw Powell, Dannycas, RussBot, Hede2000, Mark Ironie, 03haya, Wimt, Ugur Basak, NawlinWiki, Test-tools~enwiki, SigPig, Howcheng, Countakeshi, Rmky87, PhilipC, BazookaJoe, Don Williams, Jeffw57, Merishi, Th1rt3en, Ray Chason, BorgQueen, Che829, Katieh5584, Hathaldir~enwiki, Victor falk, Next362, SpLoT, Drcwright, SmackBot, YellowMonkey, Hydrogen Iodide, Rrius, Mscuthbert, RedSpruce, Dwanyewest, Kintetsubuffalo, DreamOfMirrors, Gaff, Commander Keane bot, Cool3, Gilliam, Fluri, Afasmit, Leoni2, Ecoli, Can't sleep, clown will eat me, Pevarnj, Seduisant, BostonMA, Nakon, Chris3145, GuillaumeTell, BinaryTed, SashatoBot, Akendall, Emhilradim, Žiga, Amalgamut, Llamadog903, Mets501, LaMenta3, Eastfrisian, Rickington, Clarityfiend, Captain Kirk, Flamelai, Bodukesmeltzer, Chetvorno, George100, JForget, Adam Keller, Irwangatot, Wafulz, Gr8quizzer, Liu Bei, Keithh, Johnjohnston, AndrewHowse, HalJor, Vanished user vjhsduheuiui4t5hjri, Goldfritha, Llort, WikiDomWiki, Tkynerd, DavidRF, Dferrantino, Gutterrat, Thijs!bot, HappyInGeneral, Danlibbo, Marek69, John254, Peter Gulutzan, Jennifer Brooks, AntiVandalBot, Derzsi Elekes Andor, Drewdy, Efyoo, RapidR, Chgros, Isilanes, Malcolm, Myanw, Sluzzelin, MER-C, Wildhartlivie, Pjlon, Jaysweet, VoABot II, Wikidudeman, Twsx, Whitewater97, Cgingold, Turb0flat4, Cpl Syx, JaGa, Esanchez7587, ZorkNika, Hockey90, Ratherhaveaheart, MartinBot, Timstre, Tremello, Snowybeagle, Anaxial, Maurice Carbonaro, Storm Alarm, Andareed, Canadian Scouter, NobleHelium, Thesis4Eva, MKoltnow, Idioma-bot, Oxfordoaks, Hugo999, Deor, Mrh30, Science4sail, Katydidit, Al.locke, Oshwah, Slysplace, Rdfox 76, Circusandmagicfan, Roland zh, Ponyo, Tiddly Tom, Azazyel, Malcolmxl5, Mcg85, PookeyMaster, Monegasque, Goustien, Fidelio72, TX55, Ian Clelland, Jóhann Heiðar Árnason, Mygerardromance, Dannyboy1702, Rejozenger, Tripod86, Mx. Granger, Church, ClueBot, Rumping, PipepBot, DionysosProteus, Pi zero, Mild Bill Hiccup, Leocapaldi, Piledhigheranddeeper, Cirt, Jeremiestrother, Excirial, Russ Davis, AllenHansen, Gundersen53, Paytoplay, 7, SoxBot III, Editor2020, Gotso!, Antti29, Littlebigguy, XLinkBot, AMRDeuce, Kennygollnick, Equusviride, Skarebo, Good Olfactory, Kbdankbot, Addbot, Gevorg89, Tcncv, Wgwwgw, Set1986, NjardarBot, LaaknorBot, CarsracBot, Halbwolf, Lightbot, Bermicourt, Luckas-bot, Yobot, Yngvadottir, Troymacgill, Vini 17bot5, Tempodivalse, Mdw0, AnomieBOT, OhDoTell, Jim1138, Kingpin13, Sz-iwbot, Ulric1313, Materialscientist, Bob Burkhardt, LilHelpa, Xqbot, Jebdm, Cureden, Julianhyde, Jeffrey Mall, GrouchoBot, Ad Meskens, Doulos Christos, Shadowjams, Omar35880, Vagrand, Urgos, Supergeekfreak, Codecreations, Pinethicket,

3.1. TEXT

LittleWink, RedBot, Full-date unlinking bot, Derivateur, Italiancapp31, Kgrad, Lotje, Amphicoelias, AirRuritania, Jfmantis, RjwilmsiBot, Gamonetus, DRAGON BOOSTER, Tvashtar2919, 达伟, EmausBot, Gimmetoo, K6ka, مہشیں ناهب, Josve05a, Klavierspieler, Rapunzelvern, Erget2005, Willthacheerleader18, VictorianMutant, Jfwikker, ClueBot NG, JetBlast, Stevenlin13, Loganferguson13, Soccerstars007, Barrel-Proof, JoeRoache, OlafMeding, Tellsgeschoss, Snotbot, Widr, KLBot2, Vagobot, Soerfm, Anbu121, Kelly351755, YFdyh-bot, Khazar2, JY-Bot, Foxer40, Frosty, Ouzotech, LahmacunKebab, TomSFox, Quenhitran, RGB62, OccultZone, Ithinkicahn, Mendisar Esarimar Desktrwaimar, Opencooper, Filedelinkerbot, MRD2014, KasparBot, WikiBathor, Axxxxxxxxxxaa, DatGuy, Qzd, Aideen2007, Vegan416, Bender the Bot, PrimeBOT, Justeditingtoday, CommonCry, Penskins, 2028883qc, Alexkinna12345 and Anonymous: 427

- **Yabusame** *Source:* https://en.wikipedia.org/wiki/Yabusame?oldid=788548790 *Contributors:* Phoebe, Michael Snow, Comatose51, Quadell, Fg2, Bendono, Kappa, Bart133, LordAmeth, Hijiri88, Commander Keane, BD2412, FlaBot, Adriano C., Deadhippo, Jefu, YurikBot, Quentin X, Mark Ironie, Crossfire~enwiki, Jpbowen, Shawnc, PRehse, SmackBot, Nihonjoe, Kintetsubuffalo, Betacommand, Chris the speller, Nbarth, Dreadstar, Ryulong, CmdrObot, Causantin, Ken Gallager, Montanabw, Urashimataro, Aldis90, Heliotic, Edal, Douggers, Jmills74, WinBot, Steven Walling, Bradford44, Anaxial, Marishiten, Enkyo2, WereSpielChequers, DrHacky, Oda Mari, Xavexgoem, Boneyard90, Alexbot, Lx 121, XLinkBot, MatthewVanitas, Addbot, Lightbot, Zorrobot, Luckas-bot, Yobot, Interocitor, ぎぶそん, FrescoBot, Senfrancis, Robo Cop, Lotje, EmausBot, Samuraiantiqueworld, RaptureBot, ClueBot NG, Satellizer, Justlettersandnumbers, Helpful Pixie Bot, BattyBot, Theonlytruemathnerd, Mysterious Island, Pktlaurence, KasparBot, Bender the Bot, PrimeBOT and Anonymous: 29

- **Yeoman** *Source:* https://en.wikipedia.org/wiki/Yeoman?oldid=793694678 *Contributors:* Gsl, Karen Johnson, William Avery, Ant, Daniel C. Boyer, D, Mcarling, Skysmith, Eric119, Kingturtle, Ugen64, Mxn, MasterDirk, Charles Matthews, Dino, Furrykef, Nickshanks, AnonMoos, Gentgeen, Owain, PBS, Mervyn, UtherSRG, Parasite, Gzornenplatz, Chowbok, Pgan002, Keith Edkins, Quadell, Piotrus, Billposer, Ary29, Necrothesp, Austin Hair, Neutrality, Sonett72, M1ss1ontomars2k4, Safety Cap, CALR, Rich Farmbrough, Ebelular, Dpm64, Dbachmann, KevinBot, CanisRufus, El C, Surachit, RoyBoy, West London Dweller, Func, Giraffedata, Alansohn, Gary, Couperman, WikiParker, PeteVerdon, Snowolf, Binabik80, Saga City, RainbowOfLight, Dominic, Richard Weil, Kay Dekker, Kenyon, Angr, Woohookitty, Daniel Case, Uncle G, WadeSimMiser, SDC, Ashmoo, Wachholder0, George Burgess, Ligulem, Dunkelza, FlaBot, Consumed Crustacean, DVdm, Damnbutter, Gdrbot, Bgwhite, EamonnPKeane, Albanaco, RussBot, Briaboru, Stephenb, Gaius Cornelius, Aeusoes1, Veledan, IlyaV, Rjensen, Shinmawa, Jpbowen, Vancouveriensis, Bucketsofg, Dirt, Scope creep, Jezzabr, Igiffin, Mike Selinker, JLaTondre, Lomacar, CIreland, Tom Morris, Yvwv, BonsaiViking, SmackBot, Robotbeat, OrientalHero, Pennywisdom2099, PatMcD, Hmains, Chris the speller, Quinsareth, Bduke, Colonies Chris, Yaf, HoodedMan, Snowmanradio, Matchups, Nakon, Akulkis, Thomasyen, Daniel.Cardenas, Kukini, Andrewrabbott, Esrever, LtPowers, Jimsg, John, J 1982, SilkTork, Sir Nicholas de Mimsy-Porpington, Pfold, JHunterJ, Waggers, Ryulong, Sussexman, MrDolomite, Thefuguestate, HelloAnnyong, Tawkerbot2, Dlohcierekim, Wolfdog, CmdrObot, Tinman8443, Dtrimble, ShelfSkewed, Ken Gallager, NE Ent, Shanoman, Mr Toad, Cydebot, Balaclava, Soetermans, Bpgdag, Tkynerd, Asenine, Kozuch, Jed keenan, PKT, Thijs!bot, Epbr123, Biruitorul, Rusl, Bigwyrm, Oerjan, Yeomanrycavalry, Doyley, K. Lastochka, Dawkeye, Yorkshire Phoenix, AntiVandalBot, Milton Stanley, Ambergypsy, MsDivagin, Luckz, Fayenatic london, Albany NY, TAnthony, Bongwarrior, VoABot II, Dekimasu, Mclay1, Lucas(CA), Rich257, Bleh999, LorenzoB, CharlesKiddell, MartinBot, Pupster21, Kenji 03, LittleOldMe old, J.delanoy, Rachelskit, Adavidb, Spathaky, Ginsengbomb, Panpulha, Ppgj-nzng, Wisepiglet, NewEnglandYankee, Robertgreer, Corriebertus, Mrmuk, Fingerpuppet, Calculatoronfire, Pdcook, Akechi77, Rémih, SoCalSuperEagle, Safemariner, Jeff G., Station1, Andreas Kaganov, Una Smith, Juanaquena, LeaveSleaves, Jeremy Bolwell, Billinghurst, Chad.huber, GreaterWikiholic, StAnselm, DerbyCountyinNZ, Tiddly Tom, VVVBot, Radon210, Treehill, Goustien, Mhavril39, Int21h, Henricus411, Karl2620, Msrasnw, Mygerardromance, Dabomb87, DRTllbrg, Sfan00 IMG, Tanvir Ahmmed, ClueBot, IPAddressConflict, Hutcher, The Thing That Should Not Be, SeaValeYen, Mild Bill Hiccup, RafaAzevedo, Bboutz, Gtstricky, Vivio Testarossa, Sun Creator, Iohannes Animosus, Heldane70, SchreiberBike, ChrisHodgesUK, Krome1985, MystBot, Panthos, Addbot, Grayfell, ConCompS, Fieldday-sunday, Download, LaaknorBot, 5 albert square, Hunting dog, Sophia8891, Ehrenkater, Tide rolls, Lightbot, Zorrobot, Genius101, Luckas-bot, Yobot, Fraggle81, QueenCake, Ayrton Prost, Joal o, HaldaneFan, AnomieBOT, Лудольф, Wallamoose, DAFMM, Maarten Ronteltap, Bob Burkhardt, GB fan, Ched, J04n, Joaquin008, FrescoBot, Ben Culture, D'ohBot, Tylersoron, Degen Earthfast, Neurosojourn, Supreme Deliciousness, Attilios2 notasock, Vrenator, HaiHaiRakuen, Akinderfather, GameOn, Minimac, DARTH SIDIOUS 2, Winner 42, ZéroBot, Traxs7, Midas02, Pembroke Dog, Luxie Lisbon, Erianna, SpikeballUnion, Brendanmccabe, Carmichael, TheBlackHawk11, Compactz, Turtleey, Ssvends2, ClueBot NG, Satellizer, D.justins, Widr, Paved with good intentions, BG19bot, Patrug, Zyxwv99, Kostlivec, Pratyya Ghosh, FoCuSandLeArN, Alex2564, Geongra mannus, Алексей Галушкин, LionofLondon, MRD2014, Z swagdaddy, The Sky Sword, IEditEncyclopedia, Excitedguy12, C swagmama3, Will2022, PWerger2, Jake Vonore, Invisible Guy, Z0boson and Anonymous: 356

- **Arbalest** *Source:* https://en.wikipedia.org/wiki/Arbalest?oldid=784377703 *Contributors:* Tarquin, Frecklefoot, JohnOwens, Menchi, David Latapie, Furrykef, Dhumberson, DocWatson42, Guanaco, Piotrus, ThC, Klemen Kocjancic, Epimetreus, Eyrian, Rama, Dbachmann, Blade Hirato~enwiki, OGoncho, Bart133, TaintedMustard, Japanese Searobin, Butsuri, Hairy Dude, Megapixie, Virogtheconq, SmackBot, KVDP, Hmains, Durova, Thumperward, Fuhghettaboutit, Megalophias, Tbonequeen79, ShakingSpirit, DouglasCalvert, ChristTrekker, Wandalstouring, Honeplus, Lilitu Babalon, AntiVandalBot, WinBot, Caragan1970, Fearless Son, Struthious Bandersnatch, Severo, Wrexsoul, Gun Powder Ma, Atarr, Kynikos Vodyanoi, Anaxial, Rtdixon86, Jalo, Loniousmonk, Synthebot, Roboriath, DragonBot, Xianbataar, Gnip, Berean Hunter, MystBot, Addbot, Some jerk on the Internet, OffsBlink, Luckas-bot, Yobot, Softwarestorage, AnomieBOT, BenzolBot, DivineAlpha, LittleWink, Nom du Clavier, Agent Smith (The Matrix), Rorymc1, Wormke-Grutman, ClueBot NG, Gareth Griffith-Jones, American Idiot1, Primergrey, Helpful Pixie Bot, ASCIIn2Bme, Tanyacrook, Bufo12, Magic links bot and Anonymous: 68

- **Archer's stake** *Source:* https://en.wikipedia.org/wiki/Archer'{}s_stake?oldid=723340831 *Contributors:* Bearcat, Neutrality, Dbachmann, KConWiki, WereSpielChequers, The real Marcoman, Monstrelet, Trappist the monk, RjwilmsiBot, HawkoChoco, Helpful Pixie Bot and Monkbot

- **Franc-archer** *Source:* https://en.wikipedia.org/wiki/Franc-archer?oldid=788274610 *Contributors:* Andrewman327, Aldis90, Lenticel, LittleWink, Monstrelet, Suslindisambiguator, KLBot2, GuinanDrib555, Moagim, Seu Deva, Magic links bot and Anonymous: 2

- **Gakgung** *Source:* https://en.wikipedia.org/wiki/Gakgung?oldid=768079640 *Contributors:* Chris-martin, Lou Sander, Hyacinth, Bluelake, Popolon, Dbachmann, Kjoonlee, Wipe, Bart133, Dangerous-Boy, Bhadani, FlaBot, Flowerparty, Chobot, Bgwhite, Calcwatch, Kintetsubuffalo, Mairibot, DaDoc540, LC.Lau, Ser Amantio di Nicolao, Kbarends, Richard Keatinge, Luccas, Aldis90, Krusader6, Taeguk Warrior, Magioladitis, APoincot, ACSE, Historiographer, ^demonBot2, Dcattell, Mx. Granger, Hutcher, Berean Hunter, Miami33139, XLinkBot, MystBot, Addbot, Lim-yc, Luckas-bot, Yobot, Ferromagneticmonopole, Kookyunii, Timmyshin, Vortexxman, FrescoBot, Funnyguyagency, Yunshui, Safelocked, ZéroBot, SporkBot, Dbs101dbs, Purzo3, Korakys, はぐれがらす, Mousenight, InternetArchiveBot, Bamnamu, Bender the Bot and Anonymous: 36

- **Newington Butts** *Source:* https://en.wikipedia.org/wiki/Newington_Butts?oldid=781365431 *Contributors:* Heron, Steinsky, Lproven, Tagishsimon, MRSC, Xover, Fbv65edel, Rjwilmsi, Vegaswikian, Jpbowen, Wk 85, A bit iffy, Roscelese, Eliyak, Julien Foster, ShelfSkewed, Cydebot, Marek69, Kbthompson, The Anomebot2, Ugajin, Paranomia, KylieTastic, Straw Cat, JazzWriter, Martinevans123, Adam37, Lightmouse, Alex.muller, ClueBot, Cordwangler, Mephiston999, Ehrenkater, Lightbot, Melmann, Le Deluge, RjwilmsiBot, DexDor, Winner 42, Lateg, Cobaltcigs, ClueBot NG, Gareth Griffith-Jones, Khazar2, Frosty, ArmbrustBot, Parasitaster, InternetArchiveBot, Bender the Bot and Anonymous: 15

- **Yumi** *Source:* https://en.wikipedia.org/wiki/Yumi?oldid=783298309 *Contributors:* Olivier, Marteau, Nikai, Emperorbma, Hyacinth, Morven, Yas~enwiki, RedWolf, Yosri, Nat Krause, Guanaco, Bgoldenberg, Chowbok, Aknorals, JoshG, Rama, Dbachmann, Pt, El C, Bendono, Mairi, Ypacaraí, Nborders1972, Angie Y., Pearle, Dlatrex, Alansohn, Joshbaumgartner, Swift, Pax~enwiki, TaintedMustard, LordAmeth, Jackhynes, OwenX, WadeSimMiser, Jeff3000, Miwasatoshi, Eirikr, Gryffindor, Pleiotrop3, Sango123, Chobot, YurikBot, Phantomsteve, RL0919, JSH-alive, SamuelRiv, Arthur Rubin, Katieh5584, PRehse, GrinBot~enwiki, SmackBot, Deathlibrarian, Deon Steyn, Kintetsubuffalo, Gilliam, Hmains, Charles Nguyen, Suicidalhamster, Nyletak, Tenmiles, Vina-iwbot~enwiki, Richard Keatinge, ChristTrekker, Simohell~enwiki, Aldis90, Thijs!bot, Epbr123, Julia Rossi, Awien, .anacondabot, Bongwarrior, Ebizur, Bradford44, Iwashigumo77, NewEnglandYankee, Mordrid52, Ice-Dragon64, Philip Trueman, Vipinhari, Dubtiger, DanielDeibler, Boneyard90, El bot de la dieta, Lx 121, Berean Hunter, Antediluvian67, DumZiBoT, Addbot, Fukutaro, Legobot, Yobot, AnomieBOT, Ciphers, VX, Kingpin13, Materialscientist, Citation bot, Svarthandske, TerraHikaru, Z8, Citation bot 1, Pinethicket, RedBot, Smd75jr, EmausBot, WikitanvirBot, Samuraiantiqueworld, H3llBot, Mbartelsm, Abbz9, ClueBot NG, ZarlanTheGreen, Frietjes, 自教育, B.dyck, Iqua~enwiki, Helpful Pixie Bot, The Mark of the Beast, CitationCleanerBot, BattyBot, YFdyh-bot, Dexbot, Callmemirela, AddWittyNameHere, 武士道, GreenC bot, MordeKyle, Bender the Bot, Zinniabarnes15 and Anonymous: 81

3.2 Images

- **File:'The_Victory_of_Khorgos'_('La_Victoire_de_Khorgos').jpg** *Source:* https://upload.wikimedia.org/wikipedia/commons/d/d0/%27The_Victory_of_Khorgos%27_%28%27La_Victoire_de_Khorgos%27%29.jpg *License:* Public domain *Contributors:* Christies / Musée du Louvre *Original artist:* Drawn by Attiret, engraved by Jacques-Philippe Le Bas

- **File:17th_century_salvaging.jpg** *Source:* https://upload.wikimedia.org/wikipedia/commons/4/43/17th_century_salvaging.jpg *License:* Public domain *Contributors:* Scanned from *Vasa I: the Archaeology of a Swedish Warship of 1928* ISBN 91-974659-0-9 , p. 98. *Original artist:* Peter Isotalo

- **File:Alençon_Arms.svg** *Source:* https://upload.wikimedia.org/wikipedia/commons/9/97/Alen%C3%A7on_Arms.svg *License:* CC-BY-SA-3.0 *Contributors:* SVG elements from <a href='//commons.wikimedia.org/wiki/File:Blason_Beaumont_sur_Sarthe_72.svg' class='image'><img alt='Blason Beaumont sur Sarthe 72.svg' src='https://upload.wikimedia.org/wikipedia/commons/thumb/9/93/Blason_Beaumont_sur_Sarthe_72.svg/50px-Blason_Beaumont_sur_Sarthe_72.svg.png' width='50' height='55' srcset='https://upload.wikimedia.org/wikipedia/commons/thumb/9/93/Blason_Beaumont_sur_Sarthe_72.svg/75px-Blason_Beaumont_sur_Sarthe_72.svg.png 1.5x, https://upload.wikimedia.org/wikipedia/commons/thumb/9/93/Blason_Beaumont_sur_Sarthe_72.svg/100px-Blason_Beaumont_sur_Sarthe_72.svg.png 2x' data-file-width='600' data-file-height='660' /></a> Used as reference:<a href='//commons.wikimedia.org/wiki/File:Armes_Alen%C3%A7on_ancien.png' class='image'><img alt='Armes Alençon ancien.png' src='https://upload.wikimedia.org/wikipedia/commons/thumb/9/90/Armes_Alen%C3%A7on_ancien.png/50px-Armes_Alen%C3%A7on_ancien.png' width='50' height='56' srcset='https://upload.wikimedia.org/wikipedia/commons/thumb/9/90/Armes_Alen%C3%A7on_ancien.png/75px-Armes_Alen%C3%A7on_ancien.png 1.5x, https://upload.wikimedia.org/wikipedia/commons/thumb/9/90/Armes_Alen%C3%A7on_ancien.png/100px-Armes_Alen%C3%A7on_ancien.png 2x' data-file-width='360' data-file-height='400' /></a> *Original artist:* Ipankonin

- **File:Altarpiece_of_St_Sebastian_(detail).jpg** *Source:* https://upload.wikimedia.org/wikipedia/commons/4/4b/Altarpiece_of_St_Sebastian_%28detail%29.jpg *License:* CC BY 3.0 *Contributors:* Own work *Original artist:* Gun Powder Ma

- **File:Am_Ggakji_2.jpg** *Source:* https://upload.wikimedia.org/wikipedia/commons/f/f8/Am_Ggakji_2.jpg *License:* CC BY-SA 4.0 *Contributors:* Own work *Original artist:* Ryuch

- **File:Ancient_Mechanical_Artillery._Pic_01.jpg** *Source:* https://upload.wikimedia.org/wikipedia/commons/5/5d/Ancient_Mechanical_Artillery._Pic_01.jpg *License:* CC BY-SA 2.0 *Contributors:* originally posted to **Flickr** as Artilleria experimental romana a Saalburg / Roman experimental artillery in Saalburg *Original artist:* SBA73

- **File:AnthonyRoll-2_Mary_Rose.jpg** *Source:* https://upload.wikimedia.org/wikipedia/commons/5/5d/AnthonyRoll-2_Mary_Rose.jpg *License:* Public domain *Contributors:* Anthony Roll as reproduced in *The Anthony Roll of Henry VIII's Navy: Pepys Library 2991 and British Library Additional MS 22047 With Related Documents* ISBN 0-7546-0094-7, p. 42. *Original artist:* Own scan. Photo by Gerry Bye. Original by Anthony Anthony.

- **File:Antikensammlung_Berlin_525.JPG** *Source:* https://upload.wikimedia.org/wikipedia/commons/7/76/Antikensammlung_Berlin_525.JPG *License:* CC BY-SA 3.0 *Contributors:* Picture taken by Uploader *Original artist:* Marcus Cyron

- **File:Antique_Japanese_(samurai)_daikyū_and_hankyū_yumi_3.jpg** *Source:* https://upload.wikimedia.org/wikipedia/commons/3/37/Antique_Japanese_%28samurai%29_daiky%C5%AB_and_hanky%C5%AB_yumi_3.jpg *License:* CC BY-SA 3.0 *Contributors:* Own work *Original artist:* Samuraiantiqueworld

- **File:Antique_Japanese_(samurai)_hankyū(small_yumi).jpg** *Source:* https://upload.wikimedia.org/wikipedia/commons/4/4b/Antique_Japanese_%28samurai%29_hanky%C5%AB%28small_yumi%29.jpg *License:* CC BY-SA 3.0 *Contributors:* Own work *Original artist:* Samuraiantiqueworld

- **File:Antique_Japanese_(samurai)_yumi_bukuro.jpg** *Source:* https://upload.wikimedia.org/wikipedia/commons/2/2d/Antique_Japanese_%28samurai%29_yumi_bukuro.jpg *License:* CC BY-SA 3.0 *Contributors:* Own work *Original artist:* Samuraiantiqueworld

- **File:Apollo_Artemis_Brygos_Louvre_G151.jpg** *Source:* https://upload.wikimedia.org/wikipedia/commons/c/c7/Apollo_Artemis_Brygos_Louvre_G151.jpg *License:* Public domain *Contributors:* Own work *Original artist:* Marie-Lan Nguyen

3.2. IMAGES

- **File:Apple_shooting_by_tell.JPG** *Source:* https://upload.wikimedia.org/wikipedia/commons/8/87/Apple_shooting_by_tell.JPG *License:* Public domain *Contributors:* Own workphotograph Ad Meskens *Original artist:* Ernst Stückelberg
- **File:Arbalest_(PSF).png** *Source:* https://upload.wikimedia.org/wikipedia/commons/8/82/Arbalest_%28PSF%29.png *License:* Public domain *Contributors:* Archives of Pearson Scott Foresman, donated to the Wikimedia Foundation *Original artist:* Pearson Scott Foresman
- **File:Archer'{}s_Thumb_Ring_(zihgir)_LACMA_AC1995.168.1.jpg** *Source:* https://upload.wikimedia.org/wikipedia/commons/1/13/Archer%27s_Thumb_Ring_%28zihgir%29_LACMA_AC1995.168.1.jpg *License:* Public domain *Contributors:*
- Image: http://collections.lacma.org/sites/default/files/remote_images/piction/ma-31962599-O3.jpg *Original artist:* ?
- **File:Archer_wearing_feather_headdress._Alabaster._From_Nineveh,_Iraq._Reign_of_Ashurbanipal_II,_668-627_BCE._The_Burrell_Collection,_Glasgow,_UK.jpg** *Source:* https://upload.wikimedia.org/wikipedia/commons/5/56/Archer_wearing_feather_headdress._Alabaster._From_Nineveh%2C_Iraq._Reign_of_Ashurbanipal_II%2C_668-627_BCE._The_Burrell_Collection%2C_Glasgow%2C_UK.jpg *License:* CC BY-SA 4.0 *Contributors:* Own work *Original artist:* Osama Shukir Muhammed Amin FRCP(Glasg)
- **File:Archers_frieze_Darius_palace_Louvre_AOD487.jpg** *Source:* https://upload.wikimedia.org/wikipedia/commons/6/62/Archers_frieze_Darius_palace_Louvre_AOD487.jpg *License:* Public domain *Contributors:* Jastrow (2005) *Original artist:* Unknown<a href='https://www.wikidata.org/wiki/Q4233718' title='wikidata:Q4233718'><img alt='wikidata:Q4233718' src='https://upload.wikimedia.org/wikipedia/commons/thumb/f/ff/Wikidata-logo.svg/20px-Wikidata-logo.svg.png' width='20' height='11' srcset='https://upload.wikimedia.org/wikipedia/commons/thumb/f/ff/Wikidata-logo.svg/30px-Wikidata-logo.svg.png 1.5x, https://upload.wikimedia.org/wikipedia/commons/thumb/f/ff/Wikidata-logo.svg/40px-Wikidata-logo.svg.png 2x' data-file-width='1050' data-file-height='590' /></a>
- **File:Archery_pictogram.svg** *Source:* https://upload.wikimedia.org/wikipedia/commons/8/8e/Archery_pictogram.svg *License:* Public domain *Contributors:* Own work *Original artist:* Thadius856 (SVG conversion) & Parutakupiu (original image)
- **File:Armborst_1,_Nordisk_familjebok.png** *Source:* https://upload.wikimedia.org/wikipedia/commons/d/d5/Armborst_1%2C_Nordisk_familjebok.png *License:* Public domain *Contributors:* Nordisk familjebok (1904), vol.2, p.4 [1] *Original artist:* Nordisk familjebok
- **File:Armborst_2,_Nordisk_familjebok.png** *Source:* https://upload.wikimedia.org/wikipedia/commons/a/a3/Armborst_2%2C_Nordisk_familjebok.png *License:* Public domain *Contributors:* Nordisk familjebok (1904), vol.2, p.4 [1] *Original artist:* Nordisk familjebok
- **File:Armborst_3,_Nordisk_familjebok.png** *Source:* https://upload.wikimedia.org/wikipedia/commons/b/b8/Armborst_3%2C_Nordisk_familjebok.png *License:* Public domain *Contributors:* Nordisk familjebok (1904), vol.2, p.5 [1] *Original artist:* Nordisk familjebok
- **File:Armborst_4,_Nordisk_familjebok.png** *Source:* https://upload.wikimedia.org/wikipedia/commons/6/6b/Armborst_4%2C_Nordisk_familjebok.png *License:* Public domain *Contributors:* Nordisk familjebok (1904), vol.2, p.5 [1] *Original artist:* Nordisk familjebok
- **File:Armbrustschiessen.jpg** *Source:* https://upload.wikimedia.org/wikipedia/commons/3/30/Armbrustschiessen.jpg *License:* CC-BY-SA-3.0 *Contributors:* Own work *Original artist:* Wilfried Wittkowsky
- **File:Armoiries_Jean_de_Luxembourg.svg** *Source:* https://upload.wikimedia.org/wikipedia/commons/2/22/Armoiries_Jean_de_Luxembourg.svg *License:* GFDL *Contributors:* This vector image includes elements that have been taken or adapted from this: <a href='//commons.wikimedia.org/wiki/File:Armoiries_Comtes_de_Luxembourg.svg' class='image'><img alt='Armoiries Comtes de Luxembourg.svg' src='https://upload.wikimedia.org/wikipedia/commons/thumb/9/94/Armoiries_Comtes_de_Luxembourg.svg/18px-Armoiries_Comtes_de_Luxembourg.svg.png' width='18' height='20' srcset='https://upload.wikimedia.org/wikipedia/commons/thumb/9/94/Armoiries_Comtes_de_Luxembourg.svg/27px-Armoiries_Comtes_de_Luxembourg.svg.png 1.5x, https://upload.wikimedia.org/wikipedia/commons/thumb/9/94/Armoiries_Comtes_de_Luxembourg.svg/36px-Armoiries_Comtes_de_Luxembourg.svg.png 2x' data-file-width='600' data-file-height='660' /></a> Armoiries Comtes de Luxembourg.svg. *Original artist:* Caranorn
- **File:Arms_of_Aquitaine_and_Guyenne.svg** *Source:* https://upload.wikimedia.org/wikipedia/commons/d/d3/Arms_of_Aquitaine_and_Guyenne.svg *License:* GFDL *Contributors:* This vector image includes elements that have been taken or adapted from this: <a href='//commons.wikimedia.org/wiki/File:Arms_of_William_the_Conqueror_(1066-1087).svg' class='image'><img alt='Arms of William the Conqueror (1066-1087).svg' src='https://upload.wikimedia.org/wikipedia/commons/thumb/6/6c/Arms_of_William_the_Conqueror_%281066-1087%29.svg/17px-Arms_of_William_the_Conqueror_%281066-1087%29.svg.png' width='17' height='20' srcset='https://upload.wikimedia.org/wikipedia/commons/thumb/6/6c/Arms_of_William_the_Conqueror_%281066-1087%29.svg/26px-Arms_of_William_the_Conqueror_%281066-1087%29.svg.png 1.5x, https://upload.wikimedia.org/wikipedia/commons/thumb/6/6c/Arms_of_William_the_Conqueror_%281066-1087%29.svg/34px-Arms_of_William_the_Conqueror_%281066-1087%29.svg.png 2x' data-file-width='410' data-file-height='478' /></a> Arms of William the Conqueror (1066-1087).svg (by Sodacan). *Original artist:* Adelbrecht
- **File:Arms_of_Flanders.svg** *Source:* https://upload.wikimedia.org/wikipedia/commons/0/0c/Arms_of_Flanders.svg *License:* CC BY-SA 3.0 *Contributors:* This vector image includes elements that have been taken or adapted from this: <a href='//commons.wikimedia.org/wiki/File:Generieke_vlag_van_Vlaanderen.svg' class='image'><img alt='Generieke vlag van Vlaanderen.svg' src='https://upload.wikimedia.org/wikipedia/commons/thumb/e/eb/Generieke_vlag_van_Vlaanderen.svg/30px-Generieke_vlag_van_Vlaanderen.svg.png' width='30' height='20' srcset='https://upload.wikimedia.org/wikipedia/commons/thumb/e/eb/Generieke_vlag_van_Vlaanderen.svg/45px-Generieke_vlag_van_Vlaanderen.svg.png 1.5x, https://upload.wikimedia.org/wikipedia/commons/thumb/e/eb/Generieke_vlag_van_Vlaanderen.svg/60px-Generieke_vlag_van_Vlaanderen.svg.png 2x' data-file-width='744' data-file-height='496' /></a> Vlag van Vlaanderen.svg. *Original artist:* Tom Lemmens
- **File:Arms_of_Llywelyn.svg** *Source:* https://upload.wikimedia.org/wikipedia/commons/8/83/Arms_of_Llywelyn.svg *License:* CC BY-SA 3.0 *Contributors:* Own work *Original artist:* Sodacan
- **File:Arms_of_William_the_Conqueror_(1066-1087).svg** *Source:* https://upload.wikimedia.org/wikipedia/commons/6/6c/Arms_of_William_the_Conqueror_%281066-1087%29.svg *License:* CC BY-SA 3.0 *Contributors:* Own work *Original artist:* Sodacan
- **File:Arms_of_the_Count_of_Luxembourg.svg** *Source:* https://upload.wikimedia.org/wikipedia/commons/5/5b/Arms_of_the_Count_of_Luxembourg.svg *License:* CC BY-SA 4.0 *Contributors:* Own work *Original artist:* Sodacan

- **File:Arms_of_the_Kings_of_France_(France_Ancien).svg** *Source:* https://upload.wikimedia.org/wikipedia/commons/d/d6/Arms_of_the_Kings_of_France_%28France_Ancien%29.svg *License:* CC BY-SA 4.0 *Contributors:* This vector image includes elements that have been taken or adapted from this: <a href='//commons.wikimedia.org/wiki/File:Royal_Arms_of_England_(1340-1367).svg' class='image'><img alt='Royal Arms of England (1340-1367)' src='https://upload.wikimedia.org/wikipedia/commons/thumb/1/10/Royal_Arms_of_England_%281340-1367%29.svg/17px-Royal_Arms_of_England_%281340-1367%29.svg.png' width='17' height='20' srcset='https://upload.wikimedia.org/wikipedia/commons/thumb/1/10/Royal_Arms_of_England_%281340-1367%29.svg/26px-Royal_Arms_of_England_%281340-1367%29.svg.png 1.5x, https://upload.wikimedia.org/wikipedia/commons/thumb/1/10/Royal_Arms_of_England_%281340-1367%29.svg/34px-Royal_Arms_of_England_%281340-1367%29.svg.png 2x' data-file-width='410' data-file-height='478' /></a> Royal Arms of England (1340-1367).svg. *Original artist:* Sodacan

- **File:Arms_of_the_Monarchs_of_Majorca_and_the_Balearic_Islands_(14th-20th_Centuries).svg** *Source:* https://upload.wikimedia.org/wikipedia/commons/f/fa/Arms_of_the_Monarchs_of_Majorca_and_the_Balearic_Islands_%2814th-20th_Centuries%29.svg *License:* CC BY-SA 3.0 *Contributors:* <a href='//commons.wikimedia.org/wiki/File:ISO_639_Icon_ca.svg' class='image' title='català'><img alt='català' src='https://upload.wikimedia.org/wikipedia/commons/thumb/c/c3/ISO_639_Icon_ca.svg/30px-ISO_639_Icon_ca.svg.png' width='30' height='14' srcset='https://upload.wikimedia.org/wikipedia/commons/thumb/c/c3/ISO_639_Icon_ca.svg/45px-ISO_639_Icon_ca.svg.png 1.5x, https://upload.wikimedia.org/wikipedia/commons/thumb/c/c3/ISO_639_Icon_ca.svg/60px-ISO_639_Icon_ca.svg.png 2x' data-file-width='400' data-file-height='180' /></a> [1] *Original artist:* Heralder

- **File:Arms_of_the_Prince_of_Wales_(Ancient).svg** *Source:* https://upload.wikimedia.org/wikipedia/commons/4/45/Arms_of_the_Prince_of_Wales_%28Ancient%29.svg *License:* CC BY-SA 3.0 *Contributors:*

- Coat_of_Arms_of_the_Prince_of_Wales_(Ancient).svg *Original artist:* Coat_of_Arms_of_the_Prince_of_Wales_(Ancient).svg: Sodacan

- **File:Assyriancavalry.JPG** *Source:* https://upload.wikimedia.org/wikipedia/commons/e/e9/Assyriancavalry.JPG *License:* Public domain *Contributors:* Transferred from en.wikipedia to Commons by Gikü using CommonsHelper. *Original artist:* Iglonghurst at English Wikipedia

- **File:Autoroute_icone.svg** *Source:* https://upload.wikimedia.org/wikipedia/commons/7/7f/Autoroute_icone.svg *License:* CC BY-SA 2.5 *Contributors:* SVG version of File:Road stub mini pictogram.png *Original artist:* Dake (talk · contribs), Booyabazooka (talk · contribs), Roulex 45 (talk · contribs), and Doodledoo (talk · contribs)

- **File:Balestriere1.jpg** *Source:* https://upload.wikimedia.org/wikipedia/commons/a/a2/Balestriere1.jpg *License:* CC-BY-SA-3.0 *Contributors:* Ugo Pozzati *Original artist:* User:Julo

- **File:Ballista-quadrirotis.jpeg** *Source:* https://upload.wikimedia.org/wikipedia/commons/f/f7/Ballista-quadrirotis.jpeg *License:* Public domain *Contributors:* Library of Congress, Prints & Photographs Division, LC-USZ62-110291 (b&w film copy neg.), uncompressed archival TIFF version (12 MiB), color level (adjust contrast), cropped, and converted to JPEG (quality level 88) with the GIMP 2.6.1 *Original artist:* Unknown<a href='https://www.wikidata.org/wiki/Q4233718' title='wikidata:Q4233718'><img alt='wikidata:Q4233718' src='https://upload.wikimedia.org/wikipedia/commons/thumb/f/ff/Wikidata-logo.svg/20px-Wikidata-logo.svg.png' width='20' height='11' srcset='https://upload.wikimedia.org/wikipedia/commons/thumb/f/ff/Wikidata-logo.svg/30px-Wikidata-logo.svg.png 1.5x, https://upload.wikimedia.org/wikipedia/commons/thumb/f/ff/Wikidata-logo.svg/40px-Wikidata-logo.svg.png 2x' data-file-width='1050' data-file-height='590' /></a>

- **File:Basire_Embarkation_of_Henry_VIII.jpg** *Source:* https://upload.wikimedia.org/wikipedia/commons/e/ec/Basire_Embarkation_of_Henry_VIII.jpg *License:* Public domain *Contributors:* http://www.alectouk.com/The%20Embarkation%20of%20Henry%20VIII%20at%20Dover%201520%20(2).htm Scan Alecto Editions; *Original artist:* James Basire After Unknown (1520/1550)

- **File:Bataille_de_Nicopolis_(Archives_B.N.)_1.jpg** *Source:* https://upload.wikimedia.org/wikipedia/commons/9/96/Bataille_de_Nicopolis_%28Archives_B.N.%29_1.jpg *License:* Public domain *Contributors:* Archives Bibliothèque Nationale de France *Original artist:* ?

- **File:Battle_of_crecy_froissart.jpg** *Source:* https://upload.wikimedia.org/wikipedia/commons/2/24/Battle_of_crecy_froissart.jpg *License:* Public domain *Contributors:* From Chapter CXXIX of Jean Froissart's Chronicles, example source at http://www.maisonstclaire.org/resources/chronicles/froissart/book_1/ch_126-150/fc_b1_chap129.html *Original artist:* Jean Froissart

- **File:BattleofCrecyEngraving.jpg** *Source:* https://upload.wikimedia.org/wikipedia/commons/3/32/BattleofCrecyEngraving.jpg *License:* Public domain *Contributors:* Scanned by Infrogmation (talk) from an engraving in the book "Cyclopaedia of Universial History", published 1885 *Original artist:* artist not credited

- **File:BattleofCrécyVisualisation.svg** *Source:* https://upload.wikimedia.org/wikipedia/commons/d/d3/BattleofCr%C3%A9cyVisualisation.svg *License:* CC BY-SA 4.0 *Contributors:* Own work *Original artist:* This image has been created during "DensityDesign Integrated Course Final Synthesis Studio" at Polytechnic University of Milan, organized by DensityDesign Research Lab in 2016. Image is released under CC-BY-SA licence. Attribution goes to **"Lorenzo.piazzoli, DensityDesign Research Lab"**.

- **File:BattleofSluys.jpeg** *Source:* https://upload.wikimedia.org/wikipedia/commons/b/bf/BattleofSluys.jpeg *License:* Public domain *Contributors:* http://www.gibertjoseph.com/deux-chefs-de-guerre-au-moyen-age-4818543.html image *Original artist:* Jean Froissart

- **File:Berkshire.svg** *Source:* https://upload.wikimedia.org/wikipedia/commons/0/00/Berkshire.svg *License:* CC BY-SA 4.0 *Contributors:* Own work *Original artist:*

- Vexilo

- **File:Blason_Jean_Chandos.svg** *Source:* https://upload.wikimedia.org/wikipedia/commons/d/db/Blason_Jean_Chandos.svg *License:* CC BY-SA 3.0 *Contributors:* <a href='//validator.w3.org/' data-x-rel='nofollow'><img alt='W3C' src='https://upload.wikimedia.org/wikipedia/commons/thumb/1/1a/Valid_SVG_1.1_%28green%29.svg/88px-Valid_SVG_1.1_%28green%29.svg.png' width='88' height='30' style='vertical-align: top' srcset='https://upload.wikimedia.org/wikipedia/commons/thumb/1/1a/Valid_SVG_1.1_%28green%29.svg/132px-Valid_SVG_1.1_%28green%29.svg.png 1.5x, https://upload.wikimedia.org/wikipedia/commons/thumb/1/1a/Valid_SVG_1.1_%28green%29.svg/176px-Valid_SVG_1.1_%28green%29.svg.png 2x' data-file-width='91' data-file-height='31' /></a>iThe source code of this SVG is <a data-x-rel='nofollow' class='external text' href='//validator.w3.org/check?uri=https%3A%2F%2Fcommons.wikimedia.org%2Fwiki%2FSpecial%3AFilepath%2FBlason_Jean_Chandos.svg,,&,,ss=1#source'>valid</a>.

  Original artist: Manassas

3.2. IMAGES

- **File:Blason_Lorraine.svg** *Source:* https://upload.wikimedia.org/wikipedia/commons/7/79/Blason_Lorraine.svg *License:* CC-BY-SA-3.0 *Contributors:* <a href='//validator.w3.org/' data-x-rel='nofollow'><img alt='W3C' src='https://upload.wikimedia.org/wikipedia/commons/thumb/1/1a/Valid_SVG_1.1_%28green%29.svg/88px-Valid_SVG_1.1_%28green%29.svg.png' width='88' height='30' style='vertical-align: top' srcset='https://upload.wikimedia.org/wikipedia/commons/thumb/1/1a/Valid_SVG_1.1_%28green%29.svg/132px-Valid_SVG_1.1_%28green%29.svg.png 1.5x, https://upload.wikimedia.org/wikipedia/commons/thumb/1/1a/Valid_SVG_1.1_%28green%29.svg/176px-Valid_SVG_1.1_%28green%29.svg.png 2x' data-file-width='91' data-file-height='31' /></a>iThe source code of this SVG is <a data-x-rel='nofollow' class='external text' href='//validator.w3.org/check?uri=https%3A%2F%2Fcommons.wikimedia.org%2Fwiki%2FSpecial%3AFilepath%2FBlason_Lorraine.svg,,&,,ss=1#source'>valid</a>. *Original artist:* Darkbob

- **File:Blason_de_Bretagne.svg** *Source:* https://upload.wikimedia.org/wikipedia/commons/0/0e/Blason_de_Bretagne.svg *License:* Public domain *Contributors:* Own work; Dessinée par Rinaldum le 6 mars 2004 *Original artist:* Own work

- **File:Blason_province_fr_Gascogne.svg** *Source:* https://upload.wikimedia.org/wikipedia/commons/5/5c/Blason_province_fr_Gascogne.svg *License:* CC BY-SA 3.0 *Contributors:* travail personnel (own work) using Image:Lion_rampant.svg and Image:Héraldique meuble Gerbe de blé.svg *Original artist:* Peter Potrowl

- **File:Blubber_biopsy_sample.jpg** *Source:* https://upload.wikimedia.org/wikipedia/en/8/84/Blubber_biopsy_sample.jpg *License:* PD *Contributors:* ? *Original artist:* ?

- **File:Bowmena.PNG** *Source:* https://upload.wikimedia.org/wikipedia/en/3/3d/Bowmena.PNG *License:* Public domain *Contributors:* ? *Original artist:* ?

- **File:Bronze_Demi_Cannon_Culverins_Pmoth.png** *Source:* https://upload.wikimedia.org/wikipedia/commons/7/77/Bronze_Demi_Cannon_Culverins_Pmoth.png *License:* Public domain *Contributors:* ? *Original artist:* ?

- **File:Bundesarchiv_Bild_135-S-18-07-16,_Tibetexpedition,_Volksfest,_Bogenschütze.jpg** *Source:* https://upload.wikimedia.org/wikipedia/commons/0/01/Bundesarchiv_Bild_135-S-18-07-16%2C_Tibetexpedition%2C_Volksfest%2C_Bogensch%C3%BCtze.jpg *License:* CC BY-SA 3.0 de *Contributors:* This image was provided to Wikimedia Commons by the German Federal Archive (Deutsches Bundesarchiv) as part of a cooperation project. The German Federal Archive guarantees an authentic representation only using the originals (negative and/or positive), resp. the digitalization of the originals as provided by the Digital Image Archive. *Original artist:* Ernst Schäfer

- **File:Charles_Brandon,_1st_Duke_of_Suffolk_from_NPG.jpg** *Source:* https://upload.wikimedia.org/wikipedia/commons/e/e2/Charles_Brandon%2C_1st_Duke_of_Suffolk_from_NPG.jpg *License:* Public domain *Contributors:*

National Portrait Gallery: NPG 516

Original artist: Unknown<a href='https://www.wikidata.org/wiki/Q4233718' title='wikidata:Q4233718'><img alt='wikidata:Q4233718' src='https://upload.wikimedia.org/wikipedia/commons/thumb/f/ff/Wikidata-logo.svg/20px-Wikidata-logo.svg.png' width='20' height='11' srcset='https://upload.wikimedia.org/wikipedia/commons/thumb/f/ff/Wikidata-logo.svg/30px-Wikidata-logo.svg.png 1.5x, https://upload.wikimedia.org/wikipedia/commons/thumb/f/ff/Wikidata-logo.svg/40px-Wikidata-logo.svg.png 2x' data-file-width='1050' data-file-height='590' /></a>

- **File:ChineseCrossbow.JPG** *Source:* https://upload.wikimedia.org/wikipedia/commons/5/5c/ChineseCrossbow.JPG *License:* Public domain *Contributors:* Transferred from en.wikipedia to Commons. *Original artist:* PHG at English Wikipedia

- **File:Chuangzi_Nu1.jpg** *Source:* https://upload.wikimedia.org/wikipedia/commons/8/84/Chuangzi_Nu1.jpg *License:* CC BY 1.0 *Contributors:* ? *Original artist:* ?

- **File:Claude_d'Annebault.jpg** *Source:* https://upload.wikimedia.org/wikipedia/commons/3/32/Claude_d%27Annebault.jpg *License:* Public domain *Contributors:* [1]; original at Musee Conde, Chantilly, France *Original artist:* François Clouet

- **File:Coa_England_Family_Bohun-Humphrey_de_Bohun,_C._de_Northampton.svg** *Source:* https://upload.wikimedia.org/wikipedia/commons/9/9f/Coa_England_Family_Bohun-Humphrey_de_Bohun%2C_C._de_Northampton.svg *License:* CC0 *Contributors:* Own work *Original artist:* Madboy74

- **File:Coat_of_Arms_of_Henry_VIII_of_England_(1509-1547).svg** *Source:* https://upload.wikimedia.org/wikipedia/commons/8/82/Coat_of_Arms_of_Henry_VIII_of_England_%281509-1547%29.svg *License:* CC BY-SA 3.0 *Contributors:* Own work *Original artist:* Sodacan

- **File:Coat_of_arms_of_the_Lordship_of_Ireland.svg** *Source:* https://upload.wikimedia.org/wikipedia/commons/f/f9/Coat_of_arms_of_the_Lordship_of_Ireland.svg *License:* CC BY 3.0 *Contributors:* Own work *Original artist:* NsMn

- **File:Commons-logo.svg** *Source:* https://upload.wikimedia.org/wikipedia/en/4/4a/Commons-logo.svg *License:* PD *Contributors:* ? *Original artist:* ?

- **File:Cordeliere_and_Regent.jpg** *Source:* https://upload.wikimedia.org/wikipedia/commons/b/b6/Cordeliere_and_Regent.jpg *License:* Public domain *Contributors:* David Childs, *The Warship Mary Rose: The Life and Times of King Henry VIII's flagship*, p. 108; photo credits on p. 6 *Original artist:* Unknown, photo from Mary Rose Trust

- **File:Cowdray_engraving-full-lowres.jpg** *Source:* https://upload.wikimedia.org/wikipedia/commons/6/63/Cowdray_engraving-full-lowres.jpg *License:* Public domain *Contributors:* w:en:File:Cowdray_engraving.jpg *Original artist:* Basire|James Basire] (1730-1803)

- **File:Crecy_village_sign.JPG** *Source:* https://upload.wikimedia.org/wikipedia/commons/0/0f/Crecy_village_sign.JPG *License:* CC BY-SA 3.0 *Contributors:* Own work *Original artist:* Peter Lucas

- **File:CrossbowBolt.jpg** *Source:* https://upload.wikimedia.org/wikipedia/commons/2/20/CrossbowBolt.jpg *License:* CC-BY-SA-3.0 *Contributors:* ? *Original artist:* ?

- **File:Crossbow_pistol_IMG_3841.jpg** *Source:* https://upload.wikimedia.org/wikipedia/commons/1/1c/Crossbow_pistol_IMG_3841.jpg *License:* CC BY-SA 2.0 fr *Contributors:* Own work *Original artist:* Rama

- **File:Crossbow_telescopic_sight_reticle.JPG** *Source:* https://upload.wikimedia.org/wikipedia/en/3/37/Crossbow_telescopic_sight_reticle.JPG *License:* PD *Contributors:* ? *Original artist:* ?
- **File:DaVinci_Crossbow.JPG** *Source:* https://upload.wikimedia.org/wikipedia/commons/f/f2/DaVinci_Crossbow.JPG *License:* Public domain *Contributors:* http://www.sandia.gov/tp/SAFE_RAM/CRSBW.HTM *Original artist:* Leonardo da Vinci
- **File:Dinastia_han,_lastra_parietale_a_uso_funerario_con_scena_di_caccia,_206_a.c.$-$220_dc._ca,_02.JPG** *Source:* https://upload.wikimedia.org/wikipedia/commons/d/d6/Dinastia_han%2C_lastra_parietale_a_uso_funerario_con_scena_di_caccia%2C_206_a.c.$-$220_dc._ca%2C_02.JPG *License:* CC BY-SA 3.0 *Contributors:* Own work *Original artist:* sailko
- **File:Dunker_Tell_1798.jpg** *Source:* https://upload.wikimedia.org/wikipedia/commons/0/08/Dunker_Tell_1798.jpg *License:* Public domain *Contributors:* Schweizerisches Landesmuseum, Zürich, Inventar-Nr. LM 20 965 *Original artist:* Balthasar Anton Dunker
- **File:Earthenware_architecture_models,_Eastern_Han_Dynasty,_5.JPG** *Source:* https://upload.wikimedia.org/wikipedia/commons/8/85/Earthenware_architecture_models%2C_Eastern_Han_Dynasty%2C_5.JPG *License:* CC BY-SA 3.0 *Contributors:* Self-made at the Metropolitan Museum of Art, New York *Original artist:* PericlesofAthens
- **File:Edward_III_counting_the_dead_on_the_battlefield_of_Crécy.jpg** *Source:* https://upload.wikimedia.org/wikipedia/commons/e/ec/Edward_III_counting_the_dead_on_the_battlefield_of_Cr%C3%A9cy.jpg *License:* Public domain *Contributors:* Jean Froissart, Chroniques (Vol. I) *Original artist:* Virgil Master (illuminator)
- **File:English_Archery_-_three_panels.jpg** *Source:* https://upload.wikimedia.org/wikipedia/commons/8/8d/English_Archery_-_three_panels.jpg *License:* Public domain *Contributors:* Joseph Strutt's 1801 book, *The sports and pastimes of the people of England from the earliest period* (panels appears at page 42 therein) *Original artist:* Unknown<a href='https://www.wikidata.org/wiki/Q4233718' title='wikidata:Q4233718'><img alt='wikidata:Q4233718' src='https://upload.wikimedia.org/wikipedia/commons/thumb/f/ff/Wikidata-logo.svg/20px-Wikidata-logo.svg.png' width='20' height='11' srcset='https://upload.wikimedia.org/wikipedia/commons/thumb/f/ff/Wikidata-logo.svg/30px-Wikidata-logo.svg.png 1.5x, https://upload.wikimedia.org/wikipedia/commons/thumb/f/ff/Wikidata-logo.svg/40px-Wikidata-logo.svg.png 2x' data-file-width='1050' data-file-height='590' /></a>
- **File:English_gun_used_at_Crecy.jpg** *Source:* https://upload.wikimedia.org/wikipedia/commons/0/0f/English_gun_used_at_Crecy.jpg *License:* Public domain *Contributors:* HISTORY AND DESCRIPTIVE GUIDE OF THE U.S. NAVY YARD, WASHINGTON COMPILED BY F. E. Farnham and J. Mundell. WASHINGTON, D.C.: GIBSON BROS, PRINTERS AND BOOKBINDERS. 1894. [1] *Original artist:* F. E. Farnham and J. Mundell
- **File:Englishlongbow.jpg** *Source:* https://upload.wikimedia.org/wikipedia/commons/1/1b/Englishlongbow.jpg *License:* Public domain *Contributors:* Transferred from en.wikipedia to Commons. *Original artist:* Hitchhiker89 at English Wikipedia
- **File:Evolution_Coat_of_Arms_of_Navarre-3.svg** *Source:* https://upload.wikimedia.org/wikipedia/commons/2/2d/Evolution_Coat_of_Arms_of_Navarre-3.svg *License:* CC BY-SA 3.0 *Contributors:* File:Escudo de Navarra (No oficial).svg *Original artist:* Heralder
- **File:Fergetun.jpg** *Source:* https://upload.wikimedia.org/wikipedia/commons/0/02/Fergetun.jpg *License:* CC BY-SA 3.0 *Contributors:* Own work *Original artist:* Šolon
- **File:Fish0293_-_Flickr_-_NOAA_Photo_Library.jpg** *Source:* https://upload.wikimedia.org/wikipedia/commons/8/84/Fish0293_-_Flickr_-_NOAA_Photo_Library.jpg *License:* Public domain *Contributors:* fish0293 *Original artist:* NOAA Photo Library
- **File:Flag_of_England.svg** *Source:* https://upload.wikimedia.org/wikipedia/en/b/be/Flag_of_England.svg *License:* Public domain *Contributors:* ? *Original artist:* ?
- **File:Flag_of_Switzerland.svg** *Source:* https://upload.wikimedia.org/wikipedia/commons/f/f3/Flag_of_Switzerland.svg *License:* Public domain *Contributors:* PDF Colors Construction sheet *Original artist:* User:Marc Mongenet

Credits:

- **File:Flag_of_the_United_Kingdom.svg** *Source:* https://upload.wikimedia.org/wikipedia/en/a/ae/Flag_of_the_United_Kingdom.svg *License:* PD *Contributors:* ? *Original artist:* ?
- **File:FrenchCrossbowMan.JPG** *Source:* https://upload.wikimedia.org/wikipedia/commons/2/26/FrenchCrossbowMan.JPG *License:* Public domain *Contributors:* ? *Original artist:* ?
- **File:FrenchMountedCrossbowman.JPG** *Source:* https://upload.wikimedia.org/wikipedia/commons/2/22/FrenchMountedCrossbowman.JPG *License:* Public domain *Contributors:* ? *Original artist:* ?
- **File:French_cross-bow_grenade_thrower_Arbalète_sauterelle_type_A_d'Imphy_circa_1915.jpg** *Source:* https://upload.wikimedia.org/wikipedia/commons/1/15/French_cross-bow_grenade_thrower_Arbal%C3%A8te_sauterelle_type_A_d%27Imphy_circa_1915.jpg *License:* Public domain *Contributors:* Library of Congress *Original artist:* Bain
- **File:Galleys_and_carracks_in_battle.jpg** *Source:* https://upload.wikimedia.org/wikipedia/commons/a/ad/Galleys_and_carracks_in_battle.jpg *License:* Public domain *Contributors:* David Childs, *The Warship Mary Rose: The Life and Times of King Henry VIII's flagship*, p. 108; photo credits on p. 6 *Original artist:* Frans Huys after Pieter Bruegel the Elder
- **File:Gastraphetes_-_catapult_ancestor_-_antica_catapulta.jpg** *Source:* https://upload.wikimedia.org/wikipedia/commons/e/ee/Gastraphetes_-_catapult_ancestor_-_antica_catapulta.jpg *License:* CC BY-SA 3.0 *Contributors:* Own work *Original artist:* Selinous, Aldo Ferruggia
- **File:Gastraphetes_Rekonstruktion_Saalburg.jpg** *Source:* https://upload.wikimedia.org/wikipedia/commons/a/a2/Gastraphetes_Rekonstruktion_Saalburg.jpg *License:* CC BY-SA 3.0 *Contributors:* Own work *Original artist:* Haselburg-müller
- **File:George_Carew-painting_by_Holbein.jpg** *Source:* https://upload.wikimedia.org/wikipedia/commons/b/b8/George_Carew-painting_by_Holbein.jpg *License:* Public domain *Contributors:* David Childs, *The Warship Mary Rose: The Life and Times of King Henry VIII's flagship*, p. 165; photo credits on p. 6 *Original artist:* Hans Holbein

3.2. IMAGES

- **File:Gessler_und_Tell.jpg** *Source:* https://upload.wikimedia.org/wikipedia/commons/1/18/Gessler_und_Tell.jpg *License:* Public domain *Contributors:* de.wikipedia: scannened and uploaded on 18 Sep 2004 by Dominik Hundhammer *Original artist:* Ernst Stückelberg

- **File:Giuseppe_Maria_Crespi_-_Dice_Players_-_WGA05756.jpg** *Source:* https://upload.wikimedia.org/wikipedia/commons/7/72/Giuseppe_Maria_Crespi_-_Dice_Players_-_WGA05756.jpg *License:* Public domain *Contributors:* Web Gallery of Art: <a href='http://www.wga.hu/art/c/crespi/giuseppe/diceplay.jpg' data-x-rel='nofollow'><img alt='Inkscape.svg' src='https://upload.wikimedia.org/wikipedia/commons/thumb/6/6f/Inkscape.svg/20px-Inkscape.svg.png' width='20' height='20' srcset='https://upload.wikimedia.org/wikipedia/commons/thumb/6/6f/Inkscape.svg/30px-Inkscape.svg.png 1.5x, https://upload.wikimedia.org/wikipedia/commons/thumb/6/6f/Inkscape.svg/40px-Inkscape.svg.png 2x' data-file-width='60' data-file-height='60' /></a> Image <a href='http://www.wga.hu/html/c/crespi/giuseppe/diceplay.html' data-x-rel='nofollow'><img alt='Information icon.svg' src='https://upload.wikimedia.org/wikipedia/commons/thumb/3/35/Information_icon.svg/20px-Information_icon.svg.png' width='20' height='20' srcset='https://upload.wikimedia.org/wikipedia/commons/thumb/3/35/Information_icon.svg/30px-Information_icon.svg.png 1.5x, https://upload.wikimedia.org/wikipedia/commons/thumb/3/35/Information_icon.svg/40px-Information_icon.svg.png 2x' data-file-width='620' data-file-height='620' /></a> Info about artwork *Original artist:* Giuseppe Crespi

- **File:HJRK_A_108_-_Wallarmbrust_c._1460-70.jpg** *Source:* https://upload.wikimedia.org/wikipedia/commons/a/ab/HJRK_A_108_-_Wallarmbrust_c._1460-70.jpg *License:* CC BY 3.0 *Contributors:* Own work *Original artist:* **English:** Unknown, Austria.

- **File:HJRK_A_2269_-_Crossbow_windlass,_late_15th_century.jpg** *Source:* https://upload.wikimedia.org/wikipedia/commons/8/8f/HJRK_A_2269_-_Crossbow_windlass%2C_late_15th_century.jpg *License:* CC BY 3.0 *Contributors:* Own work *Original artist:* **English:** Unknown, Southern Germany, late 15th century.

- **File:Hainaut_Modern_Arms.svg** *Source:* https://upload.wikimedia.org/wikipedia/commons/a/aa/Hainaut_Modern_Arms.svg *License:* CC-BY-SA-3.0 *Contributors:* Modified from <a href='//commons.wikimedia.org/wiki/File:Blason_Beaumont_sur_Sarthe_72.svg' class='image'><img alt='Blason Beaumont sur Sarthe 72.svg' src='https://upload.wikimedia.org/wikipedia/commons/thumb/9/93/Blason_Beaumont_sur_Sarthe_72.svg/50px-Blason_Beaumont_sur_Sarthe_72.svg.png' width='50' height='55' srcset='https://upload.wikimedia.org/wikipedia/commons/thumb/9/93/Blason_Beaumont_sur_Sarthe_72.svg/75px-Blason_Beaumont_sur_Sarthe_72.svg.png 1.5x, https://upload.wikimedia.org/wikipedia/commons/thumb/9/93/Blason_Beaumont_sur_Sarthe_72.svg/100px-Blason_Beaumont_sur_Sarthe_72.svg.png 2x' data-file-width='600' data-file-height='660' /></a> *Original artist:* Ipankonin

- **File:Henry-VIII-kingofengland_1491-1547.jpg** *Source:* https://upload.wikimedia.org/wikipedia/commons/4/45/Henry-VIII-kingofengland_1491-1547.jpg *License:* Public domain *Contributors:* www.azerbaijanrugs [dot] com/mp/eworth1.htm [link blocked by spam filter] *Original artist:* Unknown<a href='https://www.wikidata.org/wiki/Q4233718' title='wikidata:Q4233718'><img alt='wikidata:Q4233718' src='https://upload.wikimedia.org/wikipedia/commons/thumb/f/ff/Wikidata-logo.svg/20px-Wikidata-logo.svg.png' width='20' height='11' srcset='https://upload.wikimedia.org/wikipedia/commons/thumb/f/ff/Wikidata-logo.svg/30px-Wikidata-logo.svg.png 1.5x, https://upload.wikimedia.org/wikipedia/commons/thumb/f/ff/Wikidata-logo.svg/40px-Wikidata-logo.svg.png 2x' data-file-width='1050' data-file-height='590' /></a>

- **File:Henry_VIII_(reigned_1509-1547)_by_English_School.jpg** *Source:* https://upload.wikimedia.org/wikipedia/commons/e/ec/Henry_VIII_%28reigned_1509-1547%29_by_English_School.jpg *License:* Public domain *Contributors:* Berger Collection: id #69 (Denver, Colorado) *Original artist:* Unidentified painter

- **File:Henry_VIII_and_the_Barber_Surgeons,_by_Hans_Holbein_the_Younger,_Richard_Greenbury,_and_others.jpg** *Source:* https://upload.wikimedia.org/wikipedia/commons/2/2e/Henry_VIII_and_the_Barber_Surgeons%2C_by_Hans_Holbein_the_Younger%2C_Richard_Greenbury%2C_and_others.jpg *License:* Public domain *Contributors:* Stephanie Buck, *Hans Holbein*, Cologne: Könemann, 1999, ISBN 3829025831. *Original artist:* Hans Holbein

- **File:Herberstein_Muscovy_3cavalry.jpg** *Source:* https://upload.wikimedia.org/wikipedia/commons/9/9a/Herberstein_Muscovy_3cavalry.jpg *License:* Public domain *Contributors:* Немецкая гравюра. Немецкое издание Герберштейна. [1] *Original artist:* Неизвестный немецкий художник.

- **File:Hohle_Gasse.jpeg** *Source:* https://upload.wikimedia.org/wikipedia/commons/b/b7/Hohle_Gasse.jpeg *License:* CC-BY-SA-3.0 *Contributors:* [1]. If this link does not work (URLs are subject to changes), you can find the picture starting from the canton of the subject: http://www.picswiss.ch/geo.html then the location. *Original artist:* Roland Zumbühl (Picswiss), Arlesheim (Commons:Picswiss project)

- **File:Horse_back_archery_AD_4C.jpg** *Source:* https://upload.wikimedia.org/wikipedia/commons/8/8a/Horse_back_archery_AD_4C.jpg *License:* Public domain *Contributors:* http://chosun.com *Original artist:* Unknown<a href='https://www.wikidata.org/wiki/Q4233718' title='wikidata:Q4233718'><img alt='wikidata:Q4233718' src='https://upload.wikimedia.org/wikipedia/commons/thumb/f/ff/Wikidata-logo.svg/20px-Wikidata-logo.svg.png' width='20' height='11' srcset='https://upload.wikimedia.org/wikipedia/commons/thumb/f/ff/Wikidata-logo.svg/30px-Wikidata-logo.svg.png 1.5x, https://upload.wikimedia.org/wikipedia/commons/thumb/f/ff/Wikidata-logo.svg/40px-Wikidata-logo.svg.png 2x' data-file-width='1050' data-file-height='590' /></a>

- **File:Horton_Hunter_Supreme_by_IvE.jpg** *Source:* https://upload.wikimedia.org/wikipedia/commons/4/4b/Horton_Hunter_Supreme_by_IvE.jpg *License:* CC-BY-SA-3.0 *Contributors:* Transferred from de.wikipedia to Commons. *Original artist:* The original uploader was Polaris at German Wikipedia

- **File:Hulagu_1.jpg** *Source:* https://upload.wikimedia.org/wikipedia/commons/2/21/Hulagu_1.jpg *License:* Public domain *Contributors:* From en-wiki. (Scan found at http://kjv1189.egloos.com/m/1896726 ?) *Original artist:* Unknown<a href='https://www.wikidata.org/wiki/Q4233718' title='wikidata:Q4233718'><img alt='wikidata:Q4233718' src='https://upload.wikimedia.org/wikipedia/commons/thumb/f/ff/Wikidata-logo.svg/20px-Wikidata-logo.svg.png' width='20' height='11' srcset='https://upload.wikimedia.org/wikipedia/commons/thumb/f/ff/Wikidata-logo.svg/30px-Wikidata-logo.svg.png 1.5x, https://upload.wikimedia.org/wikipedia/commons/thumb/f/ff/Wikidata-logo.svg/40px-Wikidata-logo.svg.png 2x' data-file-width='1050' data-file-height='590' /></a>

- **File:Hungarian_horse_archers.jpg** *Source:* https://upload.wikimedia.org/wikipedia/commons/5/5e/Hungarian_horse_archers.jpg *License:* Public domain *Contributors:* Edit of Image:Lovasíjászok Ópusztaszer.JPG *Original artist:* Csanády, edit by László Szalai (Beyond silence)

- **File:IlkhanidHorseArcher.jpg** *Source:* https://upload.wikimedia.org/wikipedia/commons/b/b5/IlkhanidHorseArcher.jpg *License:* Public domain *Contributors:* http://www.lacma.org/khan/5/6.htm *Original artist:* Muhammad ibn Mahmudshah al-Khayyam

- **File:Insigne_Cechicum.svg** *Source:* https://upload.wikimedia.org/wikipedia/commons/7/7b/Insigne_Cechicum.svg *License:* CC BY-SA 4.0 *Contributors:* Own work *Original artist:* Ssolbergj

- **File:Japanese_archer_1878b.jpg** *Source:* https://upload.wikimedia.org/wikipedia/commons/f/f2/Japanese_archer_1878b.jpg *License:* Public domain *Contributors:* Library of Congress[1] *Original artist:* Unknown<a href='https://www.wikidata.org/wiki/Q4233718' title='wikidata:Q4233718'><img alt='wikidata:Q4233718' src='https://upload.wikimedia.org/wikipedia/commons/thumb/f/ff/Wikidata-logo.svg/20px-Wikidata-logo.svg.png' width='20' height='11' srcset='https://upload.wikimedia.org/wikipedia/commons/thumb/f/ff/Wikidata-logo.svg/30px-Wikidata-logo.svg.png 1.5x, https://upload.wikimedia.org/wikipedia/commons/thumb/f/ff/Wikidata-logo.svg/40px-Wikidata-logo.svg.png 2x' data-file-width='1050' data-file-height='590' /></a>

- **File:Johan-van-Heemskerk-Batavische-Arcadia_MGG_1334.tif** *Source:* https://upload.wikimedia.org/wikipedia/commons/5/55/Johan-van-Heemskerk-Batavische-Arcadia_MGG_1334.tif *License:* Public domain *Contributors:* Peace Palace Library *Original artist:* Jan Lamsvelt (1674 - died after 26 June 1743)

- **File:Kamakura_Yabusame.jpg** *Source:* https://upload.wikimedia.org/wikipedia/commons/e/ee/Kamakura_Yabusame.jpg *License:* CC BY-SA 4.0 *Contributors:* Own work *Original artist:* Biliana Nikolova-Lefterova

- **File:KhubilaiOnTheHunt.jpg** *Source:* https://upload.wikimedia.org/wikipedia/commons/c/cc/KhubilaiOnTheHunt.jpg *License:* Public domain *Contributors:* *Dschingis Khan und seine Erben* (exhibition catalogue), München 2005, p. 299 *Original artist:* Attributed to Liu Guandao (劉貫道)/ (of the reproduction) National Palace Museum in Taipei

- **File:Korean_archery_target.svg** *Source:* https://upload.wikimedia.org/wikipedia/commons/2/29/Korean_archery_target.svg *License:* Public domain *Contributors:* This vector image was created with Inkscape. *Original artist:* Rémi Cormier

- **File:Landesmuseum_Zürich_2010-09-20_14-38-14_ShiftN.jpg** *Source:* https://upload.wikimedia.org/wikipedia/commons/c/ce/Landesmuseum_Z%C3%BCrich_2010-09-20_14-38-14_ShiftN.jpg *License:* CC BY-SA 3.0 *Contributors:* Own work *Original artist:* Hans Sandreuter; photograph: Roland zh

- **File:Liannu.jpg** *Source:* https://upload.wikimedia.org/wikipedia/commons/0/0c/Liannu.jpg *License:* CC BY 1.0 *Contributors:* ? *Original artist:* ?

- **File:Martyrium_of_Saint_Sebastian._Pic_03.jpg** *Source:* https://upload.wikimedia.org/wikipedia/commons/9/9f/Martyrium_of_Saint_Sebastian._Pic_03.jpg *License:* CC BY-SA 3.0 *Contributors:* Own work *Original artist:* Gun Powder Ma

- **File:MaryRose-bollock_daggers.jpg** *Source:* https://upload.wikimedia.org/wikipedia/commons/1/18/MaryRose-bollock_daggers.jpg *License:* CC BY-SA 3.0 *Contributors:* Mary Rose Trust *Original artist:* Peter Crossman of the Mary Rose Trust

- **File:MaryRose-carpentry_tools1.jpg** *Source:* https://upload.wikimedia.org/wikipedia/commons/d/db/MaryRose-carpentry_tools1.jpg *License:* CC BY-SA 3.0 *Contributors:* Mary Rose Trust *Original artist:* Peter Crossman of the Mary Rose Trust

- **File:MaryRose-conservation1.jpg** *Source:* https://upload.wikimedia.org/wikipedia/commons/f/f2/MaryRose-conservation1.jpg *License:* CC BY-SA 3.0 *Contributors:* Mary Rose Trust - official webpage *Original artist:* Mary Rose Trust

- **File:MaryRose-conservation2.jpg** *Source:* https://upload.wikimedia.org/wikipedia/commons/9/92/MaryRose-conservation2.jpg *License:* CC BY-SA 3.0 *Contributors:* Mary Rose Trust *Original artist:* Mary Rose Trust

- **File:MaryRose-rigging_blocks2.JPG** *Source:* https://upload.wikimedia.org/wikipedia/commons/3/3b/MaryRose-rigging_blocks2.JPG *License:* CC BY-SA 3.0 *Contributors:* Mary Rose Trust *Original artist:* Peter Crossman of the Mary Rose Trust

- **File:MaryRose-rosary-81A1414h.jpg** *Source:* https://upload.wikimedia.org/wikipedia/commons/1/11/MaryRose-rosary-81A1414h.jpg *License:* CC BY-SA 3.0 *Contributors:* Mary Rose Trust *Original artist:* Peter Crossman of the Mary Rose Trust

- **File:MaryRose-salvage1982-above_water_edited.jpg** *Source:* https://upload.wikimedia.org/wikipedia/commons/3/3a/MaryRose-salvage1982-above_water_edited.jpg *License:* CC BY-SA 3.0 *Contributors:*

- MaryRose-salvage1982-above_water.jpg *Original artist:* MaryRose-salvage1982-above_water.jpg: Unknown photographer of the Mary Rose Trust

- **File:MaryRose-ship_hall.jpg** *Source:* https://upload.wikimedia.org/wikipedia/commons/a/af/MaryRose-ship_hall.jpg *License:* CC BY-SA 3.0 *Contributors:* Mary Rose Trust *Original artist:* Mary Rose Trust

- **File:MaryRoseMuseum1.jpg** *Source:* https://upload.wikimedia.org/wikipedia/commons/9/97/MaryRoseMuseum1.jpg *License:* CC BY-SA 3.0 *Contributors:* Wilkinson Eyre *Original artist:* Wilkinson Eyre

- **File:Mary_Rose,_Historic_Dockyard,_Portsmouth,_Hampshire_-_geograph.org.uk_-_720237.jpg** *Source:* https://upload.wikimedia.org/wikipedia/commons/2/22/Mary_Rose%2C_Historic_Dockyard%2C_Portsmouth%2C_Hampshire_-_geograph.org.uk_-_720237.jpg *License:* CC BY-SA 2.0 *Contributors:* From geograph.org.uk; transferred by User:oxyman using geograph_org2commons. *Original artist:* Christine Matthews

- **File:Mary_Rose_-_Oven_&_Cauldron.jpg** *Source:* https://upload.wikimedia.org/wikipedia/commons/3/31/Mary_Rose_-_Oven_%26_Cauldron.jpg *License:* CC BY-SA 4.0 *Contributors:* Own work *Original artist:* Forscher scs

- **File:Mary_Rose_Guns_ForeBronzeCulverin_RearWroughtIronCannon.png** *Source:* https://upload.wikimedia.org/wikipedia/commons/f/f7/Mary_Rose_Guns_ForeBronzeCulverin_RearWroughtIronCannon.png *License:* Public domain *Contributors:* w:en:File:Mary_Rose_Guns_ForeBronzeCulverin_RearWroughtIronCannon.png *Original artist:* The Land

- **File:Mary_Rose_Museum.jpg** *Source:* https://upload.wikimedia.org/wikipedia/commons/9/9e/Mary_Rose_Museum.jpg *License:* CC BY-SA 4.0 *Contributors:* Own work *Original artist:* Photograph by Mike Peel (www.mikepeel.net).

3.2. IMAGES

- **File:Mary_Rose_iron_gun_watercolor.jpg** *Source:* https://upload.wikimedia.org/wikipedia/commons/c/c0/Mary_Rose_iron_gun_watercolor.jpg *License:* Public domain *Contributors:* Scanned image from *Original artist:* Unknown, photo credit to Southsea Castle Museum
- **File:Master_Heon_Kim.jpg** *Source:* https://upload.wikimedia.org/wikipedia/commons/0/04/Master_Heon_Kim.jpg *License:* CC BY-SA 3.0 *Contributors:* Own work *Original artist:* APoincot
- **File:Maximilian_1470.png** *Source:* https://upload.wikimedia.org/wikipedia/commons/6/67/Maximilian_1470.png *License:* Public domain *Contributors:* Part of the "Triumphal Arch (woodcut) " Weißkunig, heavily illustrated with woodcuts. *Original artist:* Albrecht Dürer and his pupils
- **File:Milano-Stemma_2.svg** *Source:* https://upload.wikimedia.org/wikipedia/commons/7/7c/Milano-Stemma_2.svg *License:* CC BY-SA 3.0 *Contributors:* Own work *Original artist:* Fale
- **File:MongolCavalrymen.jpg** *Source:* https://upload.wikimedia.org/wikipedia/commons/2/26/MongolCavalrymen.jpg *License:* Public domain *Contributors:* http://afe.easia.columbia.edu/mongols/pop//conquests/cavalry_pop.htm *Original artist:* Sayf al-Vâhidî. Hérât. Afghanistan
- **File:Mongolian_draw_of_a_bowstring.jpg** *Source:* https://upload.wikimedia.org/wikipedia/commons/0/08/Mongolian_draw_of_a_bowstring.jpg *License:* CC BY-SA 3.0 *Contributors:* Transferred from en.wikipedia to Commons. *Original artist:* Llamanator at English Wikipedia
- **File:Morella_(combate-de-arquero.png** *Source:* https://upload.wikimedia.org/wikipedia/commons/3/35/Morella_%28combate-de-arquero.png *License:* Public domain *Contributors:* Hernández Pacheco, Eduardo (1924): «*Estudios de arte prehistórico, Prospección de las pinturas rupestres de Morella la Vella*». C. de I. P. y P., Madrid *Original artist:* Eduardo Hernández Pacheco
- **File:Moto_hazu_(bottom_nock).jpg** *Source:* https://upload.wikimedia.org/wikipedia/commons/8/88/Moto_hazu_%28bottom_nock%29.jpg *License:* CC BY-SA 3.0 *Contributors:* Own work *Original artist:* Samuraiantiqueworld
- **File:MuseeMarine-sabre-p1000456.jpg** *Source:* https://upload.wikimedia.org/wikipedia/commons/c/c9/MuseeMarine-sabre-p1000456.jpg *License:* CC BY-SA 3.0 fr *Contributors:* Own work *Original artist:* Rama
- **File:Newington_Butts_2008_07_09.jpg** *Source:* https://upload.wikimedia.org/wikipedia/commons/9/9e/Newington_Butts_2008_07_09.jpg *License:* CC BY-SA 3.0 *Contributors:* Own work *Original artist:* Alex.muller
- **File:Nigiri_(grip).jpg** *Source:* https://upload.wikimedia.org/wikipedia/commons/8/85/Nigiri_%28grip%29.jpg *License:* CC BY-SA 3.0 *Contributors:* Own work *Original artist:* Samuraiantiqueworld
- **File:Noix_corde_carreau_arbalette.svg** *Source:* https://upload.wikimedia.org/wikipedia/commons/7/7f/Noix_corde_carreau_arbalette.svg *License:* CC BY-SA 3.0 *Contributors:* Own work *Original artist:* Christophe Dang Ngoc Chan (Cdang (<a href='//commons.wikimedia.org/wiki/User_talk:Cdang' title='User talk:Cdang'>talk</a>))
- **File:Old_Arms_of_Blois.svg** *Source:* https://upload.wikimedia.org/wikipedia/commons/4/41/Old_Arms_of_Blois.svg *License:* CC BY-SA 3.0 *Contributors:* Early Blason *Original artist:* Heralder
- **File:OttomanHorseArcher.jpg** *Source:* https://upload.wikimedia.org/wikipedia/commons/5/59/OttomanHorseArcher.jpg *License:* Public domain *Contributors:* ? *Original artist:* ?
- **File:P_culture.svg** *Source:* https://upload.wikimedia.org/wikipedia/commons/4/4f/P_culture.svg *License:* CC-BY-SA-3.0 *Contributors:* ? *Original artist:* ?
- **File:ParthianHorseman.jpg** *Source:* https://upload.wikimedia.org/wikipedia/commons/4/4e/ParthianHorseman.jpg *License:* CC-BY-SA-3.0 *Contributors:* Palazzo Madama, Turin *Original artist:* Jean Chardin
- **File:Pavillon_royal_de_la_France.svg** *Source:* https://upload.wikimedia.org/wikipedia/commons/9/92/Pavillon_royal_de_la_France.svg *License:* CC BY-SA 3.0 *Contributors:* Own work *Original artist:* Oren neu dag (<a href='//commons.wikimedia.org/wiki/User_talk:Oren_neu_dag' title='User talk:Oren neu dag'>talk</a>)
- **File:People_viewing_the_salvage_cage_holding_the_Mary_Rose_1982.jpg** *Source:* https://upload.wikimedia.org/wikipedia/commons/7/7a/People_viewing_the_salvage_cage_holding_the_Mary_Rose_1982.jpg *License:* CC BY-SA 3.0 *Contributors:* Own work *Original artist:* Glenluwin
- **File:PistolCrossbow122.jpg** *Source:* https://upload.wikimedia.org/wikipedia/commons/8/85/PistolCrossbow122.jpg *License:* CC BY 3.0 *Contributors:* Own work *Original artist:* Vibrantspirit
- **File:Portal-puzzle.svg** *Source:* https://upload.wikimedia.org/wikipedia/en/f/fd/Portal-puzzle.svg *License:* Public domain *Contributors:* ? *Original artist:* ?
- **File:Question_book-new.svg** *Source:* https://upload.wikimedia.org/wikipedia/en/9/99/Question_book-new.svg *License:* Cc-by-sa-3.0 *Contributors:*
Created from scratch in Adobe Illustrator. Based on Image:Question book.png created by User:Equazcion *Original artist:* Tkgd2007
- **File:Rahotep_statue.jpg** *Source:* https://upload.wikimedia.org/wikipedia/commons/6/6b/Rahotep_statue.jpg *License:* Copyrighted free use *Contributors:* http://www.egyptarchive.co.uk/html/cairo_museum_06.html *Original artist:* Jon Bodsworth
- **File:Reamsa._Guillermo_Tell.jpg** *Source:* https://upload.wikimedia.org/wikipedia/commons/d/dd/Reamsa._Guillermo_Tell.jpg *License:* CC BY-SA 4.0 *Contributors:* my own collection *Original artist:* Juan Martin Garcia
- **File:Recurve_crossbow_with_bolts.jpg** *Source:* https://upload.wikimedia.org/wikipedia/commons/7/76/Recurve_crossbow_with_bolts.jpg *License:* Public domain *Contributors:* No machine-readable source provided. Own work assumed (based on copyright claims). *Original artist:* No machine-readable author provided. Liam Skoda assumed (based on copyright claims).

- **File:Ref-chamballista.jpg** *Source:* https://upload.wikimedia.org/wikipedia/commons/a/ad/Ref-chamballista.jpg *License:* CC BY 1.0 *Contributors:* ? *Original artist:* ?
- **File:Replicawrist-guard.jpg** *Source:* https://upload.wikimedia.org/wikipedia/commons/b/b5/Replicawrist-guard.jpg *License:* Public domain *Contributors:* Transferred from en.wikipedia to Commons. *Original artist:* Thefuguestate at English Wikipedia
- **File:Roman_crossbow.jpg** *Source:* https://upload.wikimedia.org/wikipedia/commons/6/6e/Roman_crossbow.jpg *License:* Public domain *Contributors:* Dictionnaire des antiquites grecques et romaines: Arcuballista, Manuballista *Original artist:* Gun Powder Ma
- **File:Royal_Arms_of_England_(1340-1367).svg** *Source:* https://upload.wikimedia.org/wikipedia/commons/1/10/Royal_Arms_of_England_%281340-1367%29.svg *License:* CC BY-SA 3.0 *Contributors:* Own work *Original artist:* Sodacan
- **File:Samurai_on_horseback.png** *Source:* https://upload.wikimedia.org/wikipedia/commons/0/00/Samurai_on_horseback.png *License:* Public domain *Contributors:* Library of Congress[1] *Original artist:* Unknown<a href='https://www.wikidata.org/wiki/Q4233718' title='wikidata:Q4233718'><img alt='wikidata:Q4233718' src='https://upload.wikimedia.org/wikipedia/commons/thumb/f/ff/Wikidata-logo.svg/20px-Wikidata-logo.svg.png' width='20' height='11' srcset='https://upload.wikimedia.org/wikipedia/commons/thumb/f/ff/Wikidata-logo.svg/30px-Wikidata-logo.svg.png 1.5x, https://upload.wikimedia.org/wikipedia/commons/thumb/f/ff/Wikidata-logo.svg/40px-Wikidata-logo.svg.png 2x' data-file-width='1050' data-file-height='590' /></a>
- **File:Sauterelle_1915.jpg** *Source:* https://upload.wikimedia.org/wikipedia/commons/e/ec/Sauterelle_1915.jpg *License:* Public domain *Contributors:* Crop of A. Sauterelle (LOC) *Original artist:* Bain News Service
- **File:Saxton_Pope_and_grizzly.jpg** *Source:* https://upload.wikimedia.org/wikipedia/en/2/29/Saxton_Pope_and_grizzly.jpg *License:* PD-US *Contributors:* ? *Original artist:* ?
- **File:Scale_of_justice_2.svg** *Source:* https://upload.wikimedia.org/wikipedia/commons/0/0e/Scale_of_justice_2.svg *License:* Public domain *Contributors:* Own work *Original artist:* DTR
- **File:Sceau_Republique_helvetique.png** *Source:* https://upload.wikimedia.org/wikipedia/commons/3/3e/Sceau_Republique_helvetique.png *License:* Public domain *Contributors:* Unknown *Original artist:* Marquard Wocher
- **File:Schranktür_1782_Tell.jpg** *Source:* https://upload.wikimedia.org/wikipedia/commons/9/95/Schrankt%C3%BCr_1782_Tell.jpg *License:* Public domain *Contributors:* http://www.bildindex.de/ – Aufnahme-Nr. C 664.176; 1959 *Original artist:* Anonymous
- **File:Searchtool.svg** *Source:* https://upload.wikimedia.org/wikipedia/en/6/61/Searchtool.svg *License:* ? *Contributors:* ? *Original artist:* ?
- **File:Self_and_composite_longbows-blank.jpg** *Source:* https://upload.wikimedia.org/wikipedia/commons/8/8d/Self_and_composite_longbows-blank.jpg *License:* CC-BY-SA-3.0 *Contributors:* Self and composite longbows.jpg, from a photograph of the english Wikipedia. *Original artist:* Sémhur ; original by Hitchhiker89
- **File:Shield_and_Coat_of_Arms_of_the_Holy_Roman_Emperor_(c.1300-c.1400).svg** *Source:* https://upload.wikimedia.org/wikipedia/commons/2/2d/Shield_and_Coat_of_Arms_of_the_Holy_Roman_Emperor_%28c.1300-c.1400%29.svg *License:* CC BY-SA 3.0 *Contributors:*
- File:Mohrenfresko MHQ detail Wappen10.jpg *Original artist:* Heralder & Tom Lemmens
- **File:Småland_vapen.svg** *Source:* https://upload.wikimedia.org/wikipedia/commons/4/46/Sm%C3%A5land_vapen.svg *License:* CC BY-SA 2.5 *Contributors:* Made by Lokal_Profil after the blasoning. *Original artist:* Lokal_Profil
- **File:South_London_Map_1800.jpg** *Source:* https://upload.wikimedia.org/wikipedia/en/a/a3/South_London_Map_1800.jpg *License:* PD-US *Contributors:*

    http://archivemaps.com/mapco/faden/faden13.htm *Original artist:*

    Topographical Map Of The Country Twenty Miles Round London 1800
- **File:Southsea_castle_from_the_east.JPG** *Source:* https://upload.wikimedia.org/wikipedia/commons/1/1c/Southsea_castle_from_the_east.JPG *License:* GFDL *Contributors:* Photo by user:geni *Original artist:* Geni
- **File:Sport_balls.svg** *Source:* https://upload.wikimedia.org/wikipedia/commons/0/0c/Sport_balls.svg *License:* GFDL *Contributors:* Own work *Original artist:* Baseball.svg: vedub4us
- **File:St_Mary'{}s_churchyard_gardens_butts.JPG** *Source:* https://upload.wikimedia.org/wikipedia/commons/6/64/St_Mary%27s_churchyard_gardens_butts.JPG *License:* CC-BY-SA-3.0 *Contributors:* Own work by the original uploader *Original artist:* Wk 85
- **File:St_marys_churchyard_playground.jpg** *Source:* https://upload.wikimedia.org/wikipedia/commons/7/7c/St_marys_churchyard_playground.jpg *License:* CC-BY-SA-3.0 *Contributors:* Own work by the original uploader *Original artist:* Wk 85
- **File:Statue_of_William_Tell_and_his_son,_City_Hall,_Tell_City,_Indiana_(looking_to_the_east,_northeast).jpg** *Source:* https://upload.wikimedia.org/wikipedia/commons/4/44/Statue_of_William_Tell_and_his_son%2C_City_Hall%2C_Tell_City%2C_Indiana_%28looking_to_the_east%2C_northeast%29.jpg *License:* CC BY-SA 3.0 *Contributors:* Own work *Original artist:* Richard G. Biever
- **File:Stückelberg_Tellensprung_1879.jpg** *Source:* https://upload.wikimedia.org/wikipedia/commons/8/87/St%C3%BCckelberg_Tellensprung_1879.jpg *License:* Public domain *Contributors:* "Von Anker bis Zünd, Die Kunst im jungen Bundesstaat 1848 - 1900", Kunsthaus Zürich, 1998, upload Dezember 2008 by Adrian Michael *Original artist:* Ernst Stückelberg
- **File:Sut_Ggakji_1.jpg** *Source:* https://upload.wikimedia.org/wikipedia/commons/c/c5/Sut_Ggakji_1.jpg *License:* CC BY-SA 4.0 *Contributors:* Own work *Original artist:* Ryuch
- **File:Tell_Deutsch_Münster_1554.jpg** *Source:* https://upload.wikimedia.org/wikipedia/commons/0/08/Tell_Deutsch_M%C3%BCnster_1554.jpg *License:* Public domain *Contributors:* Sebastian Münster, Cosmographia *Original artist:* Hans Rudolf Manuel Deutsch (1525–1571)
- **File:Text_document_with_red_question_mark.svg** *Source:* https://upload.wikimedia.org/wikipedia/commons/a/a4/Text_document_with_red_question_mark.svg *License:* Public domain *Contributors:* Created by bdesham with Inkscape; based upon Text-x-generic.svg from the Tango project. *Original artist:* Benjamin D. Esham (bdesham)

3.2. IMAGES

- **File:TheArchersCraft.jpg** *Source:* https://upload.wikimedia.org/wikipedia/en/c/ce/TheArchersCraft.jpg *License:* Fair use *Contributors:* http://www.amazon.com/The-Archers-Craft-Certain-Concerning/dp/B0000CI1VF *Original artist:* ?
- **File:The_Martyrdom_of_St_Sebastian_(detail).jpg** *Source:* https://upload.wikimedia.org/wikipedia/commons/1/18/The_Martyrdom_of_St_Sebastian_%28detail%29.jpg *License:* CC BY-SA 3.0 *Contributors:* Own work *Original artist:* Gun Powder Ma
- **File:The_meeting_of_the_Royal_British_Bowmen_in_the_grounds_of_Erthig,_Denbighshire.jpeg** *Source:* https://upload.wikimedia.org/wikipedia/commons/9/94/The_meeting_of_the_Royal_British_Bowmen_in_the_grounds_of_Erthig%2C_Denbighshire.jpeg *License:* Public domain *Contributors:* This image is available from the **National Library of Wales** *Original artist:*

Bennett, engraver.

Townshend, J., fl. 1822, artist.
- **File:Three_Indian_archer'{}s_rings.jpg** *Source:* https://upload.wikimedia.org/wikipedia/commons/0/09/Three_Indian_archer%27s_rings.jpg *License:* CC BY-SA 4.0 *Contributors:* Own work *Original artist:* Difference engine
- **File:Trebuchet.jpg** *Source:* https://upload.wikimedia.org/wikipedia/commons/2/2e/Trebuchet.jpg *License:* CC-BY-SA-3.0 *Contributors:* No machine-readable source provided. Own work assumed (based on copyright claims). *Original artist:* No machine-readable author provided. Quistnix assumed (based on copyright claims).
- **File:Tsurumaki_string_holder_1.JPG** *Source:* https://upload.wikimedia.org/wikipedia/commons/c/c7/Tsurumaki_string_holder_1.JPG *License:* CC BY-SA 3.0 *Contributors:* Own work *Original artist:* Samuraiantiqueworld
- **File:Ura_hazu_(top_nock).jpg** *Source:* https://upload.wikimedia.org/wikipedia/commons/e/e4/Ura_hazu_%28top_nock%29.jpg *License:* CC BY 3.0 *Contributors:* Own work *Original artist:* Samuraiantiqueworld
- **File:Vigiles_du_roi_Charles_VII_19.jpg** *Source:* https://upload.wikimedia.org/wikipedia/commons/e/e5/Vigiles_du_roi_Charles_VII_19.jpg *License:* Public domain *Contributors:* http://www.histoire-fr.com/valois_charles7_4.htm *Original artist:* Unknown<a href='https://www.wikidata.org/wiki/Q4233718' title='wikidata:Q4233718'><img alt='wikidata:Q4233718' src='https://upload.wikimedia.org/wikipedia/commons/thumb/f/ff/Wikidata-logo.svg/20px-Wikidata-logo.svg.png' width='20' height='11' srcset='https://upload.wikimedia.org/wikipedia/commons/thumb/f/ff/Wikidata-logo.svg/30px-Wikidata-logo.svg.png 1.5x, https://upload.wikimedia.org/wikipedia/commons/thumb/f/ff/Wikidata-logo.svg/40px-Wikidata-logo.svg.png 2x' data-file-width='1050' data-file-height='590' /></a>
- **File:WLA_vanda_gold_thumb_ring.jpg** *Source:* https://upload.wikimedia.org/wikipedia/commons/6/6f/WLA_vanda_gold_thumb_ring.jpg *License:* CC BY-SA 2.5 *Contributors:* Uploaded from the Wikipedia Loves Art photo pool on Flickr *Original artist:* Wikipedia Loves Art participant "va_va_val"
- **File:WLA_vanda_jade_thumb_ring.jpg** *Source:* https://upload.wikimedia.org/wikipedia/commons/5/58/WLA_vanda_jade_thumb_ring.jpg *License:* CC BY-SA 2.5 *Contributors:* Uploaded from the Wikipedia Loves Art photo pool on Flickr *Original artist:* Wikipedia Loves Art participant "va_va_val"
- **File:Warring_States_or_Western_Han_crossbow.jpg** *Source:* https://upload.wikimedia.org/wikipedia/commons/2/25/Warring_States_or_Western_Han_crossbow.jpg *License:* GFDL *Contributors:* Gary Lee Todd's site, Privately-owned Chinese artifacts *Original artist:* Gary Lee Todd
- **File:Warrior_of_Scithians.png** *Source:* https://upload.wikimedia.org/wikipedia/commons/8/82/Warrior_of_Scithians.png *License:* CC BY 3.0 *Contributors:* self-made; on the basis of the picture from ruWiki Скиф VIII в до Р.Х..jpg, author-S10241875 *Original artist:* Janmad
- **File:Weisses_Buch_von_Sarnen_447.jpg** *Source:* https://upload.wikimedia.org/wikipedia/commons/0/08/Weisses_Buch_von_Sarnen_447.jpg *License:* Public domain *Contributors:* Weisses Buch von Sarnen, S. 447 (fol. 211r); e-codices.unifr.ch) *Original artist:* Unknown<a href='https://www.wikidata.org/wiki/Q4233718' title='wikidata:Q4233718'><img alt='wikidata:Q4233718' src='https://upload.wikimedia.org/wikipedia/commons/thumb/f/ff/Wikidata-logo.svg/20px-Wikidata-logo.svg.png' width='20' height='11' srcset='https://upload.wikimedia.org/wikipedia/commons/thumb/f/ff/Wikidata-logo.svg/30px-Wikidata-logo.svg.png 1.5x, https://upload.wikimedia.org/wikipedia/commons/thumb/f/ff/Wikidata-logo.svg/40px-Wikidata-logo.svg.png 2x' data-file-width='1050' data-file-height='590' /></a>
- **File:Wiki_letter_w_cropped.svg** *Source:* https://upload.wikimedia.org/wikipedia/commons/1/1c/Wiki_letter_w_cropped.svg *License:* CC-BY-SA-3.0 *Contributors:* This file was derived from Wiki letter w.svg: <a href='//commons.wikimedia.org/wiki/File:Wiki_letter_w.svg' class='image'><img alt='Wiki letter w.svg' src='https://upload.wikimedia.org/wikipedia/commons/thumb/6/6c/Wiki_letter_w.svg/50px-Wiki_letter_w.svg.png' width='50' height='50' srcset='https://upload.wikimedia.org/wikipedia/commons/thumb/6/6c/Wiki_letter_w.svg/75px-Wiki_letter_w.svg.png 1.5x, https://upload.wikimedia.org/wikipedia/commons/thumb/6/6c/Wiki_letter_w.svg/100px-Wiki_letter_w.svg.png 2x' data-file-width='44' data-file-height='44' /></a>

Original artist: Derivative work by Thumperward
- **File:Wikisource-logo.svg** *Source:* https://upload.wikimedia.org/wikipedia/commons/4/4c/Wikisource-logo.svg *License:* CC BY-SA 3.0 *Contributors:* Rei-artur *Original artist:* Nicholas Moreau
- **File:Wiktionary-logo-en-v2.svg** *Source:* https://upload.wikimedia.org/wikipedia/commons/9/99/Wiktionary-logo-en-v2.svg *License:* CC-BY-SA-3.0 *Contributors:* ? *Original artist:* ?
- **File:Wilhelm_Tell_Denkmal_Altdorf_um_1900_Detail.jpg** *Source:* https://upload.wikimedia.org/wikipedia/commons/6/67/Wilhelm_Tell_Denkmal_Altdorf_um_1900_Detail.jpg *License:* Public domain *Contributors:* Wilhelm_Tell_Denkmal_Altdorf_um_1900.jpeg which is from:

Original artist: Wilhelm_Tell_Denkmal_Altdorf_um_1900.jpeg: (not named)
- **File:Wisconsin_state_coat_of_arms_(illustrated,_1876).jpg** *Source:* https://upload.wikimedia.org/wikipedia/commons/6/6f/Wisconsin_state_coat_of_arms_%28illustrated%2C_1876%29.jpg *License:* Public domain *Contributors:* Mitchell, Henry (1876) *The State Arms of the Union*, Boston: L. Prang & Co. *Original artist:*

- Restoration by Godot13
- **File:Witchery_of_Archery.jpg** *Source:* https://upload.wikimedia.org/wikipedia/commons/9/9e/Witchery_of_Archery.jpg *License:* Public domain *Contributors:* The Witchery of Archery, C. Scribner's sons *Original artist:* Maurice Thompson
- **File:Yabusame_01.jpg** *Source:* https://upload.wikimedia.org/wikipedia/commons/0/0a/Yabusame_01.jpg *License:* CC-BY-SA-3.0 *Contributors:* http://en.wikipedia.org/wiki/Image:Horse8-vi.jpg *Original artist:* Jim Mills
- **File:Yabusame_02.jpg** *Source:* https://upload.wikimedia.org/wikipedia/commons/8/89/Yabusame_02.jpg *License:* CC-BY-SA-3.0 *Contributors:* http://en.wikipedia.org/wiki/Image:Horse3-vi.jpg *Original artist:* Jim Mills (w:User:Jmills74)
- **File:Yabusame_04.jpg** *Source:* https://upload.wikimedia.org/wikipedia/commons/0/05/Yabusame_04.jpg *License:* Public domain *Contributors:* http://en.wikipedia.org/wiki/Image:Bow10ez.jpg *Original artist:* en:user:Crossfire
- **File:Yabusame_05.jpg** *Source:* https://upload.wikimedia.org/wikipedia/commons/9/96/Yabusame_05.jpg *License:* Public domain *Contributors:* http://www.whitehouse.gov/news/releases/2002/02/images/20020218-1.html *Original artist:* Unknown<a href='https://www.wikidata.org/wiki/Q4233718' title='wikidata:Q4233718'><img alt='wikidata:Q4233718' src='https://upload.wikimedia.org/wikipedia/commons/thumb/f/ff/Wikidata-logo.svg/20px-Wikidata-logo.svg.png' width='20' height='11' srcset='https://upload.wikimedia.org/wikipedia/commons/thumb/f/ff/Wikidata-logo.svg/30px-Wikidata-logo.svg.png 1.5x, https://upload.wikimedia.org/wikipedia/commons/thumb/f/ff/Wikidata-logo.svg/40px-Wikidata-logo.svg.png 2x' data-file-width='1050' data-file-height='590' /></a>
- **File:Yeoman.warder.toweroflondon.arp.jpg** *Source:* https://upload.wikimedia.org/wikipedia/commons/d/d2/Yeoman.warder.toweroflondon.arp.jpg *License:* Public domain *Contributors:* No machine-readable source provided. Own work assumed (based on copyright claims). *Original artist:* No machine-readable author provided. Arpingstone assumed (based on copyright claims).
- **File:Yumi-p1000624.jpg** *Source:* https://upload.wikimedia.org/wikipedia/commons/5/5e/Yumi-p1000624.jpg *License:* CC BY-SA 2.0 fr *Contributors:* Own work *Original artist:* Rama
- **File:YumiKai.gif** *Source:* https://upload.wikimedia.org/wikipedia/commons/f/f8/YumiKai.gif *License:* Public domain *Contributors:* Own work *Original artist:* Bicéphal
- **File:Yumi_name_of_parts.svg** *Source:* https://upload.wikimedia.org/wikipedia/commons/8/85/Yumi_name_of_parts.svg *License:* Public domain *Contributors:* own work, Yumi01.jpg *Original artist:* Nuage fou, Fukutaro
- **File:Zhugenu-payne.jpg** *Source:* https://upload.wikimedia.org/wikipedia/commons/8/86/Zhugenu-payne.jpg *License:* CC BY 1.0 *Contributors:* ? *Original artist:* ?
- **File:Аркбаллиста_на_колесном_станке_со_стальным_луком_и_зажигательный_болт.jpg** *Source:* https://upload.wikimedia.org/wikipedia/commons/f/f7/%D0%90%D1%80%D0%BA%D0%B1%D0%B0%D0%BB%D0%BB%D0%B8%D1%81%D1%82%D0%B0_%D0%BD%D0%B0_%D0%BA%D0%BE%D0%BB%D0%B5%D1%81%D0%BD%D0%BE%D0%BC_%D1%81%D1%82%D0%B0%D0%BD%D0%BA%D0%B5_%D1%81%D0%BE_%D1%81%D1%82%D0%B0%D0%BB%D1%8C%D0%BD%D1%8B%D0%BC_%D0%BB%D1%83%D0%BA%D0%BE%D0%BC_%D0%B8_%D0%B7%D0%B0%D0%B6%D0%B8%D0%B3%D0%B0%D1%82%D0%B5%D0%BB%D1%8C%D0%BD%D1%8B%D0%B9_%D0%B1%D0%BE%D0%BB%D1%82.jpg *License:* Public domain *Contributors:* [1] *Original artist:* From the medieval manuscript. Bayerische Staatsbibliothek.
- **File: 夷 -oracle.svg** *Source:* https://upload.wikimedia.org/wikipedia/commons/6/66/%E5%A4%B7-oracle.svg *License:* Public domain *Contributors:* Available Ancient Chinese Character sources : Graphic etymology - Chinese text project - sinica Database *Original artist:* Digital file creation : see **contributor name** shown in the "File history" section.

3.3 Content license

- Creative Commons Attribution-Share Alike 3.0

Made in the USA
Monee, IL
06 December 2021